B.R. Ambedkar

The Quest for Justice

Editorial Advisory Board

Anand Teltumbde
Annapurna Waughray
G. Haragopal
Kalpana Kannabiran
Laurence R. Simon
Meena Dhanda
Moses Seenarine
Rochana Bajpai
S. Japhet
Sukhadeo Thorat
Suraj Yengde
Valerian Rodrigues

B.R. Ambedkar
The Quest for Justice

VOLUME II
Social Justice

Edited by
Aakash Singh Rathore

Oxford University Press is a department of the University of Oxford.
It furthers the University's objective of excellence in research, scholarship,
and education by publishing worldwide. Oxford is a registered trademark of
Oxford University Press in the UK and in certain other countries.

Published in India by
Oxford University Press
22 Workspace, 2nd Floor, 1/22 Asaf Ali Road, New Delhi 110002, India

© Oxford University Press 2021

The moral rights of the authors have been asserted.

First Edition published in 2021

All rights reserved. No part of this publication may be reproduced, stored in
a retrieval system, or transmitted, in any form or by any means, without the
prior permission in writing of Oxford University Press, or as expressly permitted
by law, by licence, or under terms agreed with the appropriate reprographics
rights organization. Enquiries concerning reproduction outside the scope of the
above should be sent to the Rights Department, Oxford University Press, at the
address above.

You must not circulate this work in any other form
and you must impose this same condition on any acquirer.

ISBN-13 (print edition): 978-0-19-012683-4
ISBN-10 (print edition): 0-19-012683-3

ISBN-13 (eBook): 978-0-19-099164-7
ISBN-10 (eBook): 0-19-099164-X

Typeset in Trump Mediaeval LT Std 10/13
by Tranistics Data Technologies, Kolkata 700 091
Printed in India by Rakmo Press, New Delhi 110 020

Contents

List of Figures and Tables	vii
Foreword by Valerian Rodrigues	ix
Preface by S. Japhet	xi
List of Abbreviations	xix
Introduction by Aakash Singh Rathore	xxiii

1. Ambedkar's Theory of the Social:
   The Universal Condition of Recognition   1
   MARTIN FUCHS

2. B.R. Ambedkar: Visionary and Realist   26
   JAMES MANOR

3. Caste and Delivery of Social Justice: Revisiting Ambedkar   49
   G.C. PAL

4. 'Made to Think and Forced to Feel': The Power
   of Counter-Ritual   71
   MEENA DHANDA

5. Dalits in Search of Inclusion: Comparing Nepal with India   91
   DAVID N. GELLNER, KRISHNA P. ADHIKARI,
   AND ARJUN BAHADUR B.K.

6. Ambedkar, Labour, and the Political Economy
   of Dalit Conversion in Colonial Panjab   116
   NAVYUG GILL

7. The Fractured Society of the Republic	147
SHAILAJA MENON	
8. Whose State Is It Anyway? Reservation, Representation, Caste, and Power	169
KAREN GABRIEL AND PREM KUMAR VIJAYAN	
9. Reclaiming Social Justice and Deepening Democracy	197
JAGANNATHAM BEGARI	
10. Ambedkar's Internationalization of Social Justice	222
SURAJ YENGDE	
11. Foregrounding Social Justice in Indian Historiography: Interrogating the Poona Pact	252
KARTHIK RAJA KARUPPUSAMY	
12. Ambedkar and the Metaphysics of Social Justice	280
AJAY VERMA	
Index	295
Editor and Contributors	310

Figure and Tables

Figure

8.1 Representativeness of CG Employees   194

Tables

2.1 Percentages of Total Person-Days Worked   42

5.1 Dalit Sub-Groups (Castes) in Nepal by Population
and Region According to the 2011 Census   97

5.2 Migration Abroad for Work or Studies in Six Adjacent
Villages of Kaski District (Household Data)   102

8.1 Community-Wise Population Sizes   179

8.2 Community-Wise Representativeness   183

8.3 Group-Wise Distribution of HSSOs (2013)   183

8.4 Group-Wise Population (2016)   185

8.5 Group-Wise Distribution of HSSOs (Estimated for 2016)   186

8.6 OBCs in Groups (2017)   186

8.7 HSSO Employees in CG Services   188

8.8 UCH Employees in CG Services   188

Foreword

Most of the chapters included in this volume were initially presented at a momentous international conference, 'Quest for Equity: Reclaiming Social Justice, Revisiting Ambedkar', held in Bengaluru, India, from 21 June to 23 June 2017, to commemorate the 126th birth anniversary of Dr B.R. Ambedkar. Over 350 papers were presented at the seminar, and apart from common keynote presentations, there were parallel sessions in Kannada, alongside English. These sessions were open to the public, and on an average, about 10,000 people attended the presentations under the different panels. There were cultural programmes, particularly highlighting the rich folklore of Karnataka and Ambedkar-inspired Dalit cultural repertoire. The conference was organized by the Government of Karnataka, assisted by an advisory committee made of academicians and Ambedkar scholars.

The primary objective of the conference was rethinking the idea of social justice for complex, deeply diverse, and inegalitarian societies such as India by employing Ambedkar's writings and practices as a frame. By making social justice as the nodal norm, the conference sought to assess prevailing ideas, appeals, and social and political processes; to hold institutions and public policy to critical scrutiny; throw up concerns and questions afresh; and propose alternatives wherever possible. By bringing together scholars, social activists, and political leaders under a common platform, it sought to forge a critical space for theory and practice. One of the assumptions that informed this conference was the growing evidence on expanding economic and social inequality, social exclusion and violence, blatant violation of constitutional norms, and weakening of public institutions on one hand and rising tide of majoritarian nationalism and neoliberal triumphalism on the other. The central concerns that inspired this conference converged in the inspiring figure of Ambedkar, his thought, and practice. The conference venue reverberated with the message that the ideas and ideals that we cherish today and the significant strivings of social movements in quest of equity find their echo in what Ambedkar stood for all through his life.

The conference was preceded by a series of interconnected awareness-building and mobilizational activities for over a year. Social activists in Karnataka carried out a campaign across the state, making the district as a unit and institutions of higher education as their focus, to popularize certain key writings of Ambedkar and to critically probe their relevance in the present. For the purpose, local-level seminars, public meetings, and rallies were held in different districts, eventually culminating in Bengaluru. This campaign was accompanied with handy translations of some of the key writings of Ambedkar and placing them within easy reach of the youth. Further, a research team headed by Professor S. Japhet carried out a series of research projects exploring the socio-economic conditions of the scheduled castes (SCs), scheduled tribes (STs), and minorities in the state, and findings of these studies were employed as a critical pool of resource for the state-wide mobilization of vulnerable and marginal castes and communities. From all accounts, both these initiatives drew enthusiastic response from the concerned social sections. As a result, there was already in place an enthusiastic audience to listen to and interact with the proceedings of the conference.

While it is difficult to measure the impact of a conference of this scale to any appreciable extent, it definitely led to a flurry of academic publications and initiatives in India and beyond on Ambedkar and comparative studies on Dalits, Blacks, and other marginal groups. In this context, the efforts of Dr Aakash Singh Rathore to edit some of the papers presented at the conference in five volumes is truly commendable and would go a long way in reinforcing a critical sensibility to the quest for equity that the conference proclaimed aloud. This volume on social justice contains many chapters that give us a feel of not merely what went on at the conference, but the kind of research current scholarship is likely to pursue on the theme in the near future.

Valerian Rodrigues
Former Professor of Political Science, Centre for Political
Studies, Jawaharlal Nehru University

Preface

This book forms part of a five-volume publication entitled *B.R. Ambedkar: The Quest for Justice*, an ambitious project that originated during the B.R. Ambedkar International Conference, 'Quest for Equity', held at Bengaluru, India, in July 2017, with some 350 speakers and thousands of participants. That conference took place keeping in view that the values of social, political, and economic justice that were so vigorously championed by Dr Ambedkar are now under attack at several levels: constitutional norms and public institutions created to fight against dominance and subservience have proved inadequate or have been subverted; norms and policy often merely pay lip service to egalitarian considerations; and the rise of social intolerance and exclusion tends to effectively whittle down and even sabotage an inclusive conception of polity and citizenship. The complexity of the social, political, and economic environment in which the value of social justice has to be envisaged too has undergone significant changes: we understand social inequality and diversity to be layered and multidimensional; and the State has to reckon with several competing centres of religious, communal, and cultural allegiances. Despite these serious challenges, new sites for social and political assertions have re-emerged, renewing the call for justice. These five volumes are very much part of that engagement.

Social activism in India today is inspired by Dr B.R. Ambedkar's insightful lifework analysing complex social and political challenges and proposing daring and radical policy measures in response. His approach to critical intellectual and policy challenges may inspire similar interventions elsewhere in the world, particularly throughout the Global South. Thus, in the light of the conference, this five-volume collection emerged as an invitation to scholars and policymakers to substantially re-think current political, social, legal, economic, gender, racial, religious, and cultural paradigms motivated by Dr B.R. Ambedkar's imaginative and creative work.

The project has succeeded in encouraging a wide interdisciplinary engagement among academics, scholars, activists, and policymakers on each of these themes, which are treated across the five volumes. This is apparent from a review of their tables of contents:

B.R. Ambedkar: The Quest for Justice
(in five volumes)

Volume I: *Political Justice*

1. Bhikhu Parekh   *The Intellectual and Political Legacy of B.R. Ambedkar*
2. Cosimo Zene   *B.R. Ambedkar and Antonio Gramsci: Justice for the Excluded, Education for Democracy*
3. Anand Teltumbde   *Ambedkar and Democracy: Critical Reflections*
4. Neera Chandhoke   *Repairing Complex Historical Injustice*
5. Pradeep Gokhale   *Dr Ambedkar and the Trio of Principles: Liberty, Equality, and Fraternity*
6. Vidhu Verma   *Discrimination, Colonial Injustice, and the Good Society*
7. Scott Stroud   *Communication, Justice, and Reconstruction: Ambedkar as an Indian Pragmatist*
8. J. Daniel Elam   *Of Castes and Crowds: B.R. Ambedkar's Anti-colonial Endosmosis*
9. Pushparaj Deshpande   *A Constellation of Ideas: Revisiting Ambedkar and Gandhi*
10. Shaunna Rodrigues   *Self-Respect as a Primary Political Ideal: Ambedkar's Challenge to Political Theory*

Volume II: *Social Justice*

1. Martin Fuchs *Ambedkar's Theory of the Social: The Universal Condition of Recognition*
2. James Manor *B.R. Ambedkar: Visionary and Realist*
3. G.C. Pal *Caste and Delivery of Social Justice: Revisiting Ambedkar*
4. Meena Dhanda *'Made to Think and Forced to Feel': The Power of Counter-Ritual*
5. David N. Gellner, Krishna P. Adhikari, and Arjun Bahadur B.K. *Dalits in Search of Inclusion: Comparing Nepal with India*
6. Navyug Gill *Ambedkar, Labour, and the Political Economy of Dalit Conversion in Colonial Panjab*
7. Shailaja Menon *The Fractured Society of the Republic*
8. Karen Gabriel and Prem Kumar Vijayan *Whose State Is It Anyway? Reservation, Representation, Caste, and Power*
9. Jagannatham Begari *Reclaiming Social Justice and Deepening Democracy*
10. Suraj Yengde *Ambedkar's Internationalization of Social Justice*
11. Karthik Raja Karuppusamy *Foregrounding Social Justice in Indian Historiography: Interrogating the Poona Pact*
12. Ajay Verma *Ambedkar and the Metaphysics of Social Justice*

Volume III: *Legal and Economic Justice*

Part One: Legal Justice

1. Upendra Baxi *Lawless Law, Living Death, and the Insurgent Moral Reason of Babasaheb Ambedkar*
2. R. Sudarshan *B.R. Ambedkar's Exemplary Adherence to Constitutional Morality*
3. Arvind Narrain *Radical Constitutionalism: Towards an Ambedkarite Jurisprudence*
4. Antje Linkenbach *B.R. Ambedkar's Imaginations of Justice*
5. Umakant *The Significance of Rights and Rule of Law under the Indian Constitutional Framework*
6. Anupama Rao *B.R. Ambedkar and Indian Democracy*

Part Two: Economic Justice

7. Vijay Gudavarthy *Development through Informalization and Circulation of Labour: The Emerging Anatomy of an Uncivil Society*
8. Joseph Tharamangalam *India's Paradox of 'Hunger Amidst Plenty' Has a Name: Caste-Based Discrimination and Exclusion*
9. Aseem Prakash *Dalits Enter the Indian Markets as Owners of Capital: Adverse Inclusion, Social Networks, and Civil Society*
10. Pritam Singh *Ambedkar's Economic Methodology for Social Justice: The Centrality of Dalits*
11. Jawed Alam Khan *Economic Justice: Policy and Public Investment for Pasmanda Muslims*

Volume IV: *Gender and Racial Justice*

Part One: Gender Justice

1. Sanghmitra S. Acharya *Double Disadvantage of Sanitation Workers and Government Responses*
2. Mushtaq Ahmad Malla *The Shame of India: Stigma and Shame among Dalit Women in Rural Agricultural Relations*
3. Rajesh Raushan *Gender Equality and Women's Empowerment: Ambedkar in Contemporary Context*
4. Sunaina Arya *Ambedkar as a Feminist Philosopher*
5. Mala Mukherjee *Ambedkar on Women's Empowerment and the Status of Dalit Women in Karnataka*
6. Komal Rajak and N. Sukumar *Constructing a New Female Subjectivity: Ambedkar's Perspective*

Part Two: Racial Justice

7. Moses Seenarine *Organic Resistance: The Relevance of Ambedkar, Du Bois, and Garvey to Diaspora, Caste, Race, and Women's Liberation*
8. Goolam Vahed and Ashwin Desai *Racelessness and Ambedkar's Idea of Annihilation: Post-apartheid South Africa*

9. Kevin Brown and Lalit Khandare *Common Struggles? Why There Has Not Been More Cooperation between African-Americans and Dalits*
10. Goolam Vahed *Can Ambedkar Speak to Africa? Colour, Caste, and Class Struggles in Contemporary South Africa*

Volume V: *Religious and Cultural Justice*

Part One: Religious Justice

1. Laurence R. Simon *Searching for a Theology of Liberation in India*
2. Kanchana Mahadevan *Ambedkar's Critical Hermeneutics of Religion*
3. Debora Spini *Civil Religion, Uncivil Society: A Reflection on Baba Sahib Dr B.R. Ambedkar's Conception of a 'Religion for Civil Society'*
4. Priyanka Jha *The Gaze on Justice: A Genealogy from Anagarika Dharmapala to B.R Ambedkar*
5. Bansidhar Deep *B.R. Ambedkar's Philosophy of Religion*
6. Matthew H. Baxter *Two Concepts of Conversion at Meenakshipuram: Seeing through Ambedkar's Buddhism and Being Seen in EVR's Islam*

Part Two: Cultural Justice

7. Pramod K. Nayar *Marginality, Suffering, Justice: Questions of Dalit Dignity in Cultural Texts*
8. Y. Srinivasa Rao *Asura: Myth into Cultural Reality*
9. John Clammer *Cultural Rights in the Context of Ambedkarite Social Justice*
10. Raju Sakthivel *Education in a Hierarchical Culture*
11. Jadumani Mahanand *Ambedkar in/and Academic Space*

Despite the wide range of themes spread across these five volumes, the collection as a whole is oriented towards articulable specific aims and objectives. These aims and objectives are inspired by and fully consistent with the life and legacy of Dr Ambedkar, a man who was, on the one hand, a scholar of indubitable genius, and on the other hand, a dynamic agent of social and political action.

1. *B.R. Ambedkar: The Quest for Justice* seeks to explore the multifaceted idea of justice in dialogue with Ambedkar's *opus* for a society that encompasses manifold social inequalities, deep diversities, exclusion, and marginality.
2. In dialogue with Ambedkar's writings, the contributions to the collection aim in an overall way to suggest constitutional, institutional, and policy responses to the concerns of justice, and to reformulate the conceptual and policy linkages between social justice and other related norms and concerns.
3. Through high-level scholarship, this collection aims to help identify modes of thought and agency and social and political practices inimical to the pursuit of justice, and to delineate social and political agency and modes of action conducive to the furtherance of justice in line with Dr Ambedkar's own writings and mission.

Thus, in sum, Dr Ambedkar's conception of justice and his life's work shaping the idea of India offer this collection the vantage points for sustained reflection on concerns of justice and its relation to other human values. This is particularly relevant, indeed urgent, in our day, not only in India but also throughout the world.

As the convener of the organizing committee of the Dr B.R. Ambedkar International Conference, 'Quest for Equity', held at Bengaluru, India, in July 2017, where many of the chapters included in this volume were originally presented, I would like to gratefully acknowledge the people and institutions that made the conference a success and helped to make these volumes possible.

First and foremost, I must acknowledge the Government of Karnataka with Chief Minister Siddaramaiah at the helm, which hosted and funded the conference. Many put in extraordinary time and effort: Dr H.C. Mahadevappa, convenor and hon'ble minister for Public Works Department (PWD); H. Anjaneya, hon'ble minister for Social Welfare Department; Dr G. Parameshwara, hon'ble minister for home affairs; Shri T.B. Jayachandra, hon'ble minister for law and minor irrigation; Shri R. Roshan Baig, hon'ble minister for infrastructure development and information; Shri Basavaraj Rayareddy, hon'ble minister for higher education; Shrimati Umashree, hon'ble minister for women and child welfare development; Priyank M. Kharge, publicity convener and hon'ble minister for information technology and biotechnology; Krishna Byre Gowda, logistics convener and hon'ble minister for agriculture; and Captain Manivannan, secretary, Social Welfare Department. Thanks also to Dr M.C. Srinivasa, joint director, Social Welfare Department, and Dr H. Nataraj, secretary, State Safai Karmachari Commission, both nodal officers attached to Captain Manivannan, for taking care of the logistics of the conference organization. I would also like to thank Dr Nagalakshmi and Mehroz Khan, who were coordinators for the conference; Shri Srinivasulu, managing director, Ambedkar Development Corporation, attached to Krishna Byre Gowda; and Dr Nandan Kumar, officer on special duty to Priyank Kharge. I must also thank Luthfulla Atheeq, principal secretary to the chief minister; Shri Venkataiah, special advisor to Social Welfare Department; M.V. Savithri, commissioner, Social Welfare Department; and numerous other officials and staff of the Social Welfare Department, who worked so diligently.

Special thanks are due to the Scheduled Castes Department team of the All India Congress Committee: Shri K. Raju, head of the Congress President's Office, for his ideation and immense political support, and Pushparaj Deshpande, in-charge of the Quest for Equity website and other logistical support. I cannot fail to mention Oum, Navil, Deepika, and the rest of the Phase I team, who worked tirelessly.

I would like to express my profound thanks to the members of the various committees, specially members of the academic committee, Professors S. Thorat, Valerian Rodrigues, G. Haragopal, Aakash Singh Rathore, and Dr Rochana Bajpai, Sudhir Krishnaswamy, S.G. Siddaramaiah, K. Marulasiddappa, Siddalingaiah, L. Hanumanthaiah, Mallika Ganti, and K.B. Siddaiah. Special thanks are also due to the editorial advisory board for their invaluable advice and assistance throughout, including those members from the academic committee mentioned earlier, as well as Dr Suraj Yengde and Professors Anand Teltumbde, Kalpana Kannabiran, Lawrence R. Simon, and Meena Dhanda. My heartful thanks to Professor Aakash Singh Rathore for taking the responsibility of editing these volumes.

Of course, I cannot fail to mention the support of Shabin John and Chandrashekar for their office and logistics support and Dr Ramkhok Raikhan for research assistance to the editor.

S. Japhet
Professor and Vice Chancellor,
Bengaluru Central University, India

Abbreviations

AC	*Annihilation of Caste*
AISCF	All India Scheduled Caste Federation
BAMCEF	All India Backward and Minorities Central Employees Federation
BJP	Bharatiya Janata Party
BLL	Buraku Liberation League
BPA	British Philosophical Association
Capt.	Captain
CG	Central Government
DS-4	Dalit Shoshit Samaj Sangharsh Samittee
ECOSOC	Economic and Social Council
EHRC	Equality and Human Rights Commission
FIR	First Information Report
G	Gazetted
GC	Total population of *all* non-'HSSOs' (i.e., those who can only apply through the 'general category')
GDP	Gross domestic product
GEO	Government Inequalities Office
GoI	Government of India
H	Total population of 'Hindus' in India
HJS	Hindu Janajagruti Samiti
HSSO	Population of 'Hindu' SCs, STs, and OBCs
ICDS	Integrated Child Development Scheme
ILP	Independent Labour Party
ISCA	Institute of Social and Cultural Anthropology
IT&BT	Information Technology & Biotechnology
JNU	Jawaharlal Nehru University

LUISS	Libera Università Internazionale degli Studi Sociali
M	Total population of minorities in India
MANUU	Maulana Azad National Urdu University
MD	Managing Director
Mg	Population of non-'Msso' minorities in general (hence Mg)
MGNREGA	Mahatma Gandhi National Rural Employment Guarantee Act
MP	Member of Parliament
Msso	Total population of people of SC, ST, or OBC origin, in the minority communities
NAACP	National Association for the Advancement of Colored People
NCRB	National Crime Record Bureau
NDA	National Democratic Alliance
NGO	Non-Governmental Organization
OBC	Other Backward Classes
P	Total population of India
PC	Population Count
PCI	Press Council of India
PCR	Protection of Civil Rights
PH	*Philosophy of Hinduism*
PM	Prime Minister
PoA	Prevention of Atrocity
PSU	Public-sector undertaking
PWD	Public Works Department
RPI	Republican Party of India
RSS	Rashtriya Swayamsevak Sangh
SC	Scheduled Caste
SDG	Sustainable development goals
SEATO	South East Asia Treaty Organization
SOAS	School of Oriental and African Studies
SSO	Total population of *all* SCs, STs, and OBCs (including from religions where caste is not cognized)
ST	Scheduled Tribe
SWIP	Society for Women in Philosophy
TBHD	*The Buddha and His Dhamma*
UCH	Population of non-'HSSOs' amongst 'Hindus' (the upper castes, hence 'UCH')

UDALS	Una Dalit Atyachar Ladat Samiti
UK	United Kingdom
UML	Communist Party of Nepal, Unified Marxist-Leninist
UP	Uttar Pradesh
VHP	Vishva Hindu Parishad

Introduction

AAKASH SINGH RATHORE

Social Justice

At a monumental recent event in Bengaluru, India (the same which has given rise to this five-volume collection, and about which Valerian Rodrigues wrote in detail in his Foreword to this volume), many of the themes and issues that can be subsumed under the broad category of social justice were given powerful utterance in the collaborative framing and release of the Bengaluru Declaration, inspired by the life-work of B.R. Ambedkar. Dr Ambedkar is, of course, the pre-eminent authority of modern India on the subject of social justice. His preoccupations during the first half of the twentieth century remain our preoccupations in the first half of the twenty-first century. To see how all of these have been captured and articulated for our times, it would be fruitful to revisit the text of that Declaration here.

Bengaluru Declaration

PREAMBLE

Babasaheb Dr. B.R. Ambedkar once argued that 'a nation is not a people synthesised by a common culture derived from common language, common religion or common race.... Nationality is a feeling of oneness which makes those who are charged with it feel they are kith and kin.... It is a feeling of "consciousness of kind" ... it is longing to belong to one's own group. This is the essence of what is called a nationality and national feeling'.

Giving shape to that vision, and stemming from their experiences of the freedom struggle, our founders consistently strived to forge a 'consciousness of kind'. They ensured that each one of us was accorded equal opportunities to live with dignity and security, to have equitable access to a better life, and is an equal partner in this nation's growth. This has been the foundation of India's rapid growth in the last 70 years.

If India is to continue to rise to ever greater heights in the *next* 70 years, we must further the promise of the nation to all Indians through creative policies and constructive politics. We can only do that by:

1. Reasserting the fundamental principle of one person-one value
2. Reclaiming our freedom, dignity and human personality
3. Comprehensively addressing the needs and aspirations of all Indians, especially those who are most vulnerable and marginalised, such as Scheduled Castes (SCs), Scheduled Tribes (STs), other backward classes (OBCs), Women and Minorities
4. Celebrating the fact that we are stronger together, and because of each other
5. Overcoming the divisive politics that attempt to pit caste against caste, class against class, and community against community

RECOMMENDATIONS

Safeguarding the People

1. Upholding the Rule of Law: The State must be unequivocal in its protection of fundamental rights and constitutional values. To do this:
   - Irrespective of religious identities or institutional affiliations, the State needs to strictly reassert political and legal accountability for any violence. This is the only way to prevent lynchings and uphold the rule of law.
   - The police services must be freed from political control, and reformed by fully implementing police reforms, so that they become a service provider to citizens rather than a force to impose control.
   - Just like the Prevention of Sexual Harassment at Workplace Act, a special Act for the prevention of caste, religious and gender discrimination in educational institutions must be passed. This will prevent discrimination in admission, enhance access to quality education, and ensure equality as an integral part of the education process.

Introduction   xxv

- The State must uphold the Constitution in letter and spirit. Any attempt at reviewing the Constitution shall be opposed forthwith.
2. Protecting Individual Rights and Freedoms: All provisions that place constraints on freedom of speech, expression and individual rights should be reformed or removed. These include those on defamation, sedition, art/film censorship and social media.

Strengthening Democratic Institutions

3. Reform of political representation: The political party is a key institution in our democracy that organizes and channelizes the political wishes of the people. To ensure that they continue to do so, the following are proposed:
4. State funding of elections:
   - The Election Commission of India should be conferred with extensive regulatory powers to ensure that political parties mandatorily uphold fundamental rights and adhere to constitutional values, as well as comply with internal democratic procedures.
   - The ECI must also ensure that religious beliefs and practices cannot be mobilised in any form in electoral or governance practices.
   - To promote enhanced diversity and representation, a constitutional amendment institutionalising reservations for OBCs to assembly and parliament should be passed.
   - To promote gender parity in assembly and parliament, a constitutional amendment for reservations for women with an appropriate provision for representation of SC, ST, and OBC women, should be passed.
   - Reforms of the electoral system to ensure SC and ST representation better reflects the will, and are accountable to these sections.
5. Protecting media freedoms: Freedom of press is paramount for strengthening and deepening democracy. Today, the freedom of the press is compromised and individual journalists are under attack by fundamentalist elements and subject to tacit State censorship. Secondly, journalistic standards are also being systematically compromised. Thirdly, sections of the media are complicit in creating or exacerbating casteist and religious tensions. To ensure the media is able to function as a nation's conscience keeper, it is proposed:

- The Press Council of India (PCI) should be conferred with extensive regulatory powers to take suo-moto action against attacks on individual journalists and censorship.
- The PCI will also be empowered to regulate corporate monopoly and cross ownership of media.
- The PCI should also strive to ensure greater diversity in media houses by promoting representation of SC, ST, OBC, Minority and women at all levels.

6. Judicial reforms: To ensure that the judiciary is robust and reflective of the social diversity of India, reservations for SCs/STs/OBCs in the higher judiciaries must be institutionalised. Furthermore, as per the recommendation of the National Judicial Commission, an All India Judicial Services should be created with provisions of reservation for SC/STs/OBCs.

Deepening Social Justice

7. Equal Opportunities Commission: Given widespread inequities which include underrepresentation of SC, ST, OBC, Women and Minorities in employment, the State should establish an equal opportunities commission which should adopt creative strategies and policies to achieve equity in the public and private sectors. The Chairpersons of the national commissions for Scheduled Castes (SCs), Scheduled Tribes (STs), socially and educationally backward classes shall be members of the Equal Opportunities Commission.

8. Scheduled Caste Special Component and Tribal Component Legislation: A national legislation to ensure that a portion of the budget equal to the population proportion of SC & STs to support schemes to bridge the gaps in development of SCs & STs when compared to rest of the society should be brought out by the central government. These funds should be directly and exclusively meant for the welfare of SCs and STs, and not include generic expenditure.

9. Ensuring study of Dr. Ambedkar, Mahatma Jyotiba & Savitribai Phule in school and college curriculum: To inspire and educate future generations on ideas and movements of social justice, curriculum in schools and colleges should mandatorily include the study of the life and work of Dr. Ambedkar, Mahatma and Savitribai Phule.

10. Accelerated development of SC, ST, and OBC dominated habitations: Like the Multi-Sectoral Development Programme, the State should ensure that every SC, ST, and OBC household should get

access to basic civic amenities, including power supply, tapped water, sanitation and connectivity within five years.

11. Reservations in procurement and contracts: Like in Karnataka, there should be reservations in procurement and contracts for up to 100 lakhs. This will benefit SC, ST and OBC entrepreneurs.

12. Equitable access to reservations: The State shall put in place an appropriate institutional mechanism to ensure all the sub-castes among SCs & STs enjoy equal access to benefits of reservations.

13. Reservation in Promotion: The State shall amend the Constitution, if necessary, so as to ensure reservations in promotion for SCs/STs/OBCs in all government and semi-government sector.

14. English medium education to SCs, STs, OBCs, Women and Minorities: To ensure these communities are able to stand as equals with forward castes, the State shall ensure access to quality English medium education from secondary school level onwards.

15. Navodaya type residential schools for all vulnerable children: To uplift and empower through quality education, one Navodaya type of residential school from class six to class 12 should be instituted in every district, block and sub-block level for all vulnerable children, especially SCs, STs, OBCs and Minorities.

16. Universal access to hostels for SCs, STs and OBCs: To empower and give flight to their aspirations, access to hostels should be universalised for all SC, ST and OBC students.

17. Reservations for SCs, STs and OBCs in private higher educational institutions: Considering the expansion of higher educational institutions in the private section, reservations for SCs, STs and OBCs in these institutions shall be made mandatory.

18. Filling up backlog vacancies in reserved posts: Despite numerous administrative measures, backlog vacancies in government, universities and Public Sector Undertakings remain a pressing concern. The State must therefore mandatorily fill up all the backlog vacancies in reserved posts within a year and such a drive shall be repeated every year.

19. Reservations in the private sector: To ensure diversity in all sectors, the State shall bring in a legislation guaranteeing reservations for SCs, STs and OBCs in the private organised sector.

20. Economic Empowerment of SC/ST/OBCs and Minorities: The State shall ensure adequate special funds to boost entrepreneurship among the SC/STs, OBCs and Minorities, to ensure they attain economic liberty. The State shall also reserve at least 10 per cent of stakes/shares in PSUs/Corporations/Companies, for SC/STs/OBCs to enhance their participation in the economic activities of the State. For this, the State shall create a special corpus fund for SC/

ST/OBCs to buy these stakes/shares. Similar other mechanisms to increase representations of SC/ST/OBCs in Government financial institutions should also be ensured.

21. Agricultural land for landless Dalits: Landless Dalits should be provided with agricultural land as a legal entitlement and special support should be provided so that agriculture becomes an economically viable occupation including the provisions for minimum agricultural income for all people engaged in agriculture. Special legislation should be passed to this effect.

22. Universal irrigation of all SC, ST and OBC lands: Universal irrigation of all SC, ST and OBC lands should be urgently undertaken to ensure sustainable farming.

23. Institutionalising Special Tribunal to ensure ST lands are restored: A special tribunal should be institutionalised to ensure that all land belonging to STs but purchased by non-STs should be restored back to the STs.

24. Sustainable livelihoods for STs: To ensure STs are guaranteed sustainable livelihood, minimum support price for non-timber forest produce should be ensured.

25. Legislation to secure SC & ST lands: Legislation prohibiting acquisition and occupation of SC & ST lands by others should be strengthened and enacted where do they do not exist. These need to be strictly enforced.

26. Land banks to protect SC & ST land ownership: Land banks should be established to buy at market prices lands of SCs and STs who need to sell their land. Furthermore, reallotments of such land should happen only to SCs and STs so that total land ownership of SCs and STs is not diluted.

27. Permanent, not contractual employment: Safai Karmacharies in the rural and urban local bodies employed under contract system should be provided permanent employment, by abolishing contract system. Furthermore, all steps should be taken to stop manual scavenging in any forms in a time bound manner.

28. Comprehensive reform of caste-based occupational vocations: All caste-based occupational vocations must be comprehensively reformed so that they are modernised, formalised and it is ensured that those entering the particular occupation are not representative of a particular caste or community. At the same time, through the above mentioned educational and employment recommendations, the State should liberate people from caste based occupational oppression.

29. Immediate publishing of socio-economic caste census: The State shall immediately publicise the results of the socio-economic and caste census undertaken in the urban and rural areas.

Enhancing Human Development

30. Farmers Income Commission: The agricultural sector is in acute crisis, and the last three years have seen a marked decline in the economic condition of farmers. It is imperative that farmers' incomes are first protected, and then augmented. Therefore a Farmers Income Commission must be urgently institutionalised to ensure income security for India's annadatas.

31. Nine is Mine: The State should allocate six percent of the GDP for education and three percent for health. Both health and education should be universal rights.

32. Universal secondary education: Building on the Right to Education, secondary education should be universal. The State should especially focus on ensuring universal enrolment and retention of SCs, STs, OBCs and Minorities.

33. Right to Shelter and Housing: A Right to Shelter and Housing to guarantee homestead in rural India and urban areas for the poor. Special care should be taken to secure these rights for SCs, STs, OBCs and Minorities.

34. Nutritional support for children covered under the Integrated Child Development Scheme (ICDS): To improve nutritional levels at the growing stages and eliminate malnutrition, every child covered under the ICDS must receive one hot cooked meal, milk and an egg, daily.

35. Halfway homes to support employment: Tier I and II cities should have halfway homes to give free accommodation for all youth who secured employment in the cities till they find accommodation or three months (whichever is earlier).

Ensuring Responsive Governance

36. The State must establish institutionalised mechanisms for citizens to participate in all aspects of decision making in governance. This is the essence of a participatory democracy.

    – As mandated under Section 4 of the RTI Act, there must be a transparent and participatory pre-legislative process for soliciting citizen feedback before laws are passed.

    – Social audits wherein citizens and beneficiaries evaluate the impact and performance of public programmes must be extended to all areas of governance.

    – A legal framework for ensuring time bound grievance redress through a comprehensive architecture that is independent and decentralised, and incorporates provisions of social audit, public disclosures, codified citizen charter and job charts and citizen

Introduction

facilitation should be passed. This will ensure that the Right to Information organically becomes into the government's Requirement to Inform.

Promoting Social Security

37. Universal social security for unorganised sector: All labourers working in the unorganised sector should be covered with a comprehensive social security scheme providing for life, disability and health insurance. In addition, monthly pensions should be provided to those who have crossed 60 years.
38. Living wage for unorganised sector: Workers in the unorganised sector must be secured with a 'Living Wage' which ensures a decent standard of life, full enjoyment of leisure and social and cultural activities.
39. Ensuring Dignity in Retirement through enhanced pensions: To ensure that the old, disabled and widows are able to lead a dignified life, pensions will be enhanced to Rs. 1500 p.m., with an increase every year in tune with the Consumer Price Index.
40. Enhanced safety net: To uplift and empower the most vulnerable, the State's safety net should be expanded by universalising access to all poverty elimination programmes for every family where no members of the family pays income tax.
41. Fund for landless labourers: All loan waivers should have an additional 20 per cent kept aside as a fund for rehabilitating and uplifting landless labourers.
42. Low cost housing for the urban poor in all private housing layouts: To ensure affordable housing for the urban poor, all private housing layouts must allocate 20 per cent of land for low cost housing.

CONCLUSION

India's founders consciously chose to create a society where each individual—irrespective of caste, gender, ethnicity, region, religion, income capacities or ideological inclination—was to be recognised, by both the State and by every other citizen, as possessor of equal value and inalienable dignity. They sought to ensure that every person had equal access to the promise of this nation. In the last 70 years the leaders of modern India have strived to ensure that every citizen—especially SCs, STs, OBCs, Women and Minorities—enjoyed equal rights and that no one gets left, or held behind.

Regressive social and political forces have consistently resisted and tried to undermine both the constitutional idea of India and the efforts of the State in the last 70 years. These forces also seek to homogenise India and restore the principles of hierarchy, patriarchy and fundamentalism that Babasaheb Ambedkar, Jawaharlal Nehru, Jagjivan Ram, Vallabhbhai Patel, Maulana Azad and other founders rejected at the birth of the nation. Now that they enjoy State power, they are systematically dismantling the institutions that are the foundations of our society, by undermining India's holistic welfare and affirmative action architecture and by destroying the pluralistic fabric of our nation. This poses a grave threat to the idea of India espoused by the freedom movement and spelt out in the Constitution.

We need to address these concerns urgently, and resist these attacks boldly. India needs to return to its noblest ideals, the spirit of its Constitution. It is time for the Indian people to recognise the constitutional path we chose 70 years ago and dedicate ourselves to protect and enhance this legacy. In this quest, the Bengaluru Declaration hopes that all progressive forces, collectively and across party lines, will adopt and implement these recommendations to fulfil Babasaheb Ambedkar's dream of an equitable, just and egalitarian society.

The Twelve Chapters

From the first collection on political justice, in the present volume, we turn to social justice, the quintessential concern of the Bengaluru Declaration. The contributors in this volume, by means of their diversely themed engagements, illustrate the reasons why such efforts remain critical and urgent. Some of the essays constitute background, while several of the essays explicitly dialogue with the principles and recommendations set out in the Bengaluru Declaration. All of them take up issues of central relevance to exploring the nature and destiny of social justice, either as such or specifically in terms of their interpretation of Dr Ambedkar's own position.

In the first chapter, Martin Fuchs ('Ambedkar's Theory of the Social: The Universal Condition of Recognition') reconstructs Ambedkar's sociological and socio-philosophical explorations of the conditions for a just society. Fuchs focuses on what one could call Ambedkar's theory of the social, which underlies his conceptualization of religion and of social and religious change. This chapter is a fitting launch to this volume on social justice, as it starts by looking at Ambedkar's emphasis on social values and on the dispositional and attitudinal dimensions of social behaviour that affect the ways people relate to each other. The author then moves on to a discussion of Ambedkar's views of the social significance of religion and his attempts to distinguish between religion that realizes the human core values, and religion that fails on the criterion of justice. In doing so, Fuchs refers to the ontological assumptions regarding human nature and the nature of human sociality underlying Ambedkar's views. In short, he takes Ambedkar's theory of the social to be the key to his overall vision. That is, how Ambedkar conceived of society and social relations framed his ideas of religion and of possible futures. According to Fuchs, this sociological and socio-philosophical frame has still to get its full due in research on Ambedkar and in discussions about religious change, in India and beyond. In this way, the author's approach differs from those—such as predominantly in Volume I of this collection, on *Political Justice*—that focus on Ambedkar as a political actor or as a religious strategist.

James Manor ('B.R. Ambedkar: Visionary and Realist') continues to concretize Ambedkar's social vision and its lasting implications. He argues that Ambedkar has become increasingly influential and relevant in recent times because the vision that he offered was firmly anchored in a realistic analysis of India's society and culture. Manor supports this claim by evidence gathered in diverse regions of rural India on the implications of the increasing—and increasingly apparent—refusals to accept caste hierarchies by Dalits and other disadvantaged groups. But Manor is not glib about the hard-won positive developments so far achieved. He believes that Ambedkar's deep scepticism about a possible change of heart among 'higher' castes stands up especially well when considered alongside recent trends. So too, however, does his belief in the potential of laws and government actions to check abuses against Dalits, and to enhance their capabilities and autonomy. In Manor's estimation, then, Ambedkar emerges as a relevant and reliable guide as we seek to understand how things have changed, and how enlightened actors might engage effectively to promote further constructive change.

In the third chapter, G.C. Pal ('Caste and Delivery of Social Justice: Revisiting Ambedkar') argues that with the complex

Introduction xxxiii

linkages between caste and social conditions, in mainstream society, many 'unwritten laws' exist against lower-caste groups. Unless enforcement agencies are sensitive to the human rights violations against socially weaker sections and commit to upholding the legitimacy of state laws over 'caste laws', access to social justice will be an illusion. Pal cites Ambedkar's remark that the ability and efficiency of the governing class are not enough to establish the kind of governance that would ensure social justice. Thus, he argues, administrative roadblocks, judiciary bottlenecks, and lack of sensitivity need to be resolved, without which Dalits will continue to live lives of social oppression.

Meena Dhanda ('"Made to Think and Forced to Feel": The Power of Counter-Ritual') raises these concerns to a trans-national level. Fusing concerns of the second and third chapters, Dhanda turns our attention to Ambedkar's dictum that the caste Hindu must be 'made to think' and 'forced to feel that he must alter his ways'. Given the deep division within the UK's South Asian diaspora on acknowledging the salience of caste, Dhanda examines how the everyday renewal of caste relations might be disrupted through the use of counter-rituals. Dhanda observes that participation in rituals presents dual possibilities of reinforced bonding as well as ruptures. In the diaspora, everyday casteism is reproduced in distinct religious rituals, festive rituals, and marriage rituals, with costs for transgressors. Counter-rituals, as planned and deliberate challenges to entrenched ritual practices, productively deploy feelings of transgression to bring implicit caste identifications to the fore. Thus, she concludes, they may play a radical transformative role.

The fifth chapter continues the enquiry into social justice beyond India's borders. David N. Gellner, Krishna P. Adhikari, and Arjun Bahadur B.K. ('Dalits in Search of Inclusion: Comparing Nepal with India') address Nepal's separate and distinct political history from India, which means that social changes that began in India over 200 years ago have been compressed in Nepal into a quarter of that time. Electoral politics post 1990 have seen the ethnicization of caste and the emergence of five macro categories (*Khas-Arya*s or 'high' castes, *Janajati*s or tribals, Dalits, *Madheshi*s, and others). In the three-cornered fight between the three largest groups, Khas-Aryas, Janajatis, and Madheshis, the Dalits have tended to be squeezed out, despite some initial gains, thanks to the introduction of proportional representation in 2008. As the authors point out, Nepali Dalits have lacked a towering political and intellectual leader of the stature of Ambedkar. The very recent introduction of reservations in Nepal means that there is, as yet, no substantial Dalit middle class. The new 2015 Constitution gives constitutional status to the National Dalit Commission and provides for many important rights; but there is a long way to go before Nepali Dalits achieve social justice.

From the trans-national perspective, we move in the next chapter to a narrower regional or local one. In 'Ambedkar, Labour, and the Political Economy of Dalit Conversion in Colonial Panjab', Navyug Gill explores the persistence of hierarchy through the problem of lower castes formerly converting out of Hinduism, yet not out of the strictures of lowliness or casteism, in early twentieth-century Panjab. Gill begins by contextualizing what B.R. Ambedkar's undelivered 1936 Lahore speech on annihilating caste might have meant to an audience of largely landless agricultural labourers. The author then moves on to discuss the changing constellation of caste names and occupational designations for these groups amid the emergence of the *Ad Dharm* movement and its struggle to impart equality, dignity, and community to Panjabi Dalits. To understand this new sense of identity in the context of actual labour practices, the author analyses the fraught relationship between landholding cultivators and landless labourers working side by side while continuing to be separate and unequal. That a large proportion of lower castes could adopt religions other than Hinduism or even start their own and yet remain excluded and exploited reveals the limits to a politics centred on conversion. Gill concludes that it is this obstinate disjuncture between emancipation and exploitation that suggests a different horizon for overcoming caste hierarchy.

This motif of internal fissures is elaborated upon in the subsequent chapter. Shailaja Menon ('The Fractured Society of the Republic') returns our attention to a point earlier emphasized in the second chapter, that is, Ambedkar's insistence on the need to gain political power within the strategy to ameliorate the deprivations of the weaker sections of society. Ambedkar also believed as an article of faith that through political rights, the vulnerable sections would be in a position to realize social, cultural, and economic rights. This is partly rooted in his belief that state power could be a catalytic agent in bringing about this change. According to Menon, it is vital that the egalitarian ethos of the Constitution

Introduction   xxxv

is kept intact, because—as expressed poignantly throughout the Bengaluru Declaration—the last couple of years have witnessed attempts to tamper with the basic character of the Constitution and undo the gains achieved by the most marginalized sections of the population.

The next chapter continues to assess and address issues of social justice at the national level. Karen Gabriel and Prem Kumar Vijayan ('Whose State is it Anyway? Reservation, Representation, Caste, and Power') begin by foregrounding Ambedkar's observation that electoral democracy can only work if the political equality that it guarantees is matched by social and economic equality. They explore the meanings of this observation of Ambedkar in contemporary India, by examining the ways in which the idea of 'representation' has played out in the current Indian context. In relation to this, the authors discuss how non-electoral forms of representation, such as the reservation system, have fared in the current political and social scene. The focus of the chapter is on the different ways in which these understandings of representation have impacted on caste and gender, as well as on the relations between them.

Continuing along the same lines, Jagannatham Begari ('Reclaiming Social Justice and Deepening Democracy') argues that subalterns in India continue to face social discrimination, humiliation, and violence based on caste, class, gender, religion, region, and ethnicity. The author believes that the response of the state has been lackadaisical. The chapter interrogates the Una incident in Gujarat, Dalit-Muslim unity, Rohith Vemula's suicide, and other events that have led to a rise of social action and social movements. These events are discussed in conversation with the ideas and ideals of B.R. Ambedkar, especially insofar as these were articulated in the Bengaluru Declaration. Begari, thus, approaches the topic from two different sides: on the one hand, through theoretical interventions inspired by Ambedkar; and on the other hand, through mapping of the atrocities on Dalits and other subalterns in India.

Suraj Yengde raises these very same concerns at the international level. The chapter 'Ambedkar's Internationalization of Social Justice' asks what it means to look at the world through the lens of the marginalized. How do we reconcile the vision of the most oppressed under the hegemonic exclusionary theories of foreign policy? Or, simply put, do subalterns think of the global?

According to Yengde, by determining the position of the marginalized in the policy structures, close attention to Ambedkar's social and political philosophy illuminates the implications of such a global policy dialogue. This focus helps to establish the citizenry of the marginalized community in terms of social, civil, cultural, economic, and political human rights which are predominantly internationally influenced, globally inspired, and in conversation with other countries. The author argues that Dalit vision remains absent from Indian foreign policy deliberations, despite that Ambedkar was a pioneer in making internationalism and global solidarity a central concern of his project of social justice.

Just as Yengde details how Dalits are written out of India's multifaceted approach to globalization, in the next chapter, Karthik Raja Karuppusamy ('Foregrounding Social Justice in Indian Historiography: Interrogating the Poona Pact') shows how Ambedkar and the Poona Pact have been written out of Indian history. The chapter explores, elaborates, and follows the implications of such neglects and erasures through the framing of the Poona Pact in dominant historiography. Along the way, Karuppusamy offers a systematic critique of how Gandhi as a figure was used quite extravagantly without placing him in his ideological and sociopolitical trappings.

The final chapter makes another disciplinary move within the umbrella theme of social justice, now from historiography to philosophy, or metaphysics. Ajay Verma ('Ambedkar and the Metaphysics of Social Justice') takes us through Ambedkar's views on the relationship between philosophy, religion, and politics, clarifying what these terms signified for him. In this respect, the twelfth chapter loops back around to the first one, where Martin Fuchs had already referred to the ontological assumptions regarding human nature that ground social formations. In this case, basing his reading on Ambedkar's own sense of the scope and meaning of religion and philosophy, Verma aims to show how the caste system in India receives metaphysical support from Indian classical thought systems. These systems attempted to provide grounds for religious thought as it developed under the aegis of Hinduism. The author devotes most attention to Purusa Sukta, which is the heart and soul of the varna system as it came to make its appearance in Hindu society. The last part of the chapter attempts to demonstrate that an inevitable outcome of this social system is the

Introduction xxxvii

dehumanization of whole sections of society. This, clearly, bears serious implications for the idea of social justice.

Each of these twelve, broadly interrelated contributions précised here lays a single foundation stone towards erecting the pillar of social justice. This volume on social justice, in turn, serves as a unit of support for the broader edifice formed by the five volumes taken together. This broader edifice of research and scholarship may seem imposing from the academic point of view. But when viewed from the more panoramic perspective of Dr Ambedkar's lifelong quest for justice, it may rightly be seen as itself only a single foundation stone towards colossal goals. These are goals that will only be achieved by accumulating the momentum of critical masses enlightened and thundering forward. Speaking on behalf of the 70 or so participants in this particular project, I think we can take some satisfaction in the small part that we are playing through what we have achieved. The intersection and synergy between Dr Ambedkar's own profound and prolific writings with the most current scholarship and intellectual insights on offer here is a crucial step in the right direction. The Bengaluru Declaration stands as testament to the fact. But, of course, a mere declaration is not enough. Action must follow.

1

Ambedkar's Theory of the Social
*The Universal Condition of Recognition**

MARTIN FUCHS

Social justice as understood by Babasaheb Dr Bhimrao Ambedkar can be taken as shorthand for a whole bundle of values and norms that a decent society is meant to provide and which is required for each of its members to be able to lead a dignified life.[1] While Ambedkar strongly emphasized the chance for each individual to develop his or her capabilities, equality and justice for him had to be grounded in mutual respect, social recognition, and compassion, or what he, with others, called fellow feeling.

* An extended version of this article has been published under the title 'Dhamma and the Common Good: Religion as Problem and Answer—Ambedkar's Critical Theory of Social Relationality' in Fuchs and Dalmia (2019: 364–413).

This chapter owes a lot to discussions with Valerian Rodrigues. Special thanks also to Antje Linkenbach and Vasudha Dalmia who carefully read and commented on a draft of the long version of this chapter. Thanks also to the participants of colloquia and conferences at the Max-Weber-Kolleg, Erfurt, where I presented earlier drafts of the chapter, for their comments as well as to the participants and organizers of the Bengaluru conference.

[1] The concept of decent society was made prominent by Avishai Margalit (1998).

Ambedkar's attempt to achieve this in the case of his own society through political struggle and by legal means—culminating in his work on the Indian Constitution—was accompanied by his endeavour to gain deeper understanding of the mechanisms of society and explore the role of social values therein. He both explored the place and possibilities of social ethics and thought of ways of establishing such ethics that would generate a just society. It was in this context that the question of religion achieved special prominence for Ambedkar.

This chapter reconstructs Ambedkar's sociological and socio-philosophical explorations of the conditions for a just society. The focus is on what one could call Ambedkar's theory of the social, which underlies his conceptualization of religion and of social and religious change. The chapter starts by looking at Ambedkar's emphasis on social values and on the dispositional and attitudinal dimensions of social behaviour that affect the ways people relate to each other. This will be followed by a discussion on Ambedkar's views of the social significance of religion and his attempts to distinguish between religion that realizes the human core values, and religion that fails in the criterion of justice. I will briefly touch on the issue of conversion. In the course of my argument, I will refer to the ontological assumptions regarding human nature and the nature of human sociality underlying Ambedkar's views.

I consider Babasaheb's theory of the social the key to his vision. How he conceived of society and social relations frames his ideas of religion and of possible futures. This sociological and socio-philosophical frame has still to get its full due in research on Ambedkar and in discussions about religious change, in India and beyond.[2] In this, I differ from approaches that focus on Ambedkar only as a political actor or as religious strategist.

---

[2] I thus differ from D.R. Nagaraj (1993: 58) who asserted that Ambedkar's book on Buddhism, *The Buddha and His Dhamma*, reveals his 'tiredness with the social science mode of reasoning' that had guided him earlier. Valerian Rodrigues (1994: 143–4), in contrast, underlines the importance of the social sciences for Ambedkar. Rodrigues (1993) points to Fabianism besides John Dewey as influence on Ambedkar.

Ambedkar's Sociology[3]

Ambedkar's deep concern throughout his lifetime, as is well known and is being reflected in these volumes, was the plight of Dalits, their inhuman living conditions, and conditions of marginalization and oppression.[4] He did not see this only as a special problem of one group of people. Nor did he consider an adaptation to the ways and values of the upper castes (what was later labelled 'Sanskritization') an option. For him, Dalits had to be proactive, regarding their own situation and regarding society at large. At the same time, he emphasized the necessity of a thorough change of the attitudes and practices of all other members of society. Conceptually too, Ambedkar took a comprehensive view. He saw the problems that Dalits face within the wider context of the question of the constitution of society and against the backdrop of anthropological assumptions and universal conditions of human cooperation. He undertook strong efforts to gain a deeper understanding of the mechanisms as well as the potentialities of social life. He wanted to identify the possibilities and requirements for social transformation and for a change of the ways in which people relate to each other. At the same time, Dr Ambedkar's sociological approach, like that of John Dewey, the academic teacher who had impressed Ambedkar the most, combines (as he himself acknowledges;[5]) the analytical with a normative perspective.[6]

---

[3] 'Sociology' here is taken as shorthand for the conceptualization of society and the social more generally.

[4] It seems, Ambedkar first used the term *Dalit* in 1928 in his journal *Bahishkrit Bharat* (Outcaste/Boycotted India), 'where he characterized being Dalit as the experience of deprivation, marginalization, and stigmatization' (Rao 2009: 15). The term gained prominence from the 1970s onwards.

[5] Ambedkar (1987: 5).

[6] Long regarded as negligible, the significance of Dewey for Ambedkar is slowly getting more sustained, but still uneven, scholarly recognition (e.g., Kadam 1994, 1997; Rodrigues 1993, 1994, 2002; Fuchs 2001; Nanda 2001; Queen 2004; Mukherjee 2009; Škof 2011; Kumar 2015; Stroud 2016). What remains a desideratum is a systematic comparison of Dewey's and Ambedkar's social philosophies and their respective emphases. References

4 Martin Fuchs

In both theoretical and practical regards, the question of religion as social force was of core relevance to him.

Attitudes and Ideals: The Power of Social Imaginaries

Ambedkar undertook to both understand the mechanisms that led to as well as helped reproduce the suppression of Dalits and the possibilities of an alternative. While he had the structural conditions in view, Ambedkar saw the key to the reproduction of the social order elsewhere: decisive for him are the underlying values and norms that find articulation in the routinized attitudes and practices of social actors. At the same time, he ascribes high social potency to ideas and social imaginaries, anticipating later social thought.

For Ambedkar, basic values and norms are largely religiously grounded. He saw caste and social inequality among Hindus as religiously consecrated,[7] and having 'a divine basis'[8]. Equally, he sought a religious base for a more egalitarian value system and the overthrowing of caste.

On the level of everyday social action, Ambedkar focussed on the attitudes of social actors towards each other and towards other sentient beings and even towards things, inscribed into their dispositions and 'conduct',[9] giving expression to underlying norms and values.[10] People can relate to values and norms directly, but

---

to Dewey are not always given by Ambedkar and not all have so far been revealed (see Mukherjee 2009).

[7] Ambedkar (1989a: 65).

[8] Ambedkar (1989a: 69).

[9] Ambedkar (1992: 218, 284–5; 1989a: 59, 68, 78).

[10] Distinguishing three meanings of conduct, Ambedkar's main concern lies with the second one, 'conduct regulated by standards of society':

Wherever groups of men are living there are certain ways of acting which are common to the group—'folkways'. There are *approved* ways of acting, common to a group, and handed down from generation to generation. [...] The welfare of the group is regarded as in some sense imbedded in them. It becomes the duty of the individual to follow them .... We cannot strictly speaking call the conduct moral. Because the end is accepted as a standard of 'good' prescribed by society. ... it conforms to the mores and morals of the Society. It may

more importantly, the articulation of norms happens routinely, unreflectively:[11] 'Caste is a notion, it is a state of mind'.[12] 'All reform consists in a change in the notions, sentiment and *mental attitudes* of the people towards men and things'.[13] Ambedkar takes his pragmatist concept of routine action from John Dewey, but one can also see certain affinities with the fourth type in Max Weber's typology of social action, that of 'traditional' action,[14] with the concept of habitualized collective mentalities of the Annales School of historians, or with Pierre Bourdieu's concept of habitus as embodied dispositions. Like Bourdieu,[15] Ambedkar grappled with the connections between the dispositions of social actors and the reproduction of the social structure.[16]

On the conceptual level, regarding the role of ideas and ideals, Ambedkar undertakes two interesting steps. He identifies ideals, especially religious ones, as a 'social force', but a force of a particular kind. On this background, he then establishes the role of imaginary models of society and sociality that frame the thinking and the thinkable in a particular societal context.

> The ideal may be non-existent in the sense that it is something which is constructed. But although non-existent, it is real. For an

---

be called customary morality'. He, however, values particularly the third level of conduct, 'conduct regulated by individual conscience', 'which alone is truly and completely moral. That is because the individual *recognizes* the right or *chooses* the good ... and becomes personally responsible. His is reflective morality. (Ambedkar 1987: 82–3; emphases Ambedkar 82–3)

[11] Ambedkar (1989a: 73); for a discussion on this statement, see later.

[12] Ambedkar (1989a: 68).

[13] Ambedkar (1989a: 59); also see, by way of comparison, Ambedkar (1989a: 57). Emphasis added.

[14] Weber (1978: ch. 1).

[15] Bourdieu (1977).

[16] John Dewey himself, following on William James, preferred the term 'habit', appropriately understood (as denoting acquisition by prior activity, systematization of minor elements of action, projective character, operativeness, actuality), but also uses the terms disposition and attitude: 'Attitude and ... disposition suggest something latent, potential, something which requires a positive stimulus outside themselves to become active'; it also means 'predisposition'. See Dewey (2002b [1922]: 40–1); see also Dewey (2002a [1916]: 13, 379).

ideal it has full operative force which is inherent in every ideal.[17] Those who deny the importance of religion not only forget this, they also fail to realize how great is the potency and sanction that lies behind a religious ideal as [compared; correction by author] with that of a purely secular ideal.... This means'—and here we can see similarities with Max Weber—'that a religious ideal has a hold on mankind, irrespective of an earthly gain....[18] A religious ideal never fails to work so long as there is faith in that ideal. To ignore religion is to ignore a live wire.[19]

In a very sociological way, Babasaheb Ambedkar regarded ideals and religions as forces that impact on social action. At the same time, Ambedkar also propounded the concept of 'ideal society'. While there are instances in which this notion just means a society that he considers perfect,[20] he elsewhere takes the ideal as part of reality and contrasts two conflicting concepts of 'ideal society', the one based on 'the rule of graded inequality' and expressed in the idea of *chaturvarna*[21], the other 'based on righteousness' and expressed in the *sangha* 'model of society'.[22] In both cases, social life is seen as being guided by a foundational or framing image of society: 'An ideal must be practical [...] it is necessary to have *a picture of a society* working on the basis of the ideal.'[23] Ideal thus stands here for an underlying set of ideas and images, and this is meant to apply both to the concept of graded inequality and to the opposite idea of righteousness. Ambedkar anticipates aspects of the concept of social imaginary significations, as later spelt out, in

---

[17] This shows certain similarities with John Dewey (2013 [1913]: 21–2, 41, 45).

[18] Compare this with Max Weber's famous image of switches shaping civilizational developments: 'The "worldviews" that have been created by ideas have very often, like switches, decided the lines on which the dynamic of interests has propelled behaviour' (Weber 2004 [1920]: 69). The context of Weber's statement shows that what he has in mind are religious ideas and worldviews in particular.

[19] Ambedkar (1987: 23–4).

[20] Ambedkar (1989a: 64).

[21] Ambedkar (1992: 87–9, 301–3).

[22] See Ambedkar (1992: 434, 302–6). In a somewhat different way, Gopal Guru (2017) distinguishes between two conceptions of moral idealism in Ambedkar.

[23] Ambedkar (1992: 434). Emphasis added.

Ambedkar's Theory of the Social 7

slightly different ways, by Cornelius Castoriadis[25] and, after him, Charles Taylor.[26]

This concept of the social force of ideational structures gets tragically confirmed by the attitudes of those who are at the receiving end of the social order. Ambedkar saw the hierarchizing attitude so thoroughly implanted in the modes of disposition and social interaction that forms of this attitude could also be discovered among those who themselves are its victims, including untouchables themselves. As Ambedkar strongly deplores, untouchables 'are infested with the caste system in which they believe as much as does the caste Hindu'.[27]

Social values, norms, ideals, or models have both explicit and implicit dimensions. While, in order to function, it seems important that they work without being reflected, their installation is seen as a deliberate act. And deliberate policies also contribute to their perpetuation. The Brahminical ideas of hierarchy were imparted to society, and were legitimated by, the Shastras, before all else, the *Manusmriti*.[28] Ambedkar found the core of the Buddhist alternative

---

[24] Castoriadis (1987, 1997).

[25] See Taylor (2002). Some of Taylor's notions come especially close to Ambedkar's thoughts: 'The social imaginary is not a set of ideas; rather it is what enables, through making sense of, the practices of a society' (Taylor 2002: 91). Social imaginaries refer to 'a sense or an idea of moral order' implicit in people's views and actions (Taylor 2002: 93, 106, 109). 'I am thinking', writes Taylor, 'of the ways in which people imagine their social existence, how they fit together with others, how things go on between them and their fellows, the expectations that are normally met, and the deeper normative notions and images that underlie these expectations' (Taylor 2002: 106). The social imaginary refers to such presuppositions of action and interaction that are quasi-intuitively reproduced in everyday life and that one cannot think beyond, 'an implicit map of social space', or of knowing how to do things (Taylor 2002: 107, 108). Such imaginaries are not usually formulated in theoretical terms, but are articulated through images, through stories, or through legends (Taylor 2002: 106). On a deeper level, again, Taylor sees the imaginaries grounded in basic assumptions about the world and how it is constituted, that is, of notions of a 'moral *or* metaphysical order' '*beyond*' the 'immediate background' (Taylor 2002: 107).

[26] See Ambedkar (1989e: 266; 1989d: 18–21); compare with Herrenschmidt (2004: 45).

[27] Ambedkar (1989a: 68 et passim; 1987: 36–7, 45, 48, 65; 1992: 87–9, 301–3).

in canonical as well as non-canonical Buddhist literature belonging to different schools of Buddhism, giving the texts a new reading.[28] Ambedkar aims for reformation or revolution of religion, but not for rescindment of religion. It is in this sense that one has to see his statement that 'political revolutions have always been preceded by social and religious revolutions'.[29] Ambedkar's concern was how to implant these alternative ideas in people's dispositions.

What Ambedkar is headed for is something that has concerned many social theorists. He wanted to grasp the combination of the prevalence of an attitude, its connection with a worldview or social imaginary, and the social power structure connected with this or lying behind this. One can see here parallels to the theoretical reflections of Antonio Gramsci,[30] who incidentally was born in the same year as Ambedkar and whose main aim was to understand cultural hegemony, or the 'manufacture of consent', that is, the way the views, values, and norms of the dominant classes or groups, their definition of social reality, apparently became the 'common sense' values of most members of society. Gramsci, too, thought about ways of establishing counter-hegemony. Still, the problem remains: enforcement and enshrinement of values point into somewhat different directions. Experiencing values as imposed creates an immediate legitimacy crisis and directly triggers the search for alternatives and opposition or resistance; sharing values attitudinally lets them appear as one's own and makes it less likely and less easy to question them. Both perceptions (enforcement and enshrinement) show up in Ambedkar's thinking.[31]

---

[28] See Sangharakshita (1986: 147). Ambedkar mainly referred to the *Sutta* and *Vinaya Pitaka, Dhammapada, Buddhacharita*, Pali commentaries and the *Milinda-panha* (Ahir 1994: 10). For details, see the references in the new 'critical' edition of *The Buddha and His Dhamma* (Ambedkar 2011). Among the modern writers and scholars he read, we know of Thomas Rhys Davids, Edwin Arnold, Lakshmi Narasu, Dharmanand Kosambi, and K.A. Kerluskar. See also Ambedkar (2011: 313–4) and Queen (2004: 134–5), regarding the works, as so far known, that he consulted.

[29] Ambedkar (1989a: 43).

[30] See Gramsci (1998).

[31] For comparisons of the political philosophies of Gramsci and Ambedkar, see Zene (2013).

Effects of Social Dispositions

Dispositional traits and power dynamics seem to represent the prime mechanisms that reproduce the order of discrimination. Regarding the effects and consequences of this order and its underlying values, Ambedkar again focussed both on the individual and on the social structure.

Regarding the effects on individuals, Ambedkar was most concerned by the denial of dignity to those who have been termed as 'untouchables' and the contempt shown to them, the 'deliberate debasement of human personality'.[32] The hierarchical organization 'produces an ascending scale of hatred and descending scale of contempt',[33] a system that 'deadens, paralyses and cripples the people'.[34] A major consequence of this is the exclusion of people of lower-caste backgrounds from access to education and respected occupations, from intellectual culture and life chances, the lack of concern 'to develop the capacity of an individual' and appreciate a person's 'merits' 'apart from his caste'.[35]

The lack of esteem for individuals' actual abilities also meant, and here he turns to the structural consequences, that these individuals could not contribute to the flourishing of society. Society, by controlling and limiting large sections of the people, makes itself inefficient. In strong words, Ambedkar attacks the dearth of 'social efficiency' of Hindu society, which harms and weakens Indian society.[36] The segregation between castes means that 'Hindus cannot be said to form a society or a nation'.[37]

Structurally speaking, it is the division and gradation of society, which is the main effect of the attitude of deprecation that Ambedkar points out. For him, what set Hindu India apart from

---

[32] Ambedkar (1987: 36).

[33] Ambedkar (1987: 48; 1992: 91).

[34] Ambedkar (1989a: 47, 61, 63).

[35] Ambedkar (1989a: 47–8, 57).

[36] See Ambedkar (1989a: 38, 47–8; 1987: 67–8). The notion of social efficiency appears in Dewey (2002a [1916]: 109, 138–44). 'Social efficiency is attained not by negative constraint but by positive use of native individual capacities in occupations having a social meaning' (Dewey 2002a [1916]: 139). Ambedkar (1989a: 47) adapts a section of Dewey (2002a [1916]: 139–40). See also Mukherjee (2009).

[37] Ambedkar (1989a: 50, 66, 79).

other class societies is the fact that people are being assigned to separate social categories that are ordered hierarchically, and that everyone's place is assigned in advance and permanently: a 'division of labourers' and not just a division of labour.[38] The analytical term that Ambedkar later coined for this type of hierarchical order and that one can then find across his writings, but that was already entailed in AC, is that of 'graded inequality'.[39]

At the level of dispositions, this peaks in an attitude of 'indifferentism' that both lies at the origin as it is the consequence of the social division: the lack of a social or 'public' spirit and of concern for those not belonging to one's immediate group.[40] What, for Ambedkar, predominates in the society he observes is the focus by each group on the 'interests of its own', to be protected against the interests of other groups. Social diagnosis and normative critique coalesce in the designation 'anti-social spirit'.[41]

At the centre of Ambedkar's concerns are the discriminating attitudes of people and the contemptuous treatment of their respective others. What he foremost castigated is the lack of 'solidarity', 'charity', and 'sympathy to the deserving'.[42] This became

---

[38] See Ambedkar (1989a: 47; 1987: 67). Concerning 'Philosophy of Hinduism' (PH), an unpublished text discovered among Ambedkar's manuscripts after his death, the editors of his writings do not provide any clue regarding the time at which he might have had worked on this text. Academic works he refers to in the text (without full details, but whose publication dates are detectable in contemporary online catalogues) as well as certain topical and semantic similarities (see especially 1987: 67–71, 79) might suggest that he had worked on this text around (either before or after) the time at which he wrote *Annihilation of Caste* (AC), that is in the second half of the 1930s. Aishwary Kumar (2015: 142) claims that PH was written after AC and made use of key passages of AC. Others put the text post-1941.

[39] See Ambedkar (1992: 87–91, 301); Also, see Ambedkar (1989a: 47); also, other writings of Ambedkar. See also Herrenschmidt (2004: 42–7). For Ambedkar's recurrent conceptual formula for the caste order, see Ambedkar (1990: 170, 215; 1992: 91).

[40] Ambedkar (1989a: 55–7).

[41] See Ambedkar (1989a: 51–2; 1992: 324). The expressions 'interests "of its own"' of a group and 'anti-social spirit' have been already used in Dewey (2002a [1916]: 99).

[42] Ambedkar (1989a: 52, 56; 1987: 65).

his central concern in *The Buddha and His Dhamma* (TBHD), his last work.[43] In the context of his exposition of Buddhism as an alternative social model, he expanded on the feelings of solidarity, with the terms compassion, *karuna*, and *maitri* now becoming central. Inversely, he now subsumed the experiences of debasement and exclusion under the broader notion of 'suffering'. Ambedkar developed this into a general thesis about social suffering and the conditions of suffering, or 'injustice'.[44] He was not convinced by the view that takes suffering as simply a general feature of the human condition.

Instead, he conceived of Buddhist thought as a kind of a socio-analytical mode. The main causes of human suffering, as he saw them pronounced by the Buddha himself, were poverty and exploitation.[45] Suffering in the eyes of the Buddha, as Ambedkar understood him, was *human-made*. The way to overcome suffering was to get rid of 'wrong' dispositions and acquire '*the disposition to do good*': 'the training of the mind ... is the same as the training of a man's disposition'.[46] '*A good disposition is the only permanent foundation of and guarantee of permanent goodness*. That is why the Buddha gave the first place to the training of the mind ...'.[47] This he saw required on a society-wide scale.[48]

Emergent Possibilities

But what are the chances of changing inhuman behaviour and treatment of others in the face of the fact that behavioural attitudes, social value orders, and power structures are so deeply ingrained?

---

[43] *The Buddha and His Dhamma*, on which he worked until his death, remained unfinished and was published posthumously in 1957.

[44] See Ambedkar (1992: 126, 129, 254, 325). Ananya Vajpeyi (2012: ch. 5) makes this the key to Ambedkar's reading of the early texts of Indian Buddhism. She regards all other considerations on Ambedkar's side as secondary.

[45] Ambedkar (1992: 10, 91, 121, 129, 368, 510–12, 587).

[46] Ambedkar (1992: 127, 283–5); emphasis added.

[47] Ambedkar (1992: 285); emphasis Ambedkar's.

[48] 'The Buddha then told them that according to his Dhamma if every person followed (1) the Path of Purity; (2) the Path of Righteousness; and (3) the Path of Virtue, it would bring about the end of all suffering' (Ambedkar 1992: 122).

Here again, we have to distinguish between Ambedkar's principled perspective and the hard realism of his social analysis.

His political realism, underpinned by social analysis, led Ambedkar to pinpoint the factors that rendered rebellion impossible. Why, Ambedkar asks, 'have there not been social revolutions in India'?[49] His answer is complex. On the one hand, as mentioned, he saw the victims of hierarchization drawn into participating in the very value system and normative mechanisms that degrade them. Further, the gradation of castes makes it impossible to put up 'a common front'.[50] On the other hand, Ambedkar identifies two (political, economic) mechanisms to keep people down. Firstly, a systematically enforced dearth of resources on the side of the lower castes and classes, especially of means of defence (weapons) and of access to education.[51] Secondly, the enforcement of the Brahminical social order and values by law, that is, a penal system that included 'penalty of death'.[52]

Against the backdrop of this disillusioning view, Ambedkar addresses the question of change on a basal level, and this already in the writings of his middle period. Taking off from there, TBHD represents an appeal to everyone to accept the necessity and sacredness of sociality. Ambedkar, who, as we could see, is not taken in by a belief in structural determination, avoids the trap of opposing the reproduction of social relationships and social change. Structural properties—positionalities as well as belief structures—feed into social action while they have to be instantiated through actions. Change, which has to come from human action, for Ambedkar then requires the insight on the side of social actors to be able to do otherwise. Taking his clues from John Dewey, Ambedkar proposes a view of social action that integrates the potentiality for reflection and critique with a notion of routine. Similar to Dewey, Ambedkar depicts the routine ways of human life as 'habitual and unreflective'.[53] It is only when routine ways are interrupted or

---

[49] Ambedkar (1989a: 63; 1987: 70).

[50] Ambedkar (1989a: 72).

[51] Ambedkar (1989a: 62–3; 1987: 70).

[52] See Ambedkar (1989a: 60–1). Dharma points in a prototypical fashion to the combination of religious and juridical power.

[53] See Ambedkar (1989a: 73, 75). 'Routine habits are unthinking habits' (Dewey 2002a [1916]: 58).

Ambedkar's Theory of the Social   13

obstructed, and this is historically contingent, that one is made to pause and consider possibilities. Only a situation 'which presents a dilemma—a crisis' can trigger processes of reflection 'in the sense of active, persistent, and careful consideration of any belief or supposed form of knowledge in the light of the grounds that support it and further conclusions to which it tends'.[54] In the Indian case, the crisis is continuous, but, on the other hand, is usually seen by only one part of the people. What distinguishes Ambedkar from Dewey is that he is generally less optimistic than his teacher. Ambedkar regards at least the overall reconsideration of beliefs and knowledges as something 'quite rare'.[55]

On the other hand, Dr Ambedkar is a theorist who believes in the basic dynamism of social life. He defends a position that claims constant change as a basic feature of all societies. Opposing the idea of things *sanatan*, eternal, as propounded by Gandhi and other speakers of contemporary Hinduism,[56] Ambedkar insists 'that there is nothing fixed, nothing eternal ...; that everything is changing, that change is the law of life for individuals as well as for society'.[57] For Ambedkar, this is not just a factual, but also a normative statement: not only is everything changing, things, and especially values, also have to constantly change.[58] Ambedkar therefore asks to conserve and transmit only such achievements 'as make for a better future society' and to not expect the past to supply one's ideals.[59]

The idea of constant change gets an even stronger underpinning in TBHD. What looks like a pragmatist version of rationalism gets an ontological underpinning. Taking the concept of *sunyata* (Sanskrit) or *sunnata* (Pali), which he understands as 'doctrine of impermanence', Ambedkar advances his notion of constant change beyond the sphere of the social towards a general emergentist

[54] See Ambedkar (1989a: 73), quoting Dewey (1991 [1910]: 6, 11).

[55] Ambedkar (1989a: 73).

[56] 'Sanatan' refers to sanatan dharma, eternal dharma or eternal order, a concept that came into vogue in the second half of the nineteenth century. From then on, increasingly, various prominent Hindus, amongst them Gandhi, regarded themselves as '*sanatanis*'.

[57] Ambedkar (1989a: 79).

[58] See also Ambedkar (1989a: 92).

[59] See Dewey (2002a [1916]: 24); quoted in Ambedkar (1989a: 79); See Ambedkar (2003: 98); Dewey (2002b [1922]: 243–4).

theory. 'Very few realize that it is on account of Sunnyata that everything becomes possible; without it nothing in the world would be possible. It is on the impermanence of the nature of all things that the possibility of all other things depends.'[60] 'Being is becoming.'[61] Sociologically speaking, this seems a very advanced idea of social hermeneutics, of practical creativity, and of the latency of possibilities inherent in (routine) praxis. As I have shown earlier,[62] the parallels to John Dewey, even if not literal in this case, are rather striking. As Dewey stated in his book on religion, *A Common Faith*, of which it is not clear whether Ambedkar had read it, a 'new vision ... emerges through seeing, in terms of possibilities, that is of imagination, old things in new relations serving a new end which the new end aids in creating'.[63] The human condition is more than the world of necessity and of inequality—a belief in transcendence that is both imminent and immanent.

The Inherent Potentiality of Humankind

Ambedkar's thought shows a deep tension between political pessimism and ontological hope. Ambedkar was pessimistic that the ways Dalits were treated would be changed quickly. At the same time, social change, even fundamental change, would seem imminent. Underneath his pessimism, Ambedkar remained a theoretical optimist: even the worst digression from what one would consider the model of a good society points back to the ineradicable conditionalities of social life. For him, the overall direction in which social change has to go seems clear, written into the very idea of humanity he upholds. His is not belief in a teleological model of progress. References to possibilities of modern institutions, like the social opportunities offered by industrialization, the political

[60] Ambedkar (1992: 241).
[61] Ambedkar (1992: 240).
[62] Fuchs (2001).
[63] See Dewey (2013 [1934]: 46). Dewey here refers to 'aims and ideals that move us' and are generated by the imagination, but 'not made out of imaginary stuff' (2013: 45). See also Joas (2000: 114–5) and Fuchs (2001: 250, 261). This would connect to Ambedkar's remarks on the reality and social force of ideals (see earlier).

opportunities offered by parliamentary democracy, and the rule of law or the critical role of the State, are empirical and pragmatic. What Ambedkar assumes is a certain human potentiality that, in principle, always exists, a potentiality for sociality, only blocked by circumstances, especially by forces of power and by dispositions, and otherwise to be fostered or nurtured.

Basic moral values and ethical directive principles inform people about how they are supposed to treat each other. Ambedkar explicates these values and directives using two different registers. On the one hand, there is the affective-philanthropic language of 'fellow feeling', 'sympathy', 'compassion', 'charity', among other terms, ultimately being subsumed under the concepts of 'karuna' and 'maitri' (loving kindness to all human or all living or all sentient beings).[64] The other register refers to the core principles and values of equality, liberty, fraternity or solidarity, and justice. These terms point back to the European Humanist and Utilitarian traditions on the one hand, and to Buddhist traditions, which voiced these concepts much earlier, on the other hand, as well as tangentially to other religious traditions.

It is not always easy to decide how Ambedkar employs and organizes or classifies these principles. Especially, his conceptualization of 'fraternity' fluctuates. Following John Stuart Mill, and indirectly pointing back to the Scottish Enlightenment, he characterizes fraternity as a 'natural' and 'necessary' 'sentiment', a moral universal 'which leads an individual to identify himself with the goods of others', and equates it with a core term of this tradition, that of 'fellow feeling'.[65] On the other hand, he takes fraternity, together with liberty and equality, as a societal doctrine, principle, and value[66]—a doctrine or value that gives articulation to, as it develops, the moral universal. Finally, he sometimes considers fraternity, like liberty, *derivative* of 'equality *and* respect', thus introducing another and essentially relational conceptualization at the level of basic principles.[67]

---

[64] Ambedkar (1992: 128, 296–300, et passim).

[65] Ambedkar (1987: 44). He takes this from John Stuart Mill's *Utilitarianism* (orig. 1861, republished in 1910 as the first of three essays).

[66] Ambedkar (1989a: 77–8).

[67] Ambedkar (1987: 66); emphasis added.

16   Martin Fuchs

Elsewhere, liberty, equality, and fraternity together constitute what he calls the principle of justice,[68] which acts as the norm or criterion 'for judging right and wrong' in modern society (modern here including all post-antique societies and religions)[69]. While constantly appealing to these principles, Ambedkar never attempted a systematic conceptualization of their interrelationships. This had already been observed by Valerian Rodrigues.[70] For Ambedkar, the dimensions of the right, or just, and the good, more clearly differentiated in more recent debates,[71] appear as congruent; for him, there is no tension between the two in an ideal society: the core of what is good is what is just. Even if equality (be it alone or be it together with respect) constitutes the basic principle,[72] it is fraternity that marks the final goal.

Closing the circle, Ambedkar addresses the social mechanisms needed to achieve these values and implement a morally ordered society, mechanisms that respect the dignity and freedom of the individual and allow for an open, but concerted sociality. These he finds in communication and democratic practices (democracy understood in a broad sense). Fraternity is here equated with what Ambedkar calls, following Dewey, 'social endosmosis':[73] at the centre of a functioning society has to be free, equitable, open, and, in this sense, fluid communication that allows to articulate critique and fresh ideas.[74] Fraternity, instantiated through communication, then becomes 'only another name for democracy': Democracy 'is essentially an attitude of respect and reverence towards fellowmen'.[75]

[68] Ambedkar (1987: 25).

[69] Ambedkar (1987: 22).

[70] Rodrigues (1994: 143).

[71] Hans Joas (2000), especially ch. 10.

[72] Elsewhere, he calls equality, even if it may be a fiction, 'the governing principle'. See Ambedkar (1989a: 58).

[73] Ambedkar (1989a: 57). Ambedkar takes this term from John Dewey (see Dewey 2002a [1916]: 98, who seems to have used the term only once). According to Arun Mukherjee (2009: 352), the term was originally used by Henri Bergson and later by William James.

[74] 'Society continues to exist by communication[,] indeed in communication' (Ambedkar 1989a: 51; similar Dewey 2002a [1916]: 5; also see for comparison, Dewey 2002a [1916]: 96, 101).

[75] Ambedkar (1989a: 57).

The Necessity of Religion: The Discovery of *Dhamma*

Ambedkar never thought that one could pursue the principles of liberty, equality, and solidarity (or fraternity) without a religious-moral grounding. Societal change requires a fresh source, and it was clear for Ambedkar that this has to be a religious one.

Religion for Ambedkar, however, is not a given thing. Nor does he consider the term an unproblematic generic concept. He distinguishes between categories of religion: true and untrue religions; ethical, partly ethical, and non-ethical religions; or religions that put ethics at their centre and those that do not. He made at least three attempts to distinguish between 'true' and untrue religion(s). (*a*) In 1936, in AC, he makes a distinction between 'religions of rule' and 'religions of principle'. (*b*) In PH, he distinguishes between religions centred on society and religions centred on the individual. (*c*) In 1957, in TBHD, he distinguishes between religions that take morality as their essence and those religions that treat morality as only an attachment to their metaphysical system.

I will skip here the first two deliberations on religion and concentrate on the one displayed in the TBHD.[76] Here, Ambedkar deals with the concept of a religion completely based on principles. Dhamma, the teaching of the Buddha, standing for morality and thus representing what is or should be true in religion, is seen in opposition to the other religions with their fixation on God.[77]

Buddhism came, for Ambedkar, to best express the human, which means social, condition and its conversion into societal values. Buddhism had already enshrined what later thinkers, supporters of religions as well as social philosophers, formulated in new ways, but what then became an aspect of secondary relevance. At the same time, the pointed way in which Ambedkar presented the

---

[76] For a discussion on the two earlier attempts to distinguish 'true' and untrue religions, see Fuchs (2019).

[77] In TBHD, Ambedkar uses 'religion' in two different ways: on the one hand, as a generic term, as usual in religious and social studies, and on the other hand, in opposition to dhamma (see Fuchs 2001: 259). Thus, while we occasionally find him repeating the idea of 'the only real religion' applied to Buddhism (Ambedkar 1992: 452), at many other instances, dhamma does no more fall under religion for him, but appears as only 'analogous' to the 'European' concept of religion (Ambedkar 1992: 316).

argument brought into sharp relief the ambivalent status of this plea for social ethics. Social ethics, or morality, denotes a 'necessity'— 'the direct necessity for man to love man'[78]— a requirement for humans to live by, if they want a life beyond the barbaric state. On the other hand, conviviality and sociality is not a given. Humans have to work for it; they have to practise togetherness, compassion, and fellow feeling. Implicitly, Ambedkar follows up on the figure of *social contract*: morality, required to protect 'the weak', who often also are 'the best', has to be made into 'common standards' or 'rules', 'which are sacred to all'.[79] As already mentioned, 20 years earlier, already Ambedkar had approvingly quoted John Stuart Mill declaring that the 'social state', on which the sentiment of fellow or social feeling builds, is 'natural', 'habitual', as well as 'necessary'. The assumption that humans are equal leads to both, individualism and 'the understanding that the interests of all are to be regarded equally', as the two contrary but co-present consequences.[80] 'Individualism would produce anarchy. It is only fraternity which prevents it and helps to sustain the moral order among men'.[81]

Finally, one should not forget one aspect that is of highest importance for Ambedkar. It is his insistence that the argument for sociality is not just ethical or moral, but essentially rational, based on reason. Fellow feeling for Ambedkar derives logically from the notion of the human, and Buddhism in the form taught by the Buddha especially is completely rational.[82] Not to practise a humanist religion and ethics would not only be immoral, but also against reason. It is the force of reason, and not force in the sense of coercion, on which his politics and his hopes build. Ambedkar's

---

[78] Ambedkar (1992: 323).

[79] See Ambedkar (1992: 323–5). While there are only few direct references to Émile Durkheim in Ambedkar, I agree with Gail Omvedt that Ambedkar's statement at this point 'echoed' Durkheim (Omvedt 2003: 260; also see Fuchs 2019). The reference would be to chapter one of Durkheim's *Elementary Forms of the Religious Life*, in which he introduces the binary of sacred and profane as the defining concept of religion (Durkheim 1964 [1915]: 37; to compare, see Ambedkar 1989f: 179–80).

[80] Mill (1910: 29), quoted in Ambedkar (1987: 44).

[81] Ambedkar (1987: 44).

[82] Ambedkar (1992: 350–1). Similarly, Lakshmi Narasu in his *Essence of Buddhism* (quoted by G. Aloysius in the preface to Narasu [2002: xix]).

Ambedkar's Theory of the Social   19

plea for a 'moral regeneration' requires beforehand 'an intellectual regeneration' and 'intellectual emancipation', already in AC.[83]

Reason too is conceived processually. The change of circumstances means that even insights built on reason require to be constantly revisited and rethought (the concept of sunyata). A religion has to regularly check on its teachings. Ambedkar claims that the Buddha applied this argument self-referentially also to his own teachings. 'He [the Buddha] never claimed infallibility for his message. He said that it was open to anyone to question it, test it and find what truth it contained'.[84] 'His religion', Ambedkar claims the Buddha to have said,

> was based on reason and experience and ... his followers should not accept his teaching as correct and binding merely because they emanated from Him. Being based on reason and experience they were free to modify or even to abandon any of his teachings if it was found that at a given time and in given circumstances they do not apply.[85]

The Social Constraints of Conversion

Taking his overall sociological and social-philosophical approach and his both analytical and normative reasoning, it thus also becomes more transparent what conversion meant for Ambedkar and what he sought in a new religion: a complete overhaul, a new, or renewed, holistic vision. Conversion for Ambedkar was based on decisions to be taken by each individual, but his interest lay not in individual spiritual change alone, it lay in the transformation of social life. Again, there are two aspects. The final goal is the complete (self-)transformation or 'remoulding' of a whole way of life, of outlook, attitude, and values applied to society as a whole, and thus to all its members, and in that sense referring to society's religious-moral basis. Changing one's religion, shifting allegiance from one to another religion, typically by an individual or by a smaller or larger group, without transforming the religious-moral basis of society as a whole, is a more limited goal; it has to be seen against the larger background. For Ambedkar, conversion in this confined

[83] Ambedkar (1989a: 94).
[84] Ambedkar (1992: 222).
[85] Ambedkar (2003 [1950]: 98).

sense became necessary because he could not see the possibility of an overall turn-around of Hindu society.

The reflections that went into Ambedkar's final project of conversion to a non-Hindu religion are highly complex. Decisive is the criterion for the religion to be chosen: not religion as an individual path towards salvation, but religion understood as social, and this in two senses of the term—as promoting a universalist idea of humanness and sociality, and as a collective, shared, and not an individual endeavour. In the sense of the confined idea of conversion, this, for Ambedkar, was to secure a sense of brotherhood at least within the new community. Community represents for Ambedkar what society cannot give, a feeling of kinship (see his comparison of the two terms[86]). At the same time, conversion, also in the restricted sense, was intended by him to gain respect (from others) as well as from and for oneself, in the form of self-respect.[87]

TBHD, Ambedkar's last work, is meant for all humans; it is universalist in the fullest sense of the term. Buddhism, as he saw it, was not an identitarian religion; Ambedkar had at several points expressed his scepticism of identity and identity politics. But the project, and the act of conversion itself, could, under the circumstances, only be a project of Dalits, or even just the members of his own caste, the *Mahar*s, themselves. It had not been an option to lead larger sections of Indians onto this path. Nor were others in any way willing to join this act of transformation. It was thus the Dalits who embodied the universals, the basic truths, the possible future, and a culture of liberation. Conversion was meant as an idea of an inclusive, total project, that, however, remained caught in the social and political restrictions it fought against.

In Search of a Ground of Universality

Babasaheb Ambedkar was not satisfied with developing a critical social theory of the society he was part of. Nor was he satisfied with a critique of inequalities that simply refers to humanist values. What he was after was a stronger basis for the norms he defended, a ground of universality that represents the basic axes of human existence, and that thus can be used to define basic norms.

[86] Ambedkar (1989b: 416).
[87] Ambedkar (1989b: 412).

Identifying Buddhism as the site where these are enshrined allowed him a firm ground to stand on; a ground that cannot easily be disputed. Ambedkar avoided the relativistic quandary in which the majority of Hindu reformers of his time were trapped, the struggle between 'Western' and 'Indian' values, modern and traditional civilization, 'their' and 'our' traditions. Ambedkar did not have to look outside India for a universalist and humanist alternative. He found it, and in actual fact, the strongest possible version, on his own turf. In addition, establishing a special connection of those considered untouchables to this universalist strand allowed him to excavate a positive identity for Dalits.

Ambedkar saw universalism, while best expressed by Buddhism, as derived from the premises of human, which for him instantly meant social, existence. In a way, rediscovering the natural law background of sociology,[88] certain capabilities were considered as inhering in human nature, to be discovered by reason and to be realized by religion, that is, *dhamma*, respectively.

One can see in Ambedkar's thought on sociality and on the role of religion a confluence of at least three streams—besides traces of natural law traditions, these are pragmatist sociology and philosophy, and Buddhist ethics, ontology, and epistemics—all three sharing a (quasi-)transcendental grounding. It is the respect, feeling, and love for one's others—*reciprocal recognition* of the other—that is (at) the core of what it means to be human. Briefly alluding to Aristotle, but actually expressing a core concept of pragmatism, namely that of primary sociality,[89] Ambedkar emphasizes that social relationships, and more specifically social recognition—'the recognition of others and their interests'—are 'intrinsic' to the life and purposes of the individual. To quote Ambedkar a last time: 'It is impossible for any one to begin life as an individualist in the sense of radically separating himself from his social fellows. The social bond is established and rooted in the very growth of self-consciousness.'[90]

---

[88] Chernilo (2013; 2014)

[89] See Joas (1996: 270–85).

[90] Ambedkar (1989c: 424). The notion of social recognition crops up in Ambedkar's writings only exceptionally. With two influential publications by Charles Taylor (1994) and especially Axel Honneth (1996; orig. German ed. 1992), recognition became a central term of socio-philosophical, sociological, and political science debate since the 1990s and was systematically applied to the analysis of the social struggles of the Dalits (Fuchs 1999; Fuchs 2017).

References

Ahir, D.C. 1994. 'Dr. Ambedkar's Pilgrimage to Buddhism', in A.K. Narain and D.C. Ahir (eds), *Dr. Ambedkar, Buddhism and Social Change*, pp. 1–16. Delhi: B.R. Publishing Corp.

Ambedkar, B.R. 1987. 'The Philosophy of Hinduism', in Vasant Moon (ed.), *Dr. Babasaheb Ambedkar Writings and Speeches*. Vol. 3, pp. 1–92. Bombay: Education Department, Government of Maharashtra.

———. 1989a [1936/1944]. 'Annihilation of Caste—with a Reply to Mahatma Gandhi', in Vasant Moon (ed.), *Dr. Babasaheb Ambedkar, Writings and Speeches*. Vol. 1, pp. 3–96. Bombay: Education Department, Government of Maharashtra.

———. 1989b. 'Away from the Hindus', in Vasant Moon (ed.), *Dr. Babasaheb Ambedkar Writings and Speeches*. Vol. 5, pp. 403–21. Bombay: Education Department, Government of Maharashtra.

———. 1989c. 'Caste and Conversion', in Vasant Moon (ed.), *Dr. Babasaheb Ambedkar Writings and Speeches*. Vol. 5, pp. 422–5. Bombay: Education Department, Government of Maharashtra.

———. 1989d [1917]. 'Castes in India. Their Mechanism, Genesis and Development', in Vasant Moon (ed.), *Dr. Babasaheb Ambedkar, Writings and Speeches*. Vol. 1, pp. 3–22. Bombay: Education Department, Government of Maharashtra.

———. 1989e. 'Held at Bay', in Vasant Moon (ed.), *Dr. Babasaheb Ambedkar Writings and Speeches*. Vol. 5, pp. 259–71. Bombay: Education Department, Government of Maharashtra.

———. 1989f. 'The Rock on Which It Is Built', in Vasant Moon (ed.), *Dr. Babasaheb Ambedkar Writings and Speeches*. Vol. 5, pp. 170–91. Bombay: Education Department, Government of Maharashtra.

———. 1990 [1945]. 'What Congress and Gandhi Have Done to The Untouchables', in Vasant Moon (ed.), *Dr. Babasaheb Ambedkar Writings and Speeches*. Vol. 9. Bombay: Education Department, Government of India.

———. 1992 [1957]. 'The Buddha and His Dhamma', in *Dr. Babasaheb Ambedkar Writings and Speeches*. Vol. 11. Bombay: Education Department, Government of Maharashtra.

———. 2003 [1950]. 'Buddha and Future of His Religion', in Hari Narake, M.L. Kasare, N.G. Kamble, and Ashok Godghate (eds.), *Dr. Babasaheb Ambedkar. Writings and Speeches*. Vol. 17, pt. 2, pp. 97–108. Mumbai: Dr. Babasaheb Ambedkar Source Material Publication Committee, Government of Maharashtra.

———. 2011. *The Buddha and His Dhamma. A Critical Edition*, Aakash Singh Rathore and Ajay Verma (eds). New Delhi: Oxford University Press.

Bourdieu, Pierre 1977. *Outline of a Theory of Practice*. Cambridge: Cambridge University Press.

Castoriadis, Cornelius. 1987. *The Imaginary Institution of Society*. Cambridge: Polity.

———. 1997. *World in Fragments. Writings on Politics, Society, Psychoanalysis and the Imagination*. Stanford: Stanford University Press.

Chernilo, Daniel. 2013. *The Natural Law Foundations of Modern Social Theory. A Quest for Universalism*, Cambridge: Cambridge University Press.

———. 2014. 'The Idea of Philosophical Sociology', *The British Journal of Sociology*, 65 (2): 338–57.

Dewey, John. 1991 [1910]. *How We Think*. Buffalo (N.Y.): Prometheus.

———. 2002a [1916]. *Democracy and Education. An Introduction to the Philosophy of Education*. Bristol: Thoemmes.

———. 2002b [1922]. *Human Nature and Conduct. An Introduction to Social Psychology*. Amherst (N.Y.): Prometheus.

———. 2013 [1934]. *A Common Faith*. New Haven: Yale University Press.

Durkheim, Émile. 1964 [1915]. *The Elementary Forms of the Religious Life*. London: George Allen and Unwin.

Fuchs, Martin. 1999. *Kampf um Differenz. Repräsentation, Subjektivität und soziale Bewegungen—Das Beispiel Indien*. Frankfurt am Main: Suhrkamp.

———. 2001. 'A Religion for Civil Society? Ambedkar's Buddhism, the Dalit Issue and the Imagination of Emergent Possibilities', in Vasudha Dalmia, Angelika Malinar, and Martin Christof (eds), *Charisma and Canon. Essays on the Religious History of the Indian Subcontinent*, pp. 250–73. New Delhi: Oxford University Press.

———. 2017. 'Recognition across Difference: Conceptual Considerations against an Indian Background', in Dieter Gosewinkel and Dieter Rucht (eds), *Transnational Struggles for Recognition. New Perspectives on Civil Society since the Twentieth Century*, pp. 252–76. New York and Oxford: Berghahn.

———. 2019. 'Dhamma and the Common Good: Religion as Problem and Answer—Ambedkar's Critical Theory of Social Relationality', in Martin Fuchs and Vasudha Dalmia (eds), *Religious Interactions in Modern India*, pp. 364–413. New Delhi: Oxford University Press.

Fuchs, Martin and Vasudha Dalmia (eds.). 2019. *Religious Interactions in Modern India*. New Delhi: Oxford University Press.

Gramsci, Antonio. 1998. *Selections from the Prison Notebooks*, Quintin Hoare and Geoffrey Nowell Smith (eds). London: Lawrence and Wishart.

Guru, Gopal. 2017. 'Bhimrao Ramji Ambedkar's Modern Moral Idealism: A Metaphysics of Emancipation', in Jonardon Ganeri (ed.), *The Oxford Handbook of Indian Philosophy*, pp. 737–49. Oxford: Oxford University Press.

Herrenschmidt, Olivier. 2004. 'Ambedkar and the Hindu Social Order', in Surendra Jondhale and Johannes Beltz (eds), *Reconstructing the World: B.R. Ambedkar and Buddhism in India*, pp. 37–48. New Delhi: Oxford University Press.

Honneth, Axel. 1996. *The Struggle for Recognition: The Moral Grammar of Social Conflicts*. Cambridge: Polity.

Joas, Hans. 1996. *The Creativity of Action*. Cambridge: Polity.

———. 2000. *The Genesis of Values*. Cambridge: Polity.

Kadam, K.N. 1994. 'Dr. Ambedkar and Buddhism as an Instrument of Social Change', in A.K. Narain and D.C. Ahir (eds), *Dr. Ambedkar, Buddhism and Social Change*, pp. 35–48. Delhi: B.R. Publishing Corp.

———. 1997. *The Meaning of the Ambedkarite Conversion to Buddhism and Other Essays*. Mumbai: Popular Prakashan.

Kumar, Aishwary. 2015. *Radical Equality. Ambedkar, Gandhi, and the Risk of Democracy*. Stanford: Stanford University Press.

Margalit, Avishai. 1998. *The Decent Society*. Cambridge (Mass.): Harvard University Press.

Mill, John Stuart. 1910. *Utilitarianism, Liberty and Representative Government, with an introduction by A. D. Lindsay*. London: J.M. Dent.

Mukherjee, Arun P. 2009. 'B.R. Ambedkar, John Dewey, and the Meaning of Democracy', *New Literary History*, 40 (2): 345–70.

Nagaraj, D.R. 1993. *The Flaming Feet. A Study of the Dalit Movement in India*. Bangalore: South Forum Press & Institute for Cultural Research and Action (ICRA).

Nanda, Meera. 2001. 'A "Broken People" Defend Science: Reconstructing the Deweyan Buddha of India's Dalits', *Social Epistemology*, 15 (4): 335–65.

Narasu, Lakshmi. 2002. *Religion of the Modern Buddhist*, ed. and introduced by G. Aloysius. Delhi: Wordsmiths.

Omvedt, Gail. 2003. *Buddhism in India. Challenging Brahmanism and Caste*. New Delhi: SAGE.

Queen, Christopher S. 2004. 'Ambedkar's Dhamma: Source and Method in the Construction of Engaged Buddhism', in Surendra Jondhale and Johannes Beltz (eds), *Reconstructing the World: B.R. Ambedkar and Buddhism in India*, pp. 132–50. New Delhi: Oxford University Press.

Rao, Anupama. 2009. *The Caste Question. Dalits and the Politics of Modern India*. Berkeley: University of California Press.

Rodrigues, Valerian. 1993. 'Making a Tradition Critical: Ambedkar's Reading of Buddhism', in Peter Robb (ed.), *Dalit Movements and the Meanings of Labour in India*, pp. 299–338. Delhi: Oxford University Press.

———. 1994. 'Between Tradition and Modernity: The Gandhi-Ambedkar Debate', in A.K. Narain and D.C. Ahir (eds), *Dr. Ambedkar, Buddhism and Social Change*, pp. 137–61. Delhi: B.R. Publishing Corp.

——— (ed.). 2002. *The Essential Writings of B.R. Ambedkar*. New Delhi: Oxford University Press.

Sangharakshita. 1986. *Ambedkar and Buddhism*. Glasgow: Windhorse.

Škof, Lenart. 2011. 'Pragmatism and Deepened Democracy: Ambedkar between Dewey and Unger', in Akeel Bilgrami (ed.), *Democratic Culture. Historical and Philosophical Essays*, pp. 122–42. London: Routledge.

Stroud, Scott R. 2016. 'Pragmatism and the Pursuit of Social Justice in India: Bhimrao Ambedkar and the Rhetoric of Religious Reorientation', *Rhetoric Society Quarterly* 46 (1): 5–27.

Taylor, Charles. 1994. *Multiculturalism: Examining the Politics of Recognition*, Amy Gutmann (ed.). Princeton: Princeton University Press.

———. 2002. 'Modern Social Imaginaries', *Public Culture*, 14 (1): 91–124.

Vajpeyi, Ananya. 2012. *Righteous Republic. The Political Foundations of Modern India*. Cambridge (Mass.): Harvard University Press.

Weber, Max. 1978. *Economy and Society. An Outline of Interpretive Sociology*, Guenther Roth and Claus Wittich (eds). 2 Vols. Berkeley: University of California Press.

———. 2004 [1920]. 'Introduction to the Economic Ethics of the World Religions', in Sam Whimster (ed.), *The Essential Weber. A Reader*, pp. 55–80. London: Routledge.

Zene, Cosimo (ed.). 2013. *The Political Philosophies of Antonio Gramsci and B.R. Ambedkar. Itineraries of Dalits and Subalterns*. London: Routledge.

2

B.R. Ambedkar
Visionary and Realist

JAMES MANOR

Dr B.R. Ambedkar is widely recognized as a visionary, but it is equally important to stress that he was also a realist. That is crucial because visions that are unrealistic have little hope of making an enduring impact on events. Visionaries who see society or humankind not as it is but as they wish it to be cannot produce tangible results over time.

Many visionaries inspire us at the level of ideas and imaginings. But only those whose visions face up to grim realities can produce lasting, tangible impacts at the more important level of action and interactions. Realism enables relevance amid changing circumstances. As we shall see, Ambedkar's realism makes him especially relevant today.

Before considering him, it is necessary to explain—all too briefly—the study upon which the comments on Ambedkar later in this chapter are based. (In a text of this length, it is necessary to omit or to address only briefly a large number of important topics, and to pass over numerous complexities and ambiguities.) This chapter draws upon findings from extensive research conducted since 2010 in villages and among social scientists in twelve diverse regions and sub-regions of India.[1]

---

[1] The Harry Frank Guggenheim Foundation provided a grant to support this research. This study draws heavily upon advice from and writings by

This project began with a limited objective: to produce a report from the field on the declining acceptance in rural[2] areas of caste hierarchies by the so-called 'lower' castes—especially Dalits—and its *implications*. A key question was: 'Does this trigger increases in violence against Dalits or in inter-caste accommodations or in uneasy stalemates that stop short of both violence and accommodations?' It is impossible to provide precise measurements of these three things, but in short, it appears that *all three* have increased as refusals by Dalits to accept caste hierarchies have become increasingly common and evident.

The aim of the study was to open up discussion on those implications, an exceedingly important issue that has scarcely been considered. That analysis was not intended to address theoretical debates and it has, for the most part, avoided them. For example, it does not engage with disagreements on theories of caste between Dumontians and others.

Despite that, however—and rather surprisingly—the evidence from this study turns out to inform debates among political theorists and other analysts of state–society relations. Commentators differ on how best to promote constructive caste interactions, and on the roles that might be played in pursuit of that goal by a diversity of things: high-minded ideas, rhetoric, symbols, emotions, popular perceptions, laws, government actions, and material realities. An examination of those issues helps to deepen our understanding of Ambedkar, and they are examined in 'Implications for Theories of Change in Rural India', the second part of this chapter.

Before considering those topics, it is necessary to explain in the next part some of the more important findings from this writer's reading and fieldwork on how caste interactions in villages have changed in recent times.

---

numerous social scientists, mainly in India—including the papers that have appeared in Jodhka and Manor (2017).

[2] To keep this study manageable, it does not focus on urban centres. Nor does it consider *Adivasi*s, most of whom stand at one remove from caste hierarchies.

How Have Caste Interactions Changed in Rural India?

The Declining Acceptance of Caste Hierarchies

Since the mid-1990s, we have had solid evidence that the so-called 'lower' castes in rural India, especially Dalits, are increasingly refusing to accept the old caste hierarchies. The evidence has emerged from village-level studies conducted by social scientists in several different regions.[3] As Dipankar Gupta has put it, caste is increasingly coming to denote 'difference' more than 'hierarchy'.[4] Investigations by this writer in diverse regions since 2010 have confirmed that this change is a widespread reality—with inevitable variations in its strength and in matters of detail in different regions, sub-regions, and even districts.

That change is monumentally important because caste hierarchies were long a central element in the rural social (and political) order. Hierarchies have undergone greater erosion in urban centres, but when they lose potency in *rural* areas—where a solid majority of Indians still reside—it represents a seismic shift in the foundations of society. Indeed, in this writer's view, this is one of the two most important changes to occur since Indian Independence—the other being the establishment of a socially rooted democracy. It is time that we considered its implications.

When Dalits refuse to acknowledge and begin openly to challenge caste hierarchies, we might expect an increase in physical violence (against persons and property) as the so-called 'higher' castes seek to enforce old injustices. That has indeed occurred—and violent attacks have on occasion become more savage than a generation ago. Nor should anything in this chapter be taken to imply that Dalits no longer suffer humiliations and abuses that stop short of physical violence. Such outrages persist in strength. Incidents involving physical violence have also increased. (In the book on which this chapter is based, a very long litany of such incidents will be presented and analysed.) But perhaps surprisingly, alongside that increase in physical violence, we also see an increase in negotiated accommodations between Dalits and others. In many parts

---

[3] See for example, Karanth (1995; 1996: 106); Mayer (1996: 32–64); Charsley and Karanth (1998); Gupta (2004); Jodhka (2002: 1813–23); Jodhka and Louis (2003: 2923–36). See also, Manor (2010: xi–lxi).

[4] Gupta (2004).

of India (there are some exceptions), these accommodations and uneasy stalemates between castes outnumber violent incidents.

The larger study of which this chapter is just one part seeks to explain why in many areas, accommodations have predominated— so far at least.[5] Much of that explanation is provided, in summary form, later. One key point, which is developed later, must be stressed here at the outset. Those accommodations are based not on a change of *heart* among 'higher' castes, but on a change of *mind*—on cold calculations by leaders of those castes.[6] In a huge number of interviews in villages, this writer found *next to no* evidence of empathy towards Dalits among the 'higher' castes.[7]

Readers should not conclude from the comments above that caste is becoming weaker. If we consider three meanings of the word

---

[5] It is possible that they will cease to predominate. Accommodations usually depend on negotiations between elders from 'higher' and Dalit castes. Economic and social changes within villages tend to erode elders' authority *within* their castes. If that trend gains momentum, the elders may lack the authority to persuade others in their castes to accept accommodations. Greater inter-caste violence may therefore result.

[6] I am grateful to K.C. Suri for highlighting this key point during the initial phase of my research. It was consistently corroborated in further investigations across many regions.

[7] The research for this chapter found only a tiny number of faint signs of empathy across the lines separating Dalits from 'higher' castes. In only two interviews, both in southern Karnataka, Dalits and members of 'higher' castes spoke jokingly about their disagreements—which suggested the existence of minimal empathy among 'higher' castes towards Dalits. In a few villages, young people from different caste backgrounds who attend the same schools or colleges have developed the beginnings of a sense of mutuality, but these were quite tenuous. In some Indian states, enlightened civil society organizations seek to build bridges. One example, in Maharashtra, is an organization called the *Satyashodak Parishad* (the Truth Seeking Society), originally formed in the nineteenth century by the prominent figure in the non-Brahmin movement, Jyotirao Phule. In recent times, activists such as Dr Bhobade and Hanumanth Upare have sought to revive it. For a fine study of civil society organizations, Dalits, and caste interactions, see Waghmore (2013). He deals specifically with the *Satyashodak Parishad* on pp. 14, 95, and 134–5. But Waghmore reports that the organization has an almost invisible presence in that state, and that its meetings are mostly attended by Dalits. Communication from Waghmore, 25 November 2014. Also see Naregal (2001).

'caste'[8], the one that counts most at the village level—and which is thus the main concern here—is *jati*. A jati is an endogamous group—that is, a group into which people marry their children—and there are many thousands of them across India. Jati remains extremely strong—indeed, it appears to be the most resilient and durable pre-existing social institution in Asia, Africa, and Latin America. Its strength lies less in resistance to change than in its capacity to adapt and even to take strength from forces that might be expected to threaten it, such as capitalism and democracy. Thus—and this is crucial—it is not caste or jati that is in decline, but the acceptance from below of hierarchies among jatis.

Both the resilience of jatis and the waning acceptance of caste hierarchies are mainly explained by the same thing: the impact of material realities. This takes some explaining.

The Materiality of Caste

The institution of jati has always been rooted in materiality. It has not just existed in people's minds. It is not mere 'false consciousness'. Habits of the mind are important, but there is much more to it than that. Caste (jati) has long had—and still has— tangible substance. The materiality of caste is decisively important in explaining its durability. It strongly influences how people in different castes behave, interact, and change their behaviour over

---

[8] The word 'caste' refers to three quite different things: varnas, jatis, and jati-clusters.

Varnas are immensely large groups, the four traditional categories into which most of society is seen to be divided: *Brahmins*, *Kshatriyas*, *Vaisyas*, and *Sudras*. (Or rather, these are the categories into which society outside South India is divided, since there are no indigenous Kshatriyas and Vaisyas in the south.) Note that Dalits are not included in this scheme of 'society'—they count for nothing in this traditional view.

Jatis are, as we see in the text, endogamous groups (within which people tend strongly to marry their children). They are mostly quite small, and there are tens of thousands of them.

Jati-clusters (sometimes called 'caste federations') are alliances of jatis, which usually have somewhat similar traditional occupations—alliances that have been formed in recent decades to maximize numerical strength as various caste groups seek to make gains in lobbying governments for benefits, and in electoral politics.

time. If jatis had not possessed material substance, they could not have continued for so long to shape people's ideas, imaginings, and their perceptions of themselves and of others.

What is meant by the 'materiality of caste'? Material ties have long reinforced—and despite increasing diversification within castes, still greatly reinforce—links between members of the same jati. This has often entailed members of the same jati (at whatever level in the old hierarchies) sharing tangible resources preferentially with one another: funds, livestock, agricultural implements, opportunities to gain employment, leases, and sales of land and chattels at advantageous rates, and so on. When members of a particular jati have access to resources from government (funds, favours, goods, and services), they tend to share them disproportionately with their jati fellows—and to assist them in obtaining information from government sources and education often provided by governments, which can yield concrete gains. They often deny these things to members of other jatis, including, most notably, Dalits. So caste has also erected—and to a considerable degree, still sustains—tangible divisions and inequalities between people of different jatis. Thus, like class, caste has long had and still possesses materiality, which can be seen both in the structural constraints that it imposes on people, and in the benefits, opportunities, liberties, and choices that become available to them.[9]

Materiality Also Drives Change in Inter-Caste Relations

When we focus upon inter-relations *between* jatis, and thus upon the waning power of caste hierarchies, material realities again loom large. They provide most of the explanation for increasing refusals by Dalits to accept those hierarchies, and to defer to 'higher' castes. It is impossible in a short chapter to give adequate attention to the numerous, diverse causes of the decline of the old hierarchies, but here is a brief survey. Note that nearly all of these causes have

---

[9] These issues are discussed in greater detail in Manor (1989: 335–38). For further evidence on this from two reliable economists, see Munshi and Rosenzweig (2013). See also, Munshi and Rosenzweig (2009). Also important are D.L. Sheth's arguments about caste and class. See Sheth (1999: 2502–10; 2000: 237–63).

tangible impacts and—crucially—erode material bonds of dependency by Dalits upon 'higher' castes.

Among the causes are micro-level economic changes within villages. These include increasing occupational diversity among Dalits and others, problems in agriculture that have undermined the prosperity and economic leverage of landowning castes, and the increased availability of education (which Ambedkar stressed). These and other things have undermined the old *jajmani* system, in which members of various castes tended to pursue their traditional occupations, and thus the material bonds of dependency that once locked 'lower' castes into degrading roles and relationships of subordination.

The causes also include changes that flow from the wider political system, which have had material impacts: the proliferation of government programmes over the last 40 years, some of which address caste and other inequalities; and reservations for 'lower' castes in educational institutions, government employment, and posts in elected bodies.

Those bodies include *gram* panchayats (elected local councils), the importance of which has been underestimated. This requires a brief explanation. Ambedkar rightly expressed deep pessimism about villages as arenas in which Dalits might live in dignity and make gains. He therefore had serious doubts that elected councils at the local level might provide Dalits with advantages, because he expected that gram panchayats would be captured by 'higher' castes and used to deepen the disadvantages faced by Dalits. For many years, his pessimism was strongly borne out by events— and in many Indian villages that remains true today.[10] However, in recent times, dynamics within gram panchayats in many parts of the country have begun to change in modestly encouraging ways.

Numerous members of 'higher' castes have found the contestation and cross-examinations that gram panchayat politics entails to be beneath their dignity, so that they have withdrawn, which has created opportunities on the councils for members of other

---

[10] In 1999, I expressed agreement with that pessimistic view in Manor (1999), *The Political Economy of Democratic Decentralization*. But as the next comment in the text indicates, evidence in recent years from India— far more than from other countries—has forced a reconsideration of the view set out in that earlier book.

castes, including Dalits. 'Higher'-caste leaders who remain engaged have increasingly been forced to recognize that members of 'lower' castes vote in large numbers, that they possess significant numerical strength, and that—given the 'lower' castes' increasing 'political capacity' (that is, their political awareness, their confidence as political actors in the public sphere, their political skills, and their political connections to other members of the 'lower' castes and to allies in other groups[11])—their support nowadays can only be obtained if they are offered real substance and not just tokenism or empty promises. Thanks to a recent, authoritative study,[12] we now have solid evidence that across much (though certainly not all) of India, the changes associated with *panchayati raj* have enabled Dalits to assert themselves more effectively and, thereby, to make some material gains.

In 1993, the 73rd Amendment to the Constitution came into force, requiring all state governments to create panchayats. For many years, this did little to enliven panchayati raj because in most states, governments refused to devolve significant powers and resources onto panchayats. But since 2005, the Mahatma Gandhi National Rural Employment Guarantee Act (MGNREGA) has mandated that at least 50 per cent of the funds for that massive programme be managed by gram (local-level) panchayats. All but two state governments have complied with that requirement,[13] and a few states have devolved as much as 90 per cent of those funds. This substantial devolution of funds onto gram panchayats has greatly enlivened local-level politics because members of all castes have recognized that decisions with major material implications were now made locally. This drew Dalits (and, of course, other castes) more proactively into village-level politics. The MGNREGA also contained transparency mechanisms, which are more potent than in nearly all other programmes in the world. Those mechanisms sometimes enabled Dalits to overcome attempts to cheat

---

[11] This concept, and the processes leading to the enhanced 'political capacity' of disadvantaged groups, is discussed in detail in Jenkins and Manor (2017).

[12] Binswanger-Mkhize, Meenakshisundaram, and Nagarajan (2014).

[13] The exceptions are (the undivided) Andhra Pradesh, which is something of a rogue state in this respect, and, for a time, Jharkhand where chaotic state-level politics prevented compliance.

or exclude them, but a more important impact has been to make such misdeeds *visible* to Dalits. That has, as the architects of the MGNREGA intended, catalysed discontent among Dalits and other poor villagers. That has, in turn, made them more proactive politically and has enhanced their 'political capacity'—a severe shortage of which was a key element of their 'poverty'.[14] (See the additional comments on the material gains made by Dalits as a result of the MGNREGA in 'Implications for Theories of Change in Rural India', the second part of this chapter.)

The influence of material realities on the character of inter-caste relations is nothing new. It was apparent even in the period before Independence in 1947. Consider the differences between two parts of South India with contrasting levels of economic inequality. The first, princely Mysore, had the most equitable distribution of land and the lowest incidence of landlessness in the subcontinent. In the second, the areas ruled by the Nizam of Hyderabad, severe economic inequalities prevailed.

In Mysore, caste hierarchies certainly existed in villages, and Dalits suffered abuse and injustices as a result. But because many of them possessed at least small parcels of land—and thus some minimal economic autonomy—they were less dependent, materially, upon higher castes.[15] They, therefore, experienced fewer humiliations of the kind that their counterparts suffered in other parts of India, not least Hyderabad, where maltreatment by 'higher' castes was rife. As a result of the more equitable rural economy in princely Mysore, non-trivial numbers of Dalits managed—as early as the 1920s and 1930s—to obtain (without the help of reservations) enough education to become school teachers, clerks, and the like.[16] Such things were unthinkable in many other parts of India, including Hyderabad. Because of those comparatively equitable economic conditions in princely Mysore (the southern districts of the present-day state of Karnataka), groups at and near the bottom

[14] These issues are discussed in much great detail in Jenkins and Manor (2017).

[15] This persisted after Independence. The 1971 census showed that fully 27.9 per cent of Dalits in Karnataka cultivated their own land—in contrast, for example, to 2 per cent in Kerala.

[16] This comment is based on discussions with M.N. Srinivas between 1972 and 1974.

of the caste hierarchy felt less alienation than their more sorely abused counterparts in other regions.[17] In the pre-Independence period, Christian missionaries triggered mass conversion movements in places like Medak in Hyderabad state where Dalits were economically bereft, subject to vile outrages by prosperous groups, and alienated enough from the prevailing socio-economic order to respond to an alternative.[18] By contrast, evangelicals seeking to replicate this in princely Mysore found very few takers. There was insufficient alienation.

Amid Change, Material Bonds between Jatis Suffer More Erosion than Bonds within Them

We must carefully note the *location* of certain key changes that have occurred. We have seen that the disintegration of the old jajmani system—which preceded and partly caused the waning of the old hierarchies—has eroded the material bonds of dependency by groups of lower status upon landowning castes. That has minimized or removed (*a*) many of the impediments faced by those who were dependent and (*b*) the tangible benefits once enjoyed by elites.[19] But since castes (that is, jatis) have retained most of their substance amid the decline of hierarchy, *intra*-caste links, which have long provided tangible opportunities, remain extremely important. Internal diversification within jatis has eroded those links to a limited extent, but the erosion of bonds of solidarity *within* jatis has not gone as far as the erosion of bonds of dependency *between* jatis.

There are also new opportunities to be seized. Some people find work outside their villages, nearby or at great distances. The aforementioned proliferation of government programmes has provided assets, subsidies, and services that are often targeted at disadvantaged groups. If accessed—a big 'if'—they often make a material difference. A huge number of local-level political entrepreneurs shuttle back and forth between villages and

---

[17] Manor (1989).

[18] For an account that attributes this to divine intervention, see Sackett (1951).

[19] For a very telling analysis of this, and of its consequences, see Karanth, Ramaswamy, and Hogger (2004: 265–74). See also Jodhka (2014: 339–40).

36 James Manor

government offices at higher levels, seeking (often successfully) to obtain benefits from these programmes for people in their villages. Many of these entrepreneurs come from groups other than the formerly dominant landed castes, and seek to assist fellow members of their own castes—including, in a far from trivial number of cases, Dalits.[20]

Further Changes from Without

Other changes that originate outside villages have also had significant impacts. Dalit organizations, despite the internal divisions that affect some of them, have penetrated into most rural areas. Activists within them tell Dalit villagers of heroic figures and struggles from the past and distribute pamphlets which carry that message—to inspire, at the level of ideas, greater self-respect and assertiveness.[21] Those things are important (see the discussion on Martha Nussbaum's arguments subsequently), but the more telling impact of Dalit organizations has been at the level of action— and interactions. If violent incidents occur, these organizations obtain news of them and transmit this to urban centres—to eminent urban Dalits who may visit strife-torn villages to investigate and report further, to reporters who now reach into rural parts and publicize such events, to enlightened civil society organizations, to public interest lawyers and thus the courts, and to government agencies that may feel driven to respond because politicians need Dalit votes.

Another change, which originated from the national level, has been important in influencing the behaviour of members of 'higher' castes—by persuading them to exercise at least some self-restraint in their dealings with Dalits. This is the Atrocities Act of 1989.[22] (Citing it will understandably evoke sceptical responses from some readers, but see the comments later.) Under the Act, a large number of actions that stop short of physical violence are deemed to constitute 'atrocities'. It provides for the immediate incarceration without bail of alleged perpetrators—and allegations are all that

[20] See Krishna (2003: 1171–93); and Manor (2000: 816–35).

[21] For an authoritative analysis, see Narayan (2011: 1–17, 61–70).

[22] Its official title is: The Scheduled Castes and Scheduled Tribes (Prevention of Atrocities) Act, 1989.

are required. The burden of proof in ensuing court cases rests upon the accused.

Conviction rates under the Act are quite low, but this dismal reality does not mean that it has little impact. In village after village during fieldwork for this study, it became clear that the Act imposes excruciating inconveniences upon any accused—even when they correctly assume that convictions will not happen. They face years of expensive, time-consuming legal cases, which prevent them from getting on with things that they greatly value: developing their lands, investments, and businesses; arranging for their children's educations and marriages, and so on—all of which are bound up with their own and their families' material well-being.

During fieldwork for this study, it became apparent that when the so-called 'higher' castes calculate the costs of physical violence or other forms of mistreatment against Dalits, these mighty inconveniences are often carefully considered. This is true even in places where 'higher' castes still seek, quite assertively, to exercise dominance. When the Atrocity Act was discussed during preparatory work in villages in one such area, the Gwalior region—at a time when the Digvijay Singh government held power in Madhya Pradesh and seriously implemented the Act—landowning caste leaders expressed patent fear of it. When inter-caste tensions arise, the calculations noted above often play an important role in persuading 'higher'-caste leaders to exercise self-restraint, to treat Dalits with minimal civility—and to seek grudging accommodations with Dalits in their villages. The predominance, in many (though not all) regions, of accommodations over violence led a very eminent Dalit leader—who is emphatically not a starry-eyed optimist—to see in it the beginnings of the emergence of a 'reasonably civilised society'.[23]

The comments above bring us to the central theme in this chapter, Ambedkar's realism. To understand how events unfold and how changes occur in rural India—changes in power dynamics and social interactions—the *main* focus of any analysis must be

---

[23] In the spirit of Ambedkar's realism, it is important that we not idealize the inter-caste accommodations that are stressed in this chapter. They are encouraging only up to a point, since they are attended by depressing ambiguities. For a perceptive discussion on these, see Waghmore (2016: 151–76, especially 155–8).

on mundane matters. We need to concentrate on tangible material realities, and on legal provisions and political processes that affect the material well-being of key actors at the grass roots—and not on loftier things: emotions, great leaders' edifying rhetoric, concepts, or symbols.

Implications for Theories of Change in Rural India—and for Dr Ambedkar's Realism and Relevance

Four eminent and rightly respected commentators (past and present) figure in a learned and elegantly crafted book by a distinguished authority on law and political philosophy, Martha C. Nussbaum: *Political Emotions: Why Love Matters for Justice*.[24] All four have addressed the problem of caste inequality and how it should be tackled in democratic India. All of them would—in different ways and to different degrees—be disappointed by the findings presented earlier. But their disappointments are instructive.

The first commentator (a grossly inadequate word to describe him) is M.K. Gandhi. *He might have welcomed the news of self-restraint among 'higher' castes towards Dalits, and the tendency among many of them towards accommodation. But he would have been sorely disappointed to see that 'higher' castes in rural areas now feel next to no empathy or compassion towards Dalits.* He sought, earnestly and admirably, to encourage empathy across caste lines. He had some success in pursuing that goal when, *during the great satyagrahas, people from diverse caste and religious backgrounds shared prolonged hardships in the prisons of the Raj—hardships which eroded, for a time, the social barriers that divided them. But over the long years since the struggle for Independence ended, those barriers have reacquired substance.* The old empathy of two or three generations ago has largely ebbed away and is scarcely evident in India's villages today. The pursuit of it, which Gandhi championed, has largely failed.

Jawaharlal Nehru also hoped that empathy could be cultivated among prosperous, 'higher' castes towards Dalits and other

---

[24] Nussbaum (2013). It focuses heavily on India and the United States of America, and was published by the Belknap Press, Cambridge MA and London.

disadvantaged groups. Nussbaum stresses this when she quotes from his famous speech at the dawn of Independence: 'The service of India means, the service of the millions who suffer. It means the ending of poverty and ignorance and disease and inequality of opportunity.' She adds that in this speech, 'The dominant notes are compassion and determination, as all Indians are asked to look out from within their own egos to the sufferings of those who have the greatest misery, and to unite in determination to eradicate poverty'.[25]

Nehru, like Gandhi, would be disappointed by the near absence of empathy among 'higher' castes towards Dalits in villages today. He would not, however, have been greatly surprised. He shared much of Ambedkar's realism (see later), so that like Ambedkar, he worked to create legal provisions and political structures that were partly intended to change hearts but which, if little or no empathy developed, would impede injustices towards Dalits and other vulnerable groups. But Nussbaum stresses Nehru's high-minded rhetoric—including his hopes (in Nussbaum's words) for greater 'extended compassion'[26] towards the poor and Dalits. She places less emphasis upon his realism, including his suspicions that compassion might not emerge in sufficient measure.

The findings from the fieldwork for this study also raise serious questions about the arguments of Nussbaum herself. She is the third of the four commentators discussed here. In her recent book, she draws heavily on Gandhi and Nehru, as well as on the works of Rabindranath Tagore—and on Ambedkar (see next).

Nussbaum emphasizes the importance of the inspiring 'political rhetoric' of influential leaders, and of 'public ceremonies and rituals, songs, symbols, poetry art and architecture, the design of public parks and monuments, and public sports'[27] in shaping political culture (that is, habits of mind, conscious and unconscious), and the attitudes and the behaviour of ordinary people. She believes

---

[25] Nussbaum (2013: 247–8).

[26] Nussbaum (2013: 249).

[27] Nussbaum (2013: 17). See also Nussbaum (2013: 11). She does not claim that this goal has been achieved. She carefully and correctly expresses disappointment with the progress made towards it in India—and in the United States—when she refers to 'India's incomplete struggle' (Nussbaum 2013: 364).

that these lofty things—which operate at the level of emotions, ideas, and imaginings—must exercise strong influence if power dynamics, the democratic process, and social interactions among common folk are to operate constructively.[28]

For Nussbaum, it is at that level that the crucial struggle is occurring to foster empathy, respect and 'extended compassion'. But in her view, those three things are not enough. She goes further: 'respect and even sympathy, without love, is insufficient and even dangerously unstable'.[29] 'Love' is a very strong word—stronger than empathy, respect, and compassion—but she regards it as a necessary prerequisite to the emergence of a just and civilized society and polity. Note the very title of her book: 'Why Love Matters for Justice'.

Her arguments and aspirations are very far removed from the sobering realities of India's rural society today. The evidence collected by this writer plainly indicates that empathy, respect, and compassion are almost entirely absent from inter-caste relations in villages across the country. 'Love' is nowhere to be found. And yet there is also solid evidence that a 'reasonably civilised society' is beginning to emerge in many localities, as a result of change at a more prosaic, mundane level—change which has *material* substance. By insisting on 'love', Nussbaum not only sets the bar impossibly high but also she distracts us from that other important, surprising, and very welcome development.

She offers us a misleading view of how social processes and power dynamics in rural India operate—and how they change. Social and political interactions among ordinary people there (and elsewhere) are mainly influenced by mundane things. Symbols, concepts, and inspiring words are greatly outweighed by everyday material realities. These include the wealth and power of different individuals and small groups; the existence and often the erosion of material bonds of dependency between individuals and small groups; the impact of laws, elected local councils, and political actors at local and higher levels; the access of various groups to liberties and opportunities to make tangible gains; and variations in the capabilities and 'political capacity' of different

---

[28] But she attributes this incompleteness to the failure of those edifying things to penetrate adequately into the popular consciousness.

[29] Nussbaum (2013:165).

individuals (their political awareness, confidence, skills, and connections). Nussbaum refers to some of these things, but she stresses *'Political Emotions'* (the title of her book), which in her view can and must be stirred by inspiring symbols, concepts, and words. But on the evidence set out here, they do not and cannot have the kind of impact that she envisions. Her arguments foster hopes that cannot be fulfilled.

The fourth commentator (once again, an inadequate word to describe him) whom she discusses is B.R. Ambedkar. He would be dismayed to see the remarkable resilience of the institution of jati. He sought and hoped for 'the annihilation of caste'.[30] That has clearly not happened. On the other hand, he would take some reassurance from the tendency of the so-called 'higher' castes in many villages to restrain themselves in their dealings with Dalits—and when social tensions arise, to seek accommodations with them. He was deeply sceptical about the likelihood of a change of heart among 'higher' castes.

That is why he emphasized—more realistically—three things: the creation of legal impediments to the abuse of Dalits, the constructive potential of other government actions, and the enhancement of Dalit capabilities.

His belief in the capacity of constitutional and legal provisions to exert at least some influence—not on attitudes, which he thought unlikely to change much, but on behaviour—appears realistic in the light of the evidence presented here. He lived to see some of the gains achieved by reservations, but evidence on other fronts only emerged after his passing in 1956. We have seen that the 1989 Atrocities Act has exerted some influence, and we now know that government programmes—aimed in some cases specifically at Dalits and, in others, at poor, marginalized groups in general—have made a material difference. Consider two sources of evidence on those more generalized policies.

The first is an authoritative analysis by a team from India's National Council of Applied Economic Research and the University of Maryland—the India Human Development Survey. They

---

[30] For his key text on that subject, plus important addenda, see: Ambedkar, B.R. 1936. 'Annihilation of Caste'. Ambedkar.org. Available at http://www.ambedkar.org/ambcd/02.Annihilation%20of%20Caste.htm, accessed 22 November 2014.

conducted very detailed surveys among the *same* 41,554 households across India in 2004–5 and 2011–12. They found that that while per capita household incomes among high-caste Hindus (the most prosperous group) had increased by 4.6 per cent per annum during those years, significantly larger gains in percentage terms were made by *all* other categories. OBCs saw per capita incomes increase by 7.3 per cent, STs by 5.7 per cent, and Muslims by 5.4 per cent. Most crucially for this discussion, Dalit household incomes increased by still more: 7.8 per cent.[31]

Government policies played a significant role in bringing about that change. One programme was especially important: the MGNREGA. Consider the following figures in Table 2.1 on the social groups that obtained employment from it.

Clearly, Dalits and Adivasis gained disproportionately from this massive programme. A second source[32] presents detailed evidence to show that the wages that they earned under the MGNREGA have been put to constructive use by Dalit households. They have enhanced nutrition, which has reduced irreversible and incapacitating stunting among children, and the danger of illnesses that often have catastrophic economic implications. These changes strengthen the capabilities of household members for gainful employment. Their wages have also enabled modest investments in

Table 2.1 Percentages of Total Person-Days Worked

	Dalits	**STs**
Share of person-days, 2006–8	25–31%	24–36%
Share of person-days, 2008–12	28.8%	21.3%
Share of population	16.2%	8.2%

Source: This table was constructed in 2016 on the basis of data available on the official website, Mahatma Gandhi National Rural Employment Guarantee Act, 'DMU reports', available at nrega.nic.in. But since then, data on that site has been amended and supplemented, so that the original basis for the table has been obscured.

[31] Relevant analyses from the Survey are available in: Indian Human Development Survey (2010), especially chapter two on "Income, Poverty and Inequality". For access on the internet to the full set of findings and data, go to Indian Human Development Survey website, available at ihds. umd.edu. See also, Rukmini (2014).

[32] Jenkins and Manor (2017).

education, which Ambedkar stressed and which, as a result, many Dalits have pursued energetically. The MGNREGA has reduced 'distress migration', sometimes by entire families, so that children are not uprooted with damaging interruptions to their education. They have also been used to make modest investments in livestock and small enterprises, both of which improve livelihoods.

These gains are reinforced by another point that was noted in the discussion in the first part of the impact of the MGNREGA on local power dynamics, because it has enabled Dalits to enhance their 'political capacity' as actors in the village-level public sphere. Ambedkar emphasized the need for Dalits to strengthen their capabilities—to become more autonomous, and to escape bonds of dependency on 'higher' castes. That is why he focussed heavily on education. He adopted this view because he was realistic: he did not expect other castes to develop empathy towards Dalits or to do Dalits any favours. On the evidence from the fieldwork for this chapter, his belief both in the importance of Dalit self-reliance and capabilities, and in the potential of constructive government actions to strengthen them, have turned out to be well founded.

His realism also has great relevance when we consider the question of how liberal democracy in India might be enabled to work tolerably well and to foster a 'reasonably civilised society'. Nussbaum stresses the need for 'love' and 'extended compassion' to take hold among political actors from different social groups. And yet the research for this chapter has found these things to be well-nigh absent in villages, where most Indians still reside. When people from different castes interact, they are seldom motivated by these admirable things or by the noble words and symbols that great Indians have offered. Instead, more prosaic material realities preoccupy them. These include the impact of laws, and of increases in the political capacity of Dalits, on local social and political dynamics. The so-called 'higher' castes tend towards self-restraint and accommodations with Dalits, not out of 'love' or empathy but out of cold calculations about the dangers to *themselves* that violent actions pose. They act not out a change of heart, but a change of mind.

A change of heart would, of course, be preferable. But to pin our hopes on it, and to insist that only a change of heart will suffice, is to pay too little heed to an important strand in liberal political thought about what the human condition implies for the structuring of polities. As Sudipta Kaviraj has stressed,[33] from Montesquieu to Madison, liberal philosophers have operated on the assumption that human beings would remain self-interested, but that institutional ingenuity could incentivize them to act in good ways. As Martin Luther King Jr. said in 1963 in a comment that is relevant to India today, 'It may be true that the law cannot make a man love me but it can keep him from lynching me.'[34] Laws are not meant to change bad people into good, but to impede bad behaviour. That is what, on the evidence collected for this study, has begun to happen across much of rural India.

Nussbaum actually draws upon that strand of liberal thought. She writes that 'the tendency toward stigmatizing and excluding others is present in human nature itself'. She then cites with approval John Rawls who 'is proposing a society of human beings, not angels, and he knows well that human beings do not automatically pursue the common good'. Even in the ideal 'well-ordered society' envisioned by Rawls, where 'problems of exclusion and hierarchy have been overcome, they have been overcome by human beings who still have the underlying tendencies that produce those problems'.[35] But in suggesting how best to place that kind of society on a secure footing, Nussbaum relies upon the inspirational power of high-minded rhetoric, 'symbols, memories, poetry, narrative, or music'[36] to kindle compassion, empathy, and even love. And yet our evidence plainly indicates that in village India, those edifying things have had little impact. When 'higher' castes consider Dalits, compassion and empathy scarcely exist, and love is absent.

In discussing Ambedkar and Nehru, Nussbaum emphasizes their hopes for and their efforts to foster 'extended compassion', rather than two more important things: their realistic pessimism about the achievement of those goals and consequently, their efforts to discourage destructive actions that they rightly anticipated. Ambedkar did not expect changes of heart, of the kind which Nussbaum seeks, to occur. Nehru shared much of that scepticism.

[33] Communication with this writer, 21 November 2014.
[34] This was quoted by Bhattacharjee (2017).
[35] Nussbaum (2013: 9–10).
[36] Nussbaum (2013:10).

So they worked to create legal provisions and political processes that would deter destructive actions. Those things would lead not to a change of heart among 'higher' castes but to a change of mind. They (especially Ambedkar) believed—correctly as it has turned out—that while such laws and political processes would not affect the persistent lack of empathy towards Dalits (a change of heart), they could trigger a change of mind. 'Higher' castes would make calculated assessments of the material, political, and legal realities—and be persuaded that self-restraint and accommodations were preferable to violence.

To reiterate the main point here: the evidence on which this chapter is based indicates that accommodations—grudging but solidly based on careful, mundane calculations—predominate over violence in most parts of India. That trend has emerged despite the sad fact that the hopes of Gandhi, Nehru, Nussbaum, and Ambedkar are a very long way from being realized. If we wait for the annihilation of caste, or for empathy (never mind love) towards Dalits to acquire strength, we may wait forever. We will certainly wait for a generation or two.

That is the bad news, but there is countervailing news that should inspire cautious optimism. It is not necessary to annihilate caste, as Ambedkar wished, before a 'reasonably civilised society' begins to emerge. It is not necessary to develop the kind of empathy across caste lines that Gandhi tried to encourage, or the 'extended compassion' that Nehru sought, before it emerges—or before democracy can become more genuine, can check abuses against Dalits, and can produce enabling outcomes for them. Nor is it necessary for Nussbaum's 'love'—of the nation and of its highest ideals—to be extended by 'higher' castes to Dalits before we see the beginnings of a 'reasonably civilised society'. If 'love' between castes is required to make democracy work, then India's democracy is doomed. But the evidence presented here indicates, as most of us recognize, that while—like all democracies—it is imperfect, it is not doomed.

'A reasonably civilised society' has begun, tenuously, to emerge across much of rural India. It is less satisfactory or secure than if the hope for empathy could be realized. But it is a good deal more satisfactory than our worst fears about the consequences of this shift in the foundations of Indian social life—the declining acceptance of caste hierarchies by Dalits.

Ambedkar's vision, and also the realism upon which it is based, have made him a more relevant and reliable guide as we seek to understand how things have changed, and how enlightened actors might engage effectively to promote further constructive change.

References

Bhattacharjee, Manash Firaq. 2017. 'The Lynching of a Nation.' *Wire*, 25 June.

Binswanger-Mkhize, H.P., S.S. Meenakshisundaram, and H.K. Nagarajan. 2014. *Decentralization and Empowerment for Rural Development: The Case of India*. New Delhi: Cambridge University Press.

Charsley, S.R. and G.K. Karanth (eds). 1998. *Challenging Untouchability: Dalit Initiative and Experience from Karnataka*. London: Altamira Press.

Gupta, D. 2004. *Caste in Question: Identity or Hierarchy?* London and Thousand Oaks, New Delhi: SAGE.

Indian Human Development Survey. 2010. *Human Development in India: Challenges for a Society in Transition*. New Delhi: Oxford University Press.

Jenkins, R. and J. Manor. 2017. *Politics and the Right to Work: India's Mahatma Gandhi National Rural Employment Guarantee Act*. New Delhi: Orient BlackSwan.

Jodhka, S.S. 2002. 'Caste and Untouchability in Rural Punjab', *Economic and Political Weekly*, 37(19): 1813–23.

———. 2014. 'What's Happening to the Rural?: Revisiting "Marginalities" and "Dominance" in North-West India', in N. Gooptu and J. Parry (eds), *Persistence of Poverty in India*. New Delhi: Social Science Press.

Jodhka, S.S., and P. Louis. 2003. 'Caste Tensions in Punjab: Talhan and Beyond', *Economic and Political Weekly*, 38(28): 2923–6.

Jodhka, S.S., and J. Manor (eds). 2017. *Contested Hierarchies, Persisting Influence: Caste and Power in Twenty-First Century India*. New Delhi: Orient BlackSwan.

Karanth, G.K. 1995. *Change and Continuity in Agrarian Relations*. New Delhi: Concept.

———. 1996. 'Caste in Contemporary Rural India', in M.N. Srinivas (ed.), *Caste: Its Twentieth Century Avatar*. New Delhi: Penguin.

Karanth, G.K., V. Ramaswamy, and R. Hogger. 2004. 'The Threshing Floor Disappears: Rural Livelihood Systems in Transition', in R. Baumgartner and R. Hogger (eds), *In Search of Sustainable Livelihood Systems: Managing Resources and Change*. Thousand Oaks and London, New Delhi: SAGE.

Krishna, A. 2003. 'What is Happening to Caste? A View from Some North Indian Villages', *Journal of Asian Studies* 62 (4): 1171–93.

Manor, James. 1989. 'Karnataka: Caste, Class, Dominance and Politics in a Cohesive Society', in F. Frankel and M.S.A. Rao (eds), *Dominance and State Power in India: Decline of a Social Order*, pp. 323–60. Vol. 1. Delhi: Oxford University Press.

———. 1999. *The Political Economy of Democratic Decentralization*. Washington, DC: World Bank.

———. 2000. 'Small Time Political Fixers in India States: "Towel over Armpit"', *Asian Survey* 40(5): 816–35.

———. 2010. 'Prologue', in R. Kothari (ed.), *Caste in Indian Politics*, second edition. New Delhi: Orient BlackSwan.

Mayer, A. 1996. 'Caste in an Indian Village: Change and Continuity', in C.J. Fuller (ed.), *Caste Today*. New Delhi: Oxford University Press.

Munshi, K.D., and M.R. Rosenzweig. 2009. 'Why is Mobility in India So Low? Social Insurance, Inequality and Growth', NBER Working Paper no. 14850, Cambridge MA: NBER.

———. 2013. 'Networks, Commitment, and Competence: Caste in Indian Local Politics', NBER Working Paper No. w19197, Cambridge MA: NBER. Available at SSRN: http://ssrn.com/abstract=2289107, accessed 28 November 2014.

Narayan, Badri. 2011. *The Making of the Dalit Public in North India: Uttar Pradesh, 1950-Present*. New Delhi: Oxford University Press.

Naregal, V. 2001. *Language, Politics, Elites and the Public Sphere*. New Delhi: Permanent Black.

Nussbaum, Martha C. 2013. *Political Emotions. Why Love Matters for Justice*. Harvard: Harvard University Press.

Rukmini, S. 2014. 'Middle Class Better Off, But Not Well Off'. *Hindu*, 5 April. Available at Thehindu.com/news/national/middle-class-better-off-but-not-well-off/article5872988.ece.

Sackett, C. 1951. *Posnett of Medak*. London: Cargate Press.

Sheth, D.L. 1999. 'Secularisation of Caste and Making of a New Middle Class', *Economic and Political Weekly*, 34 (34–35): 2502–10.

———. 2000. 'Caste and the Secularisation Process in India', in P.R. deSouza (ed.), *Contemporary India: Transitions*. Thousand Oaks and London; New Delhi: SAGE.

Waghmore, S. 2013. *Civility against Caste: Dalit Politics and Citizenship in Western India*. Thousand Oaks, London and Singapore; New Delhi: SAGE.

————. 2016. 'Challenging Normalised Exclusion: Humour and Hopeful Rationality in Dalit Politics' in H. Gorringe, R. Jeffery, and S. Waghmore (eds.), *From the Margins to the Mainstream: Institutionalising Minorities in South Asia.* New Delhi: SAGE. Available at www.ambedkar.org/ambcd/02.Annihilation%20of%20 Caste.htm, accessed 22 November 2014.

3

Caste and Delivery of Social Justice
Revisiting Ambedkar

G.C. PAL

The Context

Given the persistence of group inequality and the wide range of human rights violations against certain groups in different spheres of life, recent years have witnessed a widespread discussion on the lifelong concerns of B.R. Ambedkar and his contributions to the process of nation-building. It is an undeniable fact that following Independence, Ambedkar, as an architect of the Indian Constitution, has played a significant role in national reconstruction. His involvements in the field of economic development and planning and contributions to multiple spheres of social life have been immense to enrich various facets of Indian national life. His idea of nation-building through the welfare of all sections of society and respect for human rights and dignity continues to remain an inspiration for the country. As a proponent of equality and social justice, his thoughts and principles are recognized as a guiding force to address the exclusion and oppression embedded in contemporary society.

In the discourse of social science research, the past few decades witnessed a lot of writings on linkages between social exclusion and inequality. This is widely believed to be because of the popularity of the term 'social exclusion' in European countries in the late 1970s and later on in other countries. However, it must be noted that Ambedkar had, long before, provided constructive insights into the problem of social exclusion of the deprived sections and the origins of social injustice within the social and cultural milieu of Indian society. His concern for the empowerment of socially depressed classes led him to have a strong view of treating them as a separate entity for the purpose of planning. His position on social democracy, as a means for social justice, is still found to have greater relevance in modern India. Although Indian society has been transforming significantly on all fronts—social, economic, and political—the thoughts and ideas of Ambedkar have pervaded the entire gamut of social life. As evident in the present context of the nation's sustainable development goals (SDGs) and its guiding principle of 'leaving no one behind', Ambedkar's vision of socio-economic equality has been the core of the planning of sustainable development.

Thus, when we recognize the socio-economic progress in society, we must acknowledge that there is pervasiveness of human rights violations against marginalized groups, having a wider impact on the life of a large section of people in contemporary society. As is evident, despite legislative interventions to prevent social oppressions against certain groups, the practices of identity-based violence and atrocities appear to be institutionalized within rigid customary norms. This very often widens the social gap in a democratic society, perpetuating further social inequality. There are several explanations for the persistence of violence and atrocities against certain caste groups. There is also evidence to suggest that a substantial proportion of victims of such oppressive behaviour continue to suffer and the State administrative and judiciary mechanisms fail to provide justice to them. The vulnerability to continued social oppressions and denial of justice, despite the accountability of the State to protect basic human rights through effective implementation, therefore, raises an important question: Why do the victims of violence and atrocities have poor access to justice? This chapter, aligning with Ambedkar's concern with the inequities and oppressions embedded in the values of the so-called mainstream society, makes a moderate attempt to shed light on identity constructions based on 'caste' and 'class' that continue to create a culture of violence against lower-caste groups across the country and also weaken the implementation and monitoring of the laws to cause social insecurity and injustice.

As Ambedkar believed, society is always composed of classes though their basis may differ. An individual in a society is always a member of a class. That is why, in his view, 'a caste is an enclosed class'.[1] He also argued: 'The study of the origin of caste must furnish us with an answer to the question—What is the class that raised this "enclosure" around itself? The customs in their strictness are obtainable only in one caste. So long as you do not achieve social liberty, whatever freedom is provided by the law is of no avail to you.'[2] He also added, 'the Hindu society, in common with other societies, is composed of classes and the earliest known are the priestly class, followed by the military class, the merchant class and finally the artisan menial class. Accordingly, particular attention needs to be paid to the fact that this is essentially a class system.'[3]

In contemporary Indian society, understanding the elements and processes that induce human rights violations and create social exclusion and disadvantages among lower-caste groups has been an important intellectual pursuit. In line with Ambedkar's thought, it is strongly believed that caste norms provide for a regulatory mechanism to enforce the caste-based social order as well as group inequalities. Certain communities continue to remain vulnerable to exclusion and violence in the name of upholding these social norms. But the fact is that there have been changes in the consciousness of lower castes (Dalits) about their rights and persona. As a result, they claim equality of treatment, status, and opportunity, and reject the advances of the 'other' castes, rather than continuing to tolerate humiliation and indignity.[4] However, while this confident assertion of dignified living has given hopes for autonomy and social justice, in many cases, it results in caste-based violence and atrocities of different forms. While Ambedkar succeeded in giving a shape to the democratic movement in India through the movement for social justice and social inclusion, this, however, makes Dalits in contemporary society subject to more oppressive behaviour against them. There has been concern over both increase in caste-based violence and atrocities and, importantly, high acquittal

[1] Ambedkar (1979a: 15).
[2] Ambedkar (1979a: 15).
[3] Ambedkar (1979a: 18).
[4] Makwana (1992).

rates in case of such human right violations. Another critical issue is that this behaviour often prevails in various public institutional sectors, denying access to justice.

Against the above backdrop, revisiting Ambedkar's thoughts on social justice and its delivery in legal contexts would be an inspiring exercise. This chapter attempts to reflect on some core ideas of Ambedkar with regard to 'social justice' and address some questions on caste violence and atrocities in contemporary society. What are the social conditions that give rise to atrocities in the presence of legislative provisions? How do the state mechanisms, which are mandated to ensure rights to justice for every person, respond to the atrocities against Dalits? Where do social and legal actions fail to ensure access to justice? What are the challenges that Dalits face in achieving their rights to justice? This chapter draws evidence from multiple sources that comprise literature on Ambedkar's writing and speeches, official data on caste-based atrocities provided by the National Crime Record Bureau (NCRB, 1995–2016), documents of civil society organizations, fact-finding reports, media reportages, and other empirical studies.

Enacting and Upholding Laws: Ambedkar's Thoughts

Enacting laws is always well intentioned. India today has numerous laws to overcome social evils in the society, protect the rights of citizens, and ensure social justice. There are the constitutional safeguards for all citizens, and some provisions specifically for disadvantaged/weaker sections. The Constitution of India guarantees all citizens equality before the law (Article 14) and prohibits discrimination against any citizen on the grounds of religion, race, caste, sex, place of birth, or any of them (Article 15). It also recognizes that any disability arising out of 'untouchability' is an offence punishable in accordance with law (Article 17). The Constitution also incorporates special provisions for the safeguarding of weaker sections. Article 46 states that 'the state shall protect the Scheduled Castes (SCs) and Scheduled Tribes (STs) from social injustice and all forms of exploitation'. In addition to the constitutional provisions, we have a number of legislative safeguards in the form of special laws, rules, and notifications at the central as well as state levels for weaker sections of society, including

SCs and STs. These provide vital ammunition to them against human rights violations and deprivation of public resources. The Untouchability (Offences) Act, 1955, provides legal safeguards against untouchability and prescribes punishment for the enforcement of any disability arising out of practicing untouchability in access to public resources and places. In order to make this act more stringent and also to give effect to the constitutional provision regarding enforcement of civil rights, the Protection of Civil Rights (PCR) Act, 1976, an amended form of the Untouchability (Offences) Act, was introduced. However, later on, it was also realized that the provisions of the PCR act are not sufficient to prevent caste-based violence against Dalits. This led to the enactment of a powerful legislation in the form of the Scheduled Castes and Scheduled Tribes (Prevention of Atrocity [PoA]) Act, 1989, to provide legal protection against caste-based violence. The Prevention of Atrocities Act Rules was introduced in 1995 with the aim of providing guidelines to the state on the specific role of several officers at the state and district levels. One of the critical issues is that under the PoA act, the 'willful negligence' by public servants in performing their duties was made a punishable offence, and this has been reiterated through the PoA Amendment Act, 2015.

Despite these specific legislations, the problems of discrimination and violence inherited from a complicated caste system continue. The increase in the incidence of caste atrocities not only undermines the legitimacy of the legislations but also raises questions about the functioning of the State machinery involved in the implementation of laws. Despite India's commitment to the international declarations on human rights and elimination of all forms of discrimination and violence based on social identities, in contemporary India, promoting social justice with the letter and spirit of the Indian Constitution has been far from reality. This very often calls for understanding the dominant factors that operate at the local level to perpetuate violence and atrocities against Dalits and effects the responses of the state machinery. Before understanding the extent of access to justice through the criminal justice system in the context of caste violence and atrocities, reflecting on the legitimacy of legislations and efficiency of the state machinery, an attempt is made here to understand what the thoughts of Ambedkar with regard to social justice and its relevance in contemporary society have been.

With the recognition that religious practices act as a detriment to the liberties and dignities of weaker sections of society, Ambedkar formulated his own idea of social justice, which largely included the unity and equality of all human beings and the regard for human rights and human dignity of all citizens. According to him, the aim of social justice is to remove all kinds of inequalities based upon various group identities with a view to create such human social conditions that ensure free and fair development of all human beings. He strongly believed that social justice can be delivered to the members of the society only if the society is based on the principles of 'equality', 'liberty', and 'fraternity'. Ambedkar enshrined these principles of social justice in the constitution, which however are not to be treated as separate items but form a united trinity in the sense that to divorce one from the other is to defeat the very purpose of democracy.[5] Each principle supplements and complements the other in the process of social justice. Ambedkar thus sought for social transformation through the establishment of social democracy in which these principles would prevail in each and every sphere of life of all members of society. For him, the other precepts of social justice include performance of duties, adherence to legal and social obligations, and finally a staunch faith in the value of justice. While social justice is the fulfilment of a bundle of human rights, it is also the yardstick for the justice of the administration system and subsumes legal justice and social well-being. For all these elaborations on social justice, Ambedkar is also known as the 'fountainhead of social justice'.

In the meeting of the Constituent Assembly of India in 1946, while speaking on the eight-point resolution moved by Jawaharlal Nehru on the aims and objectives of drawing up the Constitution for India's future governance, Ambedkar declared that while rights are the essence of social justice, remedies are even more important when rights come to be violated. He was not so convinced of delivery of justice through legal provisions and government machinery. Going by the Hindu social order, he anticipated the failure of delivery of justice. As he said: 'The principle of equal justice would strike a death blow to the established social order.... To enunciate the principle of justice is one thing, to make it effective is another thing.'[6]

[5] Ambedkar (1994).
[6] Ambedkar (1989: 103–4).

With the existence of legal frameworks to protect the weaker sections of society, if the incidence of human rights violations in the country increases, it clearly points to the failure of the law in its deterrent role. As evident from regular reportage of various forms of discriminations and violence against Dalits, both at the institutional and the social levels, they fail to enjoy equal rights. In many cases, wrongful acts at the administration and judiciary levels dilute the scope and applicability of the law, resulting in denial of justice. Thus, 'enacting law' and 'upholding law' are seen in different spectrums. In enacting laws, little attention is paid to the existing institutions that have been tasked with the implementation of the law. Although laws have their limitations, this is further accentuated with the creation of more lapses, inexplicably, at the level of implementation.

Ambedkar envisaged the role and responsibilities of the civil services towards the protection of rights and taking forward constitutional values. He contemplated extraordinary kind of protections for them through the Articles 309 to 312.[7] It must be recognized that not only the constitutional safeguards for all citizens but also these special provisions for civil services constitute a package in the scheme of delivery of justice to the marginalized sections of society. In 1949, in his reply to the debate on 'what responsibility lies on those who are called upon to work on the Constitution both in society and in government', as a matter of fact, he had cautioned about the challenging task of carrying out the constitutional message in a mission of empowerment in every practical way. As Ambedkar put it:

> However good a Constitution may be, it is sure to turn out bad because those who are called to work it, happen to be a bad lot. However bad a Constitution may be, it may turn out to be good if those who are called to work it happen to be a good lot. The working of a Constitution does not depend wholly upon the nature of the Constitution.[8]

Over the years, Ambedkar's ideas have shaped the consciousness of many weaker sections in contemporary society. The deprivation induced in lower social groups, through various forms of human

[7] Ambedkar (1989: 103–4).
[8] Ambedkar (1994: 1210).

rights violations, remains a common phenomenon, reflecting the failure of the State mechanism to protect the rights of every section of the population. Thus, Ambedkar's idea that constitutional values and other protective measures are not sufficient for protecting human rights and dispensing social justice still remains relevant. As he observed, 'the Hindu social order does not recognize the individual as a centre of social purpose, rather caste as a system provides for a regulatory mechanism to enforce the social order and the moral philosophy ... and these becomes social and binding force on all.'[9] In his view, caste is a plural phenomenon, a system of social governance, interlinked in unequal measures of social relations with each other. His quest for an egalitarian society and complete overhaul of the prevailing social structure, therefore, remains alive and relevant even today.

In modern India, even though the issue of social justice is firmly on the national agenda, political leaders swear by the cause of social justice, and the economic development focuses on socio-economic justice in the name of inclusive growth, violations of human rights of marginalized sections persist in different spheres of life. This is rooted in the social structure and social relations in such a way that marginalized groups are forced to live a life of subordination. Violence and atrocities against Dalits, in particular, continue to increase at alarming rates, a clear indicator of the oppressive nature of the caste system. Another concern is that access to social justice is inhibited by entrenched caste discrimination within the justice system, making it a more painful experience. There is a plethora of evidence to indicate that we have regressed on 'access to justice' fronts.

The existence of the criminal justice system and specific institutional and monitoring mechanisms to deal with violations of rights of marginalized groups like Dalits and, at the same time, an increase in such violations in the forms of caste-based discrimination, violence, and atrocities justify Ambedkar's fear in a democratic society. How far have the thoughts of Ambedkar on 'social justice' been relevant in contemporary society? The following two sections discuss the scenario of caste-based crimes and atrocities in contemporary India. They examine the responses of the criminal justice system and how 'interplay of caste, class and identity' at

---

[9] Ambedkar (1987: 99).

societal as well as administrative levels remains one of the critical dimensions in delivering justice to the victims of such caste-related oppressive behaviour.

Caste-based Violence and Responses of State Machinery: Some Facts

Although evidence from community experiences point towards widespread violation of civil rights of Dalits, the official data shows otherwise. It is argued that violation of civil rights and various forms of discriminatory behaviour are accompanied by violent behaviour because assertions of rights are often met with oppressive resistance.[10] An analysis of the official data on overall crimes against Dalits reveals that on an average, 32,300 cases were registered annually between 1995 and 2016. It increased from about 33,000 in 1995 to nearly 41,000 in 2016, the year 2014 witnessing the highest number of crimes. Of the total registered crimes, cases booked under the PoA act, legally known as 'atrocities', increased from about 14,000 in 1995 to 36,000 in 2016, with an annual average of about 14,000 cases. It might be noted that while there was a steady increase in the number of registered cases of atrocities till 2013, it increased significantly afterwards. The rate of crimes (defined as the number of registered cases in a year per one lakh population) indicated that on an average, it was about 21 between 2012 and 2016, a significant increase from past years. The data on various forms of atrocities against Dalits revealed that among the registered cases, the proportion of rape, kidnapping, and abduction and murder cases increased substantially over the years. However, all these figures are a gross underestimation, as many cases remain unreported or unregistered.

The important question that needs to be addressed in the context of widespread atrocities against Dalits is: How has the State machinery dealt with such human rights violations? The NCRB data clearly show that the dispensation of all crimes at the judiciary level, in particular, has been dismal. Over the years, on an average, more than 80 per cent cases remained pending for trial

[10] Pal (2014, 2015).

in courts at the end of each year. This is despite the provision of special courts under Section 14 of the PoA Act for the purpose of providing for speedy trial. The most disappointing feature has been the very low conviction rate of the charge-sheeted cases for which trials were held. The accused were convicted in less than one-third of the cases. Another concern is that the average conviction rate for the atrocities against Dalits has been extremely low compared to the overall crimes against them. An analysis of the NCRB data on number of cases under the PoA Act (excluding the cases tried under sections of the Indian Penal Code) that came for trial between 2010 and 2016 clearly shows an increase in pendency, a steady decline in the number of cases that complete trial, and a fall in conviction rates. The proportion of cases that were pending trial at the end of the year rose from 78 per cent in 2010 to 91 per cent in 2016. Of the cases in which trial was completed by the end of the year, a majority ended in acquittals. Conviction rates dropped sharply from 38 per cent in 2010 to 16 per cent in 2016. Moreover, if conviction rates were taken as a proportion of the total cases that came up for trial in each year (and not as a proportion of the total cases that completed trial), the figures were even more dismal. For instance, given the fact that in 2016, a large majority of the registered cases were PoA crimes, only 1.4 per cent of all crimes against Dalits that came up for trial ended in convictions.

What are the reasons for a low conviction rate? There is plenty of evidence to suggest that legislative provisions are highly underutilized. Victims have to face insurmountable obstacles from village-level functionaries to the administrative personnel (police), public prosecutors, and other state functionaries. The implementation of the laws has not been in true spirit for various reasons, and there has been a lack of will and commitment from the enforcing agencies, leading to the under-performance of the laws.[11] Among other things, implementing officials resort to different means that deny justice to the victims of atrocities. These include non-registration or under-registration of cases (non-registration of the cases under proper provisions of the Act), delays in filing of the first information report (FIR), not conducting on-spot investigation in many cases, shoddy investigation, delayed investigation, incorrect and biased recording of victim and witness statements, filing of charge sheets

[11] Pal (2012).

based on inappropriate and inadequate evidence, undue delay in filing of charge sheets, recording of contradictory statements in the depositions by witnesses, delayed court trials, and other unlawful tactics by the accused in alliance with State functionaries.[12] Other hurdles include inappropriate support mechanisms for the victims and witnesses by the investigating officers and public prosecutors, and even by the trial court. There are other social practices inherently prevailing in public life that conflict with state laws. Very often, the traditional caste hegemony dominates the course of investigations and court trials. The concern is that dilution of evidence by the investigating agencies, coupled with the poor responses of the judiciary, undermines the relevance of the laws and, in turn, denies justice to the victims in many cases of caste atrocities.[13] As a trial court observed: 'It is unfortunate that higher police officials themselves play into the hands of the complainant rather than examine the case in an unbiased manner and strictly enforce the provisions of law.'[14]

There are also loopholes in court trials. There are a lot of misinterpretations of the evidence. In many cases, despite taking cognizance of the loopholes in the investigation process, the judgment is given against the victims based on procedural gaps. But the truth is that a large proportion of victims of atrocities are denied justice despite a strong criminal justice system. The sixth report of the Standing Committee on Social Justice and Empowerment (2014–15), which examined the situation of atrocities against SCs and STs, during the amendment of the PoA Act in 2015, attributed the low conviction rate to the biases and 'willful negligence' by officials involved in the investigation and to the loopholes left by the investigating officials with the purpose of helping the accused belonging to the same social class as them.[15] There is also evidence to show that the courts acquitted the accused on procedural grounds (e.g., delay in FIR, investigation not done by proper authority) as well as evidential or substantive grounds (e.g., statement or personal stand of the victim(s) and witness(es) besides other general grounds such as medical evidence, place of offence not within

---

[12] Pal (2012, 2018); Pal and Lal (2010).
[13] Pal (2012, 2018); Pal and Lal (2010).
[14] Pal and Lal (2010: 153).
[15] GoI (2014–15).

public view, insufficient evidence, and the like; and other specific grounds such as no mention of accused caste, death of complaint/ victim, counter case, and so on).[16] Thus, it is evident that gaps in the implementation procedure vitiate the very purpose of justice. The progressive provisions have actually not been implemented by the authorities in any true sense. It is not simply a matter of caste background but social class defined by the caste hierarchy that often shapes the coalition between higher-caste officials and the accused to hold their social status or positions. The wider networking based on caste makes it easier to influence the system to get the judgment against victims of atrocities. The following section elaborates on this issue in reference to Ambedkar's thoughts.

Caste-Coalition and Denial of Justice: Relevance of Ambedkar's Thoughts

From the earlier discussion, it clearly emerges that the extremely low conviction rate denies justice to a large number of victims of caste atrocities. This also suggests that officials deviate from the rules prescribed for the implementation of law. The purposeful non-registration of the atrocity cases and delays in FIR, arrest of accused, and the investigation allow the accused to dilute the case through different means, the important one being the use of caste identity to mobilize people from their own caste groups in the community as well as administration to their advantage. After the filing of charge sheets, these procedural lapses or shortcomings affect the conviction adversely. In fact, if we compare the conviction rates, the rate is much higher for general population than the rate for atrocities against Dalits. That is because a lot of people in the state machinery, that is, administration and judiciary, carry the caste bias they have to their duty. There is enormous evidence to show the apathy and lack of sensitivity in handling atrocity cases. One case in point is given below:

> Regardless of the evidence providing testimony of the involvement of upper caste militia in a heinous crime of arson and killing; police did not arrest even a single person. Most of the persons involved in this crime fled away from the village. Police never pressurized

---

[16] Thorat (2017).

Caste and Delivery of Social Justice 61

their families to make an appeal to surrender. According to the villagers police never attempted to visit the locality of the accused. Police authorities including the mayor of the *Panchayat* infringed their legal jurisdiction to act as a traditional village court to force the victims to compromise and withdraw the case for money. Even the main culprits who was involved in more than forty criminal cases, was not arrested. Appeals of dalits were always put aside as false complaints.[17]

Undoubtedly, the caste atrocities are rooted in the caste system. Fight between two caste groups are, however, not for the sake of protecting caste identity but maintaining social class or position. The analysis of fact findings and case studies revealed that a majority of atrocity cases (more than two-thirds) were collective and organized in nature, where more than one accused were involved in committing atrocities against a single individual. Dominant caste groups, as a collective entity with a higher position in the social order, commit atrocities with an ultimate motive to keep Dalits under suppression, strengthen the caste norms, hold on to social power in the locality, and exhibit their dominance in everyday life. This remains one of the greatest challenges to the justice system in civil society. As Ambedkar said, 'Law is for Individuals. It can punish them when they violate laws. But when the whole community is involved in violation, law bounds to fail.'[18] The caste-based traditions and the advent of modernity together produce a new 'coalition' between higher-caste perpetrators and classes (powerful members from their caste groups in the community and also from the administration). The social and economic status of the accused and its association with a larger 'social class' plays a significant role in denial of justice. Overwhelming caste loyalties and sentiments often influence the decisions of the personnel in the administration and the judiciary. The administration, being represented majorly by the higher-caste members, very often shows apathy towards the complaints of Dalit victims. They very often accept this system of dominance as 'natural'. In this context, Ambedkar's thought appears highly relevant. He believed that the enforcement agency and the judiciary, being very much part of the caste-ridden society, cannot be free from caste prejudice. Expecting law to ensure justice

[17] Based on case study; Pal and Lal (2010: 130).
[18] Thorat (2017: 78).

to victims of caste crimes, therefore, can be an impractical solution to this perennial social problem.

Ambedkar was aware of the aspirations of the different sections of society and their conflicting interests and also the existing biases in the Indian administration and judiciary. He emphasized that the presence of elaborate legal provisions may not always guarantee rights to social justice. Whether the principle of social justice is effective or not necessarily depends upon the nature and character of the civil services who administer the principle. He expressed his views by saying: 'India has been ruled by the British but administered by the Hindus.' If the civil services, by reason of its class bias, is in favour of the established Hindu order in which the principle of equality had no place, the new order in the form of equal justice can never come into being.[19]

Ambedkar further expressed his ideas by illustrating actual practices at the administrative level. He pointed out:

> From the capital of India down to the village the whole administration is rigged by the Hindus.... If the established order has continued to exist, it is because of the unfailing support it received from the Hindu officials of the state. Their principle is not equal justice to all. Their motto is justice consistent with established order. They carry over attitude towards different classes in society under the established order into administration. This is inevitable. If an 'Untouchable' goes to a police officer with complaint against the caste Hindu, instead of receiving any protection he will receive plenty of abuses. Either he will be driven away without his complaint being recorded or if it is recorded it would be recorded quite falsely to provide a way of escape to the 'Touchable' aggressors. Further, if the Untouchable prosecutes his offenders before a Magistrate the fate of his proceeding could be foretold. He will never be able to get Hindus as witness because of the conspiracy of the villagers not to support the case of the Untouchables however just it may be. If he brings witness from the Untouchables, the Magistrate will not accept their testimony because he can easily say that they are interested and not independent witness, or, if they are independent witness the Magistrate has easy way of acquitting the accused by simply saying that the Untouchables' complaint did not strike him as a truthful witness. He can do this fearlessly knowing fully well that the higher tribunal will not reverse his findings because it is based on

[19] Ambedkar (1989: 104).

Caste and Delivery of Social Justice   63

the testimony of witness whose conduct the higher tribunal had no opportunity to observe.[20]

This practice is very much prevalent at the community level in contemporary society. As some victims of caste atrocities in a community shared their experience:

> The police/investigation authorities did not perform their duties sincerely. Beginning from registering case to the process of investigation, this case witnessed evident flaws and lack of eagerness to book the guilty before law. Moreover, there was evidence that police got influenced by the accused family. Police fabricated the family members of victims under false case and attempted to divert the case. False cases are employed as a tool to mentally torture the complainant.[21]

The caste system and the consequent graded structure was a dominant issue in Ambedkar's quest for and vision of social justice. According to Ambedkar, caste violence has a much stronger social anchorage. The class bias and antipathy towards Dalits is likely to cause the denial of protection and justice. In this context, he wrote: 'The power to administer law is not less important than the power to make laws. And the spirit of the legislators may easily be violated if not nullified by the machinery of the administrators.'[22]

For Ambedkar, the incorporation of the aspirations of the marginalized categories in the rules and policies is not enough for dispensing social justice. That is why he wanted the Dalits and other marginalized sections of the society to be part of the administration. He believed that one of the ways to deliver social justice to the individual could be to break the monopoly of the people who are in public services. He, however, was guarded in saying that this urge of self-realization in the marginalized sections who are denied justice must not be allowed into a class struggle. In the Constituent Assembly, he pointed out that the challenging task is to carry out the constitutional message in a mission of empowerment in every practical way so that what is enshrined in the constitution does not remain mere lip service. Given the structure of our society,

---

[20] Khairmode (1989: 265).

[21] Based on case study; Pal and Lal (2010: 130).

[22] Ambedkar quoted in Kumar (2007: 3).

according to Ambedkar, the work of empowerment therefore has two aspects: how to promote the assertion by the deprived classes of their rights in all spheres of life and how to sensitize all the other classes to this message of equality and social justice.

Caste atrocities also have political dimensions, where caste and class identities operate in caste conflicts. The shift in the political power from one social group to the other makes the power holder more assertive. Not only do attempts to acquire power cause conflicts but holding that power also leads to conflicts. For example, in Bihar, when a representative from the *Yadav* community was in power, the people from this community felt emancipated and powerful. When there was a shift in power to the *Kurmi* community, the members from this community also became assertive and dominant. Similar things have been observed in Uttar Pradesh as well in the context of change in political power from one party to another supported largely by specific caste groups. The political shift contributes in social confrontations resulting in caste conflicts. Various studies have indicated that political power plays such a major role that every other attempt to capture power leads to conflicts. These developments in the democratic set-up has yielded new forms of atrocity.

Thus, in the context of atrocities against Dalits, 'truth' (evidence) and 'justice' are two terms that construct the role and responsibilities of the administrative and judiciary system respectively. In India, the legal system provokes many questions about its relevance to the poor and socially excluded, such as the Dalits who neither understand the language nor the practice of the courts. Following atrocities, Dalits promptly rely on the State system to get justice. But when the registered case is put under court trial, the complicated processes involved make it a longer wait for justice; the situation often causes them to go back to community institutions that have culturally been sources of maintaining social order. But these institutions are being managed largely by dominant caste members; the casteist decisions are pronounced in this 'non-state justice system'.

Ways Forward

It is quite clear that laws fail to ensure rights of all citizens. The situation is even worse for the marginalized groups. Despite

Caste and Delivery of Social Justice   65

specific legislations and a powerful criminal justice system in India to curb the violation of human rights against marginalized groups, the continued increase in caste-based discrimination and atrocities in different spheres of life and the conspicuous denial of justice to a large number of victims who face such oppressive social behaviour remain major concerns. Evidence shows that procedural loopholes created by the administration during the investigation of the cases often take priority over the nature and content of atrocities, which result in high acquittal and, consequently, denial of justice to the victims. This chapter makes an attempt to give insights into the causal dynamics through the lens of Ambedkar's thoughts on the role of laws and State machinery in delivering justice within a rigid social structure. The larger questions therefore are (a) do State laws have limitations in bringing desired changes with the existence of rigid social norms in Indian society? or/and (b) does the State machinery fail to follow the rules under the laws to deliver justice?

In 1936, Ambedkar observed that 'people as physical entities are not wrong, but what is wrong is the religious and social ideology that determines the relationships'.[23] Even in contemporary society, the old customary rules and ideas still continue to influence the behaviour of certain groups as they believe these rules and ideas to be right. It appears that the legal provisions fail to capture the complexities of local agencies and sociocultural contexts, leading to denial of justice to the victims. Ambedkar, however, strongly believed that laws are not sufficient and their implementation is critical to the delivery of social justice. In this sense, persistence of caste atrocities and denial of justice are important pointers to the failure of the State machinery in the implementation of the laws. The National Human Rights Commission argues that the acts of omission and commission by law enforcement agencies are further reinforced by the fact that very often members of the law enforcement agencies themselves are the offenders.[24]

It is a fact that the judiciary system is assigned the task of providing justice. But the inception of justice takes shape in the investigation process itself. Any wrongful acts by the police administration have larger consequences, not in terms of dilution of the

[23] Ambedkar (1936).
[24] National Human Rights Commission (2004).

applicability of the law resulting in denial of justice to the majority of victims but also repetition of similar atrocities, as it allows offenders to act with near impunity. This also creates unsolicited conditions for the victims to force them to compromise outside the 'law of state' and deprivation of 'natural justice'; also, this deprives the compensations and benefits under the laws, resulting in the denial of social justice to the victims. The way legislations are implemented, exclusion easily gets embedded in the discourse of delivering social justice. The explanation of Ambedkar regarding why most cases of caste-based discrimination and violence end in acquittal is found true in the present context of caste atrocities.

The chapter argues that with the complex linkages between caste and social conditions, in mainstream society, many 'unwritten laws' exist against lower-caste groups. Unless the enforcement agencies are sensitive to the human rights violations against socially weaker sections and committed to upholding the legitimacy of state laws through a change in traditional 'caste laws', access to social justice will be a matter of disillusion in a democratic society. As Ambedkar said, the ability and efficiency of the governing class are not enough for good governance, which would ensure social justice; rather, the class should have the will to get freedom from internal limitations arising out of social norms and class interests. Administrative roadblocks, judiciary bottlenecks, and lack of sensitivity on the part of both administration and judiciary systems create many social disabilities to keep the social conditions for SCs and STs as is. When the agenda of 'good governance' remains a priority in every society, a lot of reforms are required in the functioning of public institutions.

How long will Dalits continue to live this life of social oppressions? Unless, this is addressed, social democracy will be in danger. While recognizing Ambedkar's ideas and thoughts to understand social problems, it is also important to use his ideas on solutions to specific problems. Ambedkar argued that the higher-caste oppressors can easily crush the attempt to seek equal rights, Dalits being in minority and dependent on them. In 1942, Ambedkar observed that:

> The existence of grim struggle between the touchable and untouchable is a fact.... It is a contest between the Hindus who are economically and socially strong and the untouchables who are economically poor and numerically small. The chief weapon in the armory of the

Caste and Delivery of Social Justice   67

upper caste Hindus is economic power which they possess over the poor untouchables living in the village. They most often succeed in suppressing the untouchables due to many causes. In a struggle to secure equal right and dignity, the untouchables fight an unequal battle and face atrocities.[25]

This is true even today. The issue is how to make Dalits economically independent of the higher caste. This is the solution to free the Dalits from the clutches of economically and demographically upper-caste groups. The Dalits and upper castes live in close proximity on economically unequal terms. In this dependent relationship, Ambedkar argued that equal access and justice to Dalits is nearly impossible. He proposed independent means of livelihood to delink the Dalits from the higher castes in villages. He argued that separate settlements and economic independence can be a solution to the atrocities in villages. Another notable fact is that cases of atrocities based on caste are on the rise, indicating the growing resistance by upper castes with violence to the efforts by Dalits to access equal status and opportunities and also individual liberty and freedom. The State, therefore, has a larger responsibility to change the attitude and behaviour of the people to encourage them to respect and practice equality in their behaviour towards Dalits and allow them to enjoy equal rights. The change in the code of behaviour of higher castes is the most important issue, which Ambedkar also emphasized. Although the laws are necessary to provide safeguards to individuals against denial of equal rights, this will have limited impact. Ambedkar was clear about the limitation of the law in a situation where the majority in the community opposed equal rights. In 1943, he observed:

> The prevalent view is that once rights are enacted in a law then they are safeguarded. This again is an unwarranted assumption. An experience proves that rights are not protected by law but the social and moral conscience of society. If social conscience is such that it is to recognize the rights which law chooses to enact, rights will be safe and secure. But (when) the fundamental rights are opposed by the community, no law, no parliament, no judiciary can guarantee them in the real sense of the words.... Social conscience is the only safeguards of all rights, fundamental or non-fundamental.[26]

[25] Ambedkar (1979c: 426).
[26] Ambedkar (1979b: 222).

In contemporary society, when social relations are still governed by social order based on religious ideology, the continuation of denial of equal rights and status to the lower-caste groups is the outcome of the limited presence of social conscience in favour of equality. This is the reason for persistence of caste conflicts despite protective and punitive legislations. That is why Ambedkar emphasized that there is a need for a shift in the norms and principles that induce people's behaviour with the spirit of equality in practice. As he argued: 'The social and moral conscience of society should be such that it recognizes the rights of individuals. Since there are no rights in the Hindu society which the moral sense of man could recognize, there is a need to create social conscience which is supportive of rights under the law.'[27]

However, in the government action, there has been less focus on the transformation of norms and belief of people in favour of equality, which is as important as the legal safeguards. In the absence of this, the traditional norms and beliefs continue to influence the behaviour of upper castes towards the Dalits, resulting in denial of equal rights and acts of social oppression. In the implementation of laws, while it is important to focus on the victims who are the sufferers, equal attention is necessary on the accused and officials who are tasked with implementation of the law in its letter and spirit. Acceptance and propagation of charter instruments such as the Bengaluru Declaration by diverse political parties would be a significant step in this direction.

References

Ambedkar, B.R. 1936. *Annihilation of Caste*, B.R. Kadrekar (ed.). Bombay: Bharat Bhusan Printing Press.

———. 1979a. 'Castes in India', in Vasant Moon (ed.), *Dr. Babasaheb Ambedkar Writing and Speeches*. Vol. 1. Bombay: The Education Department, Government of Maharashtra.

———. 1979b. 'Ranade, Gandhi, and Jinnah', in Vasant Moon (ed.), *Dr. Babasaheb Ambedkar Writing and Speeches*. Vol. 1. Bombay: The Education Department, Government of Maharashtra.

———. 1979c. 'States and Minorities', in Vasant Moon (ed.), *Dr. Babasaheb Ambedkar Writing and Speeches*. Vol. 1. Bombay: The Education Department, Government of Maharashtra.

[27] Ambedkar (1979b: 222).

———. 1987. 'The Hindu Social Order: Its Essential Features', in Vasant Moon (ed.), *Dr. Babasaheb Ambedkar Writings and Speeches*, p. 99. Vol. 3. Bombay: Education Department, Government of Maharashtra.

———. 1989. *Dr. Babasaheb Ambedkar Writing and Speeches*, Vasant Moon (ed.). Vol. 5. Bombay: Education Department, Government of Maharashtra.

———. 1994. *Dr. Babasaheb Ambedkar Writing and Speeches*, Vasant Moon (ed.). Vol. 13. Bombay: Education Department, Government of Maharashtra

GoI (Government of India). 2014–15. *Sixth Report of the Standing Committee on Social Justice and Empowerment*. The Scheduled Castes and Scheduled Tribes (Prevention of Atrocities) to consider Amendment to the Act. New Delhi: Lok Sabha Secretariat, GoI.

Kumar, V. 2007. 'Babasaheb Ambedkar's Ideas of Social Justice and Just Theory.' *Dialogue*, 9 (2). Available at: https://www.asthabharati.org/Dia_Oct%2007/viv.htm.

Khairmode, G.B. 1989. *Bhimrao Ramji Ambedkar*. Vol. 4. Pune: Sugawa Publications.

Makwana, Yogendra. 1992. 'Ambedkar—A Crusader', in Yogendra Makwana (ed.), *Ambedkar and Social Justice*, p. 68. New Delhi: Publication Division, GoI.

National Crime Record Bureau (NCRB). 1995–2016. *Crimes in India*. New Delhi: National Crime Record Bureau (NCRB), Ministry of Home Affairs, GoI.

National Human Rights Commission. 2004. *Report on Prevention of Atrocities against SCs*. New Delhi: GoI.

Pal, G.C. 2012. *Mapping Caste-Based Atrocities in Uttar Pradesh, Research Report*. New Delhi: Indian Institute of Dalit Studies.

———. 2014. 'Access to Justice: Social Ostracism Obstructs Efforts by Dalits for Equal Rights', *Journal of Social Inclusion Studies*, 1(1): 122–34.

———. 2015. 'Social Exclusion and Mental Health: The Unexplored Aftermath of Caste-Based Discrimination and Violence', *Psychology & Developing Societies*, 27(2): 189–213.

———. 2018. 'Access to Social Justice: Intersection of Caste, Class and Identity', in C. Joshua Thomas and Padmakshi Kakoti (eds.), *Towards Social Justice*, pp.7–29. New Delhi: Pentagon Press.

Pal, G.C. and L.D. Lal. 2010. *Mapping Caste-Based Atrocities in India: Status Report. Project Report No 39*. New Delhi: Indian Institute of Dalit Studies.

Thorat, S. 2017. 'Eradication of Untouchability, Caste Discrimination and Atrocities in Maharashtra: Analysis of Magnitude, Causes and Solution', Nagpur: Memorandum, Association for Social and Economic Equality.

Acts

Protection of Civil Rights (PCR) Act. 1976. *Act No. BC.12013/2/76-SCT-V*, 15 September 1977, Ministry of Social Welfare and Empowerment, GoI, New Delhi.

Scheduled Caste and the Scheduled Tribes (Prevention of Atrocities) Amendment Act. 2015. *The Gazette of India (Registered No. DL-(N) 04/0007/2003-16)*, Ministry of Law and Justice, GoI.

Scheduled Castes and Scheduled Tribes (Prevention of Atrocities) Act. 1989. *Act No. 33*, 11 September 1989, Ministry of Social Welfare & Empowerment, GoI.

Untouchability (Offences) Act. 1955. *Notification No. S.R.O.1109*, *The Official Gazette*, Ministry of Social Welfare and Empowerment, GoI, New Delhi.

4

'Made to Think and Forced to Feel'

*The Power of Counter-Ritual**

MEENA DHANDA

Dr Ambedkar argued that habitual conduct with the backing of religion is not easy to change and that salvation will come only if the caste Hindu is 'made to think and is forced to feel that he must alter his ways'.[1] He meant that the casteist conduct of the 'caste Hindu' is hard to change because it springs from an ingrained habit of the mind.[2] The impetus to change ways can come from unexpected contingencies: impersonal political junctures, very personal histories, interpersonal challenges, intra-group skirmishes, a whole network of factors that brings the habitual conduct of caste up for scrutiny. This mix of factors is quite complicated in the United Kingdom where I am located as a researcher and academic,

---

[*] This is a revised version of my keynote at the International conference on Dr B.R Ambedkar '*Quest for Equity*', at Bengaluru, India, presented on 23 July 2017. A different version was presented at the British Sociological Association annual conference on 12 April 2018. The present essay is a kind of amalgamation of the two lectures.

[1] Ambedkar in a letter to Mr Thakkar, on 14 November 1932; see Ajnat (1993: 79). See footnote 19 (p. 78) below for the full quotation from which these words are extracted.

[2] 'Caste is a notion; it is a state of mind. The destruction of caste does not therefore mean the destruction of a physical barrier. It means a notional change'. Ambedkar (2014 [1936]: 286).

72   Meena Dhanda

regularly engaging with the public. We need to think through the means of defiance against systematic oppression and stigmatization of people on the basis of caste. In this chapter, I will reflect upon whether caste might be disrupted in its everyday reproduction through the use of counter-rituals.

Research Context

From March 2017 to September 2017, the UK Government Equalities Office (GEO) conducted a public consultation on 'Caste in Great Britain and Equality Law' for British residents. Three years prior to the consultation, I led a project on 'Caste in Britain'[3] for the UK Equality and Human Rights Commission (EHRC) producing two reports[4] that were a key reference in the GEO's guidance for the public consultation on caste.[5] The consultation took place following intense lobbying by mutually opposed sides of community groups, which one could call: the 'assenters' who want Parliament to act on its duty to prohibit caste discrimination by the explicit addition of the term 'caste' in the letter of the law, and the 'refusers' who oppose such an addition of caste. The UK government announced its response to the public consultation on 23 July 2018: a decision 'to invite Parliament to repeal the duty'.[6]

---

[3] This interdisciplinary project (2013–14) had two parts: a definitional part, and a public engagement part, which resulted in two reports (Dhanda, Waughray, et al. 2014; Dhanda, Mosse, et al. 2014). The remit of the project was to explain how caste might be defined in the context of Britain, to facilitate the legal direction to include caste as an aspect of race in Section 9 of the Equality Act (EA), 2010. We addressed three specific questions: how caste should be defined in the EA, 2010; what exceptions and exclusions for caste should be placed in the EA, 2010; and how caste should be related to the Public Sector Equality Duty.

[4] Dhanda, Waughray et al. (2014); Dhanda, Mosse et al. (2014).

[5] The GEO Public Consultation document of March 2017 refers to our EHRC Report 91 (Dhanda, Waughray et al. 2014) as 'The University of Wolverhampton' report.

[6] Penny Mordaunt (minister for Women and Equalities) announced the government's response to the consultation: 'About 53% of respondents wanted to rely on the existing statutory remedy and repeal the duty, 22% rejected both options (mainly because they wished the Government to proscribe the concept of caste in British law altogether) and about 18%

As a sop to the sufferers of caste discrimination, the government has offered:

> In order to ensure that people know their rights and what sort of conduct could be unlawful under the Equality Act, we also intend to produce short guidance before the repeal legislation is introduced. We want this to be of particular use to any individual who feels they may have suffered discrimination on grounds of caste. It should also help employers, service providers and public authorities who are outside those groups most concerned with caste and who may have little awareness of caste divisions.[7]

The assenters, or the pro-legislation groups, drawn from many different communities across the country demanded that the government must follow the direction of Parliament given in April 2013 that ministers must make 'caste an aspect of race' in the UK EA, 2010. On the other side, the refusers or the anti-legislation groups are community groups led by Hindu organizations who continue to lobby against the mention of the term 'caste' in British legal statutes.

Why is there such a sensitivity about the mention of caste? Does the vehement refusal to acknowledge the potential of caste identity to lead to discrimination rest perhaps on the deeply integral role caste plays in maintaining communal bonds? If so, what can those who are desperately seeking explicit legislation against caste discrimination do in order to convince the refusers? At the political juncture of this division within the diaspora South Asian

---

of respondents wanted the duty to be implemented.' (See Mordaunt, Penny. 2018. 'Government Response to Caste Consultation: Written statement-HCWS898'. Parliament.UK, 23 July 2018. Available at https://www.parliament.uk/business/publications/written-questions-answers-statements/written-statement/Commons/2018-07-23/HCWS898/, accessed 30 March 2019.) I think the government has disingenuously reached its conclusion based on an analysis that is highly objectionable on methodological, procedural, and ethical grounds.

[7] Mordaunt, Penny. 2018. 'Government Response to Caste Consultation: Written statement-HCWS898'. Parliament.UK, 23 July. Available at https://www.parliament.uk/business/publications/written-questions-answers-statements/written-statement/Commons/2018-07-23/HCWS898/.

community groups on the matter of whether or not to explicitly acknowledge the existence of caste discrimination in order to outlaw it, I wish to step back and examine how the everyday reproduction of caste relations might be interrupted to open the possibility of critical thinking on casted relations. How can the refusers be 'made to think and forced to feel'?

Experience of racial discrimination is a factor in the explanation of the caste-related rift within South Asian communities. I suggest, without elaboration here, that although living in the diaspora invariably prepares all South Asians to expect racial discrimination, it does not uniformly make them empathize with the victims of casteism. Their own experience of discrimination does not necessarily make them sensitive to the discrimination others face. Well-meaning anti-racists do not automatically become anti-casteists. Opposition to legislation against caste discrimination from some Hindu and some Sikh groups in the United Kingdom is fed by growing transnational attempts to forge a Hindu identity. Since Hindu identity is inseparable from caste marking, many Hindu representatives view the attempt to include caste in the EA as an assault on their Hindu identity. The Alliance of Hindu organizations, including the National Council of Hindu Temples, leading the opposition to the legislation,[8] amongst other things, claims that caste discrimination does not exist in the United Kingdom. From a distinct platform, the Sikh Council UK, representing several Sikh organizations, does not deny that caste discrimination exists, but it opposes the addition of caste to the EA, 2010, preferring instead to follow the 'case law' route.[9] The positive

[8] The alliance was formed in 2013. See Hindu Council UK. 2013. 'Alliance of Hindu Organisations (AHO): Press Release'. 22 May 2013. Available at http://www.hinducounciluk.org/2013/05/22/alliance-of-hindu-organisations-aho-press-release/, accessed 30 March 2019. The UK government response to the public consultation to repeal the duty to add caste to the EA, 2010, elicited jubilant approval from the National Council of Hindu Temples (UK) (NCHTUK) who declared it an 'entirely just conclusion'. See National Council of Hindu Temples (UK). 24 July 2018. Available at http://www.nchtuk.org/index.php/extensions/hindu-temples-in-the-uk/8-news/latest-news, accessed 30 March 2019.

[9] Besides the Sikh Council UK, the Sikh Federation UK had reportedly 'lobbied for this outcome' and were clearly very pleased with the government's decision (see Rana [2018]).

outcome of the public confrontation between the assenters and the refusers is to highlight a pressing research question: How must we understand the mechanisms of the perpetuation or erosion of caste in the diaspora? Are there avenues of cultural politics providing an opening for non-state extra-legal challenges to caste prejudice and caste hierarchies?

Reproduction of Consciousness of Caste

We must understand how consciousness of caste hierarchy is reproduced in everyday life. My focus in the remainder of this essay is on rituals and counter-rituals. Participation in rituals is an important aspect of social belonging, including dual possibilities of renewed bonding as well as ruptures.[10] Social belonging is, firstly, about connectedness to others, and secondly, but not always equally, it is about acceptance—our acceptance by others, their acceptance of us. It is worth noting that one can remain connected to others who do not accept one as we may want them to, and sometimes these are the most pernicious kinds of belongings.

Connectedness is not solidarity. Belonging to people, to traditions, to places are vulnerabilities requiring careful expression, indeed, at times requiring careful cover-ups. Revelations of one's allegiances and affiliations—to whom or to what one belongs—is risky. Proclaiming one's membership as a human being to the party of humanity is a safe option. Failure to secure a place in this party, however, can be excruciatingly painful. You may feel connected to others as human beings, but they can seem unconnected to you: their eyes touch your colour, your bodies, your caste, your attire, your accent, your age, but they do not touch *you*.

Belonging to this or that caste may or may not be central to our practical identity, but in any case, because our practical identities

---

[10] Weber wrote that 'So long as the karma doctrine was unshaken, revolutionary ideas or progressivism were inconceivable. The lowest castes, furthermore, had the most to win through ritual correctness and were least tempted to innovations.' (*Religions of India*, cited by Berg [2018: 846]). Berg notes Weber's hasty presentation of the 'lowest castes' as apolitical, and as a conceptual alternative, he deploys the idea of 'embedded contingency' to explore the possibility of resistance.

are 'unstable', transformative protest has the potential to make us who we become. Elsewhere, I have argued that practical identity is negotiating the continuous process of becoming different.[11] Is it not, therefore, incumbent upon each one of us to scrutinize our inheritance and wisely perform our little acts of identification? The deniers of caste discrimination in the United Kingdom take caste identity to be, in some undefined simple sense, about 'belonging', and not about discrimination. I think they fail to see the threads of connection between the given-ness of an inherited place (inferior or superior) in the social world and the reproduction of that place through processes of identification. Their own everyday routine acts weave these threads into the fabric of caste communities.

The Challenge to Caste by an Exceptional Man

As is well known, Dr Bhimrao Ramji Ambedkar, the chair of the drafting committee of the Indian Constitution, a student of the American pragmatist philosopher John Dewey, was an untouchable by birth. He accumulated a string of international academic degrees but remained unappreciated as an intellectual until recently.[12] I turn to him to understand the lessons learnt from trying to uproot the stranglehold of casteism. Ambedkar 'exercised his talents as a sociologist in the service of a cause: he scrutinised the mechanisms of caste with the aim of annihilating this social system based on hierarchy and such an approach did not help him to be recognised as a true social scientist'.[13] Diametrically opposed to Mohandas Karamchand Gandhi, Ambedkar challenged the 'Varna' system (a mythically conflict-free, social arrangement, of four broad, occupationally defined, mutually supporting groups). He argued that a caste society divides the dominated too! Ambedkar argued that habitual conduct with the backing of religion is not easy to change. Concerted political action is needed to overturn entrenched habits. In an insightful analysis communicated in a letter to A.V. Thakkar, a Congress leader from Bombay, the general secretary of

[11] See Dhanda (2008).
[12] Rathore (2017) shows in an exemplary way how Ambedkar's thought can be mainstreamed into political theory.
[13] Jaffrelot (2005: 6).

the Anti-Untouchability League and one of the signatories on the Poona Pact in 1932, Ambedkar wrote:

> In my opinion there can be two distinct methods of approaching the task of uplifting the Depressed Classes. There is a school, which proceeds on the assumption that the act of the individual belonging to the Depressed Classes is bound up with his personal conduct. If he is suffering from want and misery, it is because he must be vicious and sinful. Starting from this hypothesis this School of social workers concentrates all its efforts and its resources on fostering personal virtue by adopting a programme which included items such as temperance, gymnasium, co-operation, libraries, schools, etc., which are calculated to make the individual a better and virtuous individual. In my opinion, there is also another method of approach to this problem. It starts with the hypothesis that the fate of the individual is governed by his environment and the circumstances he is obliged to live under and if an individual is suffering from want and misery it is because his environment is not propitious. I have no doubt that of the two views the latter is the more correct, the former may raise a few stray individuals above the level of the class to which they belong. It cannot lift the class as a whole.[14]

He then goes on the attach the aim of the Anti-Untouchability League to the second of the two approaches, urging energies to be drawn 'to effect a change in the social environment of the Depressed Classes', rather than 'to foster private virtue'.[15]

Further, whilst encouraging the depressed classes to campaign for 'the enjoyment of their civic rights such as taking water from the village wells, entry in village schools, admission to village chawdi, use of public conveyance etc.', Ambedkar warns of two obstacles.[16] First, the corruption of the police and magistracy who 'are out not to see that justice is done but to see that the dignity and interests of the caste Hindu as against the Depressed Classes are upheld'.[17] Secondly, he fears the boycott of the depressed classes in the village will lead to harassment, unemployment, and starvation. Even so,

---

[14] Ambedkar's letter to A.V. Thakhar on 14 November 1932, see Ajnat (1993: 77–8).

[15] Ajnat (1993: 77–8).

[16] Ajnat (1993: 79).

[17] Ajnat (1993: 79).

despite expecting the programme to involve 'social disturbance and even bloodshed', he is convinced that an 'alternative policy of adopting the line of least resistance' will be 'ineffective in the matter of uprooting untouchability'.[18] His reasoning is consistent and, as explanations of social psychology, prescient of theories of the nature of prejudice that took shape decades later. I quote at length again:

> The silent infiltration of rational idea among the ignorant mass of caste Hindus cannot, I am sure, work for the elevation of the Depressed Classes. First of all, the caste Hindu like all human beings follows his customary conduct in observing untouchability towards the Depressed Classes. Ordinarily, people do not give up their customary mode of behaviour because somebody is preaching against it. But when that customary mode of behaviour has or is believed to have behind it the sanction of religion mere preaching, if it is not resented and resisted, will be allowed to waft along the wind without creating any effect on the mind. The salvation of the Depressed Classes will come only when the Caste Hindu is made to think and is forced to feel that he must alter his ways. For that you must create a crisis by direct action against his customary code of conduct. The crisis will compel him to think and once he begins to think he will be more ready to change than he is otherwise likely to be. The great defect in the policy of least resistance and silent infiltration of rational ideas lies in this that they do not compel thought, for they do not produce crisis.[19]

Sadly, dominant sections of caste Hindus still do not think they need to alter their ways. Amongst Ambedkar's exceptional contemporaries, it was Gandhi who reinvented caste through a defence of hereditary occupations. As is well known, there were bitter feelings between the two towering figures of Indian nationalism. In an interview with the BBC broadcast on 31 December in 1955, Ambedkar told the world how he saw Gandhi 'in his human capacity, the bare man in him' as 'an orthodox Hindu'. Gandhi, according to Ambedkar's acerbic estimation, 'was never a reformer'. He chides Gandhi for limiting his reformist actions to 'Temple entry'. In 1930, Ambedkar had led such movements of temple entry

[18] Ajnat (1993: 79).
[19] Ajnat (1993: 79–80).

himself, albeit, with pessimism, for he had declared to his untouchable comrades:

> Your problems will not be solved by temple entry. Politics, economics, education, religion—all are part of the problem. Today's satyagraha is a challenge to the Hindu mind. Are the Hindus ready to consider us men or not; we will discover this today.... We know the god in the temple is of stone. *Darshan* and *Puja* will not solve our problems. But we will start out, and try to make a change in the minds of the Hindus.[20]

Thus, although he posed a challenge to the ritual restriction of access preventing the so-called lower castes from entering Hindu temples by advocating transgression of ritual norms, the point of such transgression, for Ambedkar, unlike Gandhi, was to establish the hollowness of the Hindu claims to equality, rather than the value of temple entry itself. It was also his way of 'energizing' the Depressed Classes. This was Ambedkar's pragmatism.

As a social theorist, Ambedkar's understanding of social relations was quite complex. He wrote:

> The touchables and the untouchables cannot be held together by law.... The only thing that can hold them together is love. Outside the family justice alone in my opinion can open the possibility of love, and it should be the duty of the Anti-Untouchability League to see that the touchable does, or failing that is made to do, justice to the Untouchable.[21]

Justice in the public realm was necessary to accommodate commensality, a genuine sharing of social space, which in the course of time may erode the 'nausea' that poisons their interactions.

Contested Cultural Inheritance

There is a deep chasm dividing those who find their cultural inheritance troubling and those others who seek to celebrate an anodized, infinitely marketable, and ecumenical version of their

---

[20] Ambedkar cited by Zelliot (2013 [2004]: 88).
[21] Ambedkar's letter to A.V. Thakkar, Ajnat (1993: 83).

traditional cultures. Stigmatizing of people through practices is a vivid everyday reality for sufferers of prejudice, but for dominant others, it is only a regrettably aberrant, soon to disappear, awkwardness. For dominant groups, the stigma has all but gone: since hierarchies have multiplied, therefore they have become meaningless, and all that remains is 'different identities'. I do not agree with this assessment. This tendency to see caste as 'defanged' has been aptly called the 'culturalisation of caste' by Balmurli Natrajan.[22] Even when, as Natrajan rightly argues, caste has powerful material effects, its effects within the cultural domain also have deep roots. Consciousness of caste, in my view, is securely embedded and works as a silent orientation in the world.

I also agree with Gopal Guru's reiteration of the importance of referring to experience in building any theory of caste. He is right to warn against 'discursive attempts' to undermine 'any specific existence in itself' to 'caste as jati'.[23] Each such attempt robs caste of its 'significance as an unique social phenomenon' and 'denies the historical production and reproduction of experience that is associated with caste'.[24]

Therefore, I suggest that seriously uprooting casteism requires regular scrutiny of one's expressionless complicity in everyday enactments of caste superiority. We can do this through reflecting upon unthinking enjoyment of privileges. Reproduction of casteism can be checked by understanding how casteism is embedded in rituals (beyond individual motivations and actions). Scholars of a materialist bent of mind have criticized purely social structural accounts of caste; for example, Arjun Appadurai shows how in Dumont's argument, hierarchy 'becomes the essence of caste, the key to its exoticism, and the form of its totality'.[25] Caste in practice is actually more than hierarchy and can persist despite 'internal criticism'[26] of caste-based hierarchy. I think there is a route to

---

[22] Title of Natrajan (2001).

[23] Guru and Sarukkai (2012: 115).

[24] Guru and Sarukkai (2012: 115).

[25] Appadurai (1988: 41).

[26] In his essay 'Caste, *Karma* and the Gita', Bimal Krishna Matilal (2015: 136–44) discusses the 'paradoxicality of caste and *karma*' and shows the presence of 'internal criticism' within the tradition about the 'prevalence of the heredity-based caste hierarchies'. He has the convincing view that 'hierarchical society was heredity-bound from time

developing a materialist but elastic, therefore, potent account of the reproduction of caste relations through understanding the role of rituals and counter-rituals. By this, I do not mean to separate the cultural from a materialist understanding; rather, I suggest that casteism persists (even in the diaspora) because transnational connections reinforce it, because it is profitable and because dominant groups continue to defend caste privilege by act or omission.

Rituals and Caste

Tradition and modernity have intersected and renewed caste in various guises, redefining and reproducing boundaries between groups. Social relations of oppression are reproduced through enactments of rituals. Discrimination involves practices, that is, not the holding of beliefs per se, but the manifestation of beliefs in behaviour. Orthopraxy, rather than orthodoxy, sustains casteism in ritual behaviour. People follow prescribed behaviour, and if you ask a participant in a ritual why they think that a person of x caste must perform p function, they may not be able to come up with a belief justifying the restriction. They are likely to say: 'we submit to what must be done as it has to be done'. There is a connection between ritual and memory.[27] In the diaspora, everyday casteism is evident in distinct caste-marked places of worship with their distinct religious rituals, in caste associations with their distinct festive rituals, and in protection of endogamy with its ritual of finding 'suitable' marriage partners: each with costs for transgressors of caste norms.

Commenting on the 'Gujarati caste phenomena in Britain', Vertovec writes: 'A caste *system* could no longer govern social, economic, ritual, or other relationships, caste *identities* among Gujaratis have continued to be of considerable importance with regards to status, marriage, social networks and formal institutions.'[28] I add that caste identity appears harmless only so

---

immemorial' and there existed 'an internal critique of this within the tradition itself' (2015: 143).

[27] Feuchtwang (2010: 283) explains the connection of ritual with memory thus: 'It is practical spacial learning-to-be and conveys an overarching sense of time'.

[28] Vertovec (2000: 92).

long as there is no interference in the patterns of its reproduction, but when there is a challenge, for example, when a leadership of a place of worship is challenged from across a caste divide, or when marriage across caste is seen as threatening caste identity, then trouble follows. Vertovec's claim that in the diaspora, caste identities are 'waning' in competition with Hindutva 'universalism' and 'ecumenical' Hinduism[29] is hard to accept partly for demographic reasons and partly from observation of the current opposition to the UK legislation on caste discrimination.

Migration statistics, on the continuing addition of new migrants from the subcontinent, point in the direction of renewal of the 'caste mind-set'. Even if British-born second/third generations are less self-conscious about their caste identity, new arrivals are likely to come with fully formed caste identities; their presence is unlikely to allow caste to wane even if the transmission of caste across generations is weakened. Opposition to the UK legislation on caste discrimination is connected to the barely hidden fear that routine practices based on caste identities will come under scrutiny.

Opponents of the legislation have accused us of immorality, inauthenticity, and suffering from 'colonial consciousness'. I have argued that such an accusation springs from 'misplaced nativism'[30]. The accusers are obsessed with the imagined fear of Christian 'hatred for Indian culture', and thus blinded, they fail to see beyond 'Orientalist' constructions of caste.[31] They ignore the indisputable fact that indigenous traditions of protest have stood for centuries against hierarchical divisions of jatis, against *Brahmanwad* and its ritualism. Of late, there have emerged counter-rituals.

Counter-Rituals

Ambedkar had warned against the dangers of spontaneous protests on the one hand and cautious confinement within 'respect for tradition' on the other. There is another possibility of protest that emerges, which I term 'counter-ritual'. Counter-rituals are planned and deliberate challenges to entrenched practices, which

---

[29] Vertovec (2000: 162).

[30] Dhanda (2015).

[31] Shah (2015). For a sharp critique of the circularity and vacuity of Shah's use of the trope of 'colonial consciousness', see Sutton (2018).

'Made to Think and Forced to Feel' 83

productively deploy deep feelings of transgression. Counter-rituals necessarily require repeated performance, redefining the rules of engagement between participants and observers, often creating unexpected intensities of feeling in both. Examples include the burning of the *Manusmriti*, a code book of laws governing relations between members of different caste groups; beef festivals;[32] runaway marriages;[33] marking the martyrdom of Mahishasura; worship of Raavan: each of these disturb normalities of habitual conduct of the so-called upper castes. In particular circumstances, the successful use of counter-rituals would rely on an assessment of the extent to which the apologists of caste are 'made to think' and 'forced to feel' when confronted with counter-rituals *as protests*. The element of protesting is the key to distinguish between two types of counter-rituals.

Every new religious tradition in its inception very likely begins with transgression of existing norms. New rituals are designed to demarcate boundaries. In time, the element of transgression vanishes and what remains is a common ritual. One can take, as an instance, the anti-idolatry religious rituals devised by the Arya Samaj. These are geared by a democratizing impulse, one of incorporation. Initially, these challenged the priestly mediation between God and the people, but gradually these rituals produced other priests.

Contrary to newly minted religious rituals, the transgressive counter-rituals, for example, burning the Manusmriti, beef-eating festivals, or worshipping Mahishasura, are deliberately *exclusionary*. They are staged protests necessarily engaging the sufferers of casteism, and as protests, they have the potential to remain transgressive. The former type of counter-ritual, the Arya Samaji one, has to reinvent the threat against which it stands as a pseudo-rebellion. The latter type of counter-ritual, which is born of imminent threat, is deliberately limited in scope. Only those who directly bear the brunt of prohibitions can feel the power of

---

[32] Gaurav J. Pathania (2016: 273) offers a critical account of beef festivals and *Asura* worshipping as counter-hegemonic practices, arguing for the 'sophisticated balancing of rejection and acceptance of opposing hegemony and carefully building a new counter-hegemony'. See also Natrajan (2018).

[33] See Dhanda (2012).

84 Meena Dhanda

transgression, and therefore, there is no pretence of democratizing participation beyond the affected.

Protests can move from the cultural to the legal sphere. Dr Goldy George, an Adivasi academic activist, reported a few months ago:

> Durga pooja and Dussehra may be a day of celebration of Brahmanic Hindus of India. But not for the Adivasis. It is also the day when their ancestors/gods are killed and their killing is being celebrated. But not anymore. A case has been slapped upon people who celebrate Mahishasuravadh. For the first time in the history of India, the Adivasis have asserted culturally against the celebration of Mahishasuravadh.[34]

In the last few years, counter-rituals of mourning the ritual killing of Mahishasura and Raavan have emerged ectopically within university settings.[35] These are meant to challenge Brahmanical history and are mainly commemoration rituals. Speaking against 'cultural imperialism of Hindutva', Digree Prasad Chauhan, a leader of Dalit Mukti Morcha, says,

> we need to break such shackles of slavery that killed our ancestors where the killers are worshiped. All those who were killed may it be Eklavya, Mahishasura, Ravana, Shambhug, Bali, Holika are our debtas and such moves needs to have a complete stop for all times. Moolnivasis [indigenous people] have to be affirmative about what their true history is.[36]

My second example is of a festive ritual—Holi, which has become the subject of Dalit and Adivasi women's protest. The myth underlying the festival is from the *Bhagavata Purana*, of the Asura king (a demon according to hegemonic Hindu view) Hiranyakashipu who asked his sister Holika to kill his son Prahlada whom he feared due to his excessive devotion to Lord Vishnu. Holika has a cloak that can save her from fire, but when she sits with her nephew Prahlada on the fire, a wind blows off the cloak and wraps it around the boy who is miraculously saved while she is burnt by the fire. Holi is celebrated as the victory of the good (devotion to God) over evil (powers that can be used to become equal to God). A bonfire with

---

[34] See George (2017).

[35] See Pathania (2016: 267–9) for 'iconic politics', including the celebration of 'Asura week' in Indian university campuses.

[36] Cited by George (2017).

'Made to Think and Forced to Feel' 85

an effigy is burnt, and the next day, dry and wet colour is sprinkled on people in riotous abandon. Often, bhang is consumed and there is a licence to touch people in the process of applying colour.

Protesting Dalit and Adivasi women question the founding myth. Was it not possible to think of Holika as having been forced to sit on the pyre by her brother? Was it not possible to think of her as having sacrificed her life to protect her nephew? If so, should we be celebrating at all, or rather, should we not be mourning her death instead?

To understand the significance of the protest, I briefly note an influential anthropological understanding of rituals. Victor Turner writes in *The Ritual Process*:

> Society (*societas*) seems to be process rather than a thing—a dialectical process with successive stages of structure and communitas. There would seem to be—if one can use such a controversial term—a human "need" to participate in both modalities. Persons starved of one in their functional day-to-day activities, seek it in ritual liminality. The structurally inferior aspire to symbolic structural superiority in ritual; the structurally superior aspire to symbolic communitas and undergo penance to achieve it.[37]

Turner describes Holi as a ritual of status reversal, with the 'blunt speaking and rough doing' of structural inferiors noted by the anthropologist McKim Marriott.[38] Sexual improprieties are noted, but not from the point of view of the women who are violated. Although, Turner does remind us that through this ecstatic behaviour, there is 'the stressing, not the overthrowing of the principle of hierarchy'.[39]

For Turner, within certain rituals, the 'liminality of status reversals' provides a 'pseudo-structure where all behavioural extravagances are possible'.[40] He adds the 'liminality of reversal did not so much eliminate as underline structural distinctions, even to the point of (often unconscious) caricature'.[41] He surmises: 'Cognitively, nothing underlies regularity so well as absurdity or

[37] Turner (1969: 203).
[38] Cited by Turner (1969).
[39] Turner (1969: 188).
[40] Turner (1969: 202).
[41] Turner (1969:189).

paradox. Emotionally, nothing satisfies as much as extravagant or temporarily permitted illicit behaviour. Rituals of status reversals accommodate both aspects.'[42]

Thus, we see on this account, the 'reasonableness' of everyday hierarchies is reinstated after festivities of status reversals are over. But something more serious is taking place in the protests against the ritual burning of Holika—a counter-ritual is emerging. The challenge to Holi, advanced by a section of women students in a top-ranking Indian university, goes like this: 'Why does Brahmanical-Patriarchal India celebrate the burning of Holika? An Asura Bahujan woman? What is Holy about Holi?'[43] By staging the protest every time Holi is celebrated as a festival of colour, they mark the casteist and misogynist colour of the festival of Holi.

Being with Others Viscerally

From these examples, it is clear that counter-rituals bring implicit caste identifications to the fore and open them to critical confrontations. The backdrop of racism against which claims of casteism are experientially registered is an inescapable predicament of the diaspora. This backdrop has the paradoxical potential to generate solidarities with the oppressed as well as routes to evasion of responsibility. One is complicit one way or another; all inaction is still action. However, I think we need to think a bit more about *being with others*, especially in non-argumentative modes. To do this, we must change our direction of thinking to grapple with the 'un-thought', not in the banal sense of that which has not yet been thought, but that which is beyond the discursive realm.

As protest, counter-rituals enact a politics of viscerality, to use Achille Mbembe's phrase.[44] They are, what he would call 'strategies of disruption'.[45] Using the first person, one can say: those who are willing to take part in these disruptions are more solidly on my side. We belong together. We feel pain together. We laugh

---

[42] Turner (1969:189).

[43] These are questions from a pamphlet distributed in Jawaharlal Nehru University (JNU) in 2016.

[44] Achille Mbembe (2016).

[45] Mbembe (2016), [23:00].

together. It is not how our bodies appears to others that seals our togetherness. Such apparent togetherness is merely a seriality, to use Sartre's term[46], and is easily ruptured. Sartre describes the 'serial' togetherness using the example of people waiting for a bus at a bus stop: 'a plurality of isolations: these people do not care about or speak to each other and, in general they do not look at one another; they exist side by side.'[47] Within a 'series', everyone lives as 'the provisional negation of their reciprocal relations with Others.'[48] In Ambedkar's words: 'It is not enough if men act in a way which agrees with the acts of others. Parallel activity, even if similar, is not sufficient to bind men into a society'.[49]

Taking the moment of 'isolation' a bit further, if we add the element of mistrust, which marks social relations coloured by caste, we notice the potential obstacles to collective praxis. Mbembe says: 'To see is no longer enough. I don't know what I'm seeing. You might be wearing a mask. If I cannot trust the face I see how do I make sure you are with me.'[50] Looking alike is no ground for solidarity. Doing things together, for example, participating in a counter-ritual, can seal our togetherness. We could be transformed through 'a real change' of 'inert activity into collective action'.[51]

If 'rituals in ongoing practice are the principal site of new history being made, and that study of the plural formal potentialities of rituals could be basic to efforts to imagine possibilities for real political change'[52], then we must pay attention to the mediation of transformative social praxis by the insertion of counter-rituals. To be bound into an 'integral whole', what is necessary is 'for a man to share and participate in a common activity, so that the same emotions are aroused in him that animate the others'.[53] The dismantling of social groups based on caste may benefit from the invocation of visceral identifications, brought to the surface

---

[46] For his explication of the relationship between people within a social ensemble he calls a 'series', see Sartre (1976: 256–76).

[47] Sartre (1976: 256).

[48] Sartre (1976: 256).

[49] Ambedkar (2014 [1936]: 244).

[50] Mbembe (2016), [1:00:02].

[51] Sartre (1976: 370).

[52] Kelly and Kaplan (1990: 141).

[53] Ambedkar (2014 [1936]: 244).

in a dialectical mediation aimed, ultimately, at the annihilation of caste. Transgressive counter-rituals may thus play a radical transformative role, at the very least to force upon us the acknowledgement that 'caste is the monster that crosses your path. You cannot have political reform, you cannot have economic reform, unless you kill this monster.'[54]

References

Ajnat, Surendra. 1993. *Letters of Ambedkar*. Jalandhar: BheemPatrika Publications.

Ambedkar, Bhimrao. 2002 [1916]. 'Castes in India: Their Origin, Mechanism and Development', in Valerian Rodrigues (ed.), *The Essential Writings of B.R. Ambedkar*. New Delhi: Oxford University Press.

———. 2014 [1936]. *The Annihilation of Caste* (The Annotated Critical Edition), S. Anand (ed.). London, New York: Verso.

Appadurai, Arjun. 1988. 'Putting Hierarchy in Its Place', *Cultural Anthropology*, 3(1): 36–49.

Berg, Dag-Erik. 2018. 'Foregrounding Contingency in Caste-Based Dominance: Ambedkar, Hegemony, and the Pariah Concept', *Philosophy and Social Criticism*, 44(8): 843–64.

Dhanda, Meena. 2008. *The Negotiation of Personal Identity*. Saarbrüken: Verlag Dr. Muller.

———. 2012. 'Runaway Marriages: A Silent Revolution?', *Economic and Political Weekly*, 47(43): 100–8.

———. 2015. 'Anti-Castism and Misplaced Nativism', *Radical Philosophy*, 192: 33–43.

Dhanda, M., A. Waughray, D. Keane, D. Mosse, R. Green, and S. Whittle. 2014. *Caste in Britain: Socio-legal Review*. Equality and Human Rights Commission Research Report no. 91. Manchester: Equality and Human Rights Commission.

Dhanda, M., D. Mosse, A. Waughray, D. Keane, R. Green, S. Iafrati, and J.K. Mundy. 2014. *Caste in Britain: Experts' Seminar and Stakeholders' Workshop*. Equality and Human Rights Commission Research Report no. 92. Manchester: Equality and Human Rights Commission.

Feuchtwang, Stephan. 2010. 'Ritual and Memory', in S. Radstone and B. Schwarz (eds), *Memory: Histories, Theories, Debates*. New York: Fordham University.

---

[54] Ambedkar (2014 [1936]: 233).

George, G. 2017. 'Adivasis Dance Today: The First Ever FIR Filed Against Durga Puja', *Countercurrents.Org*, 29 September. Available at https://countercurrents.org/2017/09/29/adivasis-dance-today-the-first-fir-filed-against-durga-puja/, accessed 12 April 2018.

Guru, Gopal and Sundar Sarukkai. 2012. *The Cracked Mirror: An Indian Debate on Experience and Theory*. New Delhi: Oxford University Press.

Jaffrelot, Christophe. 2005. *Dr Ambedkar and Untouchability: Analysing and Fighting Caste*. London: Hurst & Company.

Kelly, John D. and Martha Kaplan. 1990. 'History, Structure and Ritual', *Annual Review of Anthropology*, 19: 119–50.

Matilal, Bimal K. 2015. *The Collected Essays of Bimal Krishna Matilal: Ethics and Epics*, Jonardon Ganeri (ed.). New Delhi: Oxford University Press.

Mbembe, Achille. 2016. 'Franz Fanon and the Politics of Viscerality', Keynote delivered on 26 April 2016 at John Hope Franklin Humanities Institute, Duke University. Available at https://humanitiesfutures.org/media/achille-mbembe-frantz-fanon-politics-viscerality/, accessed 12 April 2018.

Natrajan, Balmurli. 2011. *The Culturisation of Caste*. New Delhi: Routledge.

———. 2018. 'Cultural Identity and Beef Festivals: Toward a "Multiculturalism against Caste"', *Contemporary South Asia*, DOI: 10.1080/09584935.2018.1504000.

Pathania, Gaurav J. 2016. 'Food Politics and Counter-Hegemonic Assertion in Indian University Campuses', *South Asia Research*, 36(2): 261–77.

Rana, Yudhvir. 2018. 'UK Sikhs Hail Government Backing Off on Anti-Caste Discrimination Legislation'. *Times of India*, 25 July 2018. Available at https://timesofindia.indiatimes.com/city/chandigarh/uk-sikhs-hail-government-backing-off-on-anti-caste-discrimination-legislation/articleshow/65125615.cms, accessed 30 March 2019.

Rathore, A.S. 2017. *Indian Political Theory: Laying the Groundwork for Svaraj*. Oxon: Routledge.

Sartre, Jean Paul (trans. by Alan Sheridan-Smith). 1976. *Critique of Dialectical Reason: Part 1- Theory of Practical Ensembles*, Jonathan Rée (ed.). London: Verso.

Shah, Prakash. 2015. 'Caste, Critique and Colonial Consciousness: A Response to Meena Dhanda', Indiafacts.org. Available at http://indiafacts.org/caste-critique-and-colonialconsciousness-a-response-to-meena-dhanda/, accessed July 2018.

Sutton, Deborah Ruth. 2018. '"So called caste": S. N. Balagangadhara, the Ghent School and the Politics of grievance', *Contemporary South Asia*, DOI: 10.1080/09584935.2018.1498453.

Turner, Victor. 1969. *The Ritual Process: Structure and Anti-Structure.* New Jersey: Aldine Publishing Company.

Vertovec, Steven. 2000. *The Hindu Diaspora*: *Comparative Patterns.* London: Routledge.

Zelliot, Eleanor (ed.). 2013 [2004]. *Ambedkar's World: The Making of Babasahib and the Dalit Movement.* New Delhi: Navayana.

5

Dalits in Search of Inclusion

*Comparing Nepal with India**

DAVID N. GELLNER, KRISHNA P. ADHIKARI,
AND ARJUN BAHADUR B.K.

Nepal as a Foil to India

In comparing India and Nepal—here we focus on Dalits, but the point applies more generally—there is a big asymmetry of knowledge. Many Indians tend to assume that they already know all they need to know about the country: Nepal is just a minor variation on South Asian diversity. It fits into their mental map and no special effort is needed to understand it. Indians usually think of Nepal as a place of pilgrimage, a picturesque place to go for a honeymoon,

---

* This chapter draws on our joint research in a village in Kaski District, Nepal, as part of the UK-ESRC-funded project, 'Caste, Class, and Culture: Changing Bahun and Dalit Identity in Nepal' project, funded by the UK's Economic and Social Research Council [ES/L00240X/1]. We thank the ESRC for its support and all those in the communities studied for their cooperation. We thank also the anonymous reader for the press who made some helpful suggestions for improvement. Gellner made a preliminary presentation of the argument at the 'Reclaiming Social Justice, Revisiting Ambedkar' conference in Bengaluru in July 2017. The observations made here are of necessity provisional and the comparisons are somewhat impressionistic. We hope nonetheless that the chapter may be found to be suggestive and that its claims will provoke discussion.

92 David N. Gellner, Krishna P. Adhikari, and Arjun Bahadur B.K.

or an inspiring, but perhaps ultimately moral, tale about Maoist revolution and how it can go wrong (or right). By and large and with a few honourable individual exceptions such as S.D. Muni,[1] Indians tend to be ignorant of Nepal's history and cultural specificities.[2] By contrast, ordinary Nepalis are usually fairly knowledgeable about India, or at least about northern India, if only because they speak (or at least understand) Hindi, they watch Indian TV and movies, and they often study, work, vacation, or go on pilgrimage in India. What we have just said about ordinary Indians and Nepalis applies almost equally, and taking into account the different contexts, to Indian and Nepali academics as well.[3]

This ignorance (or knowledge asymmetry) infuriates both Nepalis and scholars of Nepal, but it is a fact (a fact about the hierarchical organization of knowledge). As such, it is better to face up to it and work out how to deal with it. Exactly the same ignorance and condescension is found in England towards the less populated Celtic fringe countries of the United Kingdom, because of the same hierarchical and structurally unequal situation. The Scots, the Welsh, and the Irish find it just as irritating.[4]

Nepal and India share a unique relationship. The border between the two countries is freely open for the movement of people and is, therefore, very different from the borders that India shares with

[1] Muni (1992, 2003).

[2] Obviously, these are gross generalizations and need to be taken in the spirit in which they are made. Clearly, Indians who live in Gorakhpur, close to the Nepalese border, are well informed, at least about events in the Tarai, whereas Indians in South India, in Bengaluru, for example, see Nepal as a faraway country of little relevance to their immediate concerns.

[3] Onta (2001) documents this in detail, showing how the chronic underfunding of the Indian centres that are supposed to engage in the academic study of Nepal has impeded them from producing much of quality. He also points out that the same problem afflicts those university centres in Nepal that are supposed to be engaged in the academic study of India.

[4] Norman Davies' *The Isles* is an acclaimed revisionist history that tries to address head on this knowledge asymmetry within the United Kingdom. See Davies (1999). For some examples of what a South Asian would interpret as communal sentiments between different parts of the United Kingdom, see 'Notes and Queries'. n.d. *Guardian*. Available at www.theguardian.com/notesandqueries/query/0,5753,-18777,00.html, accessed 15 October 2017.

Dalits in Search of Inclusion 93

its other neighbours.[5] Nepalis can live and work in India without a passport (as Indians can in Nepal), a highly advantageous position to be in and the key safety valve for Nepal's poorest citizens. This applies particularly to those (many) who cannot raise the money needed to migrate for work to the Gulf, Malaysia, or South Korea. At the same time, there are many poor and working-class Indians in Nepal: almost every barber, electrician, plumber, plasterer, and mobile vegetable and/or fruit seller in Kathmandu comes from India. No doubt the same is true in other Nepalese urban centres. It should be noted that Nepal is not a 'small' or even 'tiny country', as so often claimed. It is actually a medium-sized country with a quite sizeable population nearing 30 million (it is within the top 50 countries in the world by population). Nepal only looks small because of its location between India and China.

For social scientists interested in South Asia, Nepal represents a unique comparative opportunity. Here is a sizeable society (latterly a nation-state) that was not subject to direct or indirect rule by the British Raj or any other colonial power. Yet it shares the culture and religion of its southern neighbour, which *did* experience a century and a half of colonialism. Many of the processes of Sanskritization and modernization, the amalgamation of castes, and caste politics (for example, the formation of caste associations run on 'modern' principles), started up in Nepal only decades or even centuries after being well established in India. In Nepal, a Hindu ruler remained in place as the head of state right up until 2006. Collective party politics, after a brief experiment in the 1950s, were put off until 1990. For the thirty years of the party-less panchayat system of guided democracy (1960–90), Nepal missed out on this crucial experience and did not enjoy the deepening of democracy that occurred in India during the same period. This made and still makes a difference. Nepal had a lot of catching up to do after 1990. The opportunity for systematic comparison between India and Nepal opened up by these differing historical trajectories presents itself also when the topic is the position of Dalits, as was recognized, for example, by Professor Gopal Guru.[6]

An important difference between Nepal and India is that in Nepal, caste was supported by the full force of State law until as

[5] Gellner (2013).
[6] Guru (2012). See also Jodhka and Shah (2010).

94   David N. Gellner, Krishna P. Adhikari, and Arjun Bahadur B.K.

late as 1964. Under the *Muluki Ain,* or national law code, of 1854, the population was divided into five different and ranked 'macro-categories' based on the Hindu principles of purity, namely, 'sacred-thread-wearer', 'alcohol-drinker', 'enslavable alcohol-drinker', 'impure but touchable', and 'untouchable'.[7] Punishments and rules were laid down according to category and in line with the rulings of the *dharmashastra*s. One consequence of this was that Nepal did not have significant upward mobility (Sanskritization) movements on the part of low castes, as found especially in South India, enabled by the combination of new commercial and educational opportunities and the colonial state's removal or emasculation of Hindu rulers. In Nepal, by contrast, the king remained the ultimate arbiter of whether upward mobility would be permitted or not, and usually it was not. The cases of the *Manandhar*s of Kathmandu (traditionally mustard oil pressers),[8] some *Magar* families upgraded to *Chhetri* status,[9] the 'tribal' *Rajvamshi*s,[10] and the *Rana* clan promoting themselves from *Kunwar* to *Thakuri*,[11] were rare exceptions.

Dalits As a Stigmatized and Impoverished Minority

In Nepal, just as in India, Dalits face a crucial problem with the rise of identity politics and ethnic voting in elections. The identity issue was a key reason why the first Constituent Assembly collapsed without being able to bring in a constitution in May 2012.[12] Dalits in Nepal are obliged to play an identity game that they cannot win: they do not have a territory or a separate language. They have their own caste traditions, but for the most part, they share the culture and traditions of the wider *Parbatiya* society in the Hills and the wider *Madheshi* society in the Tarai (the plains). They are traditionally often claimed to be 'lacking culture'

---

[7] Höfer (1979); Sharma (2004: 185–6). Note that these did not correspond very well to the four varna categories: both Brahmins and Kshatriyas belonged to the first group; some of the second group were thought of as Vaisyas; all the rest were different kinds of Sudras.

[8] Gellner and Quigley (1995: 22).

[9] Whelpton (1991: 8, 21).

[10] Bista (2004: 159–60).

[11] Sharma (2004: 140–1).

[12] Adhikari and Gellner (2016).

and 'lacking history'. Even some Dalits themselves say that they lack their own distinctive cultural heritage. The special situation of Dalits (lacking a 'home' territory) was recognized in the proposals put forward during the first Constituent Assembly: the idea was that there should be a 'non-territorial state' for Dalits. At that time (2008–12), political discourse was dominated by ideas of ethnicity-based federalism.[13] Starting around 2009, and gathering strength since, there has been a considerable backlash against that view. Dalit activists were, in fact, never very keen on the separate state idea. They were and are more interested in proper and enforced reservations.[14] Many Dalit activists believe they should receive compensatory reservations of more than their share of the population, to acknowledge the centuries of oppression and exclusion that they have suffered.

The temptation has always been for those Dalits who acquire education to pass as high caste. Since their language, culture, and physiognomy are no different from the high castes, it is usually not difficult to pass as Chhetri (Kshatriya), which is in any case the largest, most mixed, and diverse caste in the country.[15] But while the rational strategy for individuals and households may be assimilation and passing, for Dalits as a whole, if they are to gain any recognition and benefits from the government, that is no solution at all. This peculiar tension between the activists' path of public recognition and the ordinary upwardly mobile person's path of identity effacement is acutely felt. It is not experienced in the same way by non-Dalit groups. Just as in India, there is a tension between maintaining one's traditional caste occupation, stigmatizing though it may be, as the basis of a marginally more secure livelihood, and, on the other hand, abandoning what may be a secure (but stigmatized) niche for open competition in other fields where one is starting from the most disadvantaged position.

After 1964, with a new national law code, caste no longer had the force of law. While caste difference now had no explicit support, and untouchability was banned, two factors enabled its practice to continue almost unabated: (*a*) there were no mechanisms for *enforcing* the abolition of untouchability practices and there

---

[13] Kisan (2012).
[14] Pyakurel (2011); Kisan (2012: 65–6).
[15] Sharma (2004: 193–4).

were no punishments for practising it; any Dalit who attempted to approach the authorities (all of whom would very likely be of 'high' caste) with a complaint was likely to be met with little enthusiasm for pursuing the culprits, and instead might risk punishment themselves for disturbing the peace; (b) there was an explicit guarantee that traditional customs should be respected.

In this context, it remained difficult to do systematic research with Dalits without compromising one's relations with other castes, which goes some way to explain why there has been relatively little anthropological work on Nepali Dalits, compared to what has been done on India. Two honourable exceptions to this are the important Dalit-focussed monographs on West Nepal by Pat Caplan and Mary Cameron,[16] based on fieldwork in the 1960s and 1980s, respectively. Caplan showed how a population of *Mijar*s (*Sarki*s, cobblers) started out relatively well off, thanks to owning fertile agricultural land, but ended up having most of it appropriated by local *Bahun*s, who were able to leverage their links to the local state in order to do so. Caplan was also decades ahead of academic fashion in that she included an explicit focus on the role of migration in determining livelihoods. Cameron, also working in difficult circumstances, explored in detail the interaction of caste, gender, and livelihood. More recently, authors such as Folmar, Vasily, and Kharel have worked on Dalits, and there are encouraging signs that a new generation of young Nepali Dalit scholars, such as Amar B.K., Ramesh Sunam, Tilak Biswakarma, Bishnu Pariyar, Mitra Pariyar, and Mom Bishwakarma, are themselves beginning to produce ethnographic research on the position of Dalits in Nepalese society.[17]

Following the national census of 1991, the Nepali public discovered what in India is still kept under wraps: the precise proportions of all the castes and ethnic groups within the population. Decennial censuses demonstrate that the Dalits are spread out around the country, which means, of course, that they lack

[16] Caplan (1972); Cameron (1998).

[17] See Folmar (2007), Vasily (2009), Kharel (2010), Amar (2013), Sunam (2014), T. Biswakarma (2014, 2018), B. Pariyar (Pariyar and Lovett 2016), M. Pariyar (2018), and Mom Bishwakarma (2016, 2019). There are also PhDs on Nepali Dalits on the way by foreign scholars, e.g., Ivan Deschenaux (LSE).

the population concentrations that enable *Janajati* ('tribal') groups to have some political influence at least in those areas. Nonetheless, there are some areas where Hill Dalits are more numerous than others[18] and there are even some parts of some west Nepali districts where they constitute more than 50 per cent of the population.[19] *Vishwakarma*s, former blacksmiths, are found pretty much everywhere, except in the eastern Tarai, but there are much higher concentrations in mid- and far west Nepal.[20]

Though the population of Tarai Dalits is relatively small (4.51 per cent of the total population) compared to Hill Dalits (8.12 per cent), they are very diverse with nineteen sub-groups (contrasted with just seven Dalit groups in the Hills), as identified by the Nepal Dalit Commission (see Table 5.1).[21] For anyone who knows Bihar

Table 5.1 Dalit Sub-Groups (Castes) in Nepal by Population and Region According to the 2011 Census

Caste	Population	% nat. pop.
Hill dalits		
Bishwakarma	1,258,554	4.75
Pariyar	472,862	1.78
Mijar	374,816	1.41
Badi	38,603	0.15
Gandharva	6,791	0.03
Chyame (*Newar*)	not known	
Pode (Newar)	not known	
Sub-total	2,151,626	8.12
Tarai dalits		
Chamar, Harijan, Ram	335,893	1.27
Musahar	234,490	0.89
Dusadh, Paswan	208,910	0.79
Dhobi	109,079	0.41

(*Cont'd*)

[18] Kisan (2012: 59–60).

[19] Tamang, Chapagain, and Ghimire (2014: 85).

[20] Tamang, Chapagain, and Ghimire (2014: 89).

[21] Dalit activists persistently argue that the census underestimates the true numbers of Dalits, which is, they claim, actually nearer to 20 per cent of the population.

David N. Gellner, Krishna P. Adhikari, and Arjun Bahadur B.K.

Table 5.1 *(Cont'd)*

Caste	Population	% nat. pop.
Tarai dalits		
Tatma	104,865	0.4
Khatwe	100,921	0.38
Bantar	55,104	0.21
Dom	13,268	0.05
Kori	12,276	0.05
Sarbhang	4,906	0.02
Halkhor	4,003	0.02
Natuwa	3,062	0.01
Dharikar	2,681	0.01
Dhandi	1,982	0.01
Chidimar	1,254	0
Kalar	1,077	0
Kakaihiya	not known	
Khatik	not known	
Pasi	not known	
Sub-total	1,193,771	4.51
Dalit others	155,354	0.59
Grand total	3,500,751	13.22

Sources: NDC[24] for the names of Dalit castes; NPHC (2012: Table 20); Dahal (2014); and Tamang, Chapagain, and Ghimire (2014: 6–9) for population figures.

Notes: Chyame and Pode are listed as Dalits by the NDC but are included within Newars by the census; likewise, Kakaihiya and Khatik are not separately enumerated by the census; the Pasi are included with the Dusadh/Paswan in the census. See Dahal (2014) for discussion of whether the Chidimars should be considered Dalits or not, as well as of other contentious cases.

and eastern Uttar Pradesh (UP), the caste names of Tarai Dalits will be familiar. The social development of Tarai Dalits lags behind that of Hill Dalits. Tarai Dalits are even more likely to be landless and they have the lowest levels of representation in politics and the bureaucracy. Like other Tarai caste groups, Dalits maintain 'bread and bride relations' (*roti-beti ka sambandha*) across the border in northern India (UP and Bihar). If anything, their situation in Nepal may be worse than the position of their caste fellows within

---

[24] NDC. n.d. 'Dalit jatiya anusuchi vivaran'. Available at www.ndc.gov. np/images/category/Anusuchi_News_2074.pdf, accessed 9 July 2019.

India.[22] As might be expected, Tarai Dalits are heavily concentrated in the Tarai districts of the eastern Tarai (Parsa to Morang) and in the Madheshi-populated areas of Kapilvastu, Rupandehi, and Nawalparasi.[23]

Since 1990, when the multiparty system was reintroduced, there has been a process of politically induced change, which has produced new kinds of 'macro-category' (these are horizontal categories, rather than the vertical/hierarchical categories of the old law code).[25] A Kathmandu taxi driver tried to explain these large categories to Gellner as not *jat* (caste) but rather as a kind of *samuha* (agglomeration). In other words, these are large, politically mobilizable categories, rather similar to those found in North India: (*a*) 'forward' or 'upper' castes, recently dubbed '*Khas-Arya*'; (*b*) Janajatis, literally 'ethnic groups' or 'tribals', formerly known as *matwali* or 'alcohol-drinkers' in Nepali, who, because of their size, correspond to what would be called OBC in North India; (*c*) Dalits; (*d*) Madheshis (the most fluid and contested category, this term refers primarily to those of Indian ethnicity residing in the Tarai, but also includes Dalits, Janajatis, and Muslims from the Tarai);[26] and (*e*) Others. Muslims are not as numerous in Nepal as they are in North India, at about 4.4 per cent, but they are concentrated in certain places in the Tarai. Indeed, in several Tarai districts, they are the largest single group, and so electoral calculations must take them into account in those areas. Tarai Muslims are often, as noted, included within the Madheshi category, but also fall into 'Others' for some purposes.

[22] Preliminary ethnographic information may be found in the series published by the Central Department of Sociology/Anthropology, Tribhuvan University, for example, Dahal, Giri, and Mishra (2014) on the Musahars; Dahal, Mishra, and Mahato (2014) on the Halkhors; and Dahal and Jha (2014) on the Chamars.

[23] Tamang, Chapagain, and Ghimire (2014: 91).

[25] On the emergence of these macro-categories, see Gellner (2016, 2019).

[26] In other words, these macro-categories are not all necessarily exclusive: it is possible to be both Janajati and Madheshi, Dalit and Madheshi, and so on. However, for most people, the three categories Khas-Arya, Janajati, and Dalit *are* mutually exclusive (except that some people occasionally try to say that Dalits should be considered part of the Khas-Aryas, since they share their language and general culture).

Identity politics in Nepal, just as in India, are made powerful by the severe imbalances in reward, especially at the top of society. The top two caste groups, Bahuns and Chhetris, that is, the Khas-Aryas (31 per cent of the population), are massively over-represented in elite jobs. They have, to date, 95 per cent of the prime ministers, 88 per cent of the chief district officers (what in India would be called the DMs), 86 per cent of government ministers, 80 per cent of high court judges, and so on and so on.[27] The numbers of Dalits at this level is tiny (Hill Dalits, for example, 8.1 per cent of the population, have 0.01 per cent of top jobs). In response to these imbalances, reservations were introduced for elections. Khas-Aryas are 45 per cent in the current federal parliament, so the over-representation of Khas-Aryas is, thanks to reservations, not as marked as it might otherwise be. Reservations have also been introduced for the civil service, with 45 per cent of places filled by quota. It will, obviously, take many years for the beneficiaries of these quotas to achieve promotion and have an effect on the statistics at the highest levels. However, in what Dalit activists interpret as a high-caste backlash, the government has proposed extending reservations in some sectors to many groups that were not entitled to them previously, thereby inevitably diluting the effect they can have on Dalit advancement.[28] There have also been adjustments when adapting the quotas for different provincial and local levels that have effectively reduced the quotas available for minorities.[29]

Dalits do worse than almost everyone on most measures of welfare (only Muslims do worse on some Human Development Index measures). On top of dire levels of poverty, they face systematic

---

[27] For tables demonstrating these imbalances, see Neupane (2000); Lawoti (2005: 104–6); Maharjan (1999: 63–4); Hachhethu and Gellner (2010: 138); Sijapati (2013: 153–4); Bennett, Sijapati, and Thapa (2013); Y.B. Gurung et al. (2014). The imbalances are diagrammed by D. Gurung (2015. 'A Graph is Worth a Thousand Words... It Seems' [blog]. Available at www. dorjegurung.com/blog/2015/11/a-graph-is-worth-a-thousand-words-it-seems/, accessed 9 July 2019). On the persistent Dalit under-representation in politics, see Biswokarma (2012); Khanal, Gelpke, and Pyakurel (2012); and M. Bishwakarma (2017, 2019).

[28] Sunam and Shrestha (2019).

[29] Ghale, S. 2019. 'The Anti-Reservation Brigade'. RecordNepal. Available at www.recordnepal.com/featured/the-anti-reservation-brigade/, accessed 9 July 2019.

exclusion and prejudice, as documented in numerous places.[30] Whatever measure one takes—life expectancy, poverty, per capita income, or remittances from abroad—Dalits do worse than other groups.[31] Because they are disproportionately poor and because they are also more likely to be excluded or overlooked, Dalits have also suffered worse than other groups in the aftermath of the 2015 earthquakes.[32] Dalits' levels of schooling, scores, pass rates at high school (School Leaving Certificate), and representation in higher education are all much worse than others.[33] Within the Dalit category, some groups do worse than others. The larger groups tend to do better. The worst off are small Tarai Dalit groups, notably the Musahars, whose particularly poor position has been recognized with the designation 'Mahadalit' over the border in Bihar.

Migration

One significant difference between Nepal and India is that Nepal has a much higher per capita emigration level than India. The absolute numbers of Indians going to work in the Gulf and elsewhere are huge, of course, but the relative numbers are much higher in the Nepali case. The majority of Nepali households have at least one member who either is currently or has been in the past working or studying abroad.

Our joint research in a fairly typical cluster of hill villages not far from Pokhara, Nepal's second city, as well as in some of the villagers' in-country migration destinations, is a good illustration. Only 21.1 per cent of households have no one who has been abroad, either now or in the past. In other words, nearly four out of every five households have at least one person who has been abroad (and some households have more than one such migrant). What Table 5.2

[30] See Cameron (1998); Human Rights Watch (2001); Goyal, Dhawan, and Narula (2005); Kisan (2005); Folmar (2007); and Pariyar (2018).

[31] Central Bureau of Statistics (2005, 2011); World Bank/DFID (2006); Bennett, Sijapati, and Thapa (2013).

[32] Barron, P. 2017. 'Dalits Left Behind as Nepal Slowly Recovers'. AsiaFoundation.org, 19 April 2017. Available at asiafoundation. org/2017/04/19/dalits-left-behind-nepal-slowly-recovers/, accessed 25 July 2019; Bownas and Bishokarma (2019).

[33] Bhatta (2005).

Table 5.2 Migration Abroad for Work or Studies in Six Adjacent Villages of Kaski District (Household Data)

Has any member of the current household ever been abroad for work or studies?		Caste groups							
		Dalit-Bishwakarma	Gurung	Dalit-Pariyar	Dalit-Nepali	Chhetri/Thakuri	Bahun-non-priestly	Bahun-priestly	Total
Yes	No. of households	117	68	75	34	70	87	33	485
	(% within caste)	89.3%	88.3%	86.2%	85.0%	72.2%	71.3%	50.8%	78.2%
No	Count	14	9	12	6	27	35	32	135
	(% within caste)	10.7%	11.7%	13.8%	15.0%	27.8%	28.7%	49.2%	21.8%
Total	Count	131	77	87	40	97	122	65	620
	(% within caste)	100%	100%	100%	100%	100%	100%	100%	100%

Source: Field survey 2014–15.

demonstrates is that migration is heavily inflected by class and caste. The three Dalit castes have the highest levels of migration. The poorest group, the Bishwakarmas, have a migration rate of around 90 per cent, whereas among the richest group in local society, the priestly Brahmins, only 51 per cent of households have a member who has been abroad.

There are also differences between groups as concerns the destination or pattern of migration. The Gurungs, in the middle of the status hierarchy, are very largely oriented towards recruitment as Gurkha soldiers, in the British Army if possible, otherwise in the Indian Army, or, failing that, the Nepal Army. Members of other groups tend to migrate as labourers to the Gulf countries or to Malaysia. India is the destination for the poorest. A few, with luck, connections, and money, have succeeded in migrating to Hong Kong, the United Kingdom, or other high-earning countries.

There is a considerable degree of correlation between caste and class. We constructed seven rough and ready class categories (using a combination of wealth, assets, and income). Although there are some poor people and some well-off people among all groups, our data shows that there are almost no very poor Brahmins and, by contrast, one of the three Dalit groups has no one at all in the richest category. One Dalit group, the Mijars or Nepalis, does have some rich members, thanks to judicious acquisition of land in the city in the old days when it was cheap and not considered very desirable. The bulk of the poorest people are found among the Dalits. Differences and cleavages between castes are certainly sharper and wider in other parts of Nepal, notably in the Far West region.

The Dalit Movement in Nepal

In its early days, immediately after the fall of the Rana regime in 1951, the Dalit movement in Nepal was certainly inspired by what was happening in India—both the movement for Indian independence and movements for social reform.[34] The very few educated Dalits at the time, such as the reformer Bhagat Sarvajit

[34] On the Dalit movement in Nepal, see Kisan (2005), Cameron (2007), and Vasily (2009).

Vishwakarma (1893–1955), who was jailed by the Ranas, were educated in India. The subsequent years of the Panchayat regime, 1960 to 1990, must be regarded as lost years. The State would not allow any organizations that were not controlled from the top. The ideology of the Panchayat regime was a kind of Hindu corporatism.[35] Dalits were dealt with simply by co-opting one or two individuals and giving them symbolic positions. As mentioned above, the law banned untouchability but did nothing to punish those who practised it. There were no reservations as in India. Dalits remained backward on every measure.

After 1990, multiple Dalit organizations emerged, but they tended to be plagued by splits according to political inclination, caste, and individual competition and animosity. A noticeable feature of many Dalit (as of many ethnic) organizations is that they are essentially front organizations of particular political parties. All the political parties claim to be against untouchability and they have passed progressive laws at various points. However, the actual practice (both in politics and in personal life) of many 'upper-caste' leaders has been very disappointing to Dalit activists, who have frequently found that their concerns are dismissed as irrelevant or untimely.

It was the Maoists who really turned their minds to the Dalit issue and insisted, often at the point of a gun, that people abandon caste practices in the villages.[36] The Maoist insurgency attracted young people from all backgrounds; but the Maoists themselves consciously targeted Dalit youth. One Dalit man from the eastern hills described how he had been present at a village wedding feast during the People's War when guests were being seated separately by caste. A Maoist cadre, a Pariyar (Damai) by caste, got out his pistol, and from that moment on, such separation ceased to be practised in that particular village.

That Nepali Dalits should therefore be attracted to the more revolutionary leftist movements is not surprising, since they offer the most radical change. However, no Nepali Dalit leader seems tempted to lead a movement into Buddhism for the Dalits, as Ambedkar did in India. Although Nepali Dalit activists

---

[35] Joshi and Rose (1966: 395–6); Whelpton (2005: 173, 184).

[36] Adhikari (2014: 137–40).

revere Ambedkar and do celebrate his memory, for nationalistic reasons it would not be advisable to place an Indian, and in particular the Indian most closely associated with the writing of the Indian Constitution, at the heart of their movement's ideological strategy.

The reason why Nepali Dalits have avoided Ambedkar's religious conversion strategy is almost certainly that there already exists an established Buddhist community in Nepal. This includes those of Tibetan ethnicity, Tamangs, some Gurungs, and some Newars.[37] Some of the Newar Buddhists, although marginalized by their religion, are otherwise quite highly placed in Nepali society over all. Among Tharu and Magar activists, a kind of Ambedkarite neo-Buddhism has proved popular,[38] but they never call themselves Ambedkarite or acknowledge any debt to Ambedkar. Meanwhile, neither Dalit activists nor established Buddhist leaders (with one or two exceptions) display much enthusiasm for the idea of attempting to convert Dalits to Buddhism en masse. Buddhists in Nepal, while happy to denounce caste in general, are not about to shine a spotlight on continuing caste practices within their communities nor would they like to invite into their fold a community that might threaten to outnumber them. In contrast to Buddhism, Christianity has proved an attractive option for many Dalits with its open opposition to caste discrimination (sometimes in combination with Maoism). One Dalit activist remarked that, with their positive encouragement of inter-caste marriage, Christians were doing more even than the Maoists to overcome caste. However, converting to Christianity does nothing to remove caste stigma in the eyes of the wider society.

According to the observations of leading Indian Dalit activist and scholar Sukhadeo Thorat, the Dalit social movement in Nepal is weaker than that of India and that is the explanation why caste discrimination is worse in Nepal.[39] However, several Dalit activ-

[37] See Holmberg (1989), Mumford (1989), Gellner (1992, 2018), LeVine and Gellner (2005).

[38] Letizia (2014).

[39] Thorat, S. 2016. 'Caste Discrimination Stronger in Nepal'. *My Republica*, 15 August 2016. Available at myrepublica.nagariknetwork.com/news/caste-discrimination-stronger-in-nepal/, accessed 9 July 2019.

ists whom we interviewed claimed, quite vehemently, that the contemporary Nepali Dalit movement, for all its faults, is more vibrant than its counterpart in India. These informants asserted that whereas the academic study of Dalits is much stronger in India, because India has more Dalits in universities and other positions, the political movement is stronger in Nepal. Nepali political parties have Dalit fronts that are organized right down to the village level; and at the same time, Dalit members of Parliament (MPs) from across political parties collaborate on Dalit issues. Neither of these, the Nepalese activists claim, is equally true of India. These strongly expressed opinions may well be mistaken and they certainly seem paradoxical, given the fact that India has powerful Dalit-oriented parties (which certainly do have local organization) and given the success of figures like Mayawati (whereas Nepal has no one similar). The fact that this perception of difference exists is itself interesting. Perhaps it was justified in the past but is no longer so. When compared to other Nepali political movements, such as those of the Janajatis and the Madheshis, Nepal's Dalit movement is certainly much weaker, that is, less able to mobilize in order to force concessions from the central government.[40]

There has been no towering personality in Nepal of the stature of Ambedkar in India. Some people on the left claim that Ruplal Bishwakarma was such an intellectual figure. He argued that caste and class must be taken together in a Marxist analysis. He also forged a progressive Dalit movement in Chitwan in the 1960s. He brought marginal sections of society together in numerous campaigns against caste-based practices, such as untouchability, exploitative interest rates, land encroachment, corruption, and general exploitation by local elite groups.[41] The current Maoist leader, and two-time prime minister (PM), Prachanda (aka Pushpa Kamal Dahal), came from the same village in Chitwan District. Prachanda claims Ruplal as a guru since it was Ruplal who gave him membership of the party.[42] However, Ruplal did not have the international impact of Ambedkar and he had no role in producing the most recent or any other constitution in Nepal. His political

[40] Lawoti (2013).
[41] Bishwakarma 2068 BS (2011–12).
[42] Sharma (2013: 25).

party, the Proletarian Workers' Association, merged with other left parties to become the Nepal Communist Party (United Front) in 1991;[43] one faction of the latter launched the Maoists' 'People's War' in 1996.

Another prominent Dalit intellectual who has inspired many Dalit youth activists is Ahuti (Comrade Ahuti). Ahuti was a member of the main Maoist party. He joined as a 'full timer' in 1986 before the 1990 revolution (during which he was imprisoned for seven days and beaten by the police). His grandfather, a cobbler, had learned to read and write and had been to Calcutta. He employed many others in his workshop and became relatively well-off during the Rana period. 'My grandfather was the only Sarki man of his generation in all of the thirty-six Sarki houses of my village who could read and write and do mathematics.'[44] They lived in a Newar village on the west side of the Kathmandu Valley and so Ahuti is fluent in Newari as well as in the Nepali language. Ahuti himself was involved in socially conscious cultural production from his school days. He was a member of a different Maoist group from the faction that launched the People's War, so he was not involved in the ten years of fighting. His party merged with Prachanda's only after the war was over.

What Ahuti is really famous for is his poetry on progressive themes and his TV productions. Of poetry in Nepali, he has written, 'Sanskrit verse was used in Nepali poetry as a representative of Hindu feudalism.'[45] His poetry is widely read and is a powerful critique, infused with a Dalit aesthetic, of existing social relations and their basis in a feudal Hindu ideology. His TV serial *Dalan* ran for fifty-two episodes in 2008–9 and won many prizes for its depiction of the plight of Dalits. The serial begins its story in 1951 with a marriage between a Brahmin and a Dalit woman, for which the man is outcasted. The timing of the programme was not an accident, in that it was shown on the nation's TV screens in the most revolutionary moment, when the PM was a Maoist and the Maoists were the largest party in the new Constituent Assembly. All the talk was of building a 'new Nepal'.

[43] Bishwakarma 2069 (2012–13).
[44] Aahuti (2017: 77).
[45] Aahuti (2017: 77).

Dalits and Government Policy

Concrete positive policy measures for Dalits in Nepal were initiated only after 2000, more than fifty years after India. In 2001, the Nepal government set up a Dalit Commission with authority to address the causes of Dalit marginalization and poverty. In 2007, 45 per cent of the total available civil service positions were reserved; 9 per cent of the total were reserved for Dalits. In the 2008 elections for the first Constituent Assembly, Dalits had 13 per cent of the seats reserved for them. This was an important step forward with a historic total of 50 Dalits elected (7 in first-past-the-post [FPTP] constituencies, 43 from the proportional representation [PR] lists).[46] This fell to 41 (2 by FPTP, 39 by PR) in 2013, in the elections for the second Constituent Assembly, marking a retreat from the revolutionary times just after the end of the civil war in 2006.[47]

From 1994, a small stipend to encourage Dalits to stay in school was instituted, and from 2009–10, small welfare grants were targeted at Dalit children up to the age of five in order to help improve their nutritional status.[48] Both Dalits and people in the backward districts of the Far West and Karnali zone (the poorest region of the country) are entitled to an old-age pension from the age of 60, rather than at 70 for non-Dalits in the rest of the country.[49] In 2010, the government of PM Madhav Kumar Nepal of the UML party (Communist Party of Nepal, Unified Marxist-Leninist) introduced grants of Rs 100,000 (about $1,350 at that time) for any couple where one member of the couple was a Dalit and the other was not.[50] This was a piece of UML populism, but it could have come straight from Dr Ambedkar himself ('The real remedy for breaking caste is intermarriage. Nothing else will serve as the solvent of caste'—*The Annihilation of Caste*).[51]

[46] For interviews with eighteen of these fifty Dalit MPs, see Darnal (2009).

[47] Gellner (2014); M. Bishwakarma (2017: 169).

[48] UNICEF (2016).

[49] Drucza (2019: 5) has a useful table summarizing all the different benefits (cash transfers) available as of 2013–14.

[50] On this policy, see T. Biswakarma (2014).

[51] Available at ccnmtl.columbia.edu/projects/mmt/ambedkar/web/index.html (accessed on 8 April 2020).

Following the peace accord signed between the Maoists and the mainstream parties in 2005, several strong policy measures were enacted to protect Dalits in Nepal against caste-based discrimination and untouchability. On 16 May 2006, the newly instated parliament declared Nepal to be a *chuwachut mukta* or 'untouchability-free' country. Assigning real power and articulating punishments, and even extending the measures to the private domain, on 24 May 2011, the Caste-Based Discrimination and Untouchability (Offence and Punishment) Act, 2011, was passed. This law was amended in 2018 in order to make the terms of punishment more substantial.

In 2015, in accordance with Articles 255 and 256 of the new constitution, the Dalit Commission became a constitutionally mandated body empowered to propose policy and legislation and to monitor the government's performance on Dalit issues. On paper, at least, Nepal's 2015 Constitution provided strong protections for Dalits: rights to free government scholarships, support for traditional occupations, healthcare, social security, land, housing, and proportionate inclusion in state bodies.

In 2017, the first local government elections for 20 years were held. In the new structures, every ward had to have at least one female Dalit for every five members. (There was also a stipulation that if the mayor was male, the deputy mayor should be female.) This has very substantially increased the overall representation of Dalits, especially women, at the local level, even though very few have been elected mayor or deputy mayor.[52]

Ambedkar's Indirect Influence on Nepal

Contrary to what some anthropologists/sociologists have thought, and contrary to what some upper-middle-class and upper-caste Indians sometimes say, caste is still very important in South Asia. It is still a major determinant of life chances and it is intimately linked to class.[53] Even when Dalits do manage to acquire wealth, the chances of them passing it on to subsequent generations, or joining the ranks of the elite, are small. Numerous unseen barriers remain in place to prevent them flourishing in the ways that members of other castes frequently can.

[52] Paswan (2017).
[53] Jodhka (2015).

Nepal's Dalits face the same problems as India's Dalits, and no doubt, there is scope for even greater collaboration and knowledge exchange between India and Nepal than already occurs. Nepal's Dalits have benefited from reservations only for a very short time, so there is, as yet, only a tiny Dalit middle class in Nepal. As a consequence, and unlike in North India, there is, as yet, no Dalit-oriented political party with a mass base and significant influence. India, with its longer history of positive discrimination, certainly provides lessons and inspiration for Nepali Dalits. As in India,[54] Dalits in Nepal appreciate the allowances that they now receive from the State and have faith in the central State's attempts to ameliorate their situation, however much they mistrust its local representatives, whom they suspect, sometimes with reason, of skimming off their benefits.[55] Such State benefits increase Dalits' identification with the state and their awareness of being citizens.

Ambedkar's direct or overtly acknowledged influence in Nepal may be slight (notwithstanding the fact that he came to Nepal in 1956, the year of his death, to participate in the 2500th anniversary of the Buddha's full nirvana).[56] Yet Ambedkar's indirect influence on Nepal, via the practical and everyday example of Indian constitutionalism and the Indian reservations system, has arguably been very considerable indeed.

References

Aahuti. 2017. 'The Story of My Poetry: An Excerpt', *La.Lit: A Literary Magazine*, 8: 76–83.

Adhikari, A. 2014. *The Bullet and the Ballot Box: The Story of Nepal's Maoist Revolution*. Delhi: Aleph.

Adhikari, K.P. and D.N. Gellner. 2016. 'New Identity Politics and the Collapse of Nepal's Constituent Assembly: When the Dominant becomes "Other"', *Modern Asian Studies*, 50(6): 2009–40.

Bennett, L., B. Sijapati, and D. Thapa. 2013. *Gender and Social Exclusion in Nepal: Update*. Kathmandu: Himal Books.

---

[54] Still (2011).

[55] Drucza (2019).

[56] The Samata Foundation has published a Nepali translation of the speech Ambedkar gave on that occasion 'Buddha and Karl Marx'.

Bhatta, S. 2005. *Determinants of Student Performance in the SLC Examinations* (SLC Study Report 13). Kathmandu: Ministry of Education and Sports.

Bishwakarma, M. 2017. 'Democratic Politics in Nepal: Dalit Political Inequality and Representation', *Asian Journal of Comparative Politics*, 2(3): 261–72.

———. 2019. *Political Transformations in Nepal: Dalit Inequality and Social Justice*. London: Routledge.

Bishwakarma, R. 2068 BS (2011–12). 'Nepal Dalit Shramik Morcha: Goshanapatra', in *Viparitharuko samarupata: Dvandatmak bhautikvadko jagbata vikasit parivartan sambandhi vaigyanik niyam viparitharuko samarupatavadi darshan*, pp. 117–30. Chitwan: Roma Bishwakarma.

———. 2069 BS (2012–13). *Krantiko vikasbare hamilai lageka kehi kuraharu (Dvandatmak bhautikbadbata nirantar parivartanonmukh khoj anusandhanmulak vicharharuko sangraha)*. Kathmandu: Roma Bishwakarma.

Bista, D.B. 2004 [1967]. *People of Nepal*. Kathmandu: Ratna Pustak Bhandar.

Biswakarma, T. 2014. 'Incentives for Inter-Caste Marriage between Dalit and non-Dalit in Nepal: Challenges and Opportunities', in D.D. Tamang and M.R. Maharjan (eds), *Citizens, Societies & State Crafting an Inclusive Future for Nepal*, pp. 91–108. Kathmandu: Mandala Book Point.

———. 2018. 'Citizenship and Social Security of Landless Dalit in Nepal', *Globe: A Journal of Language, Culture and Communication* 6: 52–65.

Biswokarma, J.B (trans. by S. Maharjan). 2012. 'Vicious Cycle of Non-Representation: Electoral System and Dalit Representation in Nepal', Samata Policy Paper 2, Lalitpur: Samata Foundation.

B.K., Amar. 2013. 'The Stigma of the Name: The Making and Remaking of a Dalit Identity in Nepal', Baha Occasional Papers 6, Kathmandu: Social Science Baha.

Bownas, R. and R. Bishokarma. 2019. 'Access after the Earthquake: The Micro Politics of Recovery and Reconstruction in Sindhupalchok District, Nepal, with Particular Reference to Caste', *Contemporary South Asia*, 27(2): 179–95.

Cameron, M. 1998. *On the Edge of the Auspicious: Gender and Caste in Nepal*. Urbana: University of Illinois Press.

———. 2007. 'Considering Dalits and Political Identity in Imagining a New Nepal', *Himalaya*, 27(1-2): 13–26. Reissued in Guneratne (2010).

Caplan, P. 1972. *Priests and Cobblers: A Study of Social Change in a Hindu Village in West Nepal*. London: Intertext.

Central Bureau of Statistics (CBS). 2005. *Poverty Trends in Nepal 1995/96 and 2003/04*. Kathmandu: Central Bureau of Statistics.

———. 2011. *Poverty in Nepal*. Kathmandu: Centre Bureau of Statistics.

Dahal, D.R. 2014. 'Social Composition of the Population: Caste/Ethnicity and Religion in Nepal', in *Population Monograph of Nepal, Vol. II (Social Demography)*, pp. 1–49. Kathmandu: Central Bureau of Statistics.

Dahal, D.R., M. Giri, and S. Mishra. 2014. *Musahar of Nepal*. Kathmandu: Central Department of Sociology/Anthropology, Tribhuvan University.

Dahal, D.R, S. Mishra, and R. Mahato. 2014. *Halkhor of Nepal*. Kathmandu: Central Department of Sociology/Anthropology, Tribhuvan University.

Dahal, D.R., and S.K. Jha. 2014. *Chamar of Nepal*. Kathmandu: Central Department of Sociology/ Anthropology, Tribhuvan University.

Darnal, S. (trans. by P. Adhikari). 2009. *A Land of our Own: Conversations with Dalit Members of Constituent Assembly*. Lalitpur: Samata Foundation.

Davies, N. 1999. *The Isles: A History*. Basingstoke: Macmillan.

Drucza, K. 2019. '"At least the Government is Watching out for us Now": Dalit Perceptions of Governance and Cash Transfers in Three Villages in Sarlahi, Nepal', *Modern Asian Studies*, 53 (6): 2041–78.

Folmar, S. 2007. 'Identity Politics among Dalits in Nepal', *Himalaya, the Journal of the Association for Nepal and Himalayan Studies*, 27(1): 41–53.

Gellner, D.N. 1992. *Monk, Householder, and Tantric Priest: Newar Buddhism and its Hierarchy of Ritual*. Cambridge: Cambridge University Press.

——— (ed.). 2013. *Borderland Lives in Northern South Asia*. Hyderabad: Orient BlackSwan.

———. 2014. 'The 2013 Elections in Nepal' *Asian Affairs*, 45(2): 243–61.

———. 2016. 'The Idea of Nepal' (MC Regmi lecture). Kathmandu: Social Science Baha.

———. 2018. 'Politics of Buddhism in Nepal', *Economic and Political Weekly*, 53(3): 17–20.

———. 2019. 'Masters of Hybridity: How Activists Reshaped Nepali Society' *Journal of the Royal Anthropological Institute*, 25(2): 265–84.

Gellner, D.N. and D. Quigley (eds). 1995. *Contested Hierarchies: A Collaborative Ethnography of Caste among the Newars of the Kathmandu Valley, Nepal*. Oxford: Clarendon.

Goyal, P., P. Dhawan, and S. Narula. 2005. *The Missing Piece of the Puzzle: Caste Discrimination and the Conflict in Nepal*. NYU School of Law: Center for Human Rights and Global Justice.

Guneratne, A. 2010. *Dalits of Nepal: Towards Dignity, Citizenship and Justice*. Kathmandu: ANHS, Social Science Baha, and Himal Books. (First published in *Himalaya* 27 January 2007.)

Guru, G. 2012. *Carrier of Social Justice in India: Implications for Affirmative Action Programs in Nepal* (Samata Annual Lecture II). Lalitpur: Samata Foundation. (www.samatafoundation.org)

Gurung, Y.B., B.R. Suwal, M.S. Pradhan, and M.S. Tamang. 2014. *Nepal Social Inclusion Survey 2012: Caste, Ethnic and Gender Dimensions of Socio-Economic Development, Governance, and Social Solidarity*. Kathmandu: Central Department of Sociology/Anthropology, Tribhuvan University.

Hachhethu, K. and D.N. Gellner. 2010. 'Nepal: Trajectories of Democracy and Restructuring of the State', in P. Brass (ed.), *Routledge Handbook of South Asian Politics*, pp. 131–46. New York: Routledge.

Höfer, A. 1979. *The Caste Hierarchy and the State in Nepal: A Study of the Muluki Ain of 1854*. Innsbruck: Universitätsverlag Wagner. (Reissue 2004, Kathmandu: Himal Books.)

Holmberg, D.H. 1989. *Order in Paradox: Myth, Ritual and Exchange Among Nepal's Tamang*. Ithaca: Cornell University Press.

Human Rights Watch (HRW). 2001. *Caste Discrimination: A Global Concern*. New York: Human Rights Watch. Available at www.hrw.org/reports/2001/globalcaste/index.htm#TopOfPage, accessed 22 July 2019).

Jodhka, S. 2015. *Caste in Contemporary India*. Delhi: Routledge.

Jodhka, S. and G. Shah 2010. 'Comparative Contexts of Discrimination: Caste and Untouchability in South Asia' *EPW* XLV(48): 99–106.

Joshi, B.L. and L.E. Rose. 1966. *Democratic Innovations in Nepal: A Case Study of Political Acculturation*. Berkeley: University of California Press.

Khanal, K., F.S. Gelpke, and U.P. Pyakurel. 2012. *Dalit Representation in National Politics of Nepal*. Lalitpur: Nepal National Dalit Social Welfare Organisation.

Kharel, S. 2010. 'The Dialectics of Identity and Resistance among Dalits in Nepal'. Unpublished PhD thesis, University of Pittsburgh.

Kisan, Y.M (trans. by L. Vasily). 2005. *The Nepali Dalit Social Movement*. Lalitpur: Legal Rights Protection Society.

——— (trans. by S. Maharjan). 2012 (BS 2069). 'Federalism and Dalit Governance: Dalit-Friendly Federal System'. Samata Policy Paper 4, Lalitpur: Samata Foundation. (www.samatafoundation.org)

Lawoti, M. 2005. *Towards a Democratic Nepal: Inclusive Political Institutions for a Multicultural Society*. Delhi: SAGE.

———. 2013. 'Dynamics of Mobilization: Varied Trajectories of Dalit, Indigenous Nationalities and Madhesi Movements', in M. Lawoti and S. Hangen (eds), *Nationalism and Ethnic Conflict in Nepal:*

Identities and Mobilization after 1990, pp. 193–225. London & New York: Routledge.

Letizia, C. 2014. 'Buddhist Activism, New Sanghas and the Politics of Belonging among some Tharu and Magar Communities of Southern Nepal', in G. Toffin and J. Pfaff-Czarnecka (eds), *Facing Globalization in the Himalayas: Belonging and the Politics of the Self*, pp. 289–325. Delhi: SAGE.

LeVine, S. and D.N. Gellner 2005. *Rebuilding Buddhism: The Theravada Movement in Twentieth-Century Nepal*. Cambridge MA: Harvard University Press.

Maharjan, P. 1999. 'Problems of Democracy in Nepal', *European Bulletin of Himalayan Research* 17: 41–68.

Mumford, S.R. 1989. *Himalayan Dialogue: Tibetan Lamas and Gurung Shamans in Nepal*. Wisconsin: University of Wisconsin Press.

Muni, S.D. 1992. *India and Nepal: A Changing Relationship*. Delhi: Konark.

———. 2003. *Maoist Insurgency in Nepal: The Challenge and the Response*. Delhi: Rupa & Co.

National Population and Housing Census (NPHC). 2012. *National Population and Housing Census 2011 (Village Development Committee/ Municipality)*. Kathmandu: Central Bureau of Statistics.

Neupane, G. 2000. *Nepālko jātiya prasna: sāmājik banot ra sājhedāriko sambhāvanā* [Nepal's nationality question: Social structure and the possibilities of compromise]. Kathmandu: Centre for Development Studies.

Onta, P. 2001. 'Regional Area Studies in South Asia: Dark Days Ahead', *Nepali Journal of Contemporary Studies*, 1(2): 60–89.

Pariyar, B. and J.C. Lovett. 2016. 'Dalit Identity in Urban Pokhara, Nepal', *Geoforum* 75: 134–47.

Pariyar, M. 2018. 'Caste Discrimination Overseas: Nepali Dalits in England', in D.N. Gellner and S.L. Hausner (eds), *Global Nepalis: Religion, Culture, and Community in a New and Old Diaspora*, pp. 404–34. Delhi: Oxford University Press.

Paswan, B. 2017. 'How Quotas Provided a Footing but Left Inequality Unresolved: Dalits in the Local Election: Election Results Reveal Gender and Pahad-Terai Imbalances in Dalit Representation'. *The Record*, 29 October. Available at www.recordnepal.com/wire/features/how-quotas-provided-a-footing-but-left-inequality-unresolved-dalits-in-the-local-election/, accessed 6 August 2018.

Pyakurel, U.P. 2011. 'A Debate on Dalits and Affirmative Action in Nepal', *Economic and Political Weekly*, 46(40): 71–8.

Sharma, P.R. 2004. *The State and Society in Nepal: Historical Foundations and Contemporary Trends*. Lalitpur: Himal Books.

Sharma, S. 2013 (VS 2070). *Prayogshala: Nepali sankramanma Dilli, darbar ra Maovadi* [Laboratory: The roles of Delhi, the palace, and the Maoists in Nepal's transition]. Kathmandu: Fineprint.

Sijapati, B. 2013. 'In Pursuit of Recognition: Regionalism, Madhesi Identity and the Madhes Andolan', in M. Lawoti and S. Hangen (eds), *Nationalism and Ethnic Conflict in Nepal: Identities and Mobilization after 1990*, pp. 145–72. Abingdon: Routledge.

Still, C. 2011. 'The State in the *palli*: Dalit Perspectives on the State in Andhra Pradesh', *Contemporary South Asia*, 19(3): 315–29.

Sunam, R. 2014. 'Marginalised Dalits in International Labour Migration: Reconfiguring Economic and Social Relations in Nepal', *Journal of Ethnic and Migration Studies*, 40 (12): 2030–48.

Sunam, R. and K. Shrestha. 2019. 'Failing the Most Excluded: A Critical Analysis of Nepal's Affirmative Action Policy', in D.N. Gellner and K.P. Adhikari (eds), Contributions to Nepalese Studies, special issue: Nepal's Dalits in Transition 45(1): 143–65. Kathmandu: CNAS, TU.

Tamang, M.S., P.S. Chapagain, and P.K. Ghimire. 2014. *Social Inclusion Atlas of Nepal: Ethnic and Caste Groups*, Vol. 1. Kathmandu: Central Department of Sociology/Anthropology, Tribhuvan University.

United Nations Children's Fund (UNICEF). 2016. 'Paying Forward: Benefits of Nepal's Child Grant for Current and Future Generations'. Policy Brief, November 2016. New York: UNICEF.

Vasily, L.A. 2009. 'Struggles against Domination: Forms of Nepali Dalit Activism', in D.N. Gellner (ed.), *Ethnic Activism and Civil Society in South Asia*, pp. 215–38. Delhi: SAGE.

World Bank (WB)/ Department for International Development (DFID). 2006. *Unequal Citizens: Gender, Caste and Ethnic Exclusion in Nepal*. Kathmandu: World Bank and Department for International Development.

Whelpton, J. 1991. *Kings, Soldiers and Priests: Nepalese Politics, 1830–1857*. Delhi: Manohar.

———. 2005. *A History of Nepal*. Cambridge: Cambridge University Press.

6

Ambedkar, Labour, and the Political Economy of Dalit Conversion in Colonial Panjab[*]

NAVYUG GILL

On 12 December 1935, Bhimrao Ramji Ambedkar received an invitation from Sant Ram, the secretary of the Jat-Pat Todak Mandal ('Association for the Breaking of Caste'), to address its annual conference the following spring in Lahore. No one had studied the problem of caste as deeply as Ambedkar, wrote Ram, adding that the 'independent Harijans of Punjab are very much desirous to meet you and discuss with you their plans'.[1] Ambedkar reluctantly agreed, but after obtaining a copy of his speech, the Mandal leadership became uneasy with some of its content and requested that he make certain changes. In particular, they expressed surprised objection to passages where Ambedkar denounced the morality and sanctity of the Hindu religion and scripture, and declared his intention to ultimately leave its fold. Ambedkar resolutely refused, stating he would 'not alter a comma' and accused the Mandal of duplicity before withdrawing from the conference, which was later

[*] A modified version of this chapter has appeared as 'Limits of Conversion: Caste, Labor, and the Question of Emancipation in Colonial Punjab', *Journal of Asian Studies*, 78(1):3-22, 2019, © The Association for Asian Studies, Inc., published by Cambridge University Press, reproduced with permission.

[1] Ambedkar (1979: 27).

Dalit Conversion in Colonial Panjab   117

cancelled altogether.[2] On returning to Bombay with nearly a thousand printed copies of the speech, he decided to distribute it on his own under the title *Annihilation of Caste*. It sold out quickly, provoking two rebuttals from Mohandas Karamchand Gandhi, to which Ambedkar issued a lengthy reply in 1937. Since then, it has been considered not only one of Ambedkar's most famous texts, but also a radical and penetrating intervention into the nature of the problem of caste.[3]

The question Ambedkar addresses in his undelivered speech is how to understand, confront, and abolish the peculiar institution of hereditary hierarchy in Indian society. Untouchability is not to be overcome by mere shifts in attitude, nor is it sufficient to rely on straightforward political or economic remedies. Of activists in the Indian National Congress, he asks: 'Are you fit for political power even though you do not allow a large class of your own countrymen like the untouchables to use public schools?' Similarly, of socialists who insist on the primacy of material relations, he asks: 'Can it be said that the proletariat of India, poor as it is, recognize no distinctions except that of the rich and the poor?'[4] According to Ambedkar, the presumed unity of citizenship or class is undercut by a more intractable ideology of caste separation. This phenomenon is unique to India because it is not only a division of labour, prevalent all over the world, but *'also a division of labourers'* based on fixity, graded inequality, and pre-destination.[5] That is why efforts at inter-caste dining and marriage are ineffective and unrealizable, however laudable. The deeper problem, argues Ambedkar, is that such a hierarchy is sanctioned and indeed mandated by Hinduism through the sacred Shastras. Individual Hindus observe caste not because they are 'inhuman or wrong-headed'; rather, they do so 'because they are deeply religious'. As a result, Ambedkar declares, 'what is wrong is their religion, which has inculcated this notion of caste'.[6] The solution is as succinct as it is searing:

---

[2] Ambedkar (1979: 34–5).

[3] In an endorsement on the front flap of a recently published annotated edition of this text, the writer and activist Anand Teltumbde states: 'What *Communist Manifesto* is to the capitalist world, *Annihilation of Caste* is to caste India.' See Ambedkar (2014).

[4] Ambedkar (1979: 41, 46).

[5] Ambedkar (1979: 47). Emphasis in original.

[6] Ambedkar (1979: 68).

'the real remedy' is to 'discard the authority of the *Shastras* and destroy the religion of the *Shastras*'.[7] Only when the legitimacy of hereditary separation is overturned will there emerge the possibility of a genuinely inclusive, united, and equal society worthy of independence.

What if Ambedkar had delivered this speech in Lahore in 1936? Given the social and economic polarities of Panjabi society, his diagnosis and remedy to the sickness of caste seems strikingly incongruent with the composition of his intended audience. According to the 1931 census, over 87 per cent of the population lived in villages, of which Hindus made up less than 30 per cent, while the bulk of the remainder was 53 per cent Muslim and 15 per cent Sikh.[8] More significantly, a few years earlier, a group of activists succeeded in registering a separate religion explicitly for lower castes called Ad Dharm or 'Original Faith', drawing on the teachings of the medieval Bhagats Kabir, Namdev, and especially Ravidas. Officially, this category returned over four hundred thousand adherents, nearly a third of all depressed classes by some estimates, and may have included tens of thousands more who were misidentified, ignored, or coerced into declaring themselves differently.[9] Thus not only were alternative religious traditions without formal caste hierarchy already available in Panjabi society,

[7] Ambedkar (1979: 78). For detailed studies of Ambedkar's approach to the question of conversion, see Kumar (2015: ch. 5); and Skaria (2015).

[8] According to the 1931 census, Panjab had a total population of 28,490,857, of which 23,580,852 (82.8 per cent) were under direct British rule and 4,910,005 (17.2 per cent) under seventeen different subordinate native principalities. The overwhelming majority lived in the countryside rather than cities: 87.6 per cent rural to 12.4 per cent urban. In terms of religion, Hindus were 37.6 per cent, Muslims 51.9 per cent, Sikhs 7.3 per cent, Christians 1.9 per cent, and so-called Others 1.3 per cent of the urban population. Yet in rural areas, Hindus dropped to 29.1 per cent, Muslims remained at 52.5 per cent, and Sikhs rose to 15.3 per cent. See Khan (1933: Part 1, 11, 89, 96, 98).

[9] The colonial state usually referred to lower castes in this period as 'Depressed Classes'. Out of a population estimated at 1,422,009 in 1931, the official figure for followers of Ad Dharm is 418,789, including 113,580 from Jalandhar, 111,829 from Hoshiarpur, 50,718 from Lyallpur, and 36,262 from Ferozepur. Khan Hasan Khan, the author of the census report, briefly mentions that a 'tug-of-war' started in some districts between Ad Dharmi activists and Hindu and Sikh landowners over the religion lower castes were declaring to census enumerators. See Khan (1933: Part 1, 374, 318, 294, iii–iv).

but lower castes had effectively pre-empted the call to leave the Hindu faith by establishing their own distinct religion.[10] While Ambedkar recognized the scriptural critique of caste in Sikhism, and even invoked Guru Nanak with the Buddha as ardent opponents of the sanctity of the Shastras,[11] he neither acknowledged the Ad Dharm movement nor the circumstances of the largely landless agricultural labourers constituting Panjabi untouchables. If caste was a perverse division of labourers as much as of labour, then the programme for its annihilation appears to miss the specific logic of its operation in rural Panjab.[12]

In this chapter, I explore the politics of conversion through the problem of lower castes freeing themselves from Brahminical Hinduism but not the constraints of lowliness or casteism in early twentieth-century Panjab.[13] I begin with mapping the changing constellation of names across different religions for groups of lower castes, designated as village menials by the colonial state. Next, I trace shifts in religious affiliation of these groups amid the emergence of the Ad Dharm movement and its attempt to impart equality, dignity, and community to Panjabi Dalits. To bring this new sense of caste identity to bear on actual labour practices, I then examine the fraught relationship between landed cultivators and landless labourers working side by side yet remaining profoundly separate and unequal. That a large proportion of lower castes could adopt religions other than Hinduism or start their own *and yet* remain excluded and exploited reveals the limits to a politics centred on conversion. It is the antinomy between emancipatory discourses and exploitative relations that suggests the need for a different horizon for overcoming caste hierarchy.

---

[10] For more on the distinct politics of caste in East Panjab, see Jodhka (2000), Puri (2003); and Ram (2004).

[11] Ambedkar is unequivocal in drawing Buddhism and Sikhism together in order to condemn Hindu scripture: 'You must take the stand that Buddha took. You must take the stand which Guru Nanak took. You must not only discard the *Shastras*, you must deny their authority, as did Buddha and Nanak.' Ambedkar (1979: 69).

[12] For studies focussed on caste in relation to labour, see Breman (1974), Prakash (1990), Prashad (2000), Gidwani (2008), Rawat (2011), and Viswanath (2014).

[13] For works mapping the politics of caste hierarchy in different parts of South Asia, see Bayly (1999), Dirks (2001), Pandian (2007), Rao (2009), and Guha (2013).

Identifying Caste Labour in Rural Panjab

Who were these 'menials' who might have attended Ambedkar's speech in Lahore? According to a conventional colonial description, 'the village servants or menials are paid by the zamindars usually in grain at the time of harvest, in return for work performed during the preceding half-year'. Formally, they were divided into two groups ostensibly based on caste occupations. First were those directly connected with agricultural operations: namely, the *Tarkhan* (carpenter) making and repairing wooden ploughs and other implements as well as the apparatus for well irrigation; the *Kumhar* (potter) providing various earthen vessels for wells and domestic use; the *Lohar* (blacksmith) forging and sharpening ploughshares along with other iron tools; the Chamar (leather worker) making leather bags, whips, and blinkers for bullocks; and the *Churha* (sweeper) providing brooms, baskets, and ropes. Second were a greater variety of those more distant from agriculture but still a part of village life, mainly the *Nai* (barber), the Dhobi (launderer), the *Darzi* or the *Chhimba* (tailor), the *Julaha* (weaver), the *Jhinwar* or the *Mehra* (water carrier), and the *Mirasi* (musician), among others.[14] Although sharing some features with supposedly caste-based occupational roles elsewhere in north India, the authority of Brahmins was conspicuously absent in colonial rural Panjab.[15]

In the first group of village menials, the first three castes were fewer in number and occupied a somewhat higher status, as they worked in their own small shops at their own pace, and increasingly took on piece-work for cash remuneration. Similarly, members of

---

[14] Saunders (1873: 61–2).

[15] A well-known description of the lack of Brahmin power in rural Panjab at the turn of the century is from the autobiography of Prakash Tandon, a *Khatri* who received his education in England and went on to become a top manager in a large multinational company. 'That they [Brahmins] could be the leaders of society, in a position of privilege,' he writes, 'I only discovered when I went to live outside the Punjab. With us the Brahmins were an unprivileged class and exercised little influence on the community.' And later: 'The very address "oh Pandita" or "oh Brahmina" had a gentle sarcasm about it.' See Tandon (1968: 76–7). For another autobiographical account of rural caste politics in the early twentieth century, this time from the perspective of a *Jatt*, see Brard (2007).

Dalit Conversion in Colonial Panjab 121

the second group were also numerically few, and mostly confined to their given tasks due to the specialization of equipment and skills. The Chamars and Churhas, on the other hand, were considered the lowest and most stigmatized of castes—untouchables— and constituted the bulk of the menial population. Yet while the colonial vocabulary relied on these simplistic categories, groups identified as 'Chamars' or 'Churhas' did not use those designations for themselves, nor were they exclusively recognized by them in the wider society. The Panjabi words they adopted reveal a remarkable spectrum of emerging and intertwining caste and religious identities.

Significant conversion of lower castes to Sikhism began in the seventeenth century, to Islam hundreds of years earlier, and to Christianity in the late nineteenth century. Chamar, deriving from *chamri* for skin or more precisely animal hides, served as a generic term for leather worker, nominally Hindu. In the northern hill areas, they were sometimes termed *Dagis* or *Kolis*. Those who converted to Islam called themselves *Mochis*, closely affiliated with shoe-making, while those who became Sikh took the name *Ravidasia* after Bhagat Ravidas, which could also be given as *Ramdasia* or *Raidasia*. For a short while in the mid-twentieth century, all three, as well as some Julahas who called themselves *Kabir-panthis* after their acclaimed ancestor Kabir, identified as *Ad Dharmi* or the followers of the Ad Dharm movement.

Churha, on the other hand, is without an assumed etymological basis, but is presented in colonial writings as another untouchable caste of Hindu sweepers and scavengers. Converts to Islam became known as *Mussalis* or *Kutanas*, Sikhs identified as *Mazbis* or *Rangretas*, and Christians were termed *Masihs*. Those remaining Hindu also changed their designation, preferring to be called *Valmikis* (or *Balmikis* colloquially) after Rishi Valmiki, the author of the epic Ramayana.[16] The two generic caste names for these labourers thus conceal a diversity of identities in a continuous process of formation and reformation. And although today, it is offensive and illegal in India to refer to anyone as either a Chamar or Churha, the word 'Chamar' is still used for certain caste-oriented associations and has even been

---

[16] For a summary of the different categories of low castes in East Panjab, see Judge (2003: 2990).

invoked positively in popular music by emerging Dalit artists in East Panjab.[17]

The term 'menial' is therefore a general and specific diminution, minimizing the various labours performed by these castes as well as underscoring their exclusion from a requisite and valued role within the agrarian economy. Menial conjures up the notion of marginal, as a periphery to the already centred Jatt, a form of labour adjacent to the main, supposedly given work of being a peasant. At the same time, menial implies inchoate and provisional, an assortment of explicitly ancillary tasks without fixity or importance to the productive process. Defined as subordinate both to the landholding cultivator and to cultivation itself, the menial labourer thus occupies a position of double subalternity. The stigma of an alienated inconsequence permeates through the very language by which these groups were located within the political economy of the countryside.

A Competition for Conversion and Community

During the late nineteenth and early twentieth centuries, lower castes changed religious affiliations and consolidated community boundaries to gain a new kind of social and economic preponderance. Here, the colonial census was crucial in creating awareness of the relative strength of a group and the possibility of tracking its trajectory over time.[18] In the first comprehensive all-India census of 1881, undifferentiated Chamars numbered 1,400,000 and Churhas 1,100,000 in Panjab. This was less than Jatts (4,400,000) and Rajputs (1,700,000), roughly equal to Brahmins (1,100,000), but more than other prominent groups such as *Pathan*s (859,000),

---

[17] The Chamar Mahan Sabha, or 'Grand Chamar Society', is a prominent Jalandhar-based organization which advocates on behalf of scheduled castes in Panjab, particularly Ravidasias. In recent years, a number of songs with titles such as *'Putt Chamaran De'* ('Sons of Chamars') and lyrics boasting of the physical strength, material possessions, and self-respect of Chamars have become popular in certain lower-caste communities. The title and content of these songs can be seen as mimetic responses to perhaps one of the most famous Panjabi songs, 'Putt *Jattan* De' ('Sons of Jatts') sung by Surinder Shinda from 1981.

[18] See Cohn (1987), Jones (1981), and Appadurai (1993).

*Gujar*s (627,000), and Khatris (419,000).[19] In a process officials admitted was replete with inaccuracies, approximately 68 per cent of Chamars were returned as Hindu, 25 as Muslim, and 7 as Sikh, while 58 per cent of Churhas were Hindu, 37 Muslim, 4 Sikh, and 1 Christian. Together, Chamars and Churhas constituted the second largest caste group in Panjab and were recorded as largely following strands of what at the time was a diverse, amorphous Hinduism.

Over the next forty years, the proselytizing efforts of Christian missionaries transformed the act of conversion into a concerted competition among the Arya Samaj, the Singh Sabha, Sunni Anjumans, and the Ahmadiyya movement.[20] As a result of this protracted, multifaceted struggle, as well as different practices in counting, the distribution of lower castes across the major religions changed significantly by the 1921 census. Chamars (including Mochis and Dagis) now stood at 1,700,000, with those professing to be Hindus decreasing to 66 per cent, Muslims remaining at 25, and Sikhs increasing to 9 per cent. Churhas (with Mussalis, Mazbis, and Christians) totalled 1,400,000, but with Hindus dropping to 48 per cent, Muslims down to 26, Sikhs rising to 7, and Christians jumping to 19 per cent.[21] Thus in four decades, almost 2 per cent of Hindu Chamars (68 to 66) and 10 per cent of Hindu Churhas (58 to 48) appeared to officially leave Hinduism, mainly for Sikhism and Christianity.

A more dramatic assertion of lower-caste religious identity took place over the following decade. Rather than leaving one faith for another, however, this change entailed the creation and adoption of a new one altogether. In early June 1926, a small group of Chamars met in the village of Mugowal in Hoshiarpur District to

---

[19] In 1881, the census shows Chamars numbered 1,072,699 in addition to 349,272 Mochis, while Churhas were 1,078,739. The figures for other castes are: Jatts 4,432,750, Rajputs 1,677,569, Brahmins 1,084,193, Pathans 859,582, Gujars 627,304, and Khatris 419,139 out of a total population of 22,712,120. See Ibbetson (1883: Table No. VIII A, 4–10).

[20] For the politics of religious conversion in colonial Panjab, see Jones (1976), Oberoi (1994), and Harding (2008).

[21] In the 1921 census, there were 1,139,741 Chamars, 434,682 Mochis, and 165,164 Dagis, while there were 749,687 Churhas, 366,098 Mussalis, 281,946 Christians (without a specified caste), and 65,004 Mazbis. The religious proportions are given within each caste category. See Middleton and Jacob (1922: Table XIII, 194–254; Table XV, 264–72).

discuss ways of concentrating lower-caste power amid upper-caste co-optation and competition. The village was the birthplace of Mangoo Ram, at the time a schoolteacher who would become the leader of the movement and an influential, if somewhat overlooked, figure in Panjab politics before and after Independence. In a series of interviews with the anthropologist Mark Juergensmeyer in the 1970s, Mangoo Ram related the extraordinary details of his life, before his death in 1980 at the age of 94.

Born into a family of leather workers, Mangoo Ram's father had become a successful wholesale supplier of leather goods to the British Indian Army, and insisted that his son be educated to help with the business. Despite excelling at school, Mangoo Ram was often the only untouchable student, forced to sit at the back of the classroom or even in a separate room, listening through an open door. In 1909, he convinced his father to send him to America in order to work and support the family through remittances. While Ambedkar was studying for a master's degree at Columbia University in New York, Mangoo Ram picked fruit in the orchards of the San Joaquin Valley in California before joining the militant anti-colonial Ghadar Party in 1913.[22] Compared to the discrimination he faced growing up, he later fondly recalled the equality and camaraderie of the Ghadar militants, even though he was only one of two Chamars in a group of mostly Jatts. Two years later, he volunteered to smuggle weapons to Panjab to incite an uprising against British rule, but was discovered en route and almost executed, spending several years in jail and then in hiding in Manila. Mangoo Ram eventually made his way back to Panjab by 1925, where he founded a school, and taught briefly before turning his attention to the condition of untouchables.[23]

The 1926 meeting in Mugowal produced a group dedicated to articulating and organizing around a distinct narrative of lower-caste history, religion, and identity. Rather than strict religious piety, these individuals were inspired by restlessness and ambition, 'socially sensitive and politically astute'.[24] For Mangoo Ram, the history of Panjab was a long sequence of destruction and

---

[22] For more on the Ghadar Party, see Puri (1993); Ramnath (2011); and Grewal, Puri, and Banga (2013).

[23] See Juergensmeyer (1982: Appendix A, 283–9).

[24] Juergensmeyer (1982:44).

Dalit Conversion in Colonial Panjab

displacement for untouchables. As the original inhabitants of the land, they were first suppressed and enslaved by Aryan invaders, with each generation of Hindus worse than the one before and Manu—a mythical figure presumed to have written the ancient Brahminical law code—in paticular denounced as a 'murderer'. Islam at first held some liberating potential but quickly absorbed and reproduced the same logic of caste hierarchy, while Sikhism was little more than a momentary upsurge ending in tyranny. Against this past, Mangoo Ram and his followers argued that all untouchables—'chamars, chuhras, sansis, bhanjre [and] bhils'[25]—together constituted a separate *qaum*, usually translated as nation but here referring to religious community, equal to Hindus, Muslims, and Sikhs. To reclaim their autochthonous status, the group took the name Ad Dharm, meaning the originary or ancient faith, and identified a quartet of figures as their founders: Valmiki, Namdev, Kabir, and especially Ravidas. By recognizing themselves as Ad Dharmis, the group believed untouchables would at last achieve separate parity with other religious communities rather than continue to be manipulated and subsumed within them.

Predictably, the new assertion provoked serious conflict with existing organizations competing for untouchable allegiance. The Arya Samaj was seen as the greatest enemy. Many Ad Dharm leaders emerged from it or one of its affiliates (such as the Jat-Pat Todak Mandal), and were constantly enticed to return to work for untouchable uplift within its larger neo-Hindu framework. Faced with the threat of re-absorption, Mangoo Ram focussed on condemning the *shuddhi* or 'purification' campaign as a devious attempt to keep untouchables imprisoned within the grasp of Hinduism.[26] In a group whose name literally meant the 'Society of Aryans,' he argued, there could be no space for equality with non-Aryans.

On the other hand, the Ad Dharm both faced and exhibited hostility of a different kind towards the Singh Sabha movement. Here, the tension was more intimate: the Sikh Gurus had denounced caste and declared the equality of all; the Adi Granth included verses from lower-caste Bhagats venerated by all Sikhs; and Sikh institutions deliberately transgressed the boundaries

---

[25] Juergensmeyer (1982:45).

[26] For a different perceptive on the politics of shuddhi, see Adcock (2013).

of purity, pollution, and distance. Yet as Mangoo Ram argued, it was also true that untouchables—whether professing to be Hindu, Muslim, or Christian, or even Mazbi or Ravidasia Sikh— remained largely untouchable for both Khatri and Jatt Sikhs, and that cruel and degrading treatment continued almost unabated in Sikh-dominated villages. Lower castes still lived in separate areas, could not access the same wells, and were exploited for their labour; they were also discriminated against within many gurd- waras through outright exclusion, different seating arrangements, and restrictions on participation in the collective kitchen known as langar.[27] At the same time, some Singh Sabha activists such as Giani Ditt Singh and Kahn Singh Nabha recognized this contradic- tion and directed energies towards exhorting Sikhs to live up to the values of their own faith.[28] Nevertheless, Mangoo Ram and the Ad Dharm would not be mollified by such attempts, however sincere. To mark their separation from Sikhism, they transformed the status of Ravidas, Kabir, and Namdev. No longer were they simply respected Bhagats, but Gurus in their own right, and thus the progenitors of an entirely new faith.

Ad Dharm's efforts bore unexpected and unprecedented results in the 1931 census. A few years before, Mangoo Ram sent a petition to the Governor of Panjab demanding a separate designation: 'We are not Hindus. We strongly request the government not to list us as such. Our faith is not Hindu but Ad Dharm. We are not a part of Hinduism, and Hinduism is not a part of us.' The administra- tion readily obliged, as the Ad Dharm's hostility towards the Arya Samaj as well as Gandhi and the Congress made it seem at best

[27] Puri (2003: 2697). See also Jodhka (2002: 1814–20); Ram (2007: 4068– 70); and Hans (2016: 142–7).

[28] Giani Ditt Singh, an eminent writer and formally from a Ramdasia family, published *Nakli Sikh Prabodh* ('False Sikhs Redeem Yourselves') in 1895, castigating Sikhs who continued to practice caste, while Kahn Singh Nabha's *Ham Hindu Nahin* ('We Are Not Hindus') from 1899 reiterated Sikhism as distinct from Hinduism in part through its explicit opposition to caste. Their efforts were not entirely unsuccessful: in the 1921 census, over 60,000 Sikhs refused to state their caste, compared to only 20,000 Hindus and 7,000 Muslims. There is little doubt that this was not because these people did not know the caste of their birth, but that they refused to acknowledge it. See Puri (2003: 2697); and Middleton and Jacob (1922: 254).

Dalit Conversion in Colonial Panjab   127

indifferent to colonial rule.[29] The census results came as a shock to everyone involved. Despite a campaign of intimidation 'not infrequently bordering on terrorism,'[30] approximately 418,789 people identified themselves as Ad Dharmis, mainly in the districts of Jalandhar, Hoshiarpur, and Lyallpur. Leaders later claimed that the actual number of people wanting to identify with Ad Dharm was close to 2,000,000.[31]

Equally significant was the changing distribution of lower castes in the other religions. The population of Chamars (this time including Dagis, Mochis, and Ramdasias) increased to slightly less than 1,900,000, of which Hindus were reduced to 47 per cent, Muslims again remained at 25, Sikhs rose to 12, and Ad Dharmis became 16. Out of 1,500,000 Churhas (with Mussalis, Mazbis, and Christians), Hindus dropped even lower to 24 per cent, Muslims rose a little to 29, Sikhs to 11, while Christians surged to 30, and Ad Dharmis now made up 6. Thus, within a decade, almost one-third of Hindu Chamars and one half of Hindu Churhas changed their religion.[32] Between 1881 and 1931, the absolute number of Hindu Chamars actually decreased from 963,000 to 885,000 while Hindu Churhas went even further down from 629,000 to 367,000. As Mangoo Ram noted with satisfaction, in less than five years, the Ad Dharm converted roughly the same number as Christian missionaries did in fifty years.[33] Thus, well before Ambedkar was to give his speech vowing to leave Hinduism, lower-caste Hindus in Panjab had by and large already severed their ties, adopting Sikhism, Christianity, or their own Ad Dharm faith.

By combining existing devotional figures with new doctrines and practices within a stirring narrative, the Ad Dharm created a distinct identity for Panjabi untouchables. Its success lay in harnessing the popular respect for Ravidas, Kabir, and Namdev into a reverence bordering on deification. Mangoo Ram's comparison

---

[29] Concurring with Ambedkar on the critique of independence for a caste-ridden society, another part of the Ad Dharm programme stated: 'India should not be given independence until Untouchables are free and equal. Otherwise it would be a disgrace to the British rule.' See Juergensmeyer (1982: Appendix B, 301).

[30] Khan (1933: Part 1, iv).

[31] Juergensmeyer (1982:77).

[32] Khan (1933: Part 2, Table XVII, 282–302).

[33] Juergensmeyer (1982: 77).

128   Navyug Gill

with Christianity is therefore more than mere boasting. Whereas missionaries had to impart a totally unfamiliar history and theology to lower castes, the Ad Dharm invoked figures already a part of the local imagination and linked to a long tradition of inquiry, critique, and assertion. An iconoclastic weaver from Benares speaking in a familiar idiom resonated more intensely than a carpenter turned messiah from Nazareth.

Yet the centrality given to figures from these specific occupational backgrounds also limited the appeal of Ad Dharm and contributed to its eventual decline. Since most of its leadership were Chamars from Jalandhar and Hoshiarpur who exalted Ravidas in particular, the vast majority of adherents were also Chamars, Ravidasias, Dagis, and even Mochis. Despite its efforts, the Ad Dharm did not manage to overcome divides internal to lower castes to attract significant numbers of Churhas, Mussalis, Mazbis, or Masihs. When Mangoo Ram reached out to Ambedkar, supporting him against Gandhi's ultimatum over separate electorates in Pune and offering to merge Ad Dharm with his organization, the reply was somewhat distant. According to Juergensmeyer, Ambedkar 'wanted to join, not a separatist religious tradition, but rather an egalitarian one, which would embrace the whole of society'—hence his temporary interest in Sikhism and ultimate conversion to Buddhism in 1955.[34] Thus the very elements that had informed and advanced the Ad Dharm movement ended up isolating it.

---

[34] Juergensmeyer (1982:162). The nature of the problem of caste and Sikhism is perhaps best illustrated by a lesser-known aspect of Ambedkar's attempt to find an alternative religion for untouchables. According to Harish Puri, after declaring he would not die a Hindu in 1935, Ambedkar began research into different religions and even came close to choosing Sikhism in June 1936. Soon after, however, the plan was suspended, and then quietly dropped. While doubts remain over his ability to reach consensus with certain constituencies among his own followers, a more persuasive explanation for the change relates to conflict within the Sikh community. On the one hand, some lower-caste Panjabis (perhaps Hindu or even Mazbi or Ravidasia Sikh) conveyed to Ambedkar 'the atrocities they suffered at the hands of the dominant community of jat Sikhs and appealed to him to ensure that the untouchables never became Sikhs'. On the other hand, some upper-caste Sikhs became alarmed at what this influx would mean for them. While the potential addition of approximately six crore untouchables to the existing forty lakh Sikhs would raise their

Dalit Conversion in Colonial Panjab 129

After the watershed of the 1931 census, and another surprising showing in the 1936 legislative elections, Ad Dharm leaders became embroiled in factional controversies and political manoeuvring, and drifted from the task of developing their qaum. Although their momentum faltered and the movement declined, Juergensmeyer points out that the Ad Dharm 'established a fact which previously had been unproved'. They demonstrated 'that Untouchable castes were capable of mobilizing for their own benefits, and of organizing in ways that permitted them to compete under the conditions that governed the sociopolitical arena at large'.[35] In little over a decade, Ad Dharm transmuted untouchability from layers of negation into the basis for a new politically informed religious community in Panjab.

Dividing Labour and Labourers

The Ad Dharm assertion of a proud, originary community did not rest entirely on refuting identification with the untouchability of Hinduism. Equally important, though receiving far less scholarly attention, was its challenge to the supposedly traditional alignment between caste and occupation. The simple, stifling equation of Chamar as leather worker or Churha as sweeper was deeply implicated—and just as debilitating—as being labelled an outcaste Hindu.[36] Two stark points coming out of the programme from the 1926 meeting at Mugowal make explicit this rejection:

12. We are agriculturalists; we know our work well. But we are not paid enough in agricultural wages. We cannot take care of our

---

number fifteen-fold across India, it would also irrevocably transform the caste composition of the community. In a vulgar comment capturing the mindset of the elites, one leader is said to have explained the matter rhetorically: 'By making six crore untouchables Sikhs, should we hand over the Darbar Sahib to Chuhras?' Upper-caste Sikhs had little interest in an exponential expansion of their religion if it required a redistribution of power with lower-caste Sikhs. Puri (2003:2698); and Hans (2016: 143–8). See also Viswanathan (1988: ch. 7).

[35] Juergensmeyer (1982: 80, 152–5). See also Gilmartin (1988: chs. 4–6); and Ram (2008).

[36] For a critique of the notion of chamars as leather workers, see Rawat (2011: ch. 2–3). For an account of the evolution of Churha identity in the Delhi region, see Prashad (2000).

130   Navyug Gill

families properly. Vacant lands should be given to the Untouchable community.

13. The government should treat agriculturalists from the Untouchable class on par with agriculturalists from other communities, especially in Lyallpur, Sheikupura, Sargoda, Montgomery, and Multan. In these districts, there should be more land for Untouchables and more employment.[37]

This affirmation of agriculturalist status—emanating from the premium placed on that category in the Punjab Alienation of Land Act of 1901[38]—raises the question of untouchable *economic* as opposed to *religious* identity.

Rather fortuitously, around this same time, the Panjab administration happened to be conducting a series of investigations into the internal dynamics of the agrarian economy. The Board of Economic Inquiry, a government-funded research body established at the turn of the century, sent local interviewers to over a dozen villages for twelve months to record details of both the expenses and returns of cultivation and the patterns of consumption and reproduction by families of landholding proprietors. Just as Ambedkar was demanding separate electorates, and Mangoo Ram was enjoying the census windfall, rural labour practices were coming under new scrutiny from the colonial state.

The most startling revelation from these studies of 'peasant' cultivation is an admission of the very impossibility of that object of inquiry. R.K. Seth and Faiz Ilahi's survey of the village of Durrana Lanhana in Multan District states the problem directly:

It will thus appear that *it is not possible* to describe the working life of *an isolated cultivator* as such with any accuracy. It is invariably so much intermingled with that of his colleagues and members of his family that one might as well consider the combination as a unit for the purposes of the present inquiry.[39]

[37] Juergensmeyer (1982: Appendix B, 300–1).

[38] For more on this pivotal piece of colonial legislation, see Barrier (1966); Islam (1995: 274, 290); and Nazir (2000: 82).

[39] Seth and Ilahi (1938: 30–1). Emphasis added. The labours of women disappear into the masculine assumptions built around the categories 'cultivator', 'peasant', and 'kisan'. For more on the gendered politics of agriculture, see Chowdhry (1994).

Agrarian production could not be reduced and singularized into the discrete labours of a lone peasant. The collective nature of the enterprise meant recognizing and tracking the contributions of different groups within the village. Instead of the North Indian jajmani system,[40] however, the researchers termed what they observed as the *sepidari* system, a similar arrangement of castes performing various labours in exchange for shares in grain: Kumhars providing pots, Mehras carrying water, a Pandit or Mullah offering solace.

For instance, the study from Kala Gaddi Thamman in Lyallpur notes that for making and repairing one plough for a cultivating landowner, a Tarkhan received twenty-two kilogrammes each of wheat and maize, one bundle of un-threshed wheat, and four bundles of green fodder a year. In addition, he would receive 1 rupee plus a measure of cloth at the birth of the cultivator's first son, two rupees on the marriage of a son, 3 rupees on the marriage of a daughter, and a quarter of a rupee on the death of a family elder in exchange for several smaller duties.[41] Yet, in Panjab, this system differed for being largely a product of makeshift custom, wedded neither to age-old beliefs nor a religious order, and far less rigid than conventional representation of jajmani as a fixed law.[42] The performance of tasks seemed to matter more than the identity of the person performing them. Also, the researchers noted that sepidari itself was declining as a form of organizing village relations. From the late nineteenth century onwards, the growth of the canal colonies and military recruitment offered greater opportunities for lower-caste mobility, while the rise of commodity production, market prices, and piece-work monetized (and standardized) the process of remuneration.[43]

Beyond the village-wide constellation of castes and roles, a specific relationship captured the attention of the Board researchers. They reported a common form of labour attachment throughout Panjab called *siri*, where landholding cultivators would contract with landless labourers to provide various agricultural services for an entire season in exchange for a proportion of the harvest.

---

[40] For a critique of the study of jajmani relations, see Commander (1983) and Mayer (1993).

[41] Singh (1932: Appendix A to Ch. 1, 17–18).

[42] See Bhattacharya (1992: 154–65) and Kessinger (1974: 56–75).

[43] For more on the economic role of military recruitment, see Mazumder (2003).

This was not a form of tenancy with an absentee landowner, nor was there a fixed list of tasks to perform or items to deliver as in sepidari arrangements. Although sometimes termed field labourers, siris resembled constant yet unequal companions in agricultural operations, working alongside 'cultivators-proper' in every aspect of cultivation.[44]

Almost all landholding households in Panjab had some form of siri relations. Their payments were based on a share of the produce and food from the cultivators' home, as well as cash advances and other types of patronage. Perhaps most importantly, the kinds of labour they performed were far removed from their caste identity. Whereas a Lohar would be translated into 'blacksmith' by virtue of possessing requisite equipment, training, and capital, and therefore be expected to provide ploughshares and sickles, the vast majority of siris were Chamars and Churhas performing tasks unrelated to leather or sweeping. In the tedious gamut of colonial caste classifications, there is no 'traditional' designation for multifarious agricultural labourers because the supposed fixity of untouchable caste work unravelled precipitously in the countryside.

The study of Gaggar Bhana in Amritsar, for instance, describes how Churhas in particular diverged from their stigmatized label as sweepers, which included removing human faeces (euphemistically called 'night soil') from the homes of landlords. The 'rural Churha', explains Gian Singh, 'has nothing to do with the removal of night soil, which is the principle occupation of the town chuhra'. The reason for this discrepancy is the unique spatial configuration of the faecal economy: there is 'practically no night soil to be removed because there is no system of latrines in the villages'. Instead, 'when necessity arises the fields near the village are used'.[45] In other words, the supposedly traditional occupation of the Churhas only manifested in the confines of the modern city. In the villages of Panjab, the vast majority of Chamars, Churhas, and other lower castes performed the labours of cultivation under the sign of a siri.

---

[44] Siri labour in Panjab thereby differed sharply from the indentured or enslaved labourers of North India as explored in Gyan Prakash's (1990) *Bonded Histories* or the 'pariahs' of Tamil Nadu in Rupa Viswanathan's (1988) *The Pariah Problem*. For more, see Jodhka (2002: 1816); and Ram (2004: 899).

[45] Singh (1928: 25).

Dalit Conversion in Colonial Panjab   133

What was the nature of the relationship between cultivator and siri?[46] Fortunately, the survey of Suner in Ferozepur contains a rare translated copy of an agreement signed by two individuals on 29 June 1932. Titled 'Specimen of agreement between cultivating owner and his siri', it begins with the following sentence: 'I, Chaugutta, son of Karmun—by caste weaver—am a resident of Village Suner, Tahsil Zira,' and am taking a sum of Rs 60 from Tehl Singh, son of Hazara Singh, 'to meet my household expenses'. The loan will be repaid after a full year starting from the first of *Har* (mid-June, after the wheat harvest) but without interest because during that period 'I will be working as siri with Tehl Singh'. Chaugutta agrees to 'look after his cattle and serve him generally as I am ordered', which may entail sleeping beside the cattle at night, in return for one-fifth of the grain produced from the area cultivated by one plough. In addition, he will receive meals from the household of Tehl Singh, but will not have access to green fodder from his land. The agreement then stipulates that if Chaugutta misses more than three days of work in the year, he will be responsible for paying the day wages of any labourer Tehl Singh hires as a temporary replacement. If, for any reason, he breaks the agreement altogether, both his share in grain will be forfeited and he will have to immediately repay his original loan plus 50 per cent interest. At the bottom are the date and name of a witness (one Atma Ram) alongside Chaugutta's age (25) and space for his thumbprint.[47]

Such a short, simple document is, in fact, brimming with disparities of power. Chaugutta's use of the first-person pronoun indicates he is the speaker, but the voice of Tehl Singh resounds throughout. All of the declarations are the duties of the former to be carried out during fixed periods for certain payments against specific consequences. Tehl Singh makes few commitments beyond the initial loan. His caste and age are not disclosed, nor is there even a place for his signature, reflecting how this document was for his use, kept in his possession to add the authority of a written contract to his considerable existing leverage in case

---

[46] Perhaps the most vivid depiction of contemporary low-caste siri labourers is from the song 'Jatt te Siri da Haal' (The Condition of a Jatt and Siri) by the radical leftist poet Sant Ram Udasi from the late 1970s. See, for more, Rahi (2011).

[47] See Dawar (1936: Appendix B to Ch. 1, 24).

Chaugutta became incompliant. There is also a revealing unevenness in the details of the agreement. While it clearly states the amount of money borrowed; dates for repayment and work; entitlements for food, fodder, and the harvest; and the types of penalties, it is silent on what exactly Chaugutta is supposed to do. Aside from caring for Tehl Singh's cattle, he commits to serving 'generally' as 'ordered'. The logic of the ambiguity of labouring tasks becomes clear against the backdrop of the calendar of agricultural operations.

Most of the village studies provide month-by-month descriptions of the labours of cultivation during a given year. In Suner, for example, starting in the middle of June, most of the fields were ploughed and spread with manure while cotton was planted and the sugarcane fields irrigated from the canal. The sowing for maize began in July with regular watering from wells. After the rains in September, other crops such as oilseed and chickpeas were sown. In November, sowing of wheat and some barley began. By late December, the cotton crop was picked and oilseed harvested. In January, the wheat required a few well waterings. From February onwards, the sugarcane was pressed and its juice boiled. In March, the area for sugarcane was re-ploughed and re-planted and the chickpeas harvested. Canal water resumed in April for sowing cotton, which also marked the beginning of the wheat harvest. May and early June were dedicated to threshing wheat, transporting grain to market, and gathering straw. At that point, the new year commenced with yet more ploughing. Tasks for livestock fodder such as regular ploughing, irrigating, harvesting and re-planting, daily feeding and washing of animals, repairing fences on cotton and sugarcane fields, and clearing irrigation channels from canals also continued throughout the year. According to colonial calculations, while the average hours worked in a day ranged from just two in July to over fifteen in May, the number of workers needed per month was never fewer than three and sometimes up to nineteen.[48] These are the myriad labours that Chaugutta would do alongside Tehl Singh, his relatives, and perhaps others. Put differently, there was no single task that only one or the other would perform, and therefore no single cultivator—hence, the Ad Dharm assertion that untouchables were, in fact, agriculturalists.

[48] See Singh (1928: 33–6).

The intertwined, indistinct quality of caste labours is evident in the everyday experiences of cultivation. According to the surveys, during the summer season (April–September), a typical day for a landholder and a siri would begin at sunrise with an empty-stomach departure for the fields. After working until 7 or 8 am, they would eat a small meal consisting of lassi (buttermilk) and one or two rotis (unleavened bread) with *gheo* (clarified butter) brought to them from the cultivator's home, presumably cooked by his wife and/ or other household women. Work resumed until around midday, when a more substantial meal of several rotis with gheo, pickled or cooked vegetables along with some *gur* (unrefined sugar) and more lassi would again be delivered, followed by more work until the approach of sunset. At that point, the cultivator and siri would return to eat the last meal in the former's home, or sometimes separately, consisting of the same rotis and gheo, but now with lentils or, very rarely, some goat or chicken.[49] In Chaugutta and Tehl Singh's situation, a Julaha and presumably a Jatt would thus eat the same food, from the same source (though probably with different utensils, if used), for at least two out of their three daily meals.

Set against the levelling aspect of food consumption, the inequities of this relationship manifested most sharply at harvest. Here, the difference of ownership conferred upon the cultivator the power to pay the siri a portion of the grain they and others produced together. The survey of Gijhi in Rohtak provides a detailed account of the expenses and returns for several cultivators. 'Farmer A', for example, cultivates 28 acres of land with a siri (called a 'servant'). Throughout the winter and spring seasons, he spends approximately Rs 290 on the upkeep of three bullocks, Rs 48 on maintaining a cart, and Rs 23 on various implements (given to sepis such as the Tarkhan and Kumhar), as well as paying Rs 117 in land revenue. The siri receives the value of around Rs 8 in cash and slightly less

---

[49] With shorter days in the winter season (October–March), the number of meals would be reduced to two (at 11 am and 6 pm) but with more gheo and sometimes barley or maize replacing wheat, while during the spring harvest, a fourth meal of rotis and gur would be eaten around 4 pm. Only ex-soldiers had developed the habit of drinking tea by this time, while opium was consumed far more regularly than alcohol. Cultivators also enjoyed greater access to gheo and milk because they owned more and better producing buffalos. See Dawar (1936:170–1); Singh (1932: 153–7); Singh (1928:182–3); and Seth and Ilahi (1938:266–70).

than Rs 6 in food per month (3 *anna* a day), for a total of Rs 164. At harvest, the primary winter crops of wheat and chickpeas plus different fodders, millets, sugarcane, and cotton from the summer generates Rs 1,540. After deducting expenses from the yield, Farmer A therefore nets around Rs 898, or more than five times as much as the siri.[50] The logic of colonial revenue and the rule for calculating net assets both permitted this disparity and erased it from view. By classifying the siri as an expense for the cultivator, akin to maintaining a plough or digging a well, the political economy of this relationship is effaced by the routine keeping of accounts. A human being becomes just another reified item on the balance sheet of an agrarian enterprise.

Yet the siri was never merely an input within a process but an individual with material and social needs, desires, and agency within a changing society. The imputed formalism of the relationship is belied by brief disclosures of discontent and manoeuvring at each end of the hierarchy from the village surveys. Elements of well-being, fairness, and trust became the terrain of constant, if unspectacular, contestation. In Gaggar Bhana, the researcher notes that although siris 'are always allowed to eat as much as they want' from the cultivators' home, 'it is a common cause of grumbling among the small farmers that their laborers eat away their profits'.[51] The situation could be more acute, as in Gijhi, where some landowners would force field labourers to work for rates lower than what they could receive outside the village. 'In these circumstances it is not surprising that the relations between the zemindars and the kamins are very strained', requiring village panchayats (councils) to mediate. The struggle, however, was between uneven parties: despite the boldness of the *kamin*s, the report points out, 'the threats of the zemindars to refuse permission to the kamins to graze their cattle in the village waste, which is the property of the owners, and *fear of starvation*, soon reduced them to submission.'[52]

---

[50] There is a discrepancy in the specific numbers used for Farmer A's income and expenses over five pages of calculations and the summary chart on the last page of this section. The occupier rate of Rs 69 is also not included in the land revenue figure. In the summery, gross income is Rs 1,602 and expenses are Rs 1,014 for a profit of Rs 588. See Narain (1932: 199–203, 213–22).

[51] Singh (1928: 185).

[52] Narain (1932: 16). Emphasis added.

Dalit Conversion in Colonial Panjab   137

More obliquely, the apparent solidity of custom would bend under a shifting balance of power. At harvest, labourers were entitled to an extra bundle of un-threshed wheat at the end of each day. Usually they would take a small bundle, worth a quarter of a rupee (4 anna), but if they 'know that their employer cannot do without them they bring away as heavy a bundle as they can carry worth about 8 annas'.[53] Beyond such sleights, subversion could also be more organized, and therefore more substantial. In Suner, the researcher reports that two siris guarding the crop 'of their master' entered into 'a conspiracy and managed every day to take away some grain which they kept collecting at one place'. Soon they were caught, leading to a panchayat meeting where it was decided to settle the issue internally by making them return the stolen grain— amounting to over 450 kilogrammes—and pay a fine of Rs 10. After the resolution however, two policemen 'happened to reach the village and hearing of the matter called the two culprits and, it was alleged, took [a further] Rs. 5 each from them'.[54] In these and countless other ways, the apparent order and reciprocity between cultivators and siris was, in fact, riven with constant, if not open, turmoil. Tehl Singh's contract is so askew because Chaugutta could resort to straining customary entitlements, pilfering grain, evading tasks, and even escaping the village to preserve or improve his own meagre position.[55]

Cultivation in early twentieth-century Panjab thus permitted neither a discrete division of labour nor labourers. Indeed, siri participation interrupts the narrative of menial labourers as ancillaries in the shadow of the autonomous peasant. Throughout the colonial period and beyond, a person ploughing a field or harvesting a crop would just as likely be a Jatt as a Chamar or Churha. Their relationship might better be described as an asymmetrical agreement between two caste-bound individuals—*one with land and its entitlements and the other without*—combining their labour in order to cultivate the holdings of the former. Yet even this binary is complicated by the fact that the two parties performed parallel tasks and consumed similar foods (though not in identical quantities)

[53] Narain (1932: 17).

[54] Dawar (1936: 88).

[55] For more on reading the insurgent politics within seemingly routine, unremarkable practices, see Guha (1983: ch. 2) and Scott (1985: chs. 1–2).

while receiving disproportionate shares from the same harvest. As noted by one researcher, in rural Panjab, 'social taboo on account of the neglect of observance of caste regulations is practically unknown'.[56] The collective labours of cultivation, therefore, both erased and obfuscated caste hierarchy, by ignoring the most obvious proscriptions on segregated exertion while strictly upholding a stark disparity in returns.

Overcoming the Caste Question?

The political economy of Dalit conversion challenges the conventional framing of the question of caste in at least colonial Panjab. It reveals a critical limit to Ambedkar's arguments from AC. By the early twentieth century, the call for untouchables to abandon Hinduism had been pre-empted not only by longstanding conversion to Sikhism, Islam, and later Christianity, but also by nearly a decade of independent lower-caste organizing. After its founding in 1926, the Ad Dharm articulated a vision of untouchable Panjabis constituting a distinct qaum with its own history, beliefs, and traditions on par with other religious communities. It registered almost half a million adherents in a census five years before the undelivered Lahore speech. Although its political capacity gradually waned, Ad Dharm created educational institutions and a dispersed devotional network that continues to instil reverence for Ravidas and self-respect among Panjabi Dalits to the present.[57] While Ambedkar's efforts brought untouchable issues to the forefront of a new, all-India audience, much of the content of that struggle had longer, more radical, and compelling antecedents.

Despite their differences, Ad Dharm and Ambedkar also held a common solution to the predicament of untouchables. Both believed in and attempted to bring about emancipation in part through conversion into either a new or alternative faith (Ad Dharm or Buddhism). Answering the caste question with religious conversion invokes an adjacent debate from nearly a century earlier in Europe. Karl Marx's 1843 essay 'On the Jewish Question' analyses the limitations of liberalism to address the problem of

---

[56] Bhalla (1922: 142).

[57] For the ongoing legacy of Ad Dharm, see Juergensmeyer (1982: 152–4) and Ram (2007).

difference-as-discrimination by contrasting political and human emancipation. He begins by discussing how, during the nineteenth century, many thinkers argued that to overcome the religious bigotry faced by Jews in Christian Prussia required a secular State that recognized the equal rights of all its citizens. For Marx, however, this meant forcing individuals to live 'a double existence'—artificially split between public citizen and private individual—to only partially relate as equals in one domain of life while continuing to experience their subordination in the other. Aligning the difference of religiosity with the difference of inferiority, Marx points out that people 'do not cease to be religious by virtue of being religious in *private*'. That is why 'the state can liberate itself from a constraint [such as religion] without man himself being *really* liberated'.[58]

Since the exclusion of Jews persists even in a non-religious State, political emancipation from Christianity does not abolish religious bigotry itself, but merely displaces it from a newly constituted public sphere into a private one, where its effects become normalized as features of immutable everyday life. In this sense, the predicament of the Jew serves as a stand-in for any inequality derived from difference, religious or otherwise, that manages to live on despite its repudiation by the state. The fact that an individual could be at once both Jew and citizen—subordinate and equal—belies the very claim to overcoming religious disparity in this manner.

The same holds true of property. The 'political suppression of private property,' argues Marx, 'not only does not abolish private property; it actually presupposes its existence.'[59] In other words, restrictive ownership qualifications for participation in public life might end, but vast disparities in ownership itself would continue unabated. Crucially, Marx extends his argument to *other forms of hierarchy*, stating the 'difference between the religious man and the citizen is the same as that between the shopkeeper and the citizens, between the day-laborer and the citizen, between the landed proprietor and the citizen, between the *living individual* and the *citizen*.'[60] For that reason, while the secular State 'certainly represents a great

[58] See Marx (1978: 32, 34). Emphasis in original. For different readings of the implications of this question, see Mufti (2007: ch. 1); Birla (2009:24–7) Rao (2009:21–6); and Skaria (2015:459–62).

[59] Marx (1978: 33).

[60] Marx (1978: 34). Emphasis in original.

progress'[61] in denying sanction to certain discriminatory practices, it does not attempt to abolish those practices themselves. Inequities not only remain, but are rendered natural. In contrast, Marx offers human emancipation, a horizon where values of secularism and equality transcend the artifice of the public sphere to penetrate all dimensions of social existence. It is through this prospective, aleatory politics, realized 'when the real, individual man has absorbed into himself the abstract citizen',[62] that society might achieve an expansive, holistic emancipation worthy of its potential.

Of course, the distinctive history and shifting conditions of colonial Panjab do not permit any direct application of continental prescriptions. Discussions over religious conversion, in fact, occurred in a context markedly dissimilar to Western Europe, and with even narrower parameters.[63] Lower castes might emancipate themselves in one sense by abandoning a faith that stigmatized them as inferior and impure. They might also enact this rejection openly, as Ambedkar eventually ceased to seek entry into Hindu temples and Ad Dharm created its own distinct places of worship. The postcolonial Indian State further contributed to this process, perhaps best epitomized in making illegal the pejorative use of caste names such as 'Churha'. But within the sphere of the agrarian economy, lower castes would have little choice other than to continue in the discriminatory labours that structured their daily existence. The stigma of caste was felt not only through spiritual denigration or social distancing, or repeating the perverse injunctions of Manu. It was experienced in the routine of performing much of the same labours as a landholder, yet receiving only a fraction of the returns.

What Marx illuminates, then, is the contradictory ideology that underpinned material relations in early twentieth-century Panjabi society. To a Hindu, Sikh, or Muslim landowner, a siri identifying as Hindu, Sikh, Muslim, or even Christian or Ad Dharmi remained a menial labourer. A new qaum could not be equal to other religious communities if the extent of its demand for equality was to seek better employment conditions for its adherents from its antagonists. The politics of Ad Dharm, though effective

---

[61] Marx (1978: 35).

[62] Marx (1978: 46).

[63] For more on the rule of colonial difference, see Chatterjee (1993: ch. 2) and Birla (2009: ch. 4–5).

Dalit Conversion in Colonial Panjab   141

in rupturing the limits of colonial public/private difference, thus simultaneously encountered another set of limitations. While the world of caste may have been turned upside down, it remained at its core the same world and not a new one altogether.[64] We still await a politics with the imaginative capacity and material force to overcome rather than overturn the modern configuration of agrarian caste hierarchy.

Perhaps the real force of Ad Dharm is better appreciated elsewhere, in the realm of dignity, self-confidence, and quotidian empowerment. Just before concluding fieldwork in Jalandhar in the late 1960s, Tom Kessinger reveals a brief exchange with a Chamar interlocutor who was also his friend and roommate. Imploring the latter to hurry up and take a set of keys from him, his unnamed friend, 'while strolling slowly,' replied with a steady, striking nonchalance: 'Chamars don't run any more [sic].'[65] Ad Dharm's struggle thus cannot be measured against an ahistorical standard of 'universal' or 'human' emancipation. Higher agricultural wages and access to vacant common land continues to be a major element in the landless labour movement in both East and West Panjab today.[66] Ambedkar too was not unaware of the foundations of this inequity: as law minister of independent India, he finally abolished the Panjab Alienation of Land Act in 1952. In this sense, the

---

[64] This critique of the limits of inversion invokes Louis Althusser's famous opposition to the commonplace notion that Marx simply inverted Hegel.

This is the basic logic implied by the famous theme of the 'inversion,' the 'setting back in to its feet' of the Hegelian philosophy (dialectic), for if it were really a matter *merely of an inversion*, a restoration of what had been turned upside down, it is clear that to turn an object right round changes neither its nature nor its content by virtue merely of a rotation!. A man on his head is the same man when he is finally walking on his feet.

See Althusser (2005: 73). Emphasis in original.

[65] See Kessinger (1974: 219). For more of the theme of caste and dignity, see Guru (2009).

[66] For the current political situation of landless labourers in East Panjab, see the important collection of articles in Puri (2004); and, more recently, Sandhu (2016). For West Panjab, see Akhtar (2006).

cancellation of his speech might have been ultimately if unintentionally productive. Instead of appearing as a pragmatic appeal directed to an audience that had already taken more radical initiatives, his text circulated across colonial India and beyond as a poignant source of inquiry, provocation, and subversion.

References

Adcock, C.S. 2013. *The Limits of Tolerance: Indian Secularism and the Politics of Religious Freedom*. New York: Oxford University Press.

Akhtar, Aasim Sajjad. 2006. 'The State as Landlord in Pakistani Punjab: Peasant Struggles on the Okara Military Farms.' *Journal of Peasant Studies*, 33(3): 479–501.

Althusser, Louis (trans. by Ben Brewster). 2005. 'On the Young Marx', in *For Marx*. London: Verso.

Ambedkar, B.R. 1979. 'Annihilation of Caste', in Vasant Moon (ed.), *Dr. Babasaheb Ambedkar: Writings and Speeches*. Vol. 1. Bombay: Education Department, Government of Maharashtra.

———. 2014. *Annihilation of Caste: The Annotated Critical Edition*, S. Anand (ed.). London: Verso.

Appadurai, Arjun. 1993. 'Number in the Colonial Imagination', in Carol A. Breckenridge and Peter van der Veer (eds), *Orientalism and the Postcolonial Predicament*. Philadelphia: University of Pennsylvania Press.

Barrier, Norman G. 1966. *The Punjab Alienation of Land Bill of 1900*. Durham: Duke University Press.

Bayly, Susan. 1999. *Caste, Society and Politics in India from the Eighteenth Century to the Modern Age*. New York: Cambridge University Press.

Bhalla, Ram Lall. 1922. *Report on Economic Survey of Bairampur in the Hoshiarpur District*. Lahore: Superintendent of Government Printing.

Bhattacharya, Neeladri. 1992. 'Agricultural Labour and Production: Central and South-East Punjab, 1870–1940', in Gyan Prakash (ed.), *The World of the Rural Labourer in Colonial India*. New Delhi: Oxford University Press.

Birla, Ritu. 2009. Stages of Capital: Law, Culture, and Market Governance in Late Colonial India. Durham: Duke University Press.

Brard, Gurnam S.S. 2007. *East of Indus: My Memories of Old Punjab*. New Delhi: Hemkunt Publishers.

Breman, Jan. 1974. *Patronage and Exploitation: Changing Agrarian Relations in South Gujarat, India*. Berkeley: University of California Press.

Chatterjee, Partha. 1993. *The Nation and Its Fragments: Colonial and Postcolonial Histories*. Princeton: Princeton University Press.

Chowdhry, Prem. 1994. *The Veiled Women: Shifting Gender Equations in Rural Haryana 1880-1900*. New Delhi: Oxford University Press.

Cohn, Bernard S. 1987. 'The Census, Social Structure and Objectification in South Asia,' in *An Anthropologist among the Historians and Other Essays*. New Delhi: Oxford University Press.

Commander, Simon. 1983. 'The Jajmani System of North India: An Examination of its Logic and Status across Two Centuries.' *Modern Asian Studies*, 17 (2): 283–311.

Dawar, Lajpat Rai. 1936. *An Economic Survey of Suner, a Village in the Ferozepore District of the Punjab*. Punjab Village Surveys No. 9. Lahore: The Civil and Military Gazette Press.

Dirks, Nicholas B. 2001. *Castes of Mind: Colonialism and the Making of Modern India*. Princeton: Princeton University Press.

Gidwani, Vinay. 2008. *Capital, Interrupted: Agrarian Development and the Politics of Work in India*. Minneapolis: University of Minnesota Press.

Gill, Navyug. 2019. 'Limits of Conversion: Caste, Labor, and the Question of Emancipation in Colonial Panjab', Journal of Asian Studies, 78 (1):3—22.

Gilmartin, David. 1988. *Empire and Islam: Punjab and the Making of Pakistan*. Berkeley: University of California Press.

Grewal, J.S., Harish K. Puri, and Indu Banga (eds). 2013. *The Ghadar Movement: Background, Ideology, Action and Legacies*. Patiala: Publication Bureau of Punjabi University.

Guha, Ranajit. 1983. *Elementary Aspects of Peasant Insurgency in Colonial India*. New Delhi: Oxford University Press.

Guha, Sumit. 2013. *Beyond Caste: Identity and Power in South Asia, Past and Present*. Leiden: Brill.

Guru, Gopal (ed.). 2009. *Humiliation: Claims and Context*. New Delhi: Oxford University Press.

Hans, Raj Kumar. 2016. 'Making Sense of Dalit Sikh History', in Ramnarayan Rawat and K. Satyanarayana (eds). *Dalit Studies*. Durham: Duke University Press.

Harding, Christopher. 2008. *Religious Transformation in South Asia: The Meanings of Conversion in Colonial Punjab*. New York: Oxford University Press.

Ibbetson, Denzil Charles Jelf. 1883. *Report on the Census of the Panjab, taken in the 17th of February 1881*. Vol. 2. Calcutta: Superintendent of Government Printing.

Islam, M. Mufakharul. 1995. 'The Punjab Land Alienation Act and the Professional Moneylenders.' *Modern Asian Studies*, 29(2): 271–91.

Jodhka, Surinder Singh. 2000. 'Prejudice without Pollution? Scheduled Castes in Contemporary Punjab.' *Journal of Indian School of Political Economy* 12(3–4): 381–403.

———. 2002. 'Caste and Untouchability in Rural Punjab.' *Economic and Political Weekly*, 37(19): 1813–23.

Jones, Kenneth W. 1976. *Arya Dharm: Hindu Consciousness in 19th Century Punjab.* Berkeley: University of California Press.

———. 1981. 'Religious Identity and the Indian Census', in N. Gerald Barrier (ed.), *The Census in British India: New Perspectives.* Delhi: Manohar Publishers.

Judge, Paramjit S. 2003. 'Hierarchical Differentiation among Dalits.' *Economic and Political Weekly*, 38(28): 2990–1.

Juergensmeyer, Mark. 1982. *Religion as Social Vision: The Movement against Untouchability in 20th Century Punjab.* Berkeley: University of California Press.

Kessinger, Tom G. 1974. *Vilyatpur 1848-1968: Social and Economic Change in a North India Village.* Berkeley: University of California Press.

Khan, Khan Ahmad Hasan. 1933. *Census of India, 1931: Volume XVII, Punjab.* Part 1—Report. Lahore: The Civil and Military Gazette Press.

———. 1933. *Census of India, 1931: Volume XVII, Punjab.* Part 2—Tables. Lahore: The Civil and Military Gazette Press.

Kumar, Aishwary. 2015. *Radical Equality: Ambedkar, Gandhi, and the Risk of Democracy.* Stanford: Stanford University Press.

Marx, Karl. 1978. 'On the Jewish Question', in Robert C. Tucker (ed.), *The Marx-Engels Reader.* 2nd ed. New York: W.W. Norton & Company.

Mayer, Peter. 1993. 'Inventing Village Tradition: The Late 19th Century Origins of the North Indian "Jajmani System."' *Modern Asian Studies*, 27(2): 357–95.

Mazumder, Rajit K. 2003. *The Indian Army and the Making of Punjab.* New Delhi: Permanent Black.

Middleton, L., and S.M. Jacob. 1922. *Census of India, 1921: Punjab and Delhi.* Vol. 15, Part II. Lahore: The Civil and Military Gazette Press.

Mufti, Aamir R. 2007. *Enlightenment in the Colony: The Jewish Question and the Crisis of Postcolonial Culture.* Princeton: Princeton University Press.

Narain, Raj. 1932. *An Economic Survey of Gijhi, a Village in the Rohtak District of the Punjab.* Punjab Village Surveys No. 2. Lahore: The Civil and Military Gazette Press.

Nazir, Pervaiz. 2000. 'Origins of Debt, Mortgage and Alienation of Land in Early Modern Punjab.' *Journal of Peasant Studies*, 27(3): 55–91.

Oberoi, Harjot. 1994. *The Construction of Religious Boundaries: Culture, Identity, and Diversity in the Sikh Tradition.* Chicago: University of Chicago Press.

Pandian, M.S.S. 2007. *Brahmin and Non-Brahmin: Genealogies of the Tamil Political Present.* New Delhi: Permanent Black.

Prakash, Gyan. 1990. *Bonded Histories: Genealogies of Labor Servitude in Colonial India.* Cambridge: Cambridge University Press.

Prashad, Vijay. 2000. *Untouchable Freedom: A Social History of a Dalit Community.* New York: Oxford University Press.

Puri, Harish K. 1993. *Ghadar Movement: Ideology, Organization, and Strategy.* Amritsar: Guru Nanak Dev University Press.

———. 2003. 'Scheduled Castes in Sikh Community: A Historical Perspective.' *Economic and Political Weekly,* 38 (26): 2693–701.

———, (ed.). 2004. *Dalits in Regional Context.* Jaipur: Rawat Publishers.

Rahi, Rajinder (ed.). 2011. *Sant Ram Udasi: Jeevan ate Samuchi Rachna,* [*Life and Collected Works*]. Ludhiana: Chetna Parkashan.

Ram, Ronki. 2004. 'Untouchability in India with a Difference: Ad Dharm, Dalit Assertion, and Caste Conflicts in Punjab.' *Asian Survey,* 44(6): 895–912.

———. 2007. 'Social Exclusion, Resistance and Deras: Exploring the Myth of Casteless Sikh Society in Punjab.' *Economic and Political Weekly,* 42(40): 4066–74.

———. 2008. 'Ravidass Deras and Social Protest: Making Sense of Dalit Consciousness in Punjab (India).' *The Journal of Asian Studies,* 67(4): 1341–64.

Ramnath, Maia. 2011. *Haj to Utopia: How the Ghadar Movement Charted Global Radicalism and Attempted to Overthrow the British Empire.* Berkeley: University of California Press.

Rao, Anupama. 2009. *The Caste Question: Dalits and the Politics of Modern India.* Berkeley: University of California Press.

Rawat, Ramnarayan S. 2011. *Reconsidering Untouchability: Chamars and Dalit History in North India.* Bloomington: Indiana University Press.

Sandhu, Amandeep. 2016. 'A Growing Movement in Jhaloor Illustrates how Dalit Villagers in Punjab are Reclaiming their Right to Panchayat Land.' *The Caravan: A Journal of Politics and Culture,* 29 November 2016.

Saunders, Leslie S. 1873. *Report on the Revised Land Revenue Settlement of the Lahore District in the Lahore Division of the Panjab, 1865–69.* Lahore: Central Jail Press.

Scott, James C. 1985. *Weapons of the Weak: Everyday forms of Peasant Resistance.* New Haven: Yale University Press.

Seth, R.K., and Faiz Ilahi. 1938. *An Economic Survey of Durrana Langana, a Village in the Multan District of the Punjab*. Punjab Village Surveys No. 11. Lahore: The Civil and Military Gazette Press.

Singh, Randhir. 1932. *An Economic Survey of Kala Gaddi Thamman (Chak 73 G.B), a Village in the Lyallpur District of the Punjab*. Punjab Village Surveys No. 4. Lahore: The Civil and Military Gazette Press.

Singh, Sardar Gian. 1928. *An Economic Survey of Gaggar Bhana, a Village in the Amritsar District of the Punjab*. Punjab Village Surveys No. 1. Lahore: The Civil and Military Gazette Press.

Skaria, Ajay. 2015. 'Ambedkar, Marx and the Buddhist Question.' *South Asia: Journal of South Asian Studies*, 38(3): 450–65.

Tandon, Prakash. 1968. *Punjabi Century: 1857–1947*. Berkeley: University of California Press.

Viswanathan, Gauri. 1988. *Outside the Fold: Conversion, Modernity, and Belief*. Princeton: Princeton University Press.

Viswanath, Rupa. 2014. *The Pariah Problem: Caste, Religion, and the Social in Modern India*. New York: Columbia University Press.

7

The Fractured Society of the Republic

SHAILAJA MENON

Foregrounding Ideology

India's Constitution bore the imprint of a long nationalist movement that made choices that have shaped its trajectory. The first and most significant choice was the idea of constitutionalism itself. The Indian nationalist movement, while radical in its normative hopes, was self-consciously a constitutional movement. In its early phases, it spoke the language of English law. Even when it acquired, under Gandhi, the character of a mass movement, it was anti-revolutionary. It placed a premium on eschewing violence as a means of overturning social order or advancing political goals. Even if not expressed in the formal language of law, a grammar of constitutionalism has marked India's mainstream political choices. Although the idea of non-violence has been associated with Gandhi's legacy, its greatest political practitioners have been India's most marginalized groups. Dalits, who were India's most unimaginably oppressed social groups, with most reason to resent the structural violence of India's inherited social and political order, have, in a sense, been at the forefront of owning a constitutional culture. This is partly due to the fact that the Constitution gave political representation and representation in public jobs to Dalits, and partly due to the fact that the Constitution saw itself as a charter of social reform.[1]

---

[1] For details refer, Choudhry, Khosla, and Mehta (2016).

The Constitution bears the unmistakable stamp of Ambedkar's intellectual prowess. His life's trajectory is replete with instances where his social, economic, and political ideas have been translated into action. As a practical political philosopher, he proved himself a person of action in realizing the rights and entitlements for the depressed classes by representing them in many commissions set up by the colonial state. In 1936, Ambedkar established the Independent Labour Party (ILP), which called for fair working conditions for labour, including fair wages and the right to strike. For him, a political party does not exist merely for the sake of winning elections but for the sake of *'educating, agitating and organizing'* so that the party establishes contacts with the masses to look into the policies, ideas, and principles. The role of the party is to create class consciousness among the masses so that the present leadership can be challenged through elections. 'Therefore before passing any judgment on any scheme of politics it is essential that one must consider the ground plan, in other words to consider the social structure which has a profound effect on the political structure. It may modify it in its working, it may nullify it or it may even make a mockery of it'.[2] This struggle of Ambedkar is a pointer to his belief that political mobilization through education and awareness alone help untouchables gain representation in the political structure. In the absence of social and economic power, gaining political power is the only plausible way to secure or regain their lost self-respect. This is the only path to dignity and self-development. The sole object of political power is to pursue social and economic reform. Unfortunately, in the last seven decades, the issue of representation that Ambedkar evoked has been diluted to serve narrow caste and communal identities. The society is further polarized and people's aspirations for leading a dignified life have been ignored.

According to Ambedkar, the essentials of a free social order were set by the French Revolution. The terms of association between individuals in a society must be founded on the principles of liberty, equality, and fraternity.[3] For him, democracy is more than a form of government. Democratic society is characterized by the absence of stratification of society into classes and their willingness to reciprocate mutual interests and benefits. From this perspective,

[2] Shashi (1992: 162).
[3] Gore (1993: 260–1).

the purpose of democracy is not so much to curb an autocratic king but to bring about revolutionary changes in the social and economic life of the people without any bloodshed. He examined the caste-ridden Hindu society on the criterion of democracy and observed that the 'caste system is a grave impediment in the path of the democracy'.[4] The roots of democracy lie not in the form of government but in the social relationships and the terms of association between the people who form the society. Community of purpose, desire for welfare, loyalty to public ends, and mutuality of cooperation are the essential hallmarks of democratic society.

Ambedkar insisted on economic and social rights being included in the Constitution so that the State will have a blueprint to uphold the rights of every subject to life, liberty, pursuit of happiness, free speech, and free exercise of belief and religion. The State has a positive role to play to remove the socio-economic and political inequalities by ensuring safeguards to the minorities and downtrodden. Though supreme liberty is not possible for an individual in the society, the State exists to usher in the conditions conducive to an understanding between the authority of the State and the liberty of the individuals. Of course, constitutional methods can always be resorted to, to get the grievances against the State redressed.

This strand of thinking forms the basis and hovers around the constitutional scheme. The purpose of the Indian Constitution is not merely to create organs of the State but to limit their authority through a system of checks and balances, the absence of which may lead to tyranny and oppression. This forms the basis of the preamble, which lays down the basic objectives of liberty, equality, and fraternity. The fundamental rights consist of the basic human rights. Abolition of disabilities, including all forms of social disabilities (practices of untouchability, patriarchy, religious majoritarianism, and the like), and rights guaranteed to minorities, including women, ensures protection from exploitation. The very idea behind incorporating certain basic rights and remedies for violation of those rights in the chapter on fundamental rights is to balance individual liberty and the need for social control. This unique contribution of Ambedkar has gone a long way in the conception of social justice.

[4] Gore (1993: 260–1).

The fundamental rights reflect the revolutionary potential of the Constitution. As observed by Ambedkar, 'the object of the fundamental rights is two-fold, firstly that every citizen must be in a position to claim those rights and secondly they must be binding upon every authority'. He said, 'I shall presently explain what the word "authority" means upon every authority which has got either the power to make laws or the power to have discretion vested in it'. He added, 'It is quite clear that if the fundamental rights are to be clear, then they must be binding not only upon the central government but binding upon the provincial government'. He further added that 'they must not only be binding upon the government established in the Indian states, they must also be binding upon district local boards, municipalities, even village panchayat and taluka boards in-fact, every authority which has been created by law and which has got certain power to make rules or make laws'.[5]

In the Indian Constitution's fundamental rights chapter, three articles have been singled out for special attention by the Supreme Court: (a) Article 14, which guarantees equality before law and equal protection of laws; (b) Article 19(1), which guarantees the freedoms of speech and expression, association, assembly, and movement, and occupation, trade, or business; and (c) Article 21, which guarantees life and personal liberty. *The Supreme Court has observed that these three articles constitute a 'golden triangle', standing 'between the heaven of freedom into which Tagore wanted his country to awake and the abyss of unrestrained power'.*[6]

> However, what Articles 14, 19(1) and 21 protect against is the abyss of unrestrained *State* power. In the finest tradition of liberal philosophy, the rights to equality, to freedom, and to life constitute a bulwark for the individual against the tyranny of the majority, exercised through the coercive arms of the State. They ensure that the great disparity in power between individual and State does not translate into oppression, domination, and erasure. They preserve every person's bodily integrity and basic dignity against the arbitrary or vengeful actions of the State. It is a noble story, and one that deserves to be told and retold. It is a story that has its origins in

---

[5] Ambedkar (1994: 375).

[6] Supreme Court of India Minerva Mills Ltd. & Ors vs Union Of India & Ors on 31 July 1980. IndianKanoon.org. Available at https://indiankanoon.org/doc/1939993/, accessed 18 September 2018.

The Fractured Society of the Republic　　　151

the Enlightenment, and in the French and American Revolutions of the late-Eighteenth Century, which firmly established the 'rights of Man' (and subsequently, after substantial struggle, the rights of woman) against the despotic power of State and sovereign.[7]

Ambedkar designed the fundamental rights with the chief objective of eliminating and abolishing inequalities in society. He had fully realized that rights without legal remedies were of no use.[8] Hence, the safeguards he contemplated against the possible intervention of the State or the individual was through the judicial power guided by the due process of law. Due to Ambedkar's effort, the fundamental rights as provided in the Indian Constitution were more elaborate and comprehensive than the Bill of Rights or rights in any other constitution.[9] Ambedkar devised and incorporated the philosophy of rights based on the need for balancing individual liberty and the need for social control, which alone could provide social and economic justice.

The heart of the Constitution is that fundamental rights are guaranteed to every citizen. These fundamental rights are the result of lessons drawn from the history of the world from the events that have taken place both at the domestic and global level. The main idea behind the fundamental rights is to ensure certain basic rights to the citizens so that they are not at the mercy of the shifting opinions of the legislators. Ambedkar stated that the object of the fundamental rights is to ensure, firstly that 'every citizen must be in a position to claim those rights; secondly they must be binding on every authority'.[10]

Ambedkar, along with many other political personalities, made intense efforts to guarantee equality to the disadvantaged sections of the population (i.e., the SCs and the minorities in particular and for all citizens in general) through constitutional provisions aimed at preventing discrimination and promoting social justice. This was sought to be done through fundamental rights guaranteeing equality before law and equal protection of law (Article 14); prohibition of discrimination on grounds of religion, race, caste, sex, or place of birth (Article 15); equality of opportunity in

[7] Bhatia (2016b).
[8] Mishra (1992: 231).
[9] Kuber (1973: 249).
[10] Ramaswamy (1992: 200).

152 Shailaja Menon

matters of public employment (Article 16); abolition of untouchability (Article 17); and prohibition of traffic in human beings and forced labour (Article 23). All these forces would 'abolish social inequality, social stigma and social disabilities in our society'.[11] In this context, comprehensive legal machinery was endorsed to make the fundamental rights justiciable.

While drafting provisions to safeguard the rights of the citizens vis-a-vis the excesses committed by the State, Ambedkar was foresighted enough to include provisions to uphold human rights and dignity between the citizenry as Indian society was deeply divided on the basis of caste, religion, gender, race, and ethnicity. *The fundamental rights chapter has another 'golden triangle'. It is within this triangle that the truly revolutionary potential of the Indian Constitution is contained, which at the time of framing marked a radical break with the established way of doing things and constituted the heart of Ambedkar's Constitution.*[12]

The three points of the triangle are Articles 15(2), 17, and 23 whereby (*a*) Article 15(2) prohibits any *citizen* from discriminating against *any other citizen*, on the basis of religion, caste, sex, race, or place of birth, with regard to access to shops, public restaurants, hotels, and place of public entertainment; (*b*) Article 17 abolishes the practice of 'untouchability' in *any form*; and (*c*) Article 23 prohibits human trafficking, *begaar*, and similar forms of *forced labour*.

As Ambedkar well understood, 'force' was not limited to crude physical compulsion, but included economic compulsion as well. In the Constituent Assembly Debates, it was he who famously called for 'economic democracy', instantiated by the principle of 'one man, one value.'

> Each of these articles protects the individual not against the State, but against other individuals and against communities. And at the heart of the triangle lies Ambedkar's revolutionary insight: that the denial of human dignity, both material and symbolic, is caused not only by public power, but by private power as well—and the task of Constitutionalism is not limited to satisfactorily regulating public power in service of liberty, but extends to positively guaranteeing human freedom even against the excesses of private

[11] Ramaswamy (1992: 273).
[12] Bhatia (2016b).

power. The word 'fraternity' is as old as the French Revolution; but it is in the Indian Constitution that it first acquired sense and meaning.[13]

Interrogating Caste

The foremost mission for which Ambedkar dedicated his life and for which he carried on several battles (Bahishkrit Hitkarini Sabha, Mahad Satyagraha, and so on), revolved around the abolition of untouchability in all its forms. He championed the cause of the untouchables and fought for their liberation. He demanded the settlement of their political rights even before Independence. During the Mahad Satyagraha, he argued that the untouchables have a right to access water from the tank. Thus, with the Mahad Satyagraha, the discourse of rights entered the political lexicon of the untouchables. When he initiated the temple entry movement, he famously stated that *'the issue is not entry, but equality'*. Despite being indifferent to religion, Ambedkar realized that through the denial of equal access to religious and sacred spaces, a hierarchical society reinforces inequality.[14]

At the First Round Table Conference (RTC) in 1930, Ambedkar submitted a memorandum to the Minorities Committee, demanding equal citizenship rights for the 'Depressed classes' and proposing an 'anti-boycott' rule, which would punish whoever 'abstain[ed] from such social, professional or business relations as he would, having regard to such existing customs in the community which are not inconsistent with any fundamental right or other rights of citizenship declared in the Constitution, ordinarily maintain with such person'.[15] He quoted the State Committee report, which, two years earlier, had observed that the boycott had both social and economic consequences, since it was used to prevent 'the Depressed Classes from using the commonly used paths and the stoppage of sale of the necessaries of life by the village Bania'.[16]

---

[13] Bhatia (2016b).

[14] Bhatia (2016a).

[15] For details, see Ambedkar (2014b: 171–9).

[16] B.R. Ambedkar. 1943. 'Mr. Gandhi and the Emancipation of the Untouchables'. Dr Ambedkar Books, 1 September 1943, p. 17. Available at https://drambedkarbooks.files.wordpress.com/2009/03/mr.docp, accessed 26 January 2018.

Writing about his experiences as late as 1945, in *What Congress and Gandhi Have Done to the Untouchables*, Ambedkar reiterated this stand; and three years later, contemporaneous with the framing of the Constitution, in *The Untouchables*, he framed the unique experiences of exclusion: '[Untouchability] is not a case of social separation, a mere stoppage of social intercourse for a temporary period. It is a case of territorial segregation and of a *cordon sanitaire* putting the impure people inside a barbed wire into a sort of a cage.'[17]

The genesis of Articles 15(2) and 17, therefore, lie in Ambedkar's experiences with a society where access to basic public goods, such as roads, water, the market, and religion, was mediated by community status. The objective of these articles was to transform that reality. In the debates preceding the framing of Article 15(2), Ambedkar clarified that the word 'shops' was not limited merely to the physical space of a shop, but extended to any provision of services—or, in other words, to any economic transaction. Article 15(2), therefore, prevented citizens or groups from leveraging their economic power and dominance to exclude others from accessing the basic necessities of life through the marketplace. Similarly, in the debates surrounding Article 17, Ambedkar consistently refused to accede to demands for 'narrowing down' the scope of the article, or 'defining' the word 'untouchability' in any specific way. For Ambedkar, 'untouchability' was not a term of art, but an entire set of experiences of exclusion, stigmatization, and segregation— once again, practised by the community upon its members, with no intervention by the State.[18]

Representation and the Politics of Presence

According to Ambedkar,

[P]olitics is nothing but to be realistic, there is very little that is academic. It is therefore that before passing any judgement on any scheme of politics it is essential that one must consider the ground plan, in other words to consider the social structure which has a profound effect on the political structure. It may modify it in its working, it may nullify it or it may even make mockery of it.[19]

[17] Ambedkar quoted in Ramachandran (2016). Also see Bhatia (2016b).
[18] Bhatia (2016b).
[19] Ambedkar (2014a: 167).

The Fractured Society of the Republic 155

He endorsed and admired the conception of 'parliamentary government' as government by discussion. A democratic government, for Ambedkar, presupposes a democratic form of society. According to Rodrigues,

> Ambedkar's commitment to democracy as the mode of governance was unwavering but he argued that democracy needed to become a way of life. He developed some interesting arguments on why parliamentary democracy was the most suitable form of government for India and advocated feasible modes of representation and franchise. His writings dwell extensively on such monumental issues as the presidential versus parliamentary form of government, the relationship between the executive and legislature, the role of the judiciary and judicial review, Constitutional bodies such as the election commission, the federal division of powers, states in a federation, the role of the governor, the Constitution and the legislature, Constitutional amendments, political parties and public opinion.[20]

The formal framework of democracy is of no value and would indeed be a misfit if there was no social democracy. Ambedkar said that politicians will never realize that democracy was not a form of government but that it was a form of society. It may not be necessary for a democratic society to be marked by unity, by community of purpose, by loyalty to public ends, and by mutuality of sympathy. But it does unmistakably involve two things: it is an attitude of mind, an attitude of respect and equality towards their fellows, and secondly, it is a social organization free from rigid social barriers. For him, democracy is incompatible and inconsistent with isolation and exclusiveness resulting in the distinction between the privileged and the unprivileged. He further said that there are three important aspects that lie in the parliamentary system of government. One is the denial of hereditary rule, followed by free and fair elections from time to time. Secondly, no individual can take for granted the authority that he or she knows everything and that he or she can make the laws and carry the government; this follows by laws, which will be made by the representatives of the people. Thirdly, the elected representatives, the legislators, and ministers must enjoy the confidence of the people. Finally, in

---

[20] Rodrigues (2002: 34).

this system, the significance of rights is recognized and protected constitutionally.

Democracy rests on four principles: (*a*) The individual is an end in himself or herself. (*b*) The individual has certain inalienable rights that must be guaranteed to him or her by the Constitution. (*c*) The individual shall not be required to relinquish any of his or her constitutional rights as a condition to the receipt of a privilege. (*d*) The State shall not delegate powers to private persons to govern others.[21]

According to Ambedkar, one of the foremost conditions for the success of democracy is that there must be no glaring inequalities in society. Democracy cannot succeed in societies with a pyramidal structure with the base having to support a privileged superstructure. In a democracy, everybody has a vote, even the oppressed and the suppressed, and since we adopt majority rule as a result of majority decision, it is possible that the privileged few will not willingly and voluntarily surrender their privileges. Such structural changes are extremely difficult to manoeuvre as reflected by the approach paper to the twelfth Five Year Plan, which emphasizes social inclusion. The progress towards inclusiveness is more difficult to assess, because inclusiveness is a multidimensional concept. Inclusive growth should result in lower incidence of poverty, broad-based and significant improvement in health outcomes, universal access for children to school, increased access to higher education, and improved standards of education, including skill development. It should also be reflected in better opportunities for both wage employment and livelihood, and in improvement in provision of basic amenities such as water, electricity, roads, sanitation, and housing. Particular attention needs to be paid to the needs of the marginalized groups, especially women and children who account for 70 per cent of the population. Minorities and other excluded groups also need special programmes to bring them into the mainstream.[22]

The successful working of democracy is also based on the existence of an Opposition and a multi-party system, because democracy means a veto of power. Ambedkar believed that democracy questions and hits at the base of hereditary or autocratic authority. The Opposition means that the government is always on the anvil.

[21] Ambedkar (1979: 409).
[22] Planning Commission (2011: 7).

The government must justify every act that it does to those of the people who do not belong to its party. For him, the existence of Opposition is a condition precedent to democracy. Ambedkar pointed out that when the party in power favours its own people in administrative matters and policies, it leads to further discrimination and inequity in society. He felt that in a democracy, there must be no oppression by the majority of the minority. The minority must always feel that although the former is carrying on the government, the latter is safe. Gradually, the minorities are being made invisible in India's body politics. In the 2014 elections, the Bharatiya Janata Party (BJP) came to power without a single elected Muslim MP—in any case, it had fielded only seven Muslims (five in Jammu and Kashmir and Bengal alone) out of a total of 482 candidates. The total Muslim representation in Parliament fell to 4 per cent, the lowest since 1957.[23] However, when one political party wins an absolute majority, there is a gradual erosion of the federal structure and the Opposition is discredited. The dialogue between the various political parties is characterized by extreme bitterness and crude speech devoid of any decency. To illustrate, Amit Shah, the BJP party president, described the opposition parties as cats, dogs, and snakes, saying that the BJP is like a mega wave that has hit the Opposition hard. 'And when flood comes, all cats, dogs, snakes and mongooses take refuge under the banyan tree and unite'.[24]

Democracy is not merely numbers but also requires a moral order in society. Ambedkar envisaged it as constitutional morality. If morals and politics are segregated as different connotations, it would result in a deep crisis in governance. Democracy is a free government having immense space for social life. Citizens are free to carry on without interference of law, or if laws have to be made, the lawmakers accept that society will have enough morality in it to make the law a success. Ambedkar appreciated Harold Laski as the only person who has categorically asserted that the moral order is taken for granted in democracy.[25] The government may pass the laws and implement them but unless there is morality in the society, law cannot achieve any success. For him, politics was an endless striving for social justice. Ironically, contemporary politics

[23] Mannathukkaren (2018).
[24] *India Today* (2018).
[25] Bharill (:1977: 189).

has been reduced to seeking votes while pandering to the lowest common denominator. The political class, instead of addressing the structural roots of caste and gender oppression, poverty, and socio-economic inequities, squanders public resources in hosting god-men/women that cater to the status quo. To exemplify, the state of Haryana, notorious for violence against women and lower castes, invited a Jain monk, Tarun Sagar, to address the State Assembly. The monk was seated above the elected representatives and observed that, 'The control of dharma over politics is essential. Dharma is the husband, politics is the wife. It is the duty of every husband to protect his wife. It is the duty of every wife to accept the discipline of her husband. If there is no control of dharma over politics, it will be like an elephant out of control.'[26] *The moral republic of dharma evoked here is contrary to the constitutional morality.*

Privileging the State

Ambedkar believed that the State is an essential political organization for the welfare of society. As a necessary institution, it functions for the welfare of the people in a civilized and democratic space by by creating an enabling environment for development. The endeavour of State organization is to uphold the right of every subject to life, liberty, and pursuit of happiness and to freedom of speech and freedom of exercise of belief in religion. In other words, democracy, happiness, welfare, and the rights of the people are the basic character. The role of the State is to remove social, political, and economic inequalities by providing better opportunities to the suppressed classes. And moreover, the State is a positive institution for the protection of the downtrodden and minorities and their rights to enjoy freedom from want and fear. And finally, it has to ensure internal peace and prevent external aggression.

As a staunch supporter of parliamentary democracy and its traditions, Ambedkar preferred the American model, which was based on the theory of separation of powers between the three organs of government and was advocated by John Locke and Montesquieu. He stated that only then a sense of balance between the authority of the government and individual liberty

---

[26] Sandhu (2016).

The Fractured Society of the Republic 159

could be struck. There should be separation of powers between the legislature, executive, and judiciary. Discussing the question of the executive in India, Ambedkar disapproved of the British type of executive, because, according to him, an unalterable communal majority in India may prove oppressive to the minorities. The minorities, especially the depressed classes, may be crushed. The aim of a good executive branch of the government must be: (a) to prevent the majority from forming a government without giving any opportunity to the minorities to have a say in the matter; (b) to prevent the majority from having exclusive control over administration and thereby making the tyranny over the minority by the majority possible; (c) to prevent the inclusion by the majority party in the executive of representative of the minorities who do not have the confidence of the minorities; (d) to provide a stable executive necessary for good and efficient administration.[27]

Social changes are effected by laws made by the legislative branch of the government and the executive must implement those laws. It must not override and interfere with the power extended by the laws and the legislative branch of government. An independent and important judiciary must prevent them from overreaching their authority and also punish those who violate the rights given to the individuals in the Constitution. Democracy can only succeed if there are no glaring inequalities in society. No individual class should enjoy monopoly privileges. There is a need for a healthy Opposition to provide checks and balances in a multi-party system. The majority should never dominate the minority. The latter should feel a sense of security that their rights are protected. A truly democratic system must enable the individual to develop all his/her inherent capacities. For this to happen, it was essential to link political democracy with economic and social democracy. This was one of the main objectives of the Indian Constitution, and particularly of the directive principles. Dr Ambedkar himself put it as follows:

> Our object in framing the Constitution is really two-fold: (1) To lay down the form of political democracy, and (2) To lay down that our ideal is economic democracy and also to prescribe that every Government whatever is in power shall strive to bring about

---

[27] Ambedkar (1979).

economic democracy. The directive principles have a great value; for they lay down that our ideal is economic democracy.[28]

This revolutionary conception of democracy, however, fell into oblivion soon after Independence. Indian democracy essentially went the same way as parliamentary democracy. In short, Indian democracy is trapped in a vicious circle of exclusion and elitism. Because underprivileged sections of the population are excluded from active participation in democratic politics, their aspirations and priorities are not reflected in public policy. The elitist orientation of public policy, in turn, perpetuates the deprivations (poverty, hunger, illiteracy, discrimination, and the like) that disempowers people and prevents them from participating in democratic politics.

While defending the directive principles, Ambedkar argued that essentially in a democracy, legal action is not the only means of holding the State accountable to its responsibilities. In cases where rights cannot be enforced through the courts, they can be asserted through other democratic means, based for instance on parliamentary interventions, the electoral process, the media, international solidarity, street action, or even civil disobedience.

The root of the problem was identified quite clearly by Dr Ambedkar in the context of his argument for linking political democracy with economic and social democracy. 'On the 26th of January 1950,' he said, 'we are going to enter into a life of contradictions. In politics we will have equality and in social and economic life we will have inequality.'[29] The contradiction is still with us today, and in some respects at least, the problem is even intensifying at this time of growing inequality and elitism.

In order to ensure that all the citizens enjoy the entitlements, society requires a political organization and this role is fulfilled by the State. *It is quite interesting to note that Ambedkar relied heavily on state and constitutional methods for realizing the liberal values he espoused for the amelioration of the erstwhile*

---

[28] B.R. Ambedkar. 'Constituent Assembly Debates'. Indian Kanoon, 19 November 1948. Available at https://indiankanoon.org/docfragment/682692/?formInput=democracy, accessed 12 February 2020.

[29] See B.R. Ambedkar, Final Speech in the Constituent Assembly, 25 November 1949 in Ambedkar (1994: 1216).

untouchables. He felt that the State is an essential political organization whose endeavour is to uphold the rights of every subject to life, liberty, pursuit of happiness, free speech, and free exercise of belief and religion. The State has a positive role to play to remove the socio-economic and political inequalities by ensuring safeguards to the minorities and downtrodden. Though supreme liberty is not possible for any individual in the society, the State exists to usher the conditions conducive for understanding between the authority of the State and the liberty of the individuals. Of course, the constitutional methods can always be resorted to for redressal of the grievances against the State.

For Ambedkar, the ballot paper stood for direct and active participation in the regulation of the terms upon which the associated life shall be sustained. The franchise based on property and privilege or private ownership is absolutely wrong. While opposing the class electorates, he emphasized that 'in democracy the ultimate principle is after all self-government and that means that final decision on all matters must be made by popularly elected persons and not by experts. It is moreover noteworthy that the advice of such people is not always serviceable to the house. This strand of thinking perpetrates the entire spirit of the Constitution'.[30]

Ambedkar defended the parliamentary form of government because it embodies what he calls the principle of 'responsibility'. By this, he means that the executive will be subject to 'daily assessment'. While elections will give an opportunity for the people to engage in what he calls 'periodic assessment', the arsenal of parliamentary democracy will facilitate daily assessment in the form of resolutions to no confidence motions, debates to adjournment motions, and so on. The function of the Parliament is not so much to *represent* popular sovereignty as it is to debate and constantly question government.[31]

The Contemporary Scenario

The (Rashtriya Swayamsevak Sangh) RSS-BJP combine has fine-tuned its political strategy and, chameleon-like, forge their words to suit different occasions. Apparently, the conductor of the grand

---

[30] Ambedkar (1982: 347).
[31] Mehta (2010: 3).

orchestra is located in Nagpur. In his public utterances, PM Modi sticks to the goal of development, bringing in mothers and sisters along with soldiers as extremely valuable for nation building. He never invokes the guiding spirits of the RSS in his public addresses. In his 71st Independence Day speech, he appealed to the values derived from *sudharshan chakradhari* Mohan to *charkhadhari* Mohan. The 'nation' anyway is aware about the other 'Mohan' who is the soul force behind the 'cultural awakening' of Hindu India.

The alter ego of the PM, Amit Shah, never minces his words about the ultimate agenda of his party. 'It is only in India that mutts and religious institutions work along with the government and even more than the government for the welfare of society'.[32] If religious institutions are better than the State, why do we need the State at all? He dismissed very smoothly the entire ethos of constitutional morality, the democratic and secular country for which thousands braved the gallows and prisons in their fight against colonial rule. The RSS and its cronies were never part of this struggle and, hence, will not understand the price that ordinary Indians paid for achieving freedom, equality, and justice. Their only icon—V.D. Savarkar—cravenly begged the British to release him from the Cellular Jail. Yet another ideologue, Ram Madhav, cleverly takes forward the discourse of dharma and, in order to substantiate it, quotes another study that argues that America is essentially a nation with a conservative ethos. There is a tacit admission that India's case is also similar. He cites Vivekananda's dictum '*Dharma Praana Bharata*' (Dharma is the soul force of Bharat) and this vision of Bharat is 'reflected in the genius of the country, which is rooted in its religio-social institutions like state, family, caste, guru and festival. There is even an economic idea centered around work, sharing happiness and charity'.[33] A common citizen is supposed to pay taxes but wealthy temples are exempted from such measures. One can discern a change in the temple discourse. It has proceeded beyond dharma and karma and focuses on these worldly issues. How can one conceive of a poverty-free India when it is scripturally compelled and justified to donate to temples? At a neighbouring temple, during the evening *aarti*, the loudspeakers speak about banning cow slaughter and that the cow should be declared the

---

[32] *Indian Express* (2017: 7).
[33] Madhav (2017).

national animal. The majority of the shops in Delhi seek charity in the name of the 'mother cow'. Not surprisingly, in the Aryan heartland of UP where the lines between the temple and state have been blurred, a yogi has become a political functionary. As an MP sitting in the Opposition, he questioned the state apathy towards the children, but as the chief minister, Yogi Adityanath has proved woefully inadequate in tackling the health crisis. Here, one can find ambulances for cows, but young children are medically massacred for want of basic healthcare. One shudders to think of the repercussions if, instead of children, cows would have died. A cultural war would have been declared against the Dalits and minorities. Presumably, this reflects the new Indian 'genius' at work.

In 2017, 150 Hindu outfits met in Goa to draw up a programme to establish a 'Hindu Rashtra' in India by 2023; the BJP, the RSS, and the Vishva Hindu Parishad (VHP) had distanced themselves from this event. The conclave was organized by the Hindu Janajagruti Samiti (HJS), the sister outfit of Sanatan Sanstha, some activists of which were accused of the murder of rationalist Narendra Dabholkar in August 2013.[34] The agenda comprised the following: how to create an 'awakening' of dharma (duty), which includes lessons on how to worship, dress, comb one's hair 'as per Hindu culture', and the 'futility of Bharatiya democracy'; how to counter 'love jihad', the notion that Muslim men want to marry and convert Hindu women as part of a conspiracy to Islamize India; conversions by Christians and other acts by 'anti-Hindu sects'; how to defend yourself— 'trainers' are available—with sticks, catapults, nunchakus (to mention anything deadlier may invite unwanted attention, but members of the Samiti's sister organization, the shadowy Sanatan Sanstha, have dabbled with improvised explosive devices, on which the Maharashtra government, in 2016, sought a ban); how to oppose 'symbols of slavery', from trying to stop Valentine's Day to changing the names of some cities, such as Aurangabad and Osmanabad; how to protect temples, and, of course, cows.[35] Though the RSS, BJP, and the VHP did not participate in the conclave 'formally', their anti-constitutional strategy is explicit, wherein public lynching is the new 'normal', with orchestrated hate campaigns against people

[34] Kamath (2017).
[35] Halarnkar (2017).

who support different ideologies and practices, attacks on Swami Agnivesh and Umar Khalid, and the current arrests of human rights and Dalit activists.

The major roadblock in achieving the aforementioned objectives is the Constitution of India, which is the repository of the finest intellectual minds of the time. More significantly, the Constitution reflects Ambedkar's vision and strategies of achieving structural changes in the polity, society, and economy of India long held hostage to ascribed scriptural norms. As stated by K.S. Sudarshan, the former RSS supremo, 'the Constitution does not reflect the basic ethos of this nation.'[36] Similarly, Guru Golwalkar observed that 'there is nothing in the Constitution which we call our own'.[37]

One needs to pause and reflect as to what it is about the Constitution that rankles the Sangh Parivar. It is essential to revisit Ambedkar's philosophy and his views while the various aspects of the Constitution are being debated. The Constitution was a culmination of his relentless struggles against the injustices meted out to untouchables and other oppressed groups in Indian society. The celebratory mood of Independence was vitiated by the bloodbath of Partition and the fear of communal influence over society. Hence, the Constitution of a newly independent nation had to chart a roadmap to fulfil people's aspirations while envisioning a more egalitarian world.

To conclude, one can argue that the purpose of the Indian Constitution is not merely to create organs of the State but to limit their authority through a system of checks and balances, the absence of which may lead to tyranny and oppression. The preamble to the Constitution privileges the basic objectives of liberty, equality, and fraternity. The fundamental rights consist of the basic human rights, the abolition of social disabilities, and the guarantee of rights to minorities, including women, which ensures protection from exploitation and guarantees individual liberty. The very idea behind incorporating certain basic rights and remedies for violation of those rights in the chapter on fundamental rights is to balance individual liberty and the need for social control. This unique contribution of Ambedkar has gone a long way in the conception of social justice. As the clamour for social justice from

[36] Thapar (2018).
[37] Thapar (2018).

The Fractured Society of the Republic   165

various belaboured groups grows louder, we need to introspect as to how far we have remained true to the ideals enshrined in the Constitution.

The attempt to dilute the emancipatory potential of the Constitution under the garb of making it truly 'Indian' reflects the shallow nature of our body politic. The State, which Ambedkar privileged as the vanguard for social and economic justice, now serves the needs of crony capitalism. Unfortunately, we have failed in inculcating democratic ethos in our society. When our families are ridden with hierarchies, the challenge is to democratize our inter- and intra-personal relations, between communities and genders. With great prescience, Ambedkar demanded social democracy rather than merely electoral democracy. For him, social democracy meant a way of life, which recognized liberty, equality, and fraternity as the principle of life. A democratic form of government presupposes a democratic form of society. The formal framework of democracy is of no value and would indeed be a misfit if there was no social democracy. The politicians never realized that democracy is not a form of government; it is essentially a form of society. It may not be necessary for a democratic society to be marked by unity, by community of purpose, by loyalty to public ends, and by mutuality of sympathy. But it does unmistakably involve two things. The first is an attitude of mind, an attitude of respect and equality towards their fellows. The second is a social organization free from rigid social barriers.[38]

Our contemporary politics is marked by bitter feuds and senseless wrangling. The political debate has become exclusive when any questioning of the State leads to people being branded as 'anti-national'. The representation of the minorities in the Parliament is deteriorating and a party like the BJP is openly claiming that they do not need minorities, specifically Muslims, to win electoral battles. The diffusion of 'Constitutional morality', not merely among the majority of any community, but throughout the whole is the indispensable condition of a government at once free and peaceable, since even any powerful and obstinate minority may render the working of a free institution impracticable, without

---

[38] B.R. Ambedkar. 'Commandments of Baba Saheb Ambedkar'. Ambedkar. org. Available at http://www.ambedkar.org/Babasaheb/Commandments_ of_Baba_Saheb.htm, accessed 6 March 2015.

being strong enough to conquer ascendance for themselves.[39] There is a moral principle overarching the idea of constitutional morality.

When the Constitution was enacted, there was a self-conscious sense that in writing a text, India was finding a way to resolve major substantive debates and disputes over norms and values. The task of constitutionalism was a morality that transcended positions and disagreements on particular issues; indeed, its strength was that it gave a framework for having a common institutional life despite disagreements. The second aspect of constitutionalism was the ambition that while the Constitution would serve Indian needs, it would not be bound by any particular tradition. It would, rather, reflect and be in the service of a global conversation on law and values.[40] What kind of a political sensibility was required to make a constitution possible? Constitutions do not only allocate authority, define the limits of power, and enunciate values. They also constitute our sense of history and shape a sense of self. They often mark a new beginning and define future horizons. Despite the centrality of the Constitution to our social and political life, it has been ill-served by our historical imagination.[41]

A fractured republic needs the Ambedkarite Constitution at this critical juncture. The Indian Constitution is, in a significant sense, a cosmopolitan constitution. It is a cosmopolitan constitution in its fidelity to the universal principles of liberty, equality, and fraternity. But it is also a cosmopolitan constitution in a second sense. Its text and principles, its values, and its jurisprudence have been situated at the major cross-currents of global constitutional law. The need of the hour is to challenge the attempts to replace the Constitution with the scriptures of Hindu Rashtra, which would spell the death knell of any dialogue on rights. The principles, policies, and proposals of the Bengaluru Declaration (2017) strengthen the ideology of the Constitution as a charter of social justice. Can such coalition-inspired progressive developments help transcend the inegalitarian direction that the Right keeps pushing us towards?

[39] Lok Sabha Secretariat (1990: 107–31).
[40] Choudhry, Khosla, and Mehta (2016).
[41] Mehta (2010: 5).

References

Ambedkar, B.R. 1979. 'States and Minorities', in Vasant Moon (ed.), *Dr. Babasaheb Ambedkar: Writings and Speeches*. Vol. 1. Bombay: Education Department, Government of Maharashtra.

———. 1982. *Dr. Babasaheb Ambedkar, Writings and Speeches*, Vasant Moon (ed.). Vol. 2. Bombay: Education Department, Government of Maharashtra.

———. 1994. *Dr. Babasaheb Ambedkar: Writings and Speeches*, Vasant Moon (ed.). Vol. 13. Bombay: Education Department, Government of Maharashtra.

———. 2014a. 'Majorities and Minorities', in Vasant Moon (ed.), *Dr. Babasaheb Ambedkar: Writings and Speeches*. Vol. 1. New Delhi: Dr. Ambedkar Foundation.

———. 2014b. 'Memorandum Submitted to the Cabinet Mission', in Hari Narake, M.L. Kasare, N.G. Kamble, and Ashok Godghate (eds), *Dr. Babasaheb Ambedkar: Writings and Speeches*. Vol. 17 (Part-2). New Delhi: Dr. Ambedkar Foundation.

Bharill, Chandra. 1977. *Social and Political Ideas of B.R. Ambedkar*. Jaipur: Aalekh Publishers.

Bhatia, Gautam. 2016a. 'The Equality of Entry'. *Hindu*, 8 September.

———. 2016b. 'Why the Uniquely Revolutionary Potential of Ambedkar's Constitution Remains Untapped'. *Scroll*, 14 April.

Choudhry, Sujit, Madhav Khosla, and Pratap Bhanu Mehta. 2016. 'Our 'Un-Indian' Constitution'. *Live Mint*, 4 April.

Gore, M.S. 1993. *The Social Context of an Ideology: Ambedkar's Political and Social Thought*. New Delhi: SAGE Publications.

Halarnkar, Samar. 2017. 'Inside the Hindu Mind, a Battle for a Hindu Nation'. *Scroll*, 11 June. Available at https://scroll.in/article/840275/the-battle-for-hindu-rashtra-is-raging-inside-the-hindu-mind-and-it-is-no-longer-a-fringe-fantasy, accessed 28 August 2018.

Indian Express. 2017. 'Eye on Vokkaliga Community, Amit Shah Visits Mutt, Releases Book on Seer'. 14 August.

India Today. 2018. 'Amit Shah Sounds 2019 Election Bugle, Calls Opposition Animals Who Unite During Storm'. *India Today*, 6 April 2018. Available at https://www.indiatoday.in/india/story/amit-shah-sounds-2019-election-bugle-compares-opposition-to-animals-who-unite-during-a-storm-1206179-2018-04-06, accessed 7 April 2018.

Kamath, Naresh. 2017. '150 Hindu Outfits to Meet in Goa to Discuss 'Hindu Rashtra' by 2023, BJP, RSS to Stay Away'. *Hindustan Times*, 11 June. Available at https://www.hindustantimes.com/mumbai-news/150-hindu-outfits-to-meet-in-goa-to-discuss-possibility-of-hindu-rashtra-by-2023/story-R8HWIzIvoUdHytWeZZguRI.html, accessed 28 August 2018.

Kuber, W.N. 1973. *Dr. Ambedkar: A Critical Study*. New Delhi: Peoples Publishing House.

Lok Sabha Secretariat. 1990. *The Constitution and the Constituent Assembly Debates*. New Delhi: Government of India Press.

Madhav, Ram. 2017. 'Coming Full Circle at 70'. *Indian Express*, 15 August.

Mannathukkaren, Nissim. 2018. 'The Fast Disappearing Muslim in the Indian Republic'. *Indian Express*, 22 January. Available at https://indianexpress.com/article/opinion/the-fast-disappearing-muslim-in-the-indian-republic-bjp-mla-hindu-saffron-religion-5034205/, accessed 22 January 2018.

Mehta, P.B. 2010. 'What is Constitutional Morality?' *The Seminar*. Available at http://www.india-seminar.com/2010/615/615_pratap_bhanu_mehta.htm, accessed 30 January 2019.

Mishra, J.P. 1992. 'Ambedkar and the Constitution Making', in *Ambedkar and Social Justice, vol. I*. New Delhi: GoI, Information and Broadcasting Publications.

Planning Commission. 2011. *Faster, Sustainable and More Inclusive Growth: An Approach to the Twelfth Five Year Plan (2012-17)*. New Delhi: Planning Commission, GoI. Available at http://planningcommission.gov.in/plans/planrel/12appdrft/approach_12plan.pdf, accessed 5 February 2019.

Ramachandran, Narayan. 2016. 'Ambedkar and Idle Worship'. *Live Mint*, 18 April. Available at https://www.livemint.com/Opinion/dr55MGOs2TQwZNpLFwNABM/Ambedkar-and-idle-worship.html, accessed 19 September 2018.

Ramaswamy, K. 1992. 'Ambedkar—Cornerstone of the Constitution', in *Ambedkar and Social Justice*. Vol. I. New Delhi: GoI, Information and Broadcasting Publications.

Rodrigues, Valerian. 2002. *The Essential Writings of B.R. Ambedkar*. New Delhi: Oxford University Publishers.

Sandhu, Khushboo. 2016. 'Jain Monk, in Nude, Talks of Pakistan, Female Foeticide, Duty of Wife in Haryana Assembly.' *Indian Express*, 29 August. Available at https://indianexpress.com/article/india/india-news-india/tarun-sagar-jain-religious-leader-monsoon-session-female-foeticide-eradication-pakistan-haryana-2998501/, accessed 29 August 2016.

Shashi, S.S. 1992. *Ambedkar and Social Justice*. Vol. I. New Delhi: Publications Division, Ministry of Information and Broadcasting, Government of India.

Thapar, Karan. 2018. 'Has the RSS Ground Shifted?' *Indian Express*, 21 September.

8

Whose State Is It Anyway? Reservation, Representation, Caste, and Power

KAREN GABRIEL AND PREM KUMAR VIJAYAN

On the 26th of January 1950, we are going to enter into a life of contradictions. In politics we will have equality and in social and economic life we will have inequality. In politics we will be recognizing the principle of one man one vote and one vote one value. In our social and economic life, we shall, by reason of our social and economic structure, continue to deny the principle of one man one value. How long shall we continue to live this life of contradictions? How long shall we continue to deny equality in our social and economic life? If we continue to deny it for long, we will do so only by putting our political democracy in peril. We must remove this contradiction at the earliest possible moment or else those who suffer from inequality will blow up the structure of political democracy which this Assembly has so laboriously built up.

—B.R. Ambedkar

We, the people as a nation, constituted ourselves as a sovereign democratic republic to conduct our affairs within the four corners of the Constitution, its goals and values. We expect the benefits of democratic participation to flow to us—all of us—so that we can take our rightful place, in the league of nations, befitting our heritage and collective genius. Consequently, we must also bear the discipline, and the rigour of constitutionalism, the essence of which is accountability of power, whereby the power of the people vested in any organ of the State, and its agents, can only be used for promotion of constitutional values and vision.[1]

These are the opening words of a landmark judgment by a two-judge bench of the Supreme Court of India, banning the Salwa Judum organization. They are a trenchant reminder of a crucial political fact, one that we are increasingly encouraged to forget: that the Indian State does not *own* the people of India. Rather, it is vested with 'the power of the people' of India—it is constituted by the people, the people are not constituted by it. Certainly, the people are obliged, as citizens, to respect and uphold the laws passed by a State that is constituted *by themselves*, that is, by the people, for the people, and is with the people. But what is almost always forgotten, again, is that these laws are supposed to be *for the people*—for the benefit, security, and dignity of the people, and therefore passed in their name. This is indisputably what is meant by the words, 'We, the people as a nation, constituted ourselves as a sovereign democratic republic to conduct our affairs within the four corners of the Constitution', by the Supreme Court judgment. But when the State begins to act against the people in their name, then it is not only profoundly hypocritical and ironic, it has the makings of a monumental tragedy. When the State enacts, executes, and upholds laws that essentially separate the people from the State, that essentially serve the interests of the State rather than of the people, and that essentially aim to immunize the State from the grievances of the people, rather than protect the people from the excesses of the State—then it is time to ask: To what extent is this Indian State truly constituted of its people? Which sections of the people constituted the Indian State when it came into being, and which sections constitute it now? What has changed? For whom is the Indian State today, and in whose name does it function? Who are the people included in and by the State—who own and run the State, in the name of the people at large—and who are excluded by and from it? In other words, whose State is it anyway?

[1] Justice B. Sudershan Reddy and Justice Surinder Singh Nijjar. 2011. 'Order'. In the 'Writ Petition (Civil) No. 250 of 2007, Nandini Sundar & Ors vs State of Chattisgarh on 5 July, 2011'. Available at https://indiankanoon.org/doc/920448/, accessed 30 April 2017.

Deciding Authority: 'Evaluation' Versus 'Acquisition'

Part of the problem, of course, is that both in theory and in practice, it is difficult to distinguish between the government and the State. In international law, the 1933 Montevideo Convention on the Rights and Duties of States set forth the legal standard for evaluating an entity's claim to statehood. Under the Montevideo Convention, an entity is a State when it possesses: (a) a permanent population; (b) a defined territory; (c) a government; and (d) the capacity to enter into relations with other States (also understood as its sovereignty).[2] By this understanding, which continues to remain the most widely accepted one, 'government' is a part of 'State', and the State itself extends to include the entire population that is governed by it, through the government, within a defined territory. The problem arises when we come to the fourth criterion—sovereignty: it refers in the main to the sovereignty of each State as a political entity in relation to other States, but is as often understood as the sovereignty of each State over its own people. The problem here is that a State that is constituted of and by its people is also somehow expected to be sovereign over them—to rule and govern them. Evidently then, the people who constitute the government have to be from amongst the people who constitute the (rest of the) State—that is, the entire 'permanent population' of the 'defined territory' or country; yet, at the same time, it has to be distinct, separate, and differentiated from them.[3] How does this happen?

This differentiation takes place through two different kinds of elimination and exclusion. The first—let us call it the 'evaluatory method'—is deployed when personnelling the armed forces, the executive, and the judiciary (the legislature is constituted

---

[2] Montevideo Convention (1933: 3).

[3] Perhaps that is one of the reasons why political parties around the world have so often sought to represent themselves as 'people's' parties, or 'folk' parties, or 'national' parties (i.e., parties that have arisen out of, and belong to, the nation as a whole, rather than, say, to one region or community), or 'republican' parties. Interestingly, a rather unusual version of this is to be found in the formal name of China, that is, the 'People's Republic of China': it basically refers to the political and social sovereignty of the only political party that is allowed to operate in China, namely, the Communist Party of China.

differently, as we shall see shortly). The 'evaluatory method' is constituted of a system of evaluations conducted through examinations and interviews, for a limited, specified number of posts. These are perceived to be *professional* posts that, therefore, require a certain level of education, aptitude, and perhaps skill-training, because they carry out the actual work of governance, that is, of *running* the State—from the defence of its territories, to the administration of policies (internal and external), the implementation of laws, the maintenance of order, the regulation of the practices of its citizenry, and the judicial oversight and circumscription of each and all of these. Thus, the purported objective of this 'evaluatory method' is to identify the most suitable, capable candidates for these posts, through conditional exclusion (using filters like citizenship, age, academic performance, regions of domicile) and competitive elimination (using examination and interview performances). As such, the principle of differentiation adopted here is that of individual 'excellence' or 'merit'—a point of some significance that we shall return to.

The second method is used to people the one remaining domain of government, namely, the legislature or legislative assemblies. It is commonly referred to as the system of 'electoral representation' and refers to the process by which the various legislative bodies are constituted, from the village-level panchayats to the state-level legislative assemblies and the two houses of the national Parliament. Here again, a degree of conditional exclusion is involved (age, citizenship, reserved versus open seats, etc); but the process of competitive elimination here is not a test of abilities or personality, but of 'popularity'. It is about the number of votes that a candidate can muster in his/her favour; this is supposed to index the extent to which the voters believe him/her capable of *representing* them and their interests: s/he is supposed to be their *representative* in the legislature. That is, the representative is chosen through a process of competitive election, by majority decision. The question here, then, is not how *well* s/he can actually represent the voters and their interests nor even how well s/he can persuade them about his/her ability to do so, but simply how well s/he can garner a majority of votes, through whatever measures are legally permissible (and sometimes even through those that are not). It is simply assumed that the greater the share of votes pulled, the more completely a particular candidate represents

Whose State Is It Anyway? Reservation, Representation, Caste, and Power 173

his/her voters and their interests. The coming together of these 'elected representatives' in the various legislative forums is thus assumed to reflect, at each level of such forums, an aggregation of the various dominant perspectives, interests, and concerns of the majority of the people, at that level, that is, village panchayats, urban municipal councils, state legislative assemblies, the two houses of the national Parliament. That is, through this aggregation of issues, each such collective of representatives is supposed to represent their voters' concerns and demands in the drafting of laws and policies. The principle of differentiation, in this instance, is best described as 'accumulation' and refers to the candidates' capacity to build, hold, and expand their vote base(s); hence, the method may be referred to as the 'acquisitory method'.

These two methods of differentiation are, at first glance, themselves very different from each other. The first one specifies the various *kinds* of persons required for the various *kinds* of governance, and also for the various state apparatuses. It also specifies the *kinds* of education, training, and skills that are expected, and required, from such persons and eliminates candidates by evaluating these (extent and quality of; aptitude for), purportedly in a free and fair manner. It thus requires and relies on a much wider institutional apparatus of education, training, and testing to produce and induct personnel into the various arms of the government (excluding the legislative). The constitution of—as well as the manner of constituting—this wider apparatus therefore substantially determines the personnel it produces, who are inducted into the government. The second one, in contrast, is only applied in constituting the legislative sections of the government. Candidates require little else besides the ability to pull votes; it is simply assumed that the greater the share of votes pulled, the more completely a particular candidate represents his/her voters and their interests—and in many places where particular political parties are strong, even this is not required: it is the party (more or less regardless of the candidate), that attracts the votes. The coming together of these 'elected representatives' in the various legislative forums is thus assumed to reflect, at each level of such forums, an aggregation of the various dominant perspectives, interests, and concerns of the majority of the people, at that level, that is, village panchayats, urban municipal councils, state legislative assemblies, the two houses of the national Parliament. That is, through this aggregation of issues, each such collective of representatives is supposed to represent their voters' concerns and demands in the drafting of laws and policies.

Another important difference between the two methods is that the personnel appointed through the first method are not (supposed to be) concerned with whether or not they are representative of the people at large. In fact, because they are appointed as 'professionals' within a national bureaucracy, they are obliged to derogate and discount such concerns. In contrast, 'representativeness' and its meanings are the central, even *sole*, concerns for those appointed through the second method (for reasons that are obvious from the previous two paragraphs). These meanings usually take shape in one of two ways—along two directional vectors, so to speak, registered in the prepositions 'of' and 'to'. The 'of' registers the representative in terms of the community that s/he 'stands for' or embodies. S/he is 'of' it; it is reflected and realized in its collective memories, aspirations, and anxieties in him/her. That is, it *identifies* itself in her/him. The 'to' registers the same representative in terms of inter-community relations, that is, s/he represents his/her community 'to' other communities; other communities *identify* his/her community through and in her/him. And political appointees, that is, those appointed through the 'acquisitory' method of winning elections, usually find they have to attend to being representative in both these ways, 'of' and 'to'.

Despite these differences, these two methods of differentiation—the 'evaluatory' and the 'acquisitory'—share some very important features. One such is the fact that these personnel (whether appointed through elections or selections) constitute the 'human face' of the government for the governed: they *represent* the government to, and for, the people. At the same time, they are also the *media* through which the government *operates*, that is, through whom the various apparatuses of the State *work*. Consequently, the work they do constitutes *the working of the State itself*. Their work, that is, governance itself, then constitutes the 'non-human' aspect, as it were, of the government. It is in this sense that the State is (seen as) greater than the sum of its parts, and the part that is greater—the *excessive* part—is (seen as) both sovereign over, yet represents and embodies, the remaining parts. We will return to discuss more such common features of these two methods shortly; for now, let us briefly examine how each of them has panned out in real terms in India today, starting with the first one.

The 'Merits' of 'Evaluation'

The first method, we may recall, was the 'evaluatory method', applied to the armed forces, the executive, and the judiciary. How has this method shaped the constitution, the demographic profile, of these services? Even a cursory glance at this social profile reveals that these three branches of government are predominantly constituted of upper-caste, upper-class, urban, Hindu men. Illustratively, according to figures provided by the Ministry of Personnel, Public Grievances and Pensions to the Lok Sabha in March 2018, 'the representation of SCs, STs and OBCs in the posts and services under the Central Government as on 01.01.2016, is 17.49%, 8.47% and 21.57% respectively'.[4] This comes to a total of 47.53 per cent—which means that the remainder, that is, 52.47 per cent of the Central Government (CG) posts and services, are in the hands of the 'general category' (a combination of upper-caste 'Hindus' and members of minority religious communities). As we shall see very shortly, at least three-fourths of this 'general category' is constituted of upper-caste Hindus.

> What is remarkable is that this dominance has continued despite the introduction of reservations in government employment, initially for SCs and STs, and then for OBCs. The reservations for SCs and STs was stabilized at 15 per cent and 7.5 per cent in 1970, based on the 1961 census data; it has not changed since then. The reservations for OBC, introduced in 1993, has remained at 27 per cent. In the words of a brochure on reservation for SCs/STs and OBCs, issued by the GoI: After introduction of reservation for OBCs, total reservation for SCs, STs and OBCs comes to 49.5% in case of direct recruitment on all-India basis by open competition and 50% in case of otherwise than by open competition [sic]. As per various judgments of

---

[4] Jitendra Singh. 2018. 'Answer'. In 'Representation of SCs, STs and OBCs in the Central Government Services—Lok Sabha Unstarred Question No.5491 dated 28.03.2018'. GConnect. Available at https://www.gconnect.in/orders-in-brief/reservation/representation-of-sc-st-and-obc-in-central-government-services.html, accessed 19 October 2017.

the Supreme Court, total reservation for these communities cannot exceed the limit of 50%.[5]

Evident from this is that, firstly, even almost 50 years after the SC and ST quotas were fixed, while the quotas themselves are filled, there is almost no SC and ST presence *outside* of the reserved positions: the figures beyond the quota, stand at about 2.5 per cent for SCs and 1 per cent for STs. This essentially represents the quantum of SCs and STs who would have gained employment in CG services, *had there been no reservation* for them—a point we will return to. Secondly, even almost twenty-five years after the OBC quota was fixed, the OBC quota remains unfulfilled, and this is a recurrent feature, every year. In fact, not only is the shortfall almost *one-fourth* of the quota—that is, at least 25 per cent of the OBC reserved positions going unfilled regularly—but the 'general category' (which is mainly upper castes), at 52.47 per cent, gain at least an additional 3 per cent of positions, almost filling the one-fourth unfilled OBC positions. In other words, *had there been no reservations for them, the implication is that there would be little to no OBC representation at all, in these services.*[6] Thirdly, it is clear that—as we noted earlier—it is the strength of representation *outside* of the quotas[7] that registers the extent to which the candidates from these categories are perceived to be as 'meritorious' as the 'general category' candidates, following the 'evaluatory method'.

This pattern—of a hugely disproportionate upper-caste overrepresentation despite building concessions of various kinds into this method, through reservations—holds true for the judiciary

---

[5] GoI (2016a: 7).

[6] It is difficult to substantiate this with data because the current writers could not trace any data going back to 1993, when OBC reservations were declared. The earliest we could find were from 2003, ten years after this was implemented: at that time, government records register 4.53 per cent OBC representation in CG services. See GoI (2016b: 347). It has taken thirteen years, from 2003 to 2016, for this figure to climb by about seventeen percentage points, to 21.57 per cent.

[7] It must be clarified here that SCs, STs, and OBCs are entitled to apply for and be appointed in 'general category' positions, although the converse is not true. See Bhaskar (2017). This means that the 'General' category is an open one and grants no exclusive entitlements to the upper castes who apply through it—often a bone of much contention with them.

and defence services as well. One news report, for instance, notes that OBCs constitute just 12 per cent of the total number of judges in the lower judiciary, while SCs constitute 14 per cent and STs about 12 per cent in the lower judiciary.[8] The report also goes on to note that even the government does not have the corresponding figures for the higher judiciary. Corresponding data for the armed services—which has 4,207,250 employees[9]—is almost completely unavailable, because the reservation policy does not apply in these services. Nevertheless, there are sufficiently reliable indications that this picture—of disproportionate upper-caste presence, especially in the higher ranks—holds true for the armed services as well.[10] However, none of this is particularly new information: it has been noted and commented on by various academics, journalists, bureaucrats, and non-governmental actors.[11] The point of dwelling on it in some detail here is, firstly, to get a sense, not just of the fact of inequality, but of the extent and kinds of inequality; and secondly, and more importantly, it allows us to see that the *outcome of this 'evaluatory method' of differentiation, despite its vaunted emphasis on 'merit', continues to reflect the outcome of socio-economic, caste-based differentiation.* This has proved to be the case even with the 'evaluation' of 'merit' made conditional to performance within quotas, under the reservations policy. That is, despite decades of following a reservation policy, this method has persistently and consistently found 'merit' to reside mainly (if not solely) with the upper castes. The question is: Why?

The Failure of 'Merit'

Before we attempt to answer this question, a clarification is necessary at this point: the 'general category' also includes all strata—and not just the upper castes—of the religious minorities.

---

[8] *Times of India* (2018).

[9] According to the website Global Fire Power. 2019. 'India Military Strength'. Globalfirepower.com. Available athttps://www.globalfirepower.com/country-military-strength-detail.asp?country_id=india, accessed 19 October 2017.

[10] See, for instance, the newspaper report about a case in the Supreme Court, alleging caste discrimination in the Indian army. PTI (2013).

[11] See the 'References' section of this chapter for a variety of such studies and reports.

Although they are not recognized by their caste status officially, there are large numbers of lower-caste people who continue to be subjected to *experience*—caste discrimination, despite belonging to religions that do not formally practice, or even acknowledge, it.[12] Officially, these fall in the 'general category'. Now, taking the total population of India to be more or less 121 crores (as per the 2011 census), we can make some reasonably accurate deductions, if we do some quick number crunching around this, as in Table 8.1:

It will be noticed, firstly, that UCH constitute just ([251,195,353/ 1,210,000,000] × 100 =) 20.75 per cent of the total population. Secondly, that a large portion of the population in the last row, that is, in the 'general category', is constituted of Msso-s: that is, about ([130,398,000/494,938,000[× 100 =) 26.35 per cent of the GC population is constituted of lower-caste minorities (Msso) who, despite suffering the same social handicaps as their 'Hindu' counterparts, cannot avail the compensatory advantage of 'reservations' in education and employment, because of having converted from 'Hinduism'. It also means that the remaining 73.65 per cent of the GC is actually constituted almost completely of UCH.

Now, with specific reference to CG jobs (not including the armed services and the judiciary), a Finance Ministry report of December 2017 states that 'as on 01.03.2016, the total number of Regular Central Government Civilian Employees in position was 32.21 lakh against the sanctioned strength of 36.34 lakh and approximately 11.36% of the posts were vacant.'[15] Assuming that the appointments made in the filled positions had followed the stipulated 'reservations' policy, then 52.47 per cent of these 3,221,183 filled posts—that is, about 17 lakhs posts—is constituted of UCH and minorities. It bears reiterating that the minorities here also include converts from the 'reserved' categories, who cannot avail of the quota relaxations and are, therefore, appointed as part of the

---

[12] The discrimination is often on a lesser scale within the religious community, than outside it, but it still remains to varying degrees in all of them. The Sachar Committee Report, recognizing this, proposed that 'the three groups of Muslims in India *ashrafs*, *ajlafs* and *arzals*, (in order of "caste" hierarchy) require different types of affirmative action.' See Sachar et al. (2006) and Parker (2006: 4).

[15] GoI (2017: 4). These are the most current figures that we could find; there appears to be no more recent data available in the public domain.

Whose State Is It Anyway? Reservation, Representation, Caste, and Power 179

Table 8.1 Community-Wise Population Sizes

Nominal	Represents	Calculation	Value
P	Total population of India	Census 2011	1,210,000,000
H	Total population of 'Hindus' in India	Census 2011	966,257,353
M	Total population of minorities in India	P – H	243,742,647
HSSO	Population of 'Hindu' SCs, STs, and OBCs	74%[13] of H	715,062,000
SSO	Total population of *all* SCs, STs, and OBCs (including from religions where caste is not cognized)	69.3%[14] of P	845,460,000
UCH	Population of non-'HSSOs' amongst 'Hindus' (the upper castes, hence 'UCH')	H – HSSO	251,195,353
M_{sso}	Total population of people of SC, ST, or OBC origin, in the minority communities	SSO – HSSO	130,398,000
M_g	Population of non-'Msso' minorities in general (hence Mg)	M – Msso	113,344,647
GC	Total population of *all* non-'HSSOs' (i.e., those who can only apply through the 'general category')	M + UCH	494,938,000

Source: Created by the authors.

[13] These figures are quite dated; they are compiled in the Sachar Committee Report (Sachar et al. [2006: 7]), based on data from survey rounds 61 and 55 of the National Sample Survey Organisation. There are no figures readily available of a later date. However, all recent and available data indicates that the general distribution of castes in the services—what we might call the 'caste-to-power ratio'—remains remarkably poor.

[14] This figure is arrived at by adding the total percentages of SCs (19.7 per cent), STs (8.5 per cent), and OBCs (41.1 per cent), at the bottom of Table 1.2 of the Sachar Committee Report (Sachar [2006: 7]).

'general category'. Ideally, the composition of the GC in these jobs ought to more or less reflect its general composition in society at large. In order to test this, let us first differentiate the GC in society at large from the GCs appointed in these CG services: thus, let 'GC' refer to the 'general category' population in society at large, and 'GCr' refer specifically to the category as it is used in official reservation policies (hence the 'r'), in education and employment. Taking account of the fact that 47.53 per cent of all CG jobs are held by reserved category candidates, it then becomes clear that, of the remaining 52.47 per cent that go to the GCr under reservation, around 73.65 per cent, that is, almost three-fourths (possibly more), of these jobs are likely to go to the UCH, or upper castes. That is, at least 73.65 per cent of 17 lakhs, or 1,252,050 jobs, are held by upper castes. This means that UCH alone hold as much as (1,252,050/3,221,000 × 100 =) 38.88 per cent of all CG jobs. Or is it even more?

According to a news article, dated 6 February 2017, the minister for Minority Affairs, Mukhtar Abbas Naqvi, is reported to have stated in Parliament that currently (that is, in February 2017), 'the percentage of minorities in Central Government jobs is 9.9 per cent'.[16] That is, as much as 90 per cent of the 32.21 lakhs CG jobs—that is, almost 29 lakh CG jobs—go to the 'Hindus', and only about 3.2 lakhs jobs go to the minorities. Then, the actual number of UCH in CG services is (17 – 3.2 =) 13.8 lakhs. This is considerably more than the figure we had estimated above, of 1,252,050 jobs—a difference of 127,950. Correspondingly, the number of jobs that go to 'Hindu' upper castes is not 73.65 per cent of 17 lakhs, but 81.18 per cent. The actual percentage of minorities in the CG services is therefore not 26.35 per cent, but 19.88 per cent of 17 lakhs, or 337,960 jobs.[17] And then the UCH would hold, not 38.88 per cent but almost 43 per cent of all 32.21 lakhs CG jobs.

Clearly, here, the UCH is disproportionately larger than its counterpart categories and is much more represented than its

[16] PTI (2017).

[17] The slight variance from the minister's figure of 318,897 (a difference of a little less than 20,000) must be attributed to the variations and approximations in the data itself. Needless to say, we will use only the official figure in our calculations, and not the figure of 337,960, which we have derived here indirectly.

Whose State Is It Anyway? Reservation, Representation, Caste, and Power 181

counterparts, in these jobs. One reason for the bloat is that this 81.18 per cent is not entirely UCH, but has a small percentage of HSSOs, who despite being from the reserved categories, are appointed against 'general category'. We had earlier noted that this amounted to about 3.5 per cent (2.5 per cent for SCs and 1 per cent for STs) of 32.21 lakhs, that is, 112,735 jobs. The actual number of UCH employees is, therefore, not 13.8 lakhs, but (1,380,000 − 112,735 =) 1,267,265. Interestingly, this is quite close to the value for UCH we got earlier, by assuming that the percentage of employees in each category would correspond roughly with the population of that category as a percentage of the total population (earlier). However, if this is to hold true for the Msso as well, then the percentage of Msso-s in CG services will be ([130,398,000/1,21,00,00,000] × 100 =) 10.78 per cent of 3,221,000, that is, 347,224. But this is clearly absurd, since it exceeds both the minister's and our own estimate of the *total* number of minorities—*including* the Msso-s—in CG service. This can only mean that, in this instance, we cannot assume that the percentage of Msso employees will correspond with the percentage of Msso in the total population. In the absence of any data about the demography of CG employees of lower-caste status who have converted to other religions, we have no way of knowing their percentages and, therefore, of how well represented (or not) they may be in the services. More significantly perhaps, this statistically confirms what might have been an otherwise intuitively evident fact: that the composition of the GC—and therefore, indeed, of all these categories—in these jobs, does not, in fact, reflect its (their) general composition in society at large. Thus, *if the 'reservations' policy was supposed to facilitate a greater degree of representation, that is, a more proportional representativeness in government, then it has fallen far short of that goal.*

Two questions arise here:

1. How does the known, disproportionately large UCH representation play out, against that of the other community categories, in terms of their respective *representativeness*?
2. Is this related in any way to the question we began with, namely, why does the 'evaluatory method' continue to find 'merit' mainly in the UCH?

To address the first question first, there are four kinds of 'representativeness' entailed here. The first (let us call this R1) is in relation to the services themselves where, posed as a question, it is: 'What is the strength of a particular community (for example, an SC community or a Christian community) *within* the service in question: for example, how many SCs are there in the Indian Railway Service? Or how many Christians in the Indian Administrative Service?' This question registers the representation of that community in and to the activities of that particular government service. The second kind of 'representativeness' (R2) is in relation to the social group/community that is represented in the services: that is, how strongly is a given community represented in the services, in proportion to the size of the community itself. The third kind (R3) is a somewhat unusual one: it is the representativeness of a given community in relation to the representativeness of all such communities and is measured in terms of the proportion of a given community to the total population of India. Simply put, it answers the question: To what extent can a given community claim to be representative of the nation as a whole (understood as a confederation of such communities), in terms of sheer numbers? And the fourth and final kind (R4) is really just an extension of R2: that is, it is the relation of R2 to the nation as a whole and is measured in terms of the proportion of CG employees from a particular community, to the population of India.

If 'CG(r)' represents the number of a particular community employed in the CG services, then the following Table 8.2 gives a clear picture of how R1, R2, R3, and R4 stand in relation to each other:

How Representative is 'Representativeness'?

There are a few more data inputs that we need, to extend our understanding of 'representativeness':

Correlating Reservations and Representativeness -I

CG employees are differentiated into groups, Group A (Gazetted; hereafter, 'G'), Group B (G), Group B (non-G), and Group C (non-G).[18] As of 1 January 2013, the figures for these groups are in Table 8.3:

---

[18] According to this web-page of the Ministry of Personnel, Public Grievances and Pensions, GoI:

Table 8.2 Community-Wise Representativeness

Column 1	Column 2	Column 3	Column 4	Column 5	Column 6	Column 7	Column 8
Category	Population count (PC)	Number in services, calculation	Number in services, value [CG(r)]	%age in 32.21 lakhs CG jobs (R1)	CG(r) as %age of PC (R2)	Category %age of total population (R3)	CG(r) as %age of category population (R4)
M	243,742,647	9.9% of 3,221,183	318,897	9.9	0.131	20.14	0.026
UCH	251,195,353	1,700,000 – 318,897	1,381,103	43	0.55	20.76	0.114
HSSO	715,062,000	47.53% (17.49 + 8.47 + 21.57) of 3,221,183	15,31,028	47.5	0.214	59.1	0.127

Source: Created by the authors.

Table 8.3 Group-Wise Distribution of HSSOs (2013)

Group	Total	SCs	%	STs	%	OBCs	%
A	65,414	7,890	12.06	3,324	5.08	5477	8.37
B	141,305	22,233	15.73	8,475	5.99	14156	10.01
C	2,423,194	424,949	17.53	187,898	7.75	435704	17.98
Total	2,629,913	455,072	17.30	199,697	7.59	455,337	17.31

Source: Extracted from the table 'Representation of Schedule Castes (SCs) and Schedule Tribes (STs) in Central Government Services in India'. Indiastat. Available at https://www.indiastat.com/table/labour-and-workforce-data/380987/civil-services/28927/88094/data.aspx, accessed 12 October 2017. The current authors could not find any more recent data on this.

These figures will be elaborated in Table 8.5 later. For now, we must draw attention to the fact that these figures are often not very clear.

Let us assume that there has been no dramatic change in the general trends indicated in the Table 8.3—a safe enough assumption to make when we recall the minister's words, that 'the representation of SCs, STs and OBCs in the posts and services under the Central Government as on 01.01.2016, is 17.49%, 8.47% and 21.57% respectively'.[19] From 2013 to 2016, the percentage of SCs has gone up by just 0.19 per cent, and that of STs by a mere 0.88 per cent; and although that of the OBCs is quite discernibly more, registering a difference of 4.26 per cent, it will not negatively affect the argument we make here, namely, that the UCH continue to remain the dominant and controlling constituency of the Indian State. In fact, it further affirms it, insofar as—as we noted earlier—HSSOs hold just 3.5 per cent of CG positions falling in the 'general category'. It is, therefore, more than likely that the steadily increasing OBC presence in these CG services will suddenly begin to stagnate, once the statutory requirement of 27 per cent is met. It also affirms this stagnancy, once it sets in, to be a historical trend, and

---

Such classification broadly corresponds to the rank, status and the degree of the level of responsibility attached to the posts. Group 'A' posts carry higher administrative and executive responsibilities and include senior management positions in the ministries/departments and field organisations. The middle and junior levels of Group 'A' along with Group 'B' constitute middle management. Group 'C' posts perform supervisory as well as operative tasks and render clerical assistances in ministries and field organisations. Group 'D' posts are meant for carrying out routine duties.

See GoI. n.d. 'Classification of Government Posts.' Persmin.gov. Available at http://persmin.gov.in/DOPT/CSWing/CRDivision/2.1.1.html, accessed 19 October 2017. With the implementation of the 7th Pay Commission's recommendations, Groups 'C' and 'D' have been merged.

[19] Jitendra Singh. 2018. 'Answer'. In 'Representation of SCs, STs and OBCs in the Central Government Services—Lok Sabha Unstarred Question No.5491 dated 28.03.2018'. GConnect. Available at https://www.gconnect.in/orders-in-brief/reservation/representation-of-sc-st-and-obc-in-central-government-services.html, accessed 19 October 2017.

Whose State Is It Anyway? Reservation, Representation, Caste, and Power 185

not just the figures for a few years or even decades—a fact of some significance.

Correlating Reservations and Representativeness -II

In the last row of a table titled 'Group-Wise and Status-wise (G/NG) Estimated Number of Central Government Civilian Regular Employees as on 1.03.2016',[20] in the same Finance Ministry report mentioned earlier, we are informed that, out of a total of 3,633,935 sanctioned civilian posts in the CG, the 'number in position' (i.e., positions with appointed personnel) was more than 4 lakhs lower, standing at 3,221,183, and was distributed thus across the groups:

Now, keeping in mind that the percentages are not substantially different, between the data of 2013 and that of 2016, if we apply the percentages in Table 8.3 to the figures in Table 8.4, then, in 2016 (the date of Table 8.4 given earlier), the following picture in Table 8.5 will likely have obtained:

However, according to the figures provided by the minister above, the percentage for OBCs is actually higher, at 21.57 per cent, so the number of OBCs in CG service will also go up, correspondingly, from 551,141 to 694,809—but we have no way of knowing from this how it is distributed in the three groups. Further, a news report in the *Hindu* newspaper, dated 9 December 2017, states that according to information received under the RTI Act, 2005, only '14% of Group A officers are from the OBCs. The figures for Group B, C and D employees are 15%, 17% and 18% respectively.'[21] The corresponding figures for the different groups are given in Table 8.6:

Table 8.4 Group-Wise Population (2016)

Number in position				
A(G)	B(G)	B(NG)	C(NG)	Total
101,901	109,769	118,741	2,890,772	3,221,183

Source: Table titled 'Group-Wise and Status-wise (G/NG) Estimated Number of Central Government Civilian Regular Employees as on 1.03.2016' in GoI (2017: 35).

[20] GoI (2017: 35).
[21] Kumar (2017).

Table 8.5 Group-Wise Distribution of HSSOs (Estimated for 2016)

Group	Total	SCs		STs		OBCs		Total %age of HSSOs	%age of UCH
		Number	%	Number	%	Number	%		
A	101,901	12,289	12.06	51,766	5.08	8,529	8.37	25.51	74.49
B	228,510 (G + NG)	35,945	15.73	13,688	5.99	22,851	10.01	31.73	68.27
C	2,890,772	506,752	17.53	224,035	7.75	519,761	17.98	43.26	56.74
Total	3,221,183	554,986	17.23	289,489	9.0	551,141	17.11	43.34	56.66

Source: Created by the authors.

Table 8.6 OBCs in Groups (2017)

Group	Calculation	Number	Total %age of HSSOs	%age of UCH
A	14% of 101,901	14,266	12.06 + 5.08 + 14 = 31.14	68.86
B	15% of 228,510	34,277	15.73 + 5.99 + 15 = 36.72	63.28
C	17.5%[22] of 2,890,772	505,885	17.53 + 7.75 + 17.5 = 42.78	57.22
Total		554,428	17.21[23] + 14 + 15 = 46.21	53.79

Source: Created by the authors.

[22] The average of 17 per cent and 18 per cent, for C and D respectively, which have to be merged here as just Group C.
[23] Derived by calculating (554428÷3221183) × 100 = 17.21 per cent

The figure of 554,428 marks a shortfall of almost 1.5 lakhs from the figure of 694,809 noted earlier, for OBC presence in the CG services, and arrived at from figures provided by a government minister. Evidently then, the percentages provided by the government under the RTI Act fall far short of the figure of 21.57 per cent provided by its own minister (whether in terms of individual groups or in terms of their average, namely, 16 per cent). Additionally, we also have the following Table 8.7 from the Ministry of Personnel, Public Grievances and Pensions, which gives yet another set of figures:

If we now extend this to include the UCH, we get the following Table 8.8:

What is strikingly clear from Tables 8.5, 8.6, 8.7, and 8.8 is that, although the dominance of the UCH in all the groups is still evident from the last columns of all the tables, there is also clear evidence of a steady decline in UCH presence from 2016 to 2018. However, there is also evidence of a concomitant increase in OBC representation, suggesting that the statutorily mandated gain of the latter through reservations has led to a concomitant decrease in the former.

Here, we need to take note of a brief but very important caveat: according to E. Muralidharan, who had filed an application under the RTI Act, eleven of the largest ministries (including the Ministries of Railways, Defence, Home, and Finance), which accounted for 91.25 per cent of the CG jobs, refused to share the data and information he had sought, despite being legally obliged to do so under the RTI Act. Thus, 'In real terms, as against an estimated 31 lakh Central Government employees, the data pertains to only 2,71,375 employees'.[24] In short then, the available data is not only partial, it also appears to be quite incommensurate with itself. Nevertheless, despite its failings, this data is still sufficient for our limited purposes: our concern here is not so much with specific evidences of imbalance or discrimination, as with identifying and demonstrating trends in the data. As we shall see (and as is probably already evident), even this uneven and limited data from 2017 does not show any real departure from the direction and orientation of earlier trends. In other words, *the dominance of the UCH in the CG services continues despite reservations.*

---

[24] Kumar (2017). Emphasis added.

Table 8.7 HSSO Employees in CG Services

Group	Number of persons						
	Total number of employees	SC		ST		OBC	
		Number	Per cent	Number	Per cent	Number	Per cent
A	84,521	11,312	13.38	5,005	5.92	11,002	13.02
B	290,598	46,583	16.03	20,910	7.20	42,975	14.79
C (excluding Safai *Karamchari*)	2,833,696	489,749	17.28	246,685	8.71	641,837	22.65
C (Safai Karamchari)	48,997	22,124	45.15	3,384	6.91	7,101	14.49
TOTAL	3,257,812	569,768	17.49	275,984	8.47	702,951	21.58

Source: GoI: (2018: 49).

Table 8.8 UCH Employees in CG Services

Group	Total number of employees	Total number of HSSOs	Total number of UCH	%age of UCH
A	84,521	11,312 + 5,005 + 11,002 = 27,319	84,521 – 27,319 = 57,202	67.68
B	290,598	46,583 + 20,910 + 42,975 = 110,468	290,598 – 110,468 = 180,130	62
C (excluding Safai Karamchari)	2,833,696	489,749 + 246,685 + 641,837 = 1,378,271	2,833,696 – 1,378,271 = 1,455,425	51.36
C (Safai Karamchari)	48,997	22,124 + 3,384 + 7,101 = 32,609	48,997 – 32,609 = 16,388	33.45
Total	3,257,812	1,548,667	1,709,145	52.46

Source: Created by the authors.

Correlating Education and Representativeness

Let us recall here what we had stated at the beginning of this piece—that these jobs are perceived to be *professional* in nature, requiring a degree of education, aptitude, and skill-training. Which is why the next set of data inputs we must engage with is education-related, that is, it pertains to the fact that a certain degree of education (not just literacy) is required to even apply for a CG position—usually, minimally, matriculate (or tenth-class) pass for group C and graduate for groups B and A. The following figures provide a quick sketch of enrolment in higher education in India: the 'Total enrolment in higher education has been estimated to be 35.7 million [i.e., 3,57,00,000]',[25] and these figures are of the age group 18–23, which is, in total, 141,537,252.[26] We are also told that,

> Gross Enrolment Ratio (GER) in Higher education in India is 25.2%, which is calculated for 18-23 years of age group. GER for male population is 26.0% and for females, it is 24.5%. For Scheduled Castes, it is 21.1% and for Scheduled Tribes, it is 15.4% as compared to the national GER of 25.2%.[27]

This cohort is just about ([14,15,37,252/1,21,00,00,000] × 100 =) 11.7 per cent of the total population, and the corresponding percentage of those enrolled (out of the total population) is ([3,57,00,000/ 1,21,00,00,000] × 100 =) 2.95 per cent. The same report also notes that 'Scheduled Casts [sic] students constitute 14.2% and Scheduled Tribes students 5.1% of the total [undergraduate] enrolment. 34.4% students belong to Other Backward Classes. 4.9% students belong to Muslim Minority and 2.2% from other Minority Community.'[28] The total of these is 60.8 per cent, which means that the remaining 39.2 per cent students are UCH.[29] Given that the UCH constitute

---

[25] Ministry of Human Resource Development (2017: iv).

[26] Ministry of Human Resource Development (2017: T-38).

[27] Emphasis in original. Ministry of Human Resource Development (2017: iv).

[28] Ministry of Human Resource Development (2017: iv).

[29] Ministry of Human Resource Development (2017: iv). Admittedly, these percentages are for undergraduates; we do not have the space to undertake a more level-specific analysis, but it is probably safe to propose that these figures will likely skew increasingly in favour of the UCH, as we move higher up the education ladder. This is confirmed by Narayanan (2015).

just about 20 per cent of the total population, the fact that they constitute the single largest bloc in higher education is not only a register of their disproportionate hold on higher education, but becomes a significant factor for their subsequent dominance of the professional jobs.

Representativeness and Power

The annual report mentioned earlier, from the Ministry of Personnel, Public Grievances and Pensions, also states that 'a total of 34,71,693 applications were received and processed ... for Civil Services/Posts' in 2016–17, and that 'a total of 3,244 candidates (including 167 candidates through Reserve List) were recommended for Civil Services/Posts'.[30] That is, 347,1693 candidates, out of the eligible 7,989,409 pass-outs (or about 43.5 per cent), applied for *just 3,244* CG positions—a success ratio of 1:1070. This is not just an indicator of the competitiveness of and in the services: *it is a mark of how much they are sought after, aspired for—and thus, constitute an index of the power of the State over its subjects.* However, this index must be read alongside the ratio of the number of CG employees to the total population—which, in the Indian case, is (1,210,000,000/3,221,000 =) 1:376. If we consider only the employees of groups A and B (since group C jobs are far less powerful or influential), this goes even higher, to (1,210,000,000/375,119 =) 1:3226. By this reckoning, the greater the ratio, the greater the power of the State, and *vice versa.*

Unpacking the Data

What does all this add up to, what does it mean for the UCH and other categories? It is time now to analyse, to 'read' all this information, and see what it is telling us in terms of the 'representativeness' of these categories. In the data compiled in the tables earlier, the contours of representativeness—or lack thereof—begin to emerge quite clearly and may be graphically represented thus:

---

[30] GoI (2018: 33).

Whose State Is It Anyway? Reservation, Representation, Caste, and Power 191

A quick recap of the keys is probably useful here:

R1: Representativeness of individual communities in the CG services as a whole
R2: Representativeness of CG employees within their own individual communities
R3: Communities as percentages of the total population
R4: Community-wise representativeness of CG employees in the total population

If we recall here our discussion around the meanings of 'representativeness' at the beginning of this article, we can now see quite clearly that:

1. Bar 'R3' shows the 'of' representativeness of the different categories, in relation to the national demographic. The UCHs have a very minor presence here, barely more than the Ms. The HSSOs, contrarily, have the biggest presence, and—at least in terms of R3—have the greatest claim to be representative 'of' the nation as a whole.
2. The large UCH blocs in the other three bars registers the extent to which—in each kind of representativeness—the UCHs have gained presence over, despite being smaller than, the other communities.
3. The other three bars thus register the 'greater' representativeness of the UCH 'to' the other communities, as well as 'to' itself (as a community) and 'to' the national demographic.

These UCH claims to greater representativeness are a direct product of their (relatively much greater) ownership of the means of representation, as well as of the institutions of production of the representations themselves, that is, the education system. This is not just about the ownership of the fields of representation and, hence, of discourse; it is about ownership of the means of 'evaluation' that determine 'representativeness'. It is in this sense that, although the principle of proportional representation has driven the policy of reservations, the policy itself has become an institutionalized means to prevent HSSO representativeness from ever growing beyond their stipulated quota limits.[31] The myth of the objectivity,

---

[31] Teltumbde (2018: 63).

impartiality, and fairness of the 'merit' and 'evaluatory' system has been one of the most disingenuous ways in which social differentiation and exclusion have been naturalized. It has proved to be one of the most resilient and enduring consequences of UCH ownership of the fields of representation.

Concluding Observations

For lack of space now, we can only dwell briefly on the other method of differentiation, namely, the 'acquisitory' one. We had noted at the beginning that we would explore the similarities between these two very different methods of exclusion. If the objective of the 'evaluatory' method of differentiation and exclusion was to establish UCH dominance of the State as a 'natural' phenomenon, then the objective of the 'acquisitory' method is to hold out the promise that this dominance can be challenged, overcome (or reinforced, perpetuated, depending on one's standpoint) by racking up electoral victories for the community's representatives that will aggregate eventually into political dominance. However, in actual fact, the objective of this 'acquisitory' method is as deeply disingenuous as that of the 'evaluatory', for several reasons. We will flag just the most obvious ones here.

Firstly, unlike the long-term, 'professional' job of the average bureaucrat, political positions are mostly short-term stints in ministries, or in Parliament when it is active. The politician's sense that s/he represents his/her community and its interests in policy and decision-making forums such as the Parliament is severely undercut by the fact that most of these forums are not constituted through proportional representation, but through regional representation. Regions with relatively homogeneous demographic profiles are then likely to send up a greater number of 'their' political representatives to these forums. But not so is the national profile, which is profoundly heterogenous and diverse. This is sought to be circumvented through constituting national parties, which by promoting the nation as a singular community, through discourses of nationalism, patriotism, and citizenship, seek to minimize inter-community and intra-regional differences; and in order to project themselves as truly 'representative', they seek to maximize the votes they can acquire. But in the process,

Whose State Is It Anyway? Reservation, Representation, Caste, and Power 193

they are compelled to cease representing their communities and to take up the cause(s) of the nation. This method, arguably, could truly potentially undercut caste hierarchies and social and political power imbalances, through combining proportional representation with the acquisitory method, and ensuring that its representativeness persists with greater professionalization and longer terms. It is one of the profounder ironies of the Indian political scene that instead, this method is itself undercut, not only by getting tangled in discourses of the nation and nationalism but also by never ever having a long enough term to even dent the resilient institutions of inequality.

Secondly, it is important to understand that representation is not just about 'standing in for', or 'on behalf' of a person or community: it is about visibility. If the State is constituted of its citizens, then the nation is constituted of its citizens' imaginations of it. If the State works through and is worked by its representatives, then the nation is narrated through its representations, and the relations between the two are dynamic and mutual: the representatives of the State determine the representations of the nation to a very large extent; but the representations of the nation, as they are purveyed in its narratives from epics and mythologies to school textbooks, conversely also impact upon the representatives of the State—from their selection to their perpetuation and reproduction in the system. Whether through the acquisitory method or the evaluatory, the elected or selected representatives together constitute a profile of presences. The visibility of these presences can depend on the extent of their representativeness, but also on their contexts of working: wherever they are, they are visible as the working of the State (as we had noted at the beginning of this article), and as the state itself. It is for this reason that bars R2 and R3 in Figure 8.1 are startling in their implications: for they indicate clearly that the HSSOs, despite their large numbers, have very low visibility, while the UCHs, though barely bigger than the minorities (M), are highly visible. When the national bureaucracy, and the national Parliament, are constituted in this way, there can be little doubt then that the image of the nation, shaped by the workings of its State, will be overwhelmingly in terms set by the UCH. And for this very reason, the HSSOs will never ever be seen as a part of this UCH nation. But the elaboration of this must wait for another occasion.

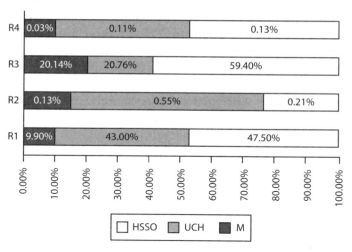

Figure 8.1 Representativeness of CG Employees
Source: Author.

References

Ambedkar, B.R. 2017 [1949]. 'Lessons for Today in Ambedkar's Last Address to the Constituent Assembly', in *Wire*, 'Lessons for Today in Ambedkar's Last Address to the Constituent Assembly', 14 April. Available at https://thewire.in/government/ambedkar-constitution-assembly-democracy, accessed 17 April 2017.

Bhaskar, Anurag. 2017. 'The Law is Clear: Reserved Category Candidates Are Entitled to General Seats on the Basis of Merit'. *Wire*, 28 April. Available at https://thewire.in/law/reservation-law-india-sc-st-obc , accessed 30 April 2017.

GoI (Government of India). 2014. *Census of Central Government Employees (As On 31st March, 2011)*. New Delhi: Ministry of Labour and Employment.

———. 2016a. *Brochure on Reservation for SCs/STs and OBCs*. New Delhi: Department of Public Enterprises, Ministry of Heavy Industries and Public Enterprises. Available at https://dpe.gov.in/sites/default/files/Reservation_Brochure-2.pdf, accessed 1 April 2018.

———. 2016b. *Handbook on Social Welfare Statistics*. New Delhi: Department of Social Justice and Empowerment, Ministry of Social Justice and Empowerment. Available at http://socialjustice.nic.in/writereaddata/UploadFile/HANDBOOK%20Social%20Welfare%20Statistice%202016.pdf, accessed 1 April 2018.

Whose State Is It Anyway? Reservation, Representation, Caste, and Power 195

———. 2017. *Annual Report on Pay and Allowances of Central Government Civilian Employees, 2016–17*. New Delhi: Department of Expenditure, Ministry of Finance. Available at https://doe.gov.in/sites/default/files/PayAllowance2016–17%28English%29.pdf, accessed 1 April 2018.

———. 2018. *Annual Report, 2017–2018*. New Delhi: Ministry of Personnel, Public Grievances and Pensions. Available at https://dopt.gov.in/reports/annual-report, accessed 7 June 2019.

Kumar, Suresh D. 2017. '24 Years On, OBC Workforce in Centre Still Short of Mandal Mark'. *Hindu*, 9 December. Available at https://www.thehindu.com/news/national/24-years-on-obc-workforce-in-centre-still-short-of-mandal-mark/article21382491.ece, accessed 12 May 2018.

Ministry of Human Resource Development. 2017. *All India Survey on Higher Education (2016–17)*. New Delhi: Department of Higher Education.

Montevideo Convention. 1933. *Montevideo Convention on the Rights and Duties of States*. 26 December. Montevideo: Montevideo Convention. Available at https://www.ilsa.org/Jessup/Jessup15/Montevideo%20Convention.pdf, accessed 12 May 2018.

Narayanan, S.V. 2015. 'Higher Education is Still a Bar Too High for Muslims, Dalits'. *Wire*, 8 September. Available at https://thewire.in/education/higher-education-is-still-a-bar-too-high-for-muslims-dalits, accessed 12 May 2018.

Parker, Priya. 2006. *Summary of Sachar Committee Report*. 7 December. New Delhi: PRS Legislative Research. Available at http://www.prsindia.org/administrator/uploads/general/1242304423~~Summary%20of%20Sachar%20Committee%20Report.pdf, accessed 22 August 2012.

PTI (Press Trust of India). 2013. 'Army Recruitment done on Caste, Region, Religion Lines, SC Told'. *Hindu*, 4 December. Available at https://www.thehindu.com/news/national/army-recruitment-done-on-caste-region-religion-lines-sc-told/article5421631.ece, accessed 30 April 2017.

———. 2017. 'Minority Percentage in Central Govt Jobs Doubled to 9.9%: Govt'. *Economic Times*, 6 February. Available at https://economic-times.indiatimes.com/news/politics-and-nation/minority-percentage-in-central-govt-jobs-doubled-to-9-9-govt/articleshow/57005855.cms, accessed 12 May 2018.

Sachar, Rajinder Saiyid Hamid, T.K. Oommen, M.A. Basith, Rakesh Basant, Akhtar Majeed, and Abusaleh Shariff. 2006. *Social, Economic and Educational Status of the Muslim Community of India: A Report*.

Prime Minister's High Level Committee (Sachar Committee). New Delhi: Cabinet Secretariat, Government of India.

Teltumbde, Anand. 2018. *Republic of Caste: Thinking Equality in the Time of Neoliberal Hindutva*. New Delhi: Navayana.

Times of India. 2018. 'Data: OBCs Just 12% of Lower Court Judges'. 29 January. Available at https://timesofindia.indiatimes.com/india/data-obcs-just-12-of-lower-court-judges/articleshowprint/62687268.cms, accessed 15 February 2018.

9

Reclaiming Social Justice and Deepening Democracy

JAGANNATHAM BEGARI

The world has moved towards modernity and globalization and is, today, considered as a global village. India is not an exemption to this trend. Despite the modernity, rights, and various provisions enshrined in the Constitution of India, the marginalized sections or subalterns in India still today continue to face social discrimination, humiliation, and violence based on caste, class, gender, religion, region, and ethnicity. The response of the State towards the heinous atrocities can be termed as lackadaisical. This disturbing trend has led to a spurt in people's movements across the country. To examine this, the chapter is an attempt to revisit the philosophy of B.R. Ambedkar. The chapter is divided into two aspects: theoretical interventions of B.R. Ambedkar and mapping of the atrocities on Dalits and other subalterns in India.

Revisiting Ambedkar's Multifaceted Personality in the Modern Era

B.R. Ambedkar had multiple agendas as well as multiple careers. His struggle was not confined merely against caste inequalities. He had a broader vision to build a society based on equality, liberty, and fraternity. Ambedkar was a lawyer, teacher, legislator, educational organizer, economist, social scientist and social activist, party builder, and minister. Notwithstanding these roles, he continued to be a prolific writer. He published books on subjects such as federalism, theology and philosophy, finance, language, constitutionalism, the social system, and so on. Ambedkar had touched upon aspects such as federalism, separate electorates for the depressed classes, women, the Kashmir issue, smaller states, minorities, and the economy. Dr B.R. Ambedkar's volumes speak about his assiduous efforts in establishing an egalitarian society.

As Ramchandra Guha has rightly mentioned, the views of Ambedkar's biographer sum up what Ambedkar had achieved for the untouchables:

> It was for the first time in the history of the past twenty-five hundred years that the sun of a better future arose on their horizon. Ambedkar, the son of their soil, their kith and kin, focused the world's attention on their civil, social and political rights and liberties, made untouchables a burning topic of the day, raised it to an international importance and gave it a global publicity. His ceaseless hard struggle and his merciless hammer forced an opening for them, and inaugurated an era of light and liberty. He awakened in them out a sense of human dignity, a feeling of self-respect and burning hatred of untouchability that was worse than slavery.[1]

Ambedkar started several social and political organizations and institutions and wrote extensively about their issues in Marathi and English. Against this backdrop, this chapter attempts to emphasize Ambedkar's understanding of democracy. Ambedkar's philosophy and his continuous interventions in search of justice, equality, liberty, freedom, and morality had enhanced, influenced, inspired, and given the perspective and framework for many, irrespective of their identities and ideologies. He started his temple entry movement in the 1920s. Ambedkar reminded the audience of their failure to secure elementary rights or equal status in Hindu society through Kalaram temple entry movement. And Ambedkar said:

> Because we have the misfortune of calling ourselves as Hindus, we are treated thus. If we were members of another Faith, none would dare treat us so. Choose any religion which gives you equality of status and treatment. We shall repair our mistake now. I had

[1] Guha (2010: 207).

the misfortune of being born with the stigma of an Untouchable. However, it is not my fault; but I will not die a Hindu, for this is in my power.[2]

Against this background, it is to be noted that B.R. Ambedkar had *rejected the Hindu religion and converted into Buddhism in the year of 1956.*

B.R. Ambedkar's Understanding of Democracy and Making of the Indian Constitution

Ambedkar envisaged a good society based on the principles of liberty, equality, and fraternity. Democracy, as he saw it, was both an end and the means for achieving this ideal. It was the end, because he ultimately considered democracy as coterminous with the realization of liberty, equality, and fraternity. At the same time, democracy was also the means through which this ideal was to be attained. Ambedkar's notion of a 'democratic government' went back to the fundamental idea of 'government of the people, by the people and for the people'. However, 'democracy' meant much more to him than democratic government. It was a way of life. 'Democracy,' for him, 'is not merely a form of government. It is primarily a mode of associated living, of conjoint communicated experience. It is essentially an attitude of respect and reverence towards one's fellow men.'[3] Another crucial feature of Ambedkar's conception of democracy is that it was geared to social transformation and human progress. In an inspiring definition of the term, he described democracy as 'a form and a method of government, whereby revolutionary changes in the economic and social life of the people are brought about without bloodshed'.[4] B.R. Ambedkar's passion for democracy was closely related to his commitment to rationality and the scientific outlook. At an obvious level, rationality is necessary for democratic government, since public debate (an essential aspect of democratic practice) is impossible in the absence of a shared adherence

---

[2] Zelliot (2013: 147).
[3] Moon (2014: Vol. 1, 57).
[4] Dreze (2005: 1–9).

to common sense, logical argument, critical enquiry, and rational thinking. He further says that science can also have a unifying influence in human affairs: the delights of scientific enquiry can be universally shared, irrespective of race, nationality, religion, or other identities. Ambedkar felt that 'morality', in the sense of social ethics, was indispensable for the realization of liberty and equality. In the absence of morality, he thought, there were only two alternatives: anarchy or the police.[5] Ambedkar's many criticisms of the caste system were that it undermines social ethics and morality. Ambedkar's emphasis on morality was well integrated with his commitment to rationality and the scientific spirit. In particular, he considered that morality was always subject to rational scrutiny. Ambedkar's vision of democracy encompassed 'political, social and economic democracy'. As he saw it, political democracy alone could not be expected to go very far, if glaring economic and social inequalities remained.[6] The apprehensions of Ambedkar are proved correct as we can still find tremendous gaps and contradictions in socio-economic and political life of the people.

G. Haragopal has rightly said that B.R. Ambedkar was aware of the iniquitous forces embedded in the social systems, economic institutions, and political organizations in India in relation to the weaker and vulnerable sections of the society and, therefore, considered it necessary to provide for specific safeguards in the Constitution in their favour.[7] The Constitution set out the fundamental rights of the citizens, especially, equality, freedom of speech and expression, protection of life and liberty, non-discrimination, abolition of untouchability, and prohibition of forced labour. The Directive Principles of State Policy envisaged a social order in which justice—social, economic, and political—will inform all institutions of national life, with minimizing of inequalities of income status and opportunities, the right to adequate means of livelihood, as well as the equitable control and ownership of material resources of the community. Protection of the interests of the weaker sections of the people from social injustice and all forms of

[5] Dreze (2005).
[6] Moon (2014: Vol. 1, 41).
[7] Haragopal (2002).

exploitation is a specific directive incorporated in Article 46 of the Constitution.[8]

The Indian Constitution is, thus, he said, a quest for equality and a just society. As eloquently expressed by Ambedkar, S.R. Sankaran said, 'We must make our political democracy a social democracy as well'.[9] Political democracy cannot last unless there lies at the base of it social democracy. What does social democracy mean? It means a way of life, which recognizes liberty, equality, and fraternity as the principles of life. S.R. Sankaran further reminded that 'we must begin by acknowledging the fact that there is complete absence of two things in Indian society: equality and fraternity'.[10] Ambedkar believed that establishing equal human and civil rights for the depressed classes alone was not sufficient in ensuring justice and welfare to them, unless it was accompanied by the legal provisions and safeguards to uphold those rights in the case of their violation and denial.[11] The tangible contribution of Ambedkar is echoed in the protective discrimination scheme or the reservation policy of the government visualized in some of the provisions of Part III and many of Part IV of the Constitution. He believed that providing rights to all citizens would not be enough since the powerful and the privileged might be able to deny these to the lower strata of society. Law, therefore, should provide remedies against the invasion of fundamental rights. Ambedkar said in the Constituent Assembly, 'All of us are aware that rights are nothing unless remedies are provided whereby people can seek to obtain redress when rights are invaded'.[12] Thorat has further noted that equality was more important than rights as he believed that without freedom, there is no question of rights. Therefore, he argued, change in the behaviour of the socially and economically privileged and elite castes is more important than solely depending on the Constitution.[13] In view of this, it is necessary to revisit Ambedkar's critique of socialism.

---

[8] Haragopal (2002: 133–59).

[9] Moon (2014: Vol. 9, 131).

[10] Kalse (2015).

[11] Thorat and Kumar (2008).

[12] Jaffrelot and Kumar (2018: 127).

[13] S.K. Thorat in Government of Karnataka (2017).

Ambedkar's Critique of Socialism

B.R. Ambedkar questioned the political-minded Hindus when the socialists and orthodox Hindus were attempting merely to bring in political reforms but were ignoring social reforms. He argued that even in the modern era, the underprivileged sections continue to face social discrimination despite constitutional protections. Hence, Dr Ambedkar maintained that a socialistic interpretation of economic empowerment does not solve social problems that the underprivileged sections are facing since centuries.[14] B.R. Ambedkar argued that economic motive is not the only motive by which man is actuated, but religion, social status, and property serve as sources of power. Ambedkar recognized that the economic interpretation of history is not necessary for the validity of the socialist contention that equalization of property is the only real reform and that it must precede everything else.[15] Therefore, resisting caste discrimination was his first priority.

As a form of division of labour, the caste system suffers from a serious defect. The division of labour, brought about by the caste system, is not a division based on choice. Individual sentiments and individual preferences have no place in it. Instead, it is based on the caste. Hence, Ambedkar argued that caste is a harmful institution, inasmuch as it involves the subordination of man's natural powers and inclinations to the exigencies of social rules. Caste prohibits persons belonging to different castes from intermarrying.[16] Even in modern times, caste still exists in all domains, though in a different modern, sophisticated, and refined form. These modern forms of discrimination are more sophisticated and are more dangerous than earlier forms of discrimination. Ambedkar put forward three propositions to end the caste system: (a) abolition of sub-castes, (b) inter-caste marriages, and (c) inter-dining.[17] These are necessary requirements, but ultimately there should be a change of mindset. The Bengaluru Declaration came up with the recommendation to end caste-based discrimination, by calling for a

---

[14] Moon (2014: Vol. 1, 41).
[15] Moon (2014: Vol. 1, 46).
[16] Moon (2014: Vol. 1, 41).
[17] Moon (2014: Vol. 1, 66–7).

Reclaiming Social Justice and Deepening Democracy　　203

comprehensive reform of caste based occupational vocations. All caste-based occupational vocations must be comprehensively reformed so that these are modernised, formalised and it is ensured that those entering the particular occupation are not representative of a particular caste or community. At the same time, reforms in education and employment can empower the State to liberate people from caste-based occupational oppression.[18]

Ambedkar, the Hindu Code Bill, and Women's Liberation

Ambedkar did not confine himself to the caste question. Instead, he fought for the liberation of women as he felt that it was due to the Indian social system and patriarchy that women were treated unequally. Women were denied entry into public spaces and the right to property. They were not free to live with dignity and enjoy a decent and dignified life. Hence, Ambedkar took up this issue as part of his larger egalitarian agenda when he was the law minister in Independent India. Ambedkar relentlessly fought for the rights of women and argued for equal rights for them in the Hindu Code Bill. It is to be noted that he had condemned the prevailing Hindu law that denied women the right of divorce, while granting to men the right to enter into multiple marriages. Ambedkar's defence of women as the law minister of India appeared in the form of the Hindu Code Bill in the Parliament. However, the bill could not withstand the opposition from the representatives of Hindu orthodoxy.

The major argument was that the bill

> aims at changing the law of marriage, the law of divorce, the law of adoption, law relating to minority and guardianship, the law of Hindu joint family, the law of succession and everything that constitute and what remains of the features of Hindu society. The very foundations not only of one pillar of all the pillars but of all the pillars on which the Hindu society rests, are shaken.[19]

In reality, the bill was a threat to patriarchy, on which the traditional family structure was founded and that was the major reason

[18] Government of Karnataka (2017: 6).
[19] Moon (2013: Vol. 14, Part II: 569).

behind the opposition. The bill sought to abolish polygamy among the Hindus. The bill tried to codify the Hindu laws, which were in a scattered form. Ambedkar proposed to reform these laws on different matters, namely, (a) the right to property of a deceased Hindu dying intestate to both the male and female heirs, (b) the order of succession among different heirs to the property of a deceased dying intestate, (c) the law of maintenance, (d) marriage, (e) divorce, (f) adoption, and (g) minority guardianship. In protest against the failure in getting the bill passed in the Parliament, Ambedkar resigned from his post as law minister.[20] Ambedkar was unhappy with the way Jawaharlal Nehru and his other colleagues in Parliament disappointed him by changing their stand from time to time with regard to the Hindu Code Bill. Although the bill was not passed, his efforts did not entirely go waste. Later, the original bill was split into four different bills with slight changes. Those were passed as: (a) the Hindu Marriage Act, 1955; (b) the Hindu Succession Act, 1956; (c) the Hindu Minority and Guardianship Act, 1956; and (d) the Hindu Adoption and Maintenance Act, 1956.[21]

Nationalism, Nation Building, and Subalterns

It is notable that the mass enthusiasm generated in the wake of Independence and the subsequent engagement in nation-building activities in the early 1950s seemed to have overcome the fissiparous tendencies visible earlier and gave us the illusion that nationalism had indeed invented the nation. But illusion it proved to be, for, as mass euphoria over the British departure receded in collective memory and as the economic front began to stagnate, exacerbating the problems of unemployment, poverty, corruption in public life, tenacious illiteracy, population explosion, and so on, centrifugal and disruptive forces reoccupied the centre stage with unprecedented vehemence. Nationalism, instead of giving birth to one national society, seems to have delivered a whole litter of communities divided from one another in terms of language, religion, region, or caste. The response of the centralizing state to this bizarre phenomenon was predictable. As Aloysius rightly mentions, true to its colonial inheritance, it has been arming itself

[20] Moon (2013: Vol. 14, Part II).
[21] Moon (2014: Vol. 14, Part I, 1326).

to the teeth, not so much against the external enemy as against its own citizens, becoming increasingly nervous about even minor and marginal struggles against any form of exploitation. That the pan-Indian polity no longer attracts the allegiance of the majority of the masses and is increasingly being replaced by smaller entities is clear from the emergence and struggle of nationalists often denigrated through charges of regionalism, linguistic chauvinism, and separatism. Communalism and communal violence are spreading to newer areas with increased intensity, becoming more frequent, and engulfing more and more sections of people. India seems to have become, instead of a nation state, one powerful state system, comprising multiple warring communities. It is, therefore, more appropriately termed as 'Upper caste Brahminical nationalism'.[22] No wonder, India seems to have become a nation in principle and procedurally, but not in spirit.

India has several nationalities in which a few socially and economically dominant sections and castes influence the polity, economy, and, of course, the social sphere. However, the underprivileged and marginalized sections, including women, were not made equal partners in the task of nation-building. It can be argued that a few elites, upper castes, continue to hold sway over all the domains. By excluding Dalits and other marginalized and weaker sections of society, the Indian State has failed to make use of their creative abilities, knowledge, and subjective experience in nation building. In other words, the underprivileged sections were set aside from nation building. It is, therefore, not surprising that the nation has not been able to properly put in place a society based on equality, liberty, fraternity, and morality.[23] It is rather unfortunate that social and economic inequalities are still evident in the present neoliberal era and the gap between the privileged and the deprived or between the powerful and the disempowered or between the wealthy and the poor is large and increasing. The elected persons who are sworn to implement the Constitution's lofty principles are mostly engaged in wilfully breaching and neglecting their constitutional responsibilities for their own gains. It is this elite section that comprises the 5 per cent, very influential section of society. Many prominent members of this section

[22] Aloysius (1997: 1–2).
[23] Begari (2016: 3).

are involved in monstrous corruption scams; yet they define what is patriotism and demand patriotism from everybody else. In this whole spectrum of development, deprived sections are further pushed from the so-called development process. Those who speak and write against injustice and speak the truth are dealt with by using coercive means. Some social activists (such as Narendra Dabholkar, Govind Pansare, and M.M. Kalburgi) are eliminated by self-appointed vigilantes or through extra-judicial killings arranged by shady and unaccountable agencies of the State.

Mapping Atrocities against Dalits in Modern India

Discrimination, humiliations, and atrocities experienced by Dalits and the cases of rape of Dalit women by the upper-caste men appear to be regular phenomena in India. It is rather distressing that atrocities against Dalits, who constitute around a sixth of the nation's population, and the consequent denial of justice in a majority of cases are an unfortunate reality of our country. It is found that there is a huge gap between constitutional pronouncements to abolish untouchability in all its forms and the actual practice on the ground level. Even in the media coverage (electronic and print), Dalit issues receive little or no attention and are soon relegated to the back pages. Some of the atrocity cases such as Mirchpur, Haryana (where a Dalit settlement was attacked by the dominant castes, killing two); Banthal, Gujarat (where Dalits were expelled en masse from the village); Jait (the Madhya Pradesh chief minister's village where Dalits were denied temple entry); Madurai (where the government itself usurped Dalit land); or Bathani Tola and Laxmanpur Bathe in Bihar[24] caused little debate in the public domain in the country.

One such incident took place on 13 April 2013 in Pabnava village of Kaithal District of Haryana state. Here, a Dalit youth Suryakant (24) broke the caste rules and married his classmate, Meena (22), a *Rod-Maratha* girl. The Rods were unable to digest this transgression and threatened the family of Suryakant, asking him to divorce Meena. Suryakant did not agree to this suggestion. As a result, the parents and Dalit families of the village

---

[24] New Socialist Initiative (2010: 23).

Reclaiming Social Justice and Deepening Democracy   207

were attacked by the goons belonging to the Rod community. However, there was no substantial response from the police and the administration. In another case in the state of Odisha, an entire Dalit *pada* (hamlet) was burnt to ashes by upper castes in Lathore village, Khaprakhol block, Balangir District (2012). Similarly, in February, in Kamadhenukote village of Dhenkanal District of the state, twenty-two Dalit houses were burnt down on suspicion of not voting for a particular candidate in the Panchayat elections (2012). Besides these, it is prerequisite to examine atrocity cases such as the Karamchedu massacre, Tsundur massacre, attacks on Dalits in Laxmipet, attacks in Andhra Pradesh, and Khairlanji massacre in Maharashtra. The gruesome brutal murder of four members of a Dalit family in Khairlanji village (Mohadi Taluka, District Bhandara) shocked the nation.[25] In a few cases, they went up to the higher courts and Supreme Court; however, there was no considerable justice done to the Dalit victims. The result was severe—expulsion from the villages, humiliation, and killings of Dalits. This is largely because of the emergence of an educated class due to their access to education, employment, electoral politics, and the like. All these cases act as an evidence of the atrocities committed against Dalits in modern India.

Interrogating Discrimination and Humiliation in Modern India

Gopal Guru argues that the Dalit assertion is an active process basically through asymmetries of intersecting sets of attitudes: arrogance and obeisance, self-respect and servility, and reverence and repulsion.[26] It continues to survive in different forms depending upon the specific social context. This involves the dynamics of social life with contradictory responses offered by the modern elite. Thus, on the one hand, the dynamics of social life shakes these social elite from the humiliating social protocols that regulate feudal society. On the other hand, these so-called modern social elites tend to reproduce structures, both institutional (state) and moral (friendship) that underlie and renew the phenomenon

[25] All India Team (2007).
[26] Guru (2009).

of humiliation. The reorganization of modern society was largely based on the division between the private and public spheres, which was accompanied by the possibility of misrecognition, degradation, and humiliation. Transgression of the boundaries between the private and the public spheres was considered as the context for humiliation.[27]

S.K. Thorat has posited that there is not only social discrimination but also economic discrimination in the modern era.[28] The people from SCs have been excluded from access to agricultural land and a high proportion of atrocities and violence against them are mainly related to the issues of land. It is due to landlessness that Dalits continue to face discrimination. The prevalence of market discrimination against certain social groups creates adverse consequences for economic growth and income distribution and can lead to inter-group conflict. Market discrimination leads to income inequalities and a high degree of deprivation for the discriminated groups and it induces inter-group conflict.[29]

Teltumbde argues that, after Independence in 1947, rural India was transformed through a modernizing project that included, among other things, land reforms and the capital-intensive technologies of the Green Revolution in agriculture.[30] Capitalist production relations came to the villages and seemed to shake the caste structure to its roots—but caste survived nonetheless. Since the mid-1980s, neoliberal India has taken remarkable strides towards globalizing its economy and, with an impressive recent growth record, has increasingly been projecting itself as an emerging superpower. The world is dazzled by its success. Caste was expected to fall away under the pressure of the global order. But this has not happened. On the contrary, it appears to have grown far more vicious, if caste atrocities are taken as a proxy measure. Indeed, caste has showed a remarkable resilience. It has survived feudalism, capitalist industrialization, a republican Constitution, and today, despite all denial, the institution of caste is well alive under neoliberal globalization.[31]

---

[27] Guru (2009: 1–2).
[28] Thorat (2007).
[29] Thorat (2007: 3–9).
[30] Teltumbde (2010).
[31] Teltumbde (2010: 2).

Higher Educational Institutions as Hubs of Discrimination

The notion of discrimination, humiliation, and exclusion are inbuilt in the very structure of the educational institutions, including in higher education. This can be seen in the curriculum, pedagogy, approach of the administration, the negative approach of the teaching faculty towards the Dalit students, and discrimination in the evaluation of their answer sheets. The discrimination is sometimes visible and many times invisible, and in fact, most of the time, these are found in very subtle forms. These are disguised in the ornamental and metaphorical language used, body gestures, and in the garb of implementing objective institutional rules. It is the individual experience—each being a different and unique form of discrimination that the Dalit students face.[32] Sharmila Rege has rightly pointed out that 'New times' in the university are marked by narratives that bemoan a 'decline in plurality and standards', especially in places where a new generation of scholars and students from historically disadvantaged sections in Indian society are posing challenges to the social homogeneity of the classroom, Boards of Studies, and other academic bodies, leading to obvious frictions on issues related to a decline in standards and merit. Mahatma Phule, in the first modern Marathi play *Trutiya Ratna*, draws complex linkages between religious-cultural and educational authority and reimagines education as the *Trutiya Ratna* (third eye) that has the potential for enabling the oppressed to understand and to transform the relation between power and knowledge. Ambedkar, in a speech in Nagpur in 1942, called upon his followers to 'Educate-Agitate-Organise', arguing that this was central to the battle for freedom.[33]

Rohith's Suicide and Resistance for Democratization

At this, juncture, it is necessary to examine the suicide of Rohith Vemula. The suicide of a Dalit student was not the first of its kind in the University of Hyderabad. In fact, it has been reported that

[32] Kumar (2016: 12–15).
[33] Rege (2010: 88–98).

over six students have resorted to this extreme step. A common thread in all these suicides had been that all were due to caste discrimination. Rohith's suicide has been in the public domain as there was direct political interference from the government in the affairs of the university. In light of this, it is posited that it is due to reservations that students from marginalized sections are entering educational institutions. When they enter the universities, they start asserting their rights and resist the social discrimination. In other words, the educated youth from the Dalit community are currently questioning the superior and condescending behaviour of the administration, the teaching faculty, and the State. However, such an assertive response of these students is leading to their suppression in higher learning institutions. A case in point is the suspension of five Dalit students, including Rohith Vemula, which led to his suicide. The callous and atrocious response of the State and political elite towards the marginalized sections has further accelerated the discrimination against the Dalit students in other universities in India—such as filing sedition cases against students, suspension, arresting students, and not permitting students to hold meetings. The committee that was constituted by the GoI to enquire into Rohith Vemula's death came out with a biased report. Instead of detailing the reasons that led to his death, it had entirely confined itself to the question of which caste Rohith Vemula belongs to. It is a clear reflection of the negative attitude of the State. As a result of Rohith Vemula's suicide, his mother and brother converted to Buddhism.[34] Even in Gujarat, after the Una incident, more than 200 Dalits converted to Buddhism.[35] After conceptualizing these cases, it is prerequisite to refer to the words of B.R. Ambedkar as he said,

> The position of Scheduled Castes today so far as I see, it is the same before, the same old tyranny, the same old oppression, the same old discrimination which exists before, exists now, and perhaps in a worst form.[36]

[34] Vemula (2016).
[35] Dabhi (2016).
[36] Moon (2013: Vol. 14, Part II, 1320).

Reclaiming Social Justice and Deepening Democracy 211

The Una Incident in Gujarat State and Dalit–Muslim Unity: A Way Forward

The Una tragedy reveals that the Gujarat model of development has failed to ensure justice for the most deprived and exploited sections of society. The claims of the Gujarat government that it is the best governed state and ranks first in terms of the indices of development are under serious question now. The findings of several studies based on a survey say that the practice of manual scavenging and untouchability is still prevalent in many parts of Gujarat. It finds that in more than half of the villages in Gujarat surveyed, Dalits did not have access to wells, temples, tea stalls, panchayat offices, barbers, non-Dalit mid-wives, and midday meals due to non-implementation of the SC and ST (PoA) Act, 1989.[37] Dalits are being targeted in various parts of the country in the name of cow protection. In the state of Gujarat, four Dalit youths were publicly flogged by a cow vigilante group on 11 July 2016. Members of the Gau Raksha Samiti (Committee of Cow Protection) came across a Dalit family skinning the carcass of a dead cow in the village of Mota Samadhiyala in Unataluka of Gir Somnath District. Accusing them of cow slaughter, these vigilantes beat up the entire family and then picked up four youths, stripped them to the waist, chained them to the back of a car, and drove it to Una town, where they were again beaten up close to a police station. This uncivilized behaviour of cow vigilantes once again reminds the entire nation about the social discrimination against Dalits, which has been in existence in spite of a modern, democratic, and secular nation. Thousands of Dalits took a pledge in the rally meeting *not to remove cow carcasses* and demanded five acres of land for each family. Members of the Muslim community came out in large numbers to support the Dalit community in their campaign. The activists in Gujarat called for a march to Una, after a series of localized protests. The *gaurakshak*s have targeted Muslims and Dalits, forging a bond between them without clearly intending to.

Muslims and Dalits see a commonality of purpose and it is also indispensable to resist the anti-Dalit and anti-Muslim groups. The slogan '*Dalits-Muslims bhai-bhai*' (brotherhood between Dalits and Muslims) reflects the spirit of the unity between Dalits and

---

[37] Jaffrelot (2016).

Muslims. Under the banner of Una Dalit Atyachar Ladat Samiti (UDALS), they started a march from Ahmedabad to Una and raised a slogan, 'You take cow's tail, give us land' and took a pledge 'not to be in the business of skinning of cows and to abandon the practice of cleaning the underground drains by going down manholes'. This has created enormous awareness among subalterns in India.

The Dadri incident of killing Mohammad Akhlaq struck new fear amongst the Muslims. The Muzaffarnagar violence was part of the campaign of anti-Muslim groups against what is termed 'love jihad' and the hapless Dadri villager was killed as part of the 'gauraksha' campaign launched by the same forces. The lynching in Dadri and the flogging in Una would have remained isolated incidents had it not been that both were carried out by cow vigilantes through a public display of intolerance that left India shocked. Mobs who attacked Muslims claim to protect the cow; they dragged out a Muslim man from his home and beat him to death in a village in Dadri in September 2015. However, instead of bringing the anticipated kudos, it generated deep anger, not only in Gujarat but across the country. The suicide by Rohith Vemula and the subsequent politics by the National Democratic Alliance (NDA) government shifted equations rapidly and moved the youth into a pattern of resistance. Rohith Vemula's mother was constantly pilloried by the government and BJP for not being a Dalit. These incidents, in fact, raised apprehensions about the political leaders and functioning of India's democracy.

Appropriation, Identity, and Assertions: A Perspective from Below

India celebrated the 126th birth anniversary of B.R. Ambedkar in a grand way this year. The GoI had directed all the higher educational institutions to celebrate B.R. Ambedkar's birth anniversary. The State had purchased the house of Ambedkar in London where he had stayed for some time. This is a positive aspect of the State. On the one hand, the State and political elites intend to use the figure of Ambedkar for their political gains. On the other hand, they are not serious about implementing his ideals, values, practices, and the egalitarian vision for which he fought. The government of Maharashtra has demolished the historical building that was the house of Ambedkar, *Rajgriha*, in Dadar

(East Mumbai), where he had stayed during his productive years and from where he led the movement against the social inequalities and the stigma of untouchability, in the name of development of Ambedkar's memorial. Therefore, it is argued that the State does not make substantial efforts to stop atrocities on Dalits, does not stop heinous acts against women, and does not provide confidence to Dalits, tribals, women, and other religious minorities. On the other hand, the State cuts down the funds for higher education, stops fellowships for the students from weaker sections, and initiates the process of strict surveillance on the students. The administration of higher learning institutes continues to discriminate against Dalit students, rusticates them from the universities, and harasses them psychologically, mentally, and physically. Some universities have gone to the extent of suspending and arresting Dalit teachers, students, and other opinion-makers, branding those who stood by the democratic cause as anti-nationals and putting them under electronic surveillance legitimized by the State.

The dual nature of the State, political elite, and government is a treacherous threat to the very fundamental principles of the Indian Constitution. Notwithstanding the conventional celebrations initiated by the GoI, the people of India, particularly, the marginalized sections, celebrate and take a pledge to carry forward the vision and objectives of B.R. Ambedkar and resist the discriminations in the social, economic, and political domains. Foreign countries, such as Canada, the United Kingdom, and the United States of America, too have installed statues of B.R. Ambedkar in their countries, celebrated his birth anniversary, and organized seminars to honour him and get stimulation from his ideas, philosophy, thoughts, and relentless struggles against the unjust Hindu social order and towards building a modern nation based on egalitarian values.

These countries consider Ambedkar a symbol of egalitarian principles. However, the political elite in India play a dubious role in honouring and respecting Ambedkar's contribution. It is found that a set of scholars deliberately avoid mentioning, theorizing, and recognizing the philosophy of B.R. Ambedkar. Nonetheless, they try to find faults with his interventions. The same set of scholars try to put all efforts into denigrating the philosophy of Ambedkar and fail to differentiate between the dimensions of Dalit assertions and Dalit politics. When Dalits speak, write, and assert their rights, it is easy to brand their assertions as Dalit politics, caste politics, and identity politics and to forget to recognize their assertions and articulations as alternative democratic voices. A few intellectuals who get recognition due to their Dalit identity ignore Dalits and criticize Dalit scholars. They try to have cordial relations with or get a platform in the platforms of others or align with so-called Marxist scholars. It is to be noted that there are limitations, internal problems which need to be corrected, and efforts to be initiated within the Dalit movement. It argued that it is essential that one has to speak, write, assert, and create consciousness among the masses about the problems related to caste and about social problems that marginalized sections have been facing since centuries. It is to be noted that Dalit politics are different from that of Dalit assertions though both are equally concerned about the welfare of Dalits; however, the aim of political parties who represent Dalits and weaker sections of society is to get political power like other conventional political parties. Even a few scholars who talk of the caste problem do not like to recognize themselves with Dalit assertions as they are based on the identity of caste. Ambedkar took active part in Indian politics, formed political organizations and a political party, played an active role in policymaking, and participated in social activism. We have to make a note here that politics is not completely ruthless or useless; politics in any democratic country or set-up has the potential to find solutions to the problems.

There are essentially two kinds of politics: politics against hegemony and politics of the hegemonic class. Dalit politics and Dalit assertions come under the purview of politics against hegemony, caste, and gender inequalities. Dalit politics comes under the purview of politics against hegemony. Instead of aligning with and supporting Dalit assertions and Dalit movements, political parties, political leaders, and a few intellectuals who claim that they represent Dalits and their problems deprive Dalits and discriminate against Dalits. Self-criticality is an important aspect among the scholars who narrow down Dalit assertions. These negative trends among the scholars need to be resisted at all levels. Otherwise, other anti-progressive groups would further widen the gap among progressive forces and make use of it for their political, cultural, and religious prosperity. It will be again a threat to the ethos of India's democracy that Ambedkar envisaged.

Scholars in academia affiliate with theory as a specialization. Theorizing is a passion for them. But the question arises as to what and who one is theorizing. It is to be noted that theorizing shall involve not merely passion, but compassion, ethics, and morality as well. Theorizing on social discrimination, caste discrimination, humiliation, gender discrimination, equality, and so on, requires morality and ethics. It is interesting to note that a set of scholars and students of theory lack moral values. If one does not qualify as a moral being, one is not qualified to be a theoretician or a student of theory. The notion of morality also has its own limitations; political, spiritual, and social prejudices; and economic biases. Even for Ambedkar, the notion of morality, ethics, and fraternity was vital to his understanding of democracy and in his egalitarian project. One has to be morally correct and ethically truthful, so that the theory carries sanctity. Otherwise, it would be another futile exercise. The notion of morality and ethics are part of Buddhism, which has shown the way for democratic movements in the world.[38]

Ambedkar's theories, response, and resistance against the social discrimination and against unethical incidents are based on morality, legality, and a larger egalitarian agenda. The committed adherents of Ambedkar must understand that his scholarship and his engagement with the social stigma that the lower strata of the society faces are based on morality. The language, assertion, and theoretical interventions of Ambedkar and his response to his contemporaries (M.K. Gandhi and others) relied upon the context, history, and response of the other contemporaries. Therefore, his interventions are close to moral, legal, concrete, realistic, and historical. One should not compare Ambedkar with other modern thinkers of his period. Another way to conceptualize Ambedkar is that he is not merely confined to one stream of thinking, concerns, and section. He is not merely a conventional social reformer, scholar, social activist, and thinker, unlike others. He is above all and he touched the hearts of all subaltern thinkers and democratic voices of the world. His philosophy does not merely confine itself to India but has spread across the world. Eventually, Ambedkar has taken all aspects in fighting injustice and in striving for an egalitarian society. Therefore, if anyone confines and narrows down the contributions of Ambedkar and his resistance, morality, ethics, and scholarship, I argue that they are doing injustice to Ambedkar and his scholarship and egalitarian agenda. Therefore, any scholar

[38] Guru (2017).

identifying with the anti-caste movements and leadership must strive to strengthen Ambedkar's movement, rather than merely critiquing them further and disappointing his other adherents who are carrying forward the egalitarian agenda of Ambedkar.

Post-Ambedkar Buddhist Conversion: The Path Way

According to Ambedkar, Buddhism evolved to fight against the social inequalities existent in Hinduism. Buddhism stands for universal principles. Ambedkar fought for the same values for underprivileged sections of society. Buddhism has produced an alternative discourse to subalterns in India. Therefore, Ambedkar converted to Buddhism at Nagpur with lakhs of followers. The conversion to Buddhism is still going on. The Dalit political discourse has produced a concrete alternative to the mainstream nationalist formulations in all the realms of public reason. The discourse legitimizes the thirst for social change and political power, as its prime instrument is to bring a radical change in social relationships. On one hand, rejection of political dominance by the 'Manuvadis' (proponents who believes the ethos of a society governed by Manusmriti) became the mantra of the new Dalit political ideology. And on the other hand, the Ambedkarite Buddhist identity challenges the 'immoral', unscientific, and regressive mode of social system and is hopeful of building a modern social order based on the human values of Buddhism. This alternative conceptualization of religious identity relates the Dalits to a proud historic legacy of Buddhism and helps them to imagine a new culture, social and political. Both the assertion of a new political identity and conversion to Buddhist identity become essentially important to understand the aspirations of the modern Dalit, as these supplement equally well the radical agenda of social transformations.

Harish argues that the modern Buddhist identity offers the notion of dignity to the new assertive Dalit self, without which he/she will be identified as a wretched, degraded, lower-caste 'Hindu self'.[39] At this juncture, it is essential to analyse the intent of B.R. Ambedkar's conversion. In 1935, Ambedkar announced his decision that 'though he was born as Hindu, but he would not die a Hindu'. Buddhism was seen as an alternative for the Dalits. Ambedkar was

[39] Wankhede (2008: 50–1).

aware of the increased intellectual interest in Buddhism. Eleanor Zelliot has argued that 'efforts to gain education, and efforts to secure political rights such as special representation in legislative bodies, had been fairly successful. However, efforts to claim religious rights had generally ended in failure'.[40] After the great conversion announcement of 1935–6, however, there was a hiatus of twenty years before Ambedkar's formal conversion to Buddhism took place in the year of 1956 at Nagpur. Zelliot argues that converting to Buddhism means relief from the concept of pollution and striving for freedom and respect.[41]

The important reason for the long delay between the conversion announcement in 1935 and Ambedkar's actual conversion twenty years later were that none of the available choices were intellectually and politically suitable to him, and, more importantly, he had the opportunity to work for constitutional change, a method more suited to his abilities than working for a change of heart among the caste Hindus or building a religious movement among untouchables. It is to be noted that he did some organizational work among the 'untouchables' to prepare them for conversion. After condemnation of Hinduism as a religion founded on neither morality nor equality, he expressed an optimistic view of Buddhism's future in India. Eleanor Zelliot argues that Ambedkar's rejection of Hinduism may be read as an attempt to force Hindus to 'modernise their theology, allowing a religious development parallel to the partial modernisation of occupation and political structure'.[42] This trend continued even after Ambedkar's death and lakhs of people converted to Buddhism as a challenge to India's social inequalities.

Bengaluru Declaration and Its Recommendations in the Quest for Justice

On one hand, the present regime and a few political parties evolved the strategy to use the symbol of Ambedkar for their political gains. On the other hand, they violate the rights of marginalized sections and exclude them from the public domain—such as educational

[40] Zelliot (2015: 193).
[41] Zelliot (2015:192–6).
[42] Zelliot (2013: 149).

institutions, development process—and suspect the nationality of Muslim minorities and Dalits. Against this backdrop, the government of Karnataka organized a three-day international conference on 'Reclaiming Social Justice and Revisiting B.R. Ambedkar' in 'Quest for Equity' at Bengaluru from 21 July 2017 to 23 July 2017 and came out with the Bengaluru Declaration. It recognized that the NDA government at the centre is systematically dismantling the institutions that are the foundations of our society, undermining India's holistic welfare and affirmative action architecture, and destroying the pluralistic fabric of India. This poses a grave threat to the idea of India espoused by the freedom movement and spelt out in the Constitution. Therefore, it felt that all progressive forces need to address these concerns urgently and resist the attacks on Dalits and minorities.[43] The declaration has proposed an 'alliance of equity' of all progressive forces committed to safeguarding the idea of India. The declaration believed that 'we can only do that by reasserting the fundamental principle of one person-one value; reclaiming freedom, dignity and human personality, comprehensively addressing the needs and aspirations of all Indians, especially, subalterns'.[44]

Therefore, revisiting the philosophy of B.R. Ambedkar and his relentless struggle is essential to reclaim social justice and a quest for equity. In the absence of equality, rights may not be very effective in fighting for an egalitarian society. One of the important means to attain an egalitarian society and empower marginalized sections, minorities, and women is through free and compulsory education. The Constitution of India clearly states that the State shall take steps and formulate policies in this holistic direction. It is found that no sincere efforts are being made to stop inhuman incidents by consecutive governments. The state, institutions, and intellectuals are becoming mute spectators and sometimes they become party to suicides. This disturbing trend has further deteriorated the spirit of our democracy. Therefore, it can be argued that it is indispensable for everybody, particularly, policymakers and administrators, to respect the Constitution of India. Intellectuals, opinion-makers, and media, both the electronic and print, should break their silence and speak out for the weak and marginalized

[43] Government of Karnataka (2017: 8).
[44] Government of Karnataka (2017: 1).

sections. This chapter intends to argue that one has to respect the assertions of subalterns, particularly assertions of Dalits. Therefore, revisiting the philosophy, struggles, and scholarship of B.R. Ambedkar is indispensable. Ambedkar's mantra of 'educate, agitate and organise' can be very effective in fighting injustice and discrimination in the modern era.

References

All India Team. 2007. *Suppressing the Voice of the Oppressed State Terror on Protests against the Khairlanji Massacre*. Nagpur: Fact Finding Committee, PUCL. Available at http://www.pucl.org/major_reports/Report%20on%20Khairlanji%20Massacre,%202007-2.pdf, accessed 14 February 2020.

Aloysius, G. 1997: *Nationalism without a Nation in India*. New Delhi: Oxford University Press.

Begari, Jagannatham. 2016. *Mapping Human Rights and Subalterns of Modern India*. New Delhi. Kalpaz Publications.

Dabhi, Parimal A. 2016. 'Over 200 Dalits Convert to Buddhism in Gujarat'. *Indian Express*, 12 October. Available at http://indianexpress.com/article/india/india-news-india/dalit-gujarat-atrocities-una-convert-buddhism-3077677/.

Dreze, Jean. 2005. 'Dr. B.R. Ambedkar and the Future of Indian of Democracy.' *Indian Journal of Human Rights*, 9(1&2): 1–9.

Government of Karnataka. 2017. *Bengaluru Declaration*: '*Deepening the Promise of India*'. Bengaluru: Government of Karnataka.

Guha, Ramchandra. 2010. *Makers of Modern India*. New Delhi: Penguin.

Guru, Gopal. 2009. *Humiliation: Claims and Context*. New Delhi: Oxford University Press.

———. 2017. 'Ethics in Ambedkar's Critique of Gandhi'. *Economic and Political Weekly*, 52(15): 95–100.

Haragopal, G. 2002. 'Rights of Dalits: Values and Reality'. *Journal of National Human Rights Commission*, 1: 133–59.

Jaffrelot, Christophe. 2016. 'Complicity and Inequality: The Plight of Dalits in Gujarat cannot be Attributed only to BJP Rule. Congress Must Share the Blame.' Indian Express, 8 August. Available at https://indianexpress.com/article/opinion/columns/dalit-protests-gujarat-una-dalit-flogging-bjp-congress-2960221/ , accessed 14 February 2020.

Jaffrelot, Christophe and Narendra Kumar. 2018. *Dr. Ambedkar and Democracy: An Anthology*. New Delhi: Oxford University Press.

Kalse, Anant. 2015. *Speeches Delivered by Babasaheb Ambedkar Before the Constituent Assembly of India*. Mumbai: Government of Maharashtra.

Kumar, Vivek. 2016. 'Discrimination on Campuses of Higher Learning: A Perspective from Below.' *Economic and Political Weekly*, 51(6): 12–15.

Moon, Vasant (ed.). 2013. *Dr. Babasaheb Ambedkar: Writings and Speeches*. Vol. 14 Part 2. New Delhi: Ambedkar Foundation, GoI.

———. 2014. *Dr. Babasaheb Ambedkar: Writings and Speeches*. New Delhi: Ambedkar Foundation, GoI.

New Socialist Initiative. 2010. 'Atrocities on Dalits'. *Economic and Political Weekly*, 45(4).

Rege, Sharmila. 2010. 'Education as Trutiya Ratna: Towards Phule-Ambedkarite Feminist Pedagogical Practice'. *Economic and Political Weekly*, 45(44): 88–98.

Srinivaasulu, K., A.K. Patnaik, and K.Y. Ratnam. 2012. 'Laxmipet Dalit Killings'. *Economic and Political Weekly*, 47(47/48): 26–8.

Sunani, Khuturam, Nigam, Ranjana Padhi, and Debaranjan Sarangi. 2012. 'The Price of Dalit Assertion on the Burning down of Dalit Houses in Lathore, Odisha'. *Economic and Political; Weekly*, 47(35): 19–21.

Teltumbde, Anand. 2010. *The Persistence of Caste: The Khairlanji Murders and India's Hidden Apartheid*. London: Zed Books.

———. 2016. 'Dalit Protest in Gujarat'. *Economic and Political Weekly*, 51(32): 10.

Thorat, S.K. 2007. 'Economic Exclusion and Poverty: India's Experience of Remedial against Exclusion', draft prepared for 'Agricultural and Rural Development for Reducing Poverty and Hunger in Asia: In Pursuit of Inclusive and Sustainable Growth', lecture, International Food Policy Research Institute and Asian Development Bank (ADB), ADB Headquarters, Manila, Philippines). Available at http://conferences.ifpri.org/2020chinaconference/pdf/manilac_Thorat.pdf, accessed 14 February 2020.

Thorat, Sukhadeo and N. Kumar. 2008. *B.R. Ambedkar: Perspective on Social Exclusion and Inclusive Politics*. New Delhi: Oxford University Press.

Rodrigues, Valerian. 2004. *The Essential Writings and Speeches of B.R. Ambedkar*. New Delhi: Oxford University Press.

Vemula, Raju. 2016. 'Rohith Vemula's Brother Converts to Buddhism, Says Won't Rest till Suicide Probed.' *Indian Express*, 14 April. Available at http://indianexpress.com/article/india/india-news-india/rohith-vemulas-dalit-ambedkar-suicide-buddhism-convert-appa-rao-hyderabad-full-text/, accessed 14 February 2020.

———. 2016. 'Conversion Letter, Mumbai'. *Indian Express*, 14 April. Available at http://indianexpress.com/article/india/india-news-india/rohith-vemula-suicide-jnu-du-students-detained-enroute-to-protest-3076153/, accessed 14 February 2020.

Wankhede, S. Harish. 2008. 'The Political and Social in the Dalit Movement Today'. *Economic and Political Weekly*, 43(6): 50–1.

Zelliot, Eleanor. 2013. *Ambedkar's World: Making of Babasaheb and Dalit Movement*. New Delhi: Navyana Publications.

——— 2015. *From Untouchable to Dalit*. New Delhi: Manohar Publications.

10

Ambedkar's Internationalization of Social Justice

SURAJ YENGDE[*]

Beyond the Nation

Strange, isn't it, that the first common sense on the subject, strongly and publicly enunciated by a political leader of stature, comes from a spokesman of the Harijan Caste.

—Lester B. Granger.

United States National Urban League leader, civil rights activist, and labour organizer Lester B. Granger, while reflecting on global foreign policy programmes, invoked B.R. Ambedkar to describe the failing policies of peaceful coexistence and neutralism famous in the 1950s.[1] This chapter explores the historical intersectional struggle of Dalit rights in global politics. In order to understand it better, I suggest looking at the ideas of Ambedkar, one of the founding figures of modern Indian democracy, on national state formation. Various studies have commented on the international

[*] This chapter is dedicated to the memory of Rajkumar Kamble (1954–2018), who pioneered the Ambedkar-inspired international Dalit movement. It is a slightly modified version of Suraj Yengde. 2018. 'Ambedkar's Foreign Policy and the Ellipsis of the "Dalit" from International Activism', in Suraj Yengde and Anand Teltumbde eds. *The Radical in Ambedkar: Critical Reflections*. Penguin Random House.

[1] Granger (1954: 16).

Ambedkar's Internationalization of Social Justice 223

political imagination of Indian nationalist leaders, namely, Lala Lajpat Rai, Jawaharlal Nehru, and M.K. Gandhi, alongside a stream of other privileged-caste leaders, M.N. Roy included. However, there is not a single study that analyses the international outlook of Ambedkar. The reasons have to do, perhaps, with ignorance about Ambedkar and the prejudice of the dominant privileged-caste academia.[2] The Brahminical historiography of India as well as the country's national narratives bear the responsibility for the egregious omission. This chapter attempts to shed light on the global thinking of subalterns. With the story of Ambedkar, I wish to present the geopolitical thought process of marginalized groups to understand how under-represented groups envision(ed) their location in the international movements of human rights athwart civil and political representation.

In the post-Independence period, the Indian democracy bureaucratized the modus operandi of the social order. In the area of foreign policy especially, the Brahminical class was overwhelmingly appointed to the coveted posts of ambassadors, emissaries, and experts and in the state delegations to various committees of international government bodies. Foreign policy is the international mediation of a country's domestic policies with the rest of the world. It is an arena that guarantees global dialogue on mutual terms. Therefore, by promoting the Brahminical class, the postcolonial Indian State ensured strict control over the global scrutiny of its internal policies.

Extrapolating from this, we may ask what it means to look at the world through the lens of the marginalized. How do we reconcile the vision of the most oppressed under the hegemonic exclusionary theories of foreign policy? Or, simply put, do subalterns think of the global? By determining the position of the marginalized in the policy structures, close attention to Ambedkar's political philosophy illuminates the implications of such a global policy dialogue. This focus could help establish the citizenry of the marginalized community in terms of social, civil, cultural, economic, and political human rights, which are predominantly internationally influenced, globally inspired, and in conversation with other countries. This will also help critically examine how the postcolonial Indian State,

---

[2] Barring one exception: Gaikwad (1999). The author confessed in his preface that the book does not claim to be a complete research work.

224   Suraj Yengde

which was essentially inherited from the colonial regime, kept the foreign policy stance the same by excluding the marginalized community from its deliberations. It ensured that the internal strife between the majority and minority communities remained muted on international platforms.

Internationalist Ambedkar

Ambedkar has been primarily confined to the emancipatory politics of the SC community of India, along with being bestowed with other laurels such as Constitution-maker. However, little is spoken of his role in the colonial and postcolonial Indian foreign policy make-up and in international human rights movements. Ambedkar was a keen observer of India's foreign policy and it constituted one of the cornerstones of his political visions. The All India Scheduled Caste Federation (AISCF), in its election manifesto in 1951 authored by Ambedkar, had a special column titled 'Problems of Foreign Policy', referring to the collapsing state of the Indian foreign programme. In it, Ambedkar made suggestions about the Kashmir issue that had been plaguing the South Asian region. He had also proposed India getting permanent membership of the United Nations Organization (UNO) way back in 1951, making him perhaps the first person who considered that India had a legitimate and rightful place in the international body.

Nationalist histories as well as the organized Left's counter-narratives overlooked these facets of the internationalist Ambedkar. Vernacular writings in India, which are rich in the narratives of the Ambedkar movement and the Dalit movement's 'counter publics',[3] also blatantly overlooked the Dalits' interface with international rights movements. Foreign policy was very dear to Ambedkar. He observed 'foreign affairs' to be the 'most important subject from

---

[3] Sharmila Rege argues that the emergence of 'counter-publics' in the popular Dalit discourse was to challenge Brahminical patriarchy. She finds 'booklet culture' consisting of humongous booklets produced in vernacular languages, and the music troupe ('gayan party') as authentic interpretations to understand the expression of the body politic. In these media too, there is no exemplified version of engaging with foreign policy dossiers and Ambedkar Rege (2013).

Ambedkar's Internationalization of Social Justice — 225

[a] social, political and financial point of view'.[4] By taking a keen interest in foreign policy, Ambedkar was perhaps trying to extend his political constituency beyond India. This enthusiasm is seen in his efforts to communicate with other political movements, such as his famous letter to W.E.B. Du Bois, N. Sivaraj's[5] visit to the Pacific Relations Committee conference in Quebec as a representative of the AISCF in 1942, and the Buddhist country diplomacy with South East Asian countries, which he thought of in terms of potential solidarity to help the emancipatory struggle of the Dalits. Despite the eventual failures of all these measures, they serve as testimony to his international outlook. However, even though he led one of the world's most important civil rights movements, Ambedkar fell short of unifying it with other civil and political rights movements the world over. He confined his approach to State-sponsored organizations such as the United Nations (UN). This singular focus isolated the Dalit movement from other global social justice movements.

Ambedkar's international outlook matured during his stay in the US and the UK in pursuit of his education in the early decades of the twentieth century. Eleanor Zelliot argues that his vision towards the US had taken cues from non-Brahmin movement leaders such as Jyotiba Phule, who was inspired by America's initiative to abolish Black slavery.[6] Maharaja Sayajirao Gaikwad had introduced the American education system after his visit to the US in 1893. The students who were being educated in Marathi, Hindi, and English read about George Washington and *Uncle Tom's Cabin* instead of British-centred education. This inspired the anti-caste movement to draw inspirations from other parallel examples in the

---

[4] Ambedkar (1979d: 322).

[5] N. Sivaraj was a president of the AISCF. He had experienced the power of working with international allies. Ambedkar had deputed Sivaraj to represent the cause of the untouchables as a depressed class delegation at the Pacific Relations Committee hosted in Mont Tremblant, Quebec, in December 1942. Sivaraj made the demand for separate settlements in separate villages. The report of the 1942 conference also stated that the depressed classes representative desired prior assurance of special protection and opposed the idea of a constituent assembly that would undermine their representation Sivaraj (1943: 68–9). Also see, Sivaraj (1995: 143–5); Kshirsagar (1994: 150–1).

[6] Zelliot (1992).

US and not the British Empire.[7] Due to this American influence, Ambedkar was selected for a scholarship by the Maharaja of Baroda to go to a university in the US and not the UK—then a general practice among Indians.

Ambedkar's arrival in the US coincided with the era of the American Dream. It was a vibrant time for the US economy and appeals for social and political equality to ethnic groups such as the Irish, Italians, and Jews in New York was gaining momentum. The vibrancy of the Harlem Renaissance permeated the academic and social circles of New York, where Ambedkar was staying. Zelliot suggests that these observations helped Ambedkar build a theory of cultural unification as a prerequisite to the political and social unity of a nation.[8]

Upon Ambedkar's arrival in 1913 at Columbia University, which was in its 'Golden Age', the US was undertaking major reforms in the finance and banking system and management. Frederick Winslow Taylor had revolutionized management thinking with the publication of his book *The Principles of Scientific Management* (1911). The Federal Reserve System was established in 1913. The Ford automobile was increasing its productivity. In 1914, President Woodrow Wilson officially declared his neutral position in the European conflict that led to the First World War. The communication gap was shrinking when Graham Bell telephoned San Francisco from New York in 1915, while 1916, Ambedkar's last year in the US, coincided with Wilson's second-term victory. Along with this, the Harlem neighbourhood in New York was expending the artistic and cultural articulations of immigrant communities— Black and non-Black. The Black figures deliberated and presented their struggle through their experiences. This emphasized the emergence of a stronger identity movement that helped export the literary and musical creativity of African Americans to the world. The art-based movement offered an internationalist identity to the Black figures, who acted as ambassadors of Black culture, advocating for their rights. World-famous figures such as Louis Armstrong, W.E.B. Du Bois, Alain Locke, Marcus Garvey, Duke Ellington, Paul Robeson, and Claude McKay were the leading names that popularized their struggles in the literary canon, in newspapers, and in

[7] Immerwahr (2007: 278).
[8] Zelliot (1992).

performances on stage. It is unlikely that Ambedkar was ignorant about these developments. However, there is no direct evidence that he took interest in the social upheavals in his locale, and it is neither reflected in his early writings or speeches nor in the Dalit rights movement he launched in India.

Following his stint at Columbia, Ambedkar moved to London to pursue his DSc (Doctor of Science) degree at the London School of Economics in 1916 and returned to India in 1917. His five years of education in Europe and America became one of the cornerstones of his grand public life and was to shape the course of his struggle against the millennium-old oppression of untouchables. Even after assuming his responsibility as a civil rights activist and as the leader of India's untouchables, he had many occasions to travel overseas.

Asserting the Indian Sovereign Right

In their attempts to construct an Indian image for the world, various works have been published that project the Brahminical classes (the Congress, socialists, and communists) as anti-imperial. The 'Nehru doctrine', for example, receives enormous commentary, and almost every biographer of Nehru lauds his ingenuity towards strengthening Third Worldism.[9]

In contrast, Ambedkar is completely ignored as someone who had important insights to offer in international politics. However, he observed the dismal relationship among the former English colonies in the Commonwealth and demanded the 'status of equal partnership'—an equal share and role in its activities. If not, warned Ambedkar, it would herald the invocation of a new master-slave relationship; he rhetorically stated, 'No new masters, please!'[10] In the expanded thesis, 'India and the British Commonwealth', Ambedkar had pivotal observations on building a strong identarian international character. The thesis also measured India's position in the Commonwealth, with Ambedkar denouncing its unfair representation, which had to do with India's negligent role in 'the making of events that bring on war and ... in the making of terms

[9] Akbar (1988); Kennedy (2015: 92–103).
[10] Ambedkar (2014 [2003a]: 310–11).

which often instead of ending war only adjourn war'.[11] Ambedkar was trying to find ways to operate in the imperial government that was leading the First World War efforts by subordinating Indian interests.

From the 1930s to the 1950s, the ILP formed by him made important interventions in asserting India's sovereign right. During the Second World War, the ILP critically commented on India's losing stand. It rejected outright Nazi Germany's proposition of the mono-race rule, that is, the idea of the Nordic race dominating over other races. It took serious offence to this position, considering it 'obnoxious' to the people of India.[12]

Foreign policy was among Ambedkar's principal grievances with independent India's general policies, leading to his frustrated resignation from the portfolio of law minister in Nehru's cabinet.[13] Ambedkar's relationship with the Congress and Gandhi was set on ambiguous lines. His criticism of Gandhi was followed by his acceptance of a position in the Constitutional Assembly, and later, his standing by the Congress's policy of country first, and winding up with his resignation. There are various readings of this moment. Gail Omvedt[14] argues that it was Ambedkar's commitment to a strong, centralized state that paved the way for his taking up the post in Nehru's cabinet that came with no strings attached. Sekhar Bandyopadhyay argues that owing to the AISCF's defeat in the 1946 elections, Ambedkar had few avenues in which to confront the Congress. Thus, a hostile attitude would have alienated and further marginalized the Dalit constituency. This was an after-effect of the power struggle among the Dalit leadership that begun in 1917, leading to a fragmented version of Dalit political discourse. It was so shaken that Dalit politics was threatened with 'extinction' by the hegemonic Congress in the late 1940s.[15]

Anand Teltumbde sees it as Gandhi's strategic masterstroke to obligate Ambedkar by inducting him at his desperate moment into the Constituent Assembly and also the first all-party cabinet headed

---

[11] Ambedkar (2014 [2003a]:308).
[12] Ambedkar (2014 [2003a]:308–13).
[13] Ambedkar (2014 [2003b]: 404).
[14] Omvedt (1994).
[15] Bandyopadhyay (2000: 895).

by Nehru.[16] The former extended to making him chairperson of the most important committee in the Constituent Assembly, giving him the epitaph of the maker of the Constitution. The strategy was to make the lowest strata of Indian society emotionally attach itself to the Constitution through its icon, Ambedkar. It was an ideal political choice.[17] Two years before Independence, in 1945, Ambedkar had 'wholly opposed' the proposal of the Constituent Assembly. He regarded it as the 'most dangerous project' that had the potential to incite 'civil war' in the country should it follow the upper-caste Hindu and Muslim dominance as decided by the Sapru Committee. (Hindus and Muslims were offered fifty-one reserved seats each of the total of 160. This would have given them a larger footing in incorporating a majority in the Constituent Assembly.)[18]

Ambedkar had indirectly created a space for himself in the elite circles of the Constituent Assembly by rejecting it outright in the first instance. In his rejection, he emphasized that the responsibility of the communal problem could not be entrusted to it. He believed it would not be a true representative body of the minorities who were to be chosen in joint electorates that were wholly dependent on caste Hindu votes and disproportionate sharing of seats between Hindus and Muslims.

Notwithstanding this, I argue that it was Ambedkar's best rhetorical tactic wherein he gestured to the Indian government that he was exploring the possibility of taking India to the UN. This move could have caused serious embarrassment to the Indian government as India was presenting itself as a nation that stood against racism and other forms of oppression; it was a tactic that worked for both, Ambedkar and the Congress. However, this relationship was short-lived. Nehru persisted in consciously ignoring Ambedkar,

[16] Teltumbde (2017).

[17] Ambedkar was an incomparable intellect in the country and a perfect candidate for the position. He had demonstrated his calibre when he drafted a memorandum in 1947 on behalf of the AISCF that was viewed as a draft Constitution of India. The memorandum consisted of a preamble, fundamental rights, provisions for the protection of minorities, special responsibilities regarding higher education and separate settlement, and protection of SCs. In spite of this, he was excluded from the States Committee of the Constituent Assembly formed in 1947. See Ambedkar (1979e: Ch. 10).

[18] Ambedkar (1979c: 360).

right from withdrawing his support to the Hindu Code Bill to the important deliberations offered in various memorandums on the situations of minorities. On the other hand, Ambedkar could not build strategic alliances with other oppressed groups using his powerful political portfolio. And his radical strategy to take India to the UN remained a statement without any developments from the AISCF. Ambedkar chose instead to resign in protest from Nehru's cabinet.

The resignation made headlines the world over, with even the *New York Times* reporting the incident. Ambedkar stated in his resignation letter dated 10 October 1951: 'It may be said that my resignation is out of time and that if I was dissatisfied with the Foreign Policy of the Government and the treatment accorded to Backward Classes and the Scheduled Castes I should have gone earlier.'[19]

Additionally, India's 'colossal' expenditure on building defence capabilities, Ambedkar suspected, was owing to the grim foreign policy that was directed by the postcolonial elite Brahminical class, which participated in the framing of casteist policies in the deliberations in the UN. The recent unearthing of archival materials confirms this.[20]

The mid-twentieth century was divided by two ideologies that were racing to establish their dominance in the world—the imperialist division amongst capitalist countries on the one hand and the Communism-inspired nationhood on the other, both of which had created a bipolar opposition. Ambedkar sympathized with India's 'dislike' for capitalism, but he feared that taken to its extreme, it could lead to Communism. His concern was that while avoiding capitalism, parliamentary democracy should not be weakened; if care were not taken, it would be 'like throwing the baby out of the bath but in emptying it of dirty water'.[21] This was also an outcome of his worries with Communism, which he found to be too dictatorial and violent and thus unsuitable to India's fragile democracy.[22]

---

[19] Ambedkar (1995: 1317–18).

[20] Thakur (2016); On the theme of post-colonial Brahminical elitism in the International Relations, see Sankaran (2015: 139–56).

[21] Ambedkar (2014) [2003a]: 396).

[22] Ambedkar (2014 [1992]: 441–64).

He chose not to align with any 'isms' as stated in the AISCF election manifesto:

> the policy of the Party is not tied to any particular dogma or ideology such as *Communism, or Socialism, Gandhism, or any other ism.* The Party will be ready to adopt any plan of social and economic betterment of the people irrespective of its origin and provided it is consistent with its principles. Its outlook on life will be *purely rational and modern, emperistic* and *not academic.*[23]

This approach makes a case for Ambedkar's strategic political pragmatism—aligning with socialist ideals[24] and, at the same time, not discarding capitalism. However, his socialist idealism was totally different from that of the socialists of privileged classes and castes—he kept them at arm's length in deciding strategies for reclaiming the rights of the depressed classes. This was a shift from his earlier position, when he had declared capitalism as one part of the Dalits' enemy duo, the other being Brahminism.[25]

Ambedkar and the UN

Founded in 1920, the League of Nations preceded the formation of the UN. Ambedkar wanted it to be concerned with the issue of untouchability. In an interview to the *New York Times* in London on 30 November 1930, Ambedkar centred untouchability as a global problem affecting the social and economic well-being of the world. He sought to bring it under the ambit of the League of Nations in the same vein as slavery and drug trafficking. He believed that the international standpoint on untouchability could bring about enough pressure for it to be eradicated. Ambedkar said, 'Nothing less than the aroused opinion of the world can do it.'[26]

The dealings between the UN and Ambedkar date back to the early years of its formation. He sought its intervention to address the problems faced by SCs by stating that the UN had jurisdiction

[23] Ambedkar (2014 [2003a]: 388). Emphasis added.

[24] Ambedkar's work on economics, for example, is understood in the context of individual development in relation to national development as a collective.

[25] Teltumbde (2017).

[26] Selden (1930: 1).

over 'eight crore Scheduled Castes'. The working committee of the AISCF, under the chairmanship of N. Sivaraj, adopted a resolution on 17 January 1947 to submit a memorandum prepared by Ambedkar to the UN Assembly to highlight 'the sufferings of the Scheduled Castes in India against the Hindus for their acts of social, economic and political tyranny'.[27] The working committee instructed the president of the AISCF to ensure the delivery of the memorandum to the UN secretary general and advised sending an AISCF delegation to the UN to present their grievances.[28] This was eventually halted as Ambedkar 'did not submit it'. He 'felt that it would be better to wait until the Constituent Assembly and the future Parliament was given a chance to deal with the matter'.[29]

Ambedkar perhaps chose to consciously oversee the potential of the 'upper-caste' state that was coming into being in postcolonial India. There were ample evidences of it during the parleys with the Cabinet Mission, the heat of which he had himself experienced. With all his compromises with the Congress to get into the Constitution and his ultimate prominent role in writing it, he could not go beyond the writ of the party. He realized his folly within two years when, in 1953, he said the following words during a Rajya Sabha debate: 'Sir, my friends tell me that I made the Constitution. But I am quite prepared to say that I shall be the first person to burn it out. I do not want it. It does not suit anybody.'[30]

Facing the liberal as well as Hindu orthodoxy of the Congress at every turn, Ambedkar explicated that his alliance with the party was not amicable and not without conflict. Taking from this experience, he chose to induct an international lobby rather than overtly relying on the Indian government. Thus, he started corresponding with other affected groups who were fighting for

[27] Ambedkar (2014 [2003a]: 358).

[28] N. Sivaraj, while presiding over the iconic All India Conference of the Depressed Classes in 1942, which was a precursor to the All India Schedule Castes Federation, had assured the gathering that the problem of the untouchables would be taken to the 'Grand Tribunal of the United Nations'. He was confident in this endeavour that he affirmed to the conference 'we will receive consideration which has not hitherto been bestowed on [us] by the British Government', referring to the rights granted to the untouchables. Sivaraj (2009: 25).

[29] Ambedkar (2014 [1995]): 1320).

[30] Ambedkar's Rajya Sabha speech delivered on 2 September 1953.

recognition in the UN (see later for the recorded communication with W.E.B Du Bois). Ambedkar drew parallels with the black population in the United States, Indians in South Africa, and SCs in India.

The efforts to draw inspiration from these groups and engage them in conversation reflected the working style of the Ambedkarite leadership. N. Sivaraj, in his presidential address at the All India Scheduled Caste Conference in 1942, drew parallels with the world atrocities committed by colonizers and white men upon non-white peoples. Talking about the atrocities upon the 'Australian Bushman by the Colonizers, that of the Negroes by the Ku-Klux-Klan and of the Jews by the Nazis', Sivaraj submitted that these were comparatively 'less heinous than the suffering ... subjected to Depressed Classes in the name of religion, caste and the like by the Hindus'. He remarked that it was 'slow poisoning'.[31] This remark came at a time when the League of Nations had acknowledged the issue of racism.

Post Independence, the Indian government took on the White apartheid government in South Africa on the issue of racism that was affecting the rights and dignity of Indians in the country.[32] Almost twenty-four resolutions were passed by the UN in Nehru's presence.[33] In the fourth session of the UN General Assembly on 20 September 1949, India sought the intervention of the UN to offer justice to the South African Indian community.[34] In the midst of the diplomatic deadlock over India's stand on racism, Ambedkar drew attention in Parliament to the situation of the SCs, arguing that the 'tyranny and the constant and shameless resort to violence by Hindus ... [was] far worse than the position of Indians in South Africa'.[35] He went on to add that the experiences of apartheid in South Africa were akin to the condition of Indian untouchable groups. To impress upon the situation, he said that 'South Africa is replicated in every Indian village' as segregation was sanctioned in India.[36]

[31] Sivaraj (2009: 22).
[32] Pachai (1971).
[33] Vahed (2015: 54–84).
[34] *Indian News Chronicle.* 1949. 'India, South Africa and the U.N.O'. South African Communist Party, sacp.org, 25 September. Available at http://www.sacp.org.za/docs/history/dadoo-38.html, accessed 25 March 2016.
[35] Ambedkar (2014 [1995]: 1320).
[36] Ambedkar (2016: 197).

234 Suraj Yengde

Even though he acknowledged the segregation, he did not make a conscious effort to establish links with the colonized groups of South Africa to make an international united front. In spite of the Dalit diaspora's vast expanse in the British Empire, South Africa in particular,[37] Ambedkar did not reach out to these Indian groups striving for freedom from the colonial regime in their respective countries. Indian delegations would visit India to solicit support for their movement in the 1940s, meeting elite members of the Congress in New Delhi. As Ambedkar was part of the colonial government, it is difficult to imagine that he missed noticing these activities as they were part of the Indian state policy.

Experiencing repeated failures at the hands of the Indian government, Ambedkar sought to fight the battle on his own. Thus, he started communicating with the leaders of the African-American struggle. He told the press in India that he was in conversation with African-American leaders in the US, mentioning W.E.B Du Bois particular, the foremost Black intellectual and civil rights activist 'who was fighting for political, economic and social rights of Negroes in that country'.[38] The two activists had famously exchanged letters, discussing an appeal to the UN to build a coalition to unify the struggle against dominating oppressive groups in their respective societies. Ambedkar wrote to Du Bois explaining his position:

I have been a student of the Negro problem and have *read your writings throughout*. There is *so much similarity* between the position of the Untouchables in India and of the position of the Negroes in America that the study of the latter is not only natural but necessary.

I was very much interested to read that the Negroes of America have filed a petition to the UNO. The Untouchables of India are also thinking of following suit. Will you be so good as to secure for me two or three copies of this representation by the Negroes and send them to my address. I need hardly say how very grateful I shall be for your troubles in this behalf.[39]

[37] Desai and Vahed (2010).
[38] Ambedkar (2014 [2003a]: 359).
[39] Ambedkar (2017). Emphasis added. Also see Immerwahr (2007: 275–301).

Du Bois promptly replied to Ambedkar and said that he too had read his works and was aware of him and 'of course have every sympathy with the Untouchables of India', expressing to offer 'any service ... if possible in the future'.[40] After this exchange, there is no evidence of these two figures communicating with each other. There is also no extended record that the African-American community took the cause of the untouchables' struggle to the UN alongside the topic of racism. However, Du Bois had furthered this cause with the National Association for the Advancement of Colored People (NAACP). In a letter written on 1 August 1946 to Walter Francis White who was then heading the NAACP, Du Bois suggested an NAACP petition to the General Assembly of the UN for taking up the issue of situation of African Americans. Stressing the importance of such a petition, Du Bois mentioned that similar groups especially, the 'Indians of South Africa, the Jews of Palestine, the Indonesians and others are making similar petitions'. Du Bois continued: 'I have on my desk a letter from Dr. [B. R.] Ambedkar of the Untouchables of India, in which he intimates that they may make an appeal. It would be, I am sure, an omission not easily to be explained if the NAACP did not make a petition and statement of this sort.'[41]

Furthering this work, Martin Luther King Jr, after his India visit in 1959, 'sought to making a study of untouchability' and started collecting the relevant materials in this regard.[42] This effort too did not see the light of day.

The connection between Indian untouchables and the American blacks can trace its provenance back to the nineteenth century when Phule sought to bring attention to the plights of the Sudras and Ati-Sudras to the world. Dedicating his book to the abolitionists, referring to them as the 'Good People of the United States', in *Slavery* (1873), Phule observed the condition of blacks in America as a defining moment in the universal recognition of suppressed groups.[43] Thus, the cause of black slavery was seen as similar to that of India's untouchables. Likewise, the black community of America expressed its solidarity with the situation of Dalits in India.

---

[40] Du Bois (1946).
[41] Du Bois (1978: 163).
[42] King (1959).
[43] Phule (2019).

Following this, several efforts were made to draw parallels between the two marginalized groups,[44] with Ambedkar himself stating that the struggle of black Americans was similar to that of the SCs, that like 'Negros were "tyrannized by the white Americans"', Scheduled Castes were tormented by the Caste Hindus'.[45] This departs from his earlier argument about the caste system being devoid of racial proliferation. In AC, Ambedkar argued against the biological defence of the caste system. 'Caste system does not demarcate racial division. Caste system is a social division of people of the same race.'[46] In his two major works, *Castes in India: Their Mechanism, Genesis and Development* (1917)[47] and *Who Were the Shudras?* (1946),[48] Ambedkar rejected the racial logic of differentiation among caste groups. He argued in a 1917 paper that it was the 'imitation' of endogamy that was practised by the dominating Brahmin community that strengthened the purist tendency of the caste system and resulted in social inequality in society, caste being one of the leading factors.

The Black-centric magazine *The Crisis*, started by W.E.B. Du Bois and later edited by Roy Wilkins, carried stories of the 'Negroes of India' in its 1942 and 1943 editions, explaining the resonance between Indian untouchables and the African-Americans in the US. It credited Ambedkar for being 'one of the finest scholars of the country' and a 'single leader of sixty million untouchables'.[49] Ambedkar's stellar foreign policy acumen received accolades in African-American circles. Granger described Ambedkar as 'the best known leader of India's Harijan caste' in the established African-American newspaper, the *New York Amsterdam News*, and as the 'first Indian voice of authority to challenge Prime Minister Nehru's dream-eyed policy of "neutralism" for South Asia and "peaceful co-existence" with a rapaciously aggressive China'.[50] He also praised Ambedkar's statement and hoped that people like him, invoking a plural denomination as the 'Ambedkars',

---

[44] Prashad (2000: 189–201).
[45] Ambedkar (2014 [2003a]: 260).
[46] Ambedkar (1979a: 48–9).
[47] Ambedkar (1979b: 3–22).
[48] Ambedkar (2014 [1987, 1946]).
[49] Paxton (1943: 378).
[50] Granger (1954: 16).

would be successful with Nehru than 'Negro leaders have thus far been with President Eisenhower, Truman, or Roosevelt and their advisors'.[51]

The Pragmatic Internationalist

The book *What Congress and Gandhi Have done to the Untouchables* was primarily an international statement of an internationalist Ambedkar who was now turning to the world to seek justice for his community, a shift from his earlier stance of reliance on the Indian government. This was primarily the outcome of the political battles between the Congress and Ambedkar. Both were fighting to claim an 'exclusive space' for Dalit polity in India. The former, however, under facile intentions, chose to plot against the subservient Dalits to 'represent', rather than lead, the Dalit struggle. Thus, time and again, Ambedkar had to face obstacles that pushed him to initiate strategic steps that, at times, did not succeed.[52] He had to confront enormous barriers at the hands of 'Congress–High class Hindu rule'[53]—a triumvirate of the Indian Congress, the Hindu Mahasabha, and Gandhi.[54]

In the book, Ambedkar delineates the way orthodox Hindu groups dominated by Brahmins undermined every effort to genuinely eradicate the menace of untouchability.[55] He found no genuine concern in Gandhi or Congress-affiliated organizations such as the Social Conference established in 1887 in Madras. The Social Conference focussed on eradicating the social injustices imposed on untouchable groups in India. According to Ambedkar, the 'Social Conference was a body which mainly concerned itself with the reform of the high-caste Hindu family'.[56] It did not believe in agitating for the abolition of caste and had no special interest in it as much as it did for child marriage and enforced widowhood. This was because the latter occurred in elite Brahmin families, thus making them personally invested in their eradication. Contrastingly,

---

[51] Granger (1954: 16).
[52] Bandyopadhyay (2000: 900).
[53] Bandyopadhyay (2000: 915).
[54] Bandyopadhyay (2000: 909).
[55] Ambedkar (2014 [1990]).
[56] Ambedkar (1979a: 41–2).

every attempt to include the issue of untouchable emancipation was suppressed by the same band of caste elites. This suppression continued in important foreign policy interventions too, where the depressed classes were not involved in deliberating over the future of the country. This led to an irresponsible international outlook in the post-Independence phase and resulted in India's position with 'no friends, if not actual enemies'.[57] The AISCF observed three reasons for such incapacitation: one was due to the Kashmir issue, the second was the admission of Communist China in the UNO, and the third was its intervention in the Korean War in the 1950s.

On permanent membership to the UNO, the AISCF in its election manifesto of 1951 ridiculed India's position to 'fight the battle for' China's permanent membership in the UNO when China was self-sufficient. Instead, it argued for India's permanent membership in the UNO. 'India is spending herself in fighting the battle of Mao as against Chaing KaiShek. This quixotic policy of saving the world is going to bring about the ruination of India and the sooner this suicidal foreign policy is reversed the better for India.'[58]

The manifesto also questioned the intentions of the Indian delegate fighting the battle for Communist China, which had irrevocably invited antagonism between India and the United States. During parliamentary proceedings in 1954, Ambedkar contended that Nehru was hostile towards the US due to the conflict of ideology that had fostered feelings of distaste in Nehru for anything that came from there.[59] The US, during those days, was an important ally to have on one's side because it had significant control over technology and global finance. Postcolonial India partially relied on US aid in terms of technical and financial assistance in reconstructing the economy via industrialization. Ambedkar was a proponent of industrialization as he foresaw it as an ideal way to improve

---

[57] Ambedkar (2014 [2003a]: 395); Ambedkar (2014 [1995]: 1321).

[58] Ambedkar (2014 [2003a]: 397).

[59] Ambedkar (2014 [1997]: 874–86, 875–81). In addition, Ambedkar had refused to offer insights on the ailing foreign policy in the later part of his life to the public. In response to a request from Marathi newspapers such as *Kesari* and *Maratha*, Ambedkar stated in his letter dated 15 July 1954 that due to the overhauling influence of Nehru on the nation's mind, any opinion contrary to Nehru's was unwelcome; as it was 'one man's traffic in public affairs it was very difficult to maintain one's interest in the foreign affairs'. See Ambedkar (2014 [2003a]: 386).

Ambedkar's Internationalization of Social Justice 239

the low productivity caused by archaic agricultural technologies.[60] He was leading infrastructure projects that relied on US technical expertise,[61] including the colossal Damodar Valley project. As a member of labour in the viceroy's cabinet, Ambedkar established the Department for Irrigation and Navigation Commission (which was later renamed the River Control Board, Central Water Power Commission) to control the river and flood; advance irrigation; and produce energy.[62] For this project, a team of four engineers from the United States were invited to establish a 'Technical Team' that would advise on the design and construction of the first two dams in India.[63]

Furthermore, there was a wise suggestion to seek every aid possible in order to strengthen the 'self' first before 'championing the cause of Asiatic countries'. This was a time of apotheosis for the Third Worldism that was gaining significant attention among the postcolonial elite who wanted to imagine their future void of Western interference. The Ambedkar-led party, however, had an alternative to offer to the enthusiastic objective of becoming an Asian power.[64] Ambedkar observed that the norm of 'Asia for Asiatics' was good in so far as colonialism was concerned, but in the postcolonial condition, this was a farcical principle where war and strife amongst Asians was turning the region into totalitarian statehood; the Korean War, the China–Japan conflict, and South East Asian instability were cited as examples. Ambedkar was also critical of India's policy on non-alignment. He held the view that non-alignment understated important American contacts that would strategically assist in development projects critical for an independent nation.[65] In the Rajya Sabha, he led a charge against Nehru's policy of peaceful coexistence, contending that it did not fare well, especially in the cases of Tibet, Indo-China, and Korea.

[60] Ambedkar (1979e: 381–452).

[61] Martin Luther King Jr had also expressed a similar view about the extension of US technical assistance to India in 1959 to tackle unemployment and India's development growth. King (1959: 84–92).

[62] Ambedkar (2014 [2003]: 387–8).

[63] Ambedkar (2014 [1991]: 289).

[64] *Indian News Chronicle.* 1949. 'India, South Africa and the U.N.O'. South African Communist Party, sacp.org, 25 September. Available at http://www.sacp.org.za/docs/history/dadoo-38.html, accessed 25 March 2016.

[65] Zelliot (1992: 84).

240   Suraj Yengde

Ambedkar is reported to have rebuked this policy as purchasing peace 'at the price of portioning countries' to which he maintained strong objections.[66] Ambedkar warned Nehru that too much affection with Communist Russia could be a harmful antidote to the politics of regionalism that was decided in the SEATO (South East Asia Treaty Organization) conference. Ambedkar had reservations about Russia's expansionist tendencies and said that Nehru's foreign policy ought to be examined in this context. The *Canberra Times* reported this news as a headline in the 28 August 1954 edition, as did another Australian paper, the *Armidale Express*.[67] Ambedkar again endorsed his commitment to pragmatism by overlooking the ideological imbalances his views had favoured. He preferred an alliance with burgeoning imperial power America as long as it brought benefits to Indian development projects.

Ambedkar's Spectre Haunts Brahmin Savoir Faire

Pondering over the current situation, one can see the Indian government's conscious suppression of caste dialogues at the UN. Post-Independence governments continued to maintain their hostility to engage with the issue on international forums. In 2001, at the World Conference against Racism in Durban, a delegation led by Omar Abdullah, then minister of state for external affairs in the BJP government, strenuously rejected a resolution on caste.[68] Seventy-six paragraphs that mentioned caste were removed by the Indian government.[69] Their logic declared caste to be an internal matter that was adequately covered in the Indian Constitution. This is the repeated excuse offered by the Indian government on every discussion of caste. The same applies to non-governmental discussions on Dalit human rights. Many international non-government organizations (NGOs) are rejected by the Indian State from getting the affiliation of the Economic and Social Council (ECOSOC), an

[66] Granger (1954: 16). Also see Ambedkar (2014 [2003]).
[67] *Canberra Times* (1954: 1); Ambedkar (1954: 1).
[68] Prashad (2000: 189–201); Prashad (2008: 133–50).
[69] Dalit Women Fight. 2018. 'Dr Ruth Manorama Speaks on the History of Dalit Womens' International Advocacy'. YouTube [video], 25 June. Available at https://www.youtube.com/watch?v=U-_nKGQ9K5Q, accessed 7 October 2018

executive body of the UN that endorses NGOs to deliberate in its proceedings. The Indian government's consistent blocking of Dalit solidarity groups focussed on working towards caste-based issues gives it the notoriety of the 'longest pending NGO application' in UN history.[70]

Another glaring example is the Indian government's continuous disfavouring of UN-appointed independent experts' findings on caste. On 28 January 2016, Special Rapporteur on Minority Issues Rita Izsák-Ndiaye presented her report to the UN. The Indian representative dismissed the report, noting that it was unclear why 'minority status' had been applied to the caste system.[71] Izsák-Ndiaye had to clarify her position—she explained that the interpretative meaning of 'minorities' could easily cover the complex issues facing victims of caste discrimination throughout the world, saying it thus fell under her mandate.[72] This can be contrasted with Ambedkar's description of the situation of SCs as much worse and vulnerable than the existing Indian minorities in 1947. He argued that SCs were more than a minority and that 'any protection given to the citizens and to the minorities will not be adequate for the Scheduled Castes ... [they] would require special safeguards (against) the tyranny and discrimination of the majority'.[73]

Dalit Movement's Blind Spots of Internationalist Vision

Given the ongoing theatrics between the Indian State on the one hand and the UN and civil society on the other, it arguably makes a stronger case to constitute a separate mandate on the issues of caste-based discrimination by having an independent body within the UN and other regional bodies such as the European Union

---

[70] International Solidarity Network (ISDN). 2014. 'IDSN Application for ECOSOC Status—the Longest Pending NGO Application'. ISDN. org. Available at http://idsn.org/wp-content/uploads/pdfs/Briefs/IDSN_ECOSOC_Application_Fact_Sheet_October_2014.pdf, accessed 10 February 2016.

[71] Mitra (2016).

[72] Izsák-Ndiaye (2016).

[73] Ambedkar (1979e: 382–4).

that exclusively concentrates on the rights and dignities of caste subjects. Currently, there is not a single organization that actively engages and consistently follows up with the international community on caste-related issues. It was, after all, Ambedkar's desire to work with the UN, one that he was unsuccessful in achieving. Governments across various parties that express admiration for Ambedkar overlook the important Dalit intervention in the UN forum, including those who claim an affinity with his ideology.

The Bahujan Samaj Party formed the government in UP four times and was also an active partner of the ruling powers in the centre. In spite of this, it did not consider launching an international policy-specific programme for developing alliances with other oppressed groups in the world. Barring Kanshi Ram's visit to the first International Dalit Conference held in Kuala Lumpur on 10–11 October 1998, there have been no significant efforts to create an international outreach programme by the political Dalit leadership.[74] The visit of Kanshi Ram was not aimed at launching cross-border solidarity initiatives at that particular moment and efforts in that direction never took place afterwards.[75] However, prior to this, Kanshi Ram had, in fact, treaded in that direction. He had formal contacts with the Buraku Liberation League (BLL), a foremost *Burakumin* (outcastes of the Japanese society) organization.[76] The BLL had invited Kanshi Ram as the chairperson of All India Backward and Minorities Central Employees Federation (BAMCEF) and Dalit Shoshit Samaj Sangharsh Samittee (DS-4) alongside Roma, British Asian, NAACP, France, and Philippines representatives.[77]

---

[74] Bahujan Sanghatak. 1998. 'We Need to Become Ruling Class if We Want to Form a Casteless Society'. Ambedkar.org, 16 November. Available at http://www.ambedkar.org/News/rulingclass.html, accessed 19 March 2018.

[75] Kanshi Ram mentions the Dalit diaspora in his classic *Chamcha Age: An Era of Stooges* (1982) as another category of stooges who try to use their influence to subjugate to the hegemonic power structures of the Brahminical political parties. Perhaps, because of this, we can assume that Kanshi Ram did not initiate any significant steps towards establishing an international anti-caste movement.

[76] I am grateful to Rahul Gajbhiye for directing to me this and Kanshi Ram's other international travel documents reported in the *Oppressed Indian*.

[77] Uesugi (1983).

Ambedkar's Internationalization of Social Justice 243

This connection was in line with the continuation of Ambedkar's contact with the foremost Buraku leader Jiichiro Matsumoto who had extended conversation with Ambedkar upon his visit to India and, on another occasion, with P.N. Rajbhoj, the general secretary of AISCF in Kyoto.[78] BLL continued to maintain contacts with the Dalits after World War II. It supported the cause of untouchables alongside Buraku in their submission to the Second World Conference to Combat Racism and Racial Discrimination in 1983 and various international human rights conferences.[79] In 1985, Kanshi Ram was invited by the Ambedkarites based in the United Kingdom to get a closer perspective on his movement. It being his first visit to the United Kingdom, the local Ambedkarite hosts and the gathering wanted to understand Kanshi Ram's objectives as he was then considered as a suspicious outsider trying to tarnish Ambedkar-led Republican Party of India (RPI) and the Buddhism movement.[80]

Some section of post-Ambedkar leadership that was influential in the political brokerage started to become disengaged with the issues of socialist policies like those concerning land and control over resources and production, which could have given them the desired platform to connect with other postcolonial countries' socialist movements fighting for a similar cause. A progressive Dalit socialist block would certainly have fit the stature of a universalist Dalit movement; it would not have remained an isolated bubble and, instead, would have become a global concern. By overlooking such political solidarities, the Dalit movement leadership was unable to fix the fault lines of Ambedkar's misplaced pragmatic political solidarity projects that rejected untimely ideological anchors. While Ambedkar's approach helped India build its post-Independence development projects and increase its industrial capability in terms of technology and knowledge-sharing, it also created a huge vacuum for the Dalit identity, which is now at the helm of NGOs, who, by virtue of their international presence,

---

[78] Neary (2010: 185).

[79] There were six appeals made to the Second World Conference on Race and Racism on behalf of the BLL. Appeal number 2 read: 'Discriminatory problems originating in the historically established class system, such as the Buraku problems in Japan, the problems of untouchables in India, etc. shall be solved through international cooperation'. Uesugi (1983:147).

[80] Kanshi Ram (1985).

244 Suraj Yengde

are privileged to describe Dalit identity to the rest of the world. International NGOs have been persistent in raising the issue of caste-affected citizens at the UN and on other international government and non-government platforms. Their understanding undermines the ideological categorization of the Dalit identity that emerges from the Dalit movement. The extraneous affirmation to identify caste within ambiguous frameworks of 'descent-based discrimination' has undermined an 'autonomous' categorization of caste violence and discrimination, and thereby its accountability in South Asia, Africa, Japan, and other countries with Indian diaspora.

The impetuous refusal of the Indian State to acknowledge the issue of caste has led Dalit diaspora groups across the world to recognize the obnoxious state of affairs in the intransigent caste Hindu society. As caste-related incidents continue to occur in different countries, Dalit associations organize regular activities to raise awareness, making it a global concern. Groups inspired by Ambedkar across North America, Europe, the Middle East, and the Far East are known as Ambedkar International Missions and Ambedkar International Associations.[81] These are run by professional expats who make a stronger case to theorize the shibboleth of caste among the diaspora.[82] There are also groups in the name of Ambedkar, Ravidas, and Valmiki along with Dalit Christian

[81] The list of United States–based Ambedkarite organizations is: Ambedkar International Mission; Ambedkar International Center; Ambedkar Association of North America; Ambedkarite Buddhist Association of Texas; Boston Study Group; Ambedkarites International Mission Society, Canada; Ambedkarites International Co-ordinating Society, British Columbia, Canada; and many anti-caste Guru Ravidass Organizations in the United States and Canada.

[82] The first intervention to the UN was made by E.V. Chinniah on behalf of the untouchables to the UN Secretary General U. Thant on 6 December 1968. Chinniah was the editor of *Prajabandhu*, a fortnightly journal started in 1971 and published from Hyderabad. Chinniah authored a Telugu biography of Ambedkar titled *Dr Ambedkar Jeevitha Charirtra* and also represented the cause of Dalit rights at the International Conference on Human Rights at Washington. Following his intervention, the second testimony was delivered by Laxmi Berwa to the UN Sub-commission on Human Rights (1982), then Bhagwan Das to United Nations Commission on Prevention of Discrimination of Minorities held at Geneva (1983). Berwa (1996: 9).

churches that single-handedly inspire the diaspora movement of the marginalized.[83] Using advancements in technology and social media, these groups—whom I refer to as the 'Millennial Dalit diaspora'—place their activities in conversation with the Indian situation.

Annual lectures, gatherings on the important days of Dalit calendars, and regular collections of funds to sponsor education-related projects in India explain the nature of these overseas Dalit groups. These are remarkable activities that remain unknown due to the organizational limitation of publication incentives and lack of interest within the scholarly world about such epochal activism. In addition, marginalized caste diaspora groups internalize the inter-group behaviour, thus ending up functioning as subordinate groups among the existing ethnic minority diaspora groups calling for a separate identity. This complex diversity hinges towards the reification of independent identities moving away from the common ethnic clubbing of divergent identities.[84] In spite of this and the efforts to establish a separate Dalit identity in the purview of ethnic diversity, there have been limited efforts by Dalit diaspora to make common cause with other oppressed groups.

Solidarity beyond Rhetoric

Ambedkar's engagement with African-American groups to solicit support for the Dalit cause at the international level and his simultaneous overlooking of African and other colonized spaces as potential partners hint at some of his shortfalls. His belief in pragmatism over ideological singularity—that is, relying entirely on one ideology—resulted in benefiting post-Independence Indian development programmes and policies. However, this came at the

[83] Although increasingly large in number, there is no accurate statistical caste census of Indians living abroad. It is commonly argued that in the post-Mandal era, there has been a swift rise in the population of Dalits and OBCs who benefited from the reservation movement and enrolled in higher educational institutions. From the pipeline of Indian IT personnel, many Dalits joined the trade and came into diaspora spaces. However, owing to the lack of organizational reach or discomfort from identifying the self as a Dalit, many have remained in the diaspora closet.

[84] Kumar (2009: 53–74).

cost of his unfulfilled promise of creating international Dalit solidarity. As time passed, after two decades (1930 to 1950) of active political engagement on Indian foreign policy matters, Ambedkar had to cede his interests in the area owing to the predominance of Nehru's overshadowing presence as a PM. Ambedkar confirmed that he had 'ceased to take the same degree of interest in the foreign affairs of the country which I used to take at one time'.[85]

Various policies and committees of the Indian foreign services have an inadequate representation of Dalit-nominated representatives. Ambedkar-inspired activism in foreign countries strives towards political intervention. The exclusion of historically marginalized communities from important interventions in India's foreign policy matters adds to the casteist make-up of the postcolonial bureaucratic order. Ambedkar's story as a staunch critic of postcolonial nationalism demands a critical appraisal of the postcolonial conditions in the global south countries. Dalit diaspora activism is yet to take a radical stand against the Indian State, which remains a passive agent in the face of persistent Dalit atrocities.

Ambedkar's famous statement to the Pacific Relations Committee detailed ten demands.[86] He was quick to add that athwart imperialism, racism, anti-Semitism, and free traffic (refugees), there was an issue of untouchability that faced a larger risk of being ignored.[87] Ambedkar took a particularist view of the question of untouchability by withdrawing its notional international significance with other oppressed groups. This reaction was perhaps in response to the false propaganda of the ruling castes in India on the question of the problems of Dalits and untouchability. Nehruvian foreign policy ensured that race could be used as an important intervention to determine India's commitment to anti-imperialism. At the same time, it gave India an upper hand to not disclose its own fallacies of caste oppression and untouchability.

The global Dalit appeal as part of the world's oppressed communities was established by the Dalit Panthers, a radical Ambedkarite outfit in Maharashtra that not only marshalled an international

[85] Ambedkar (2014 [2003a]: 386).

[86] These demands were later published in booklet format entitled 'Mr. Gandhi and the Emancipation of the Untouchables', in Ambedkar (2014 [1990, 1943]).

[87] Ambedkar (2014 [1990, 1943]: 397).

solidarity initiative but aimed to connect across race, caste, and national boundaries. They presented themselves as an inclusive category—the Dalits—with the worldly oppressed. As they declared in their manifesto: 'The Dalit Panthers aspire to join hands with the Dalits (oppressed) of the world which includes the oppressed and the exploited people in Cambodia, Vietnam, Africa, Latin America, Japan and even in US (specially with the Blacks).'[88]

However, this effort has largely remained confined to literary rhetoric and is not an action-based programme. The Dalit Panthers, disabled by state oppression, could not seek out active collaboration with the aforementioned movements. While in politics, in later years, too, the leaders of the Dalit Panthers did not utilize their offices to build active partnerships with social movements around the world.

References

Akbar, M.J. 1998. *Nehru: The Making of India*. New York: Viking.

Ambedkar, B.R. 1954. 'Warning to Nehru'. *Armidale Express*, 28 August.

———. 1979a. 'Annihilation of Caste', in Vasant Moon (ed.), *Dr. Babasaheb Ambedkar: Writings and Speeches*. Vol. 1. Bombay: Government of Maharashtra.

———. 1979b. 'Castes in India: Their Mechanism, Genesis and Development' in Vasant Moon (ed.), *Dr. Babasaheb Ambedkar: Writings and Speeches*. Vol. 1. Bombay: Government of Maharashtra.

———. 1979c. 'Communal Deadlock and a Way to Solve It, Address delivered at the session of the All India Scheduled Caste Federation held in Bombay on May 6, 1945', in Vasant Moon (ed.), *Dr. Babasaheb Ambedkar: Writings and Speeches*. Vol. 1. Bombay: Government of Maharashtra. [reprint Dr. Ambedkar Foundation 2014].

———. 1979d. 'Federation Versus Freedom', in Vasant Moon (ed.), *Dr. Babasaheb Ambedkar: Writings and Speeches*. Vol. 1. Bombay: Government of Maharashtra. [reprint Dr. Ambedkar Foundation 2014].

———. 1979e. 'States and Minorities, What are Their Rights and How to Secure Them in the Constitution of Free India', in Vasant Moon (ed.), *Dr. Babasaheb Ambedkar: Writings and Speeches*. Vol. 1. Bombay: Government of Maharashtra. [reprint Dr. Ambedkar Foundation 2014].

---

[88] Slate (2012: 127–43).

———. 1995. 'Statement by Dr. B.R. Ambedkar in Explanation of his Resignation', in Vasant Moon (ed.), *Dr. Babasaheb Ambedkar: Writings and Speeches*. Vol. 14, part 2. Bombay: Government of Maharashtra. [reprint Dr. Ambedkar Foundation 2013].

———. 2014 (1943, 1990). 'Mr. Gandhi and the Emancipation of the Untouchables', in Vasant Moon (ed.), *Dr. Babasaheb Ambedkar: Writings and Speeches*. Vol. 9. Mumbai: Government of Maharashtra. [reprint: Dr Ambedkar Foundation, 2014].

———. 2014 (2003a). 'Dr. B.R. Ambedkar and His Egalitarian Revolution: Struggle for Human Rights', in H. Narke, N.G. Kamble, M.L. Kasare, A. Godghate (eds), *Dr. Babasaheb Ambedkar: Writings and Speeches*. Vol. 17, part 2. Mumbai: Government of Maharashtra. [reprint: Dr Ambedkar Foundation, 2014].

———. 2014 (2003b). 'Resignation Not Due to Illness', in H. Narke, N.G. Kamble, M.L. Kasare, A. Godghate (eds), *Dr. Babasaheb Ambedkar: Writings and Speeches*. Vol. 17, part 2. Mumbai: Government of Maharashtra. [reprint: Dr Ambedkar Foundation].

———. 2014 (1990). 'What Congress and Gandhi Have Done to the Untouchables', in Vasant Moon (ed.), *Dr. Babasaheb Ambedkar: Writings and Speeches*. Vol. 9. Mumbai: Government of Maharashtra. [reprint: Dr Ambedkar Foundation, 2014].

———. 2014 (1946, 1987). 'Who Were the Shudras? How They Came to be the Fourth Varna in the Indo-Aryan Society', in Vasant Moon (ed.), *Dr. Babasaheb Ambedkar: Writings and Speeches*. Vol. 3. Mumbai: Government of Maharashtra. [reprint: Dr Ambedkar Foundation, 2014].

———. 2014 (1992). 'Buddha and Karl Marx', in Vasant Moon (ed.), *Dr. Babasaheb Ambedkar: Writings and Speeches*. Vol. 3. Mumbai: Government of Maharashtra. [reprint: Dr Ambedkar Foundation 2014].

———. 2014 (2003a). 'Election Manifesto of the Scheduled Castes Federation', in H. Narke, N.G. Kamble, M.L. Kasare, A. Godghate (eds), *Dr. Babasaheb Ambedkar: Writings and Speeches*. Vol. 17, part 2. Mumbai: Government of Maharashtra. [reprint: Dr Ambedkar Foundation, 2014].

———. 2014 (2003). 'Flood Control Use of Atomic Power' in H. Narke, N.G. Kamble, M.L. Kasare, A. Godghate (eds), *Dr. Babasaheb Ambedkar: Writings and Speeches*. Vol. 17, part 2. Mumbai: Government of Maharashtra. [reprint: Dr Ambedkar Foundation, 2014].

———. 2014 (1997). 'International Situation', in *Dr. Babasaheb Ambedkar: Writings and Speeches*. Vol. 15. Mumbai: Government of Maharashtra. [reprint: Dr Ambedkar Foundation, 2014].

———. 2014 (1991). 'Multi-purpose Development of Damodar Valley, Labor Member's Speech at Calcutta Conference', in Vasant Moon (ed.), *Dr. Babasaheb Ambedkar: Writings and Speeches*. Vol. 10.

Mumbai: Government of Maharashtra. [reprint: Dr Ambedkar Foundation, 2014].

———. 2014 (1995). 'Statement by Dr. B.R. Ambedkar in Parliament in Explanation of his Resignation from the Cabinet, 10 October, 1951', in *Dr. Babasaheb Ambedkar: Writings and Speeches*. Vol. 14, part 2. Mumbai: Government of Maharashtra. [reprint: Dr Ambedkar Foundation 2014].

———. 2016. 'An Appeal to Join the Republican Party of India', in P. Gaikwad (ed.), *Dr. Babasaheb Ambedkaranchi Samagra Bhashane*. Vol. 10. Nagpur: Kshitij Publications.

———. 2017. 'Letter from B.R. Ambedkar to W.E.B. Du Bois, ca. July 1946', in *W.E.B. Du Bois Papers (MS 312)*. Amherst: Special Collections and University Archives, University of Massachusetts Amherst Libraries.

Bandyopadhyay, Sekhar. 2000. 'Transfer of Power and the Crisis of Dalit Politics in India'. *Modern Asian Studies*, 34(4): 893–942.

Berwa, Laxmi. 1996. 'Globalizing the Dalit Issue'. *Dalit International Newsletter*, June.

Canberra Times. 1954. 'Dr. Ambedkar Warns Pandit Nehru on "Communist Giant"'. 28 August.

Desai, Ashwin and Goolam Vahed. 2010/2014. *Inside Indian Indenture: A South African Story, 1860–1914*. Pretoria: HSRC Press.

Du Bois, W.E.B. 1946. 'Letter from W.E.B. Du Bois to B.R. Ambedkar, July 31, 1946', in *W.E.B. Du Bois Papers (MS 312)*. Amherst: Special Collections and University Archives (University of Massachusetts Amherst Libraries). Available at http://credo.library.umass.edu/view/full/mums312-b109-i133, accessed 21 March 2018.

Du Bois, W.E.B. and Herbert Aptheker. 1978. *The Correspondence of W.E.B. Du Bois. Vol. 3, Selections, 1944–1963*. Amherst: University of Massachusetts Press.

Gaikwad, Vijay. 1999. *Dr Ambedkar's Foreign Policy and Its Relevance*. Mumbai: Vaibhav Prakashan.

Granger, L.B. 1954. 'Manhattan and Beyond'. *New York Amsterdam News*, 11 September.

Immerwahr, Danile. 2007. 'Caste or Colony? Indianizing Race in the United States'. *Modern Intellectual History*, 4(2): 275–301.

Izsák-Ndiaye, Rita 2016. *Report of the Special Rapporteur on Minority Issues*. Thirty-first session agenda item 3 A/HRC/31/56. Geneva: Human Rights Council.

Kennedy, A.B. 2015. 'Nehru's Foreign Policy', in D. Malone, C.R. Raja, and Srinath Raghavan (eds), *The Oxford Handbook of Indian Foreign Policy*. Oxford: Oxford University Press.

King, Martin Luther Jr. 1959. 'My Trip to India'. *Ebony*, July.

Kshirsagar, R. 1994. *Dalit Movement in India and Its Leaders, 1857–1956*. New Delhi: MD Publications.

Kumar, Vivek. 2009. 'Dalit Diaspora: Invisible Existence'. *Diaspora Studies*, 2(1): 53–74.

Mitra, D. 2016. 'Stung by UN Report on Caste Discrimination, India Cries Foul'. *Wire*, 25 March. Available at http://thewire.in/2016/03/25/stung-by-un-report-on-caste-discrimination-india-hits-back-25909, accessed 30 March 2016.

Neary, Ian. 2010. *The Buraku Issue and Modern Japan: The Career of Matsumoto Jiichiro*. Routledge: London.

Omvedt, Gail. 1994. *Dalits and the Democratic Revolution: Dr. Ambedkar and the Dalit Movement in Colonial India*. New Delhi: SAGE.

Pachai, B. 1971. *The International Aspects of the South African Indian Question 1860–1971*. Cape Town: Struik.

Paxton, H.P. 1943. 'The Negroes of India'. *The Crisis*, December.

Phule, Jotiba. 2019. *Slavery*. Delhi: Samyak Prakasha.

Prashad, Vijay 2000. 'Afro-Dalits of the Earth, Unite!'. *African Studies Review*, 43(1):189–201.

———. 2008. 'Cataracts of Silence: Race on the Edge of Indian Thoughts', in M. Bhagavan and A. Feldhaus (eds), *Claiming Power from Below Dalits and the Subaltern Question in India*. New Delhi: Oxford University Press.

Ram, Kanshi. 1982. *Chamcha Age: An Era of Stooges*. Delhi: Samyak Prakashan.

———. 1985. 'My 1st Visit to England'. *The Oppressed Indian*, July.

Rege, Sharmila. 2013. *Against the Madness of Manu: B.R. Ambedkar's Writings on Brahminical Patriarchy*. New Delhi: Navayana.

Sankaran, Krishna. 2015. 'A Postcolonial Racial/Spatial Order: Gandhi, Ambedkar and the Construction of the International', in Alexander Anievas, Nivi Manchanda, and Robbie Shilliam (eds), *Race and Racism in International Relations: Confronting the Global Colour Line*. New York: Routledge.

Selden, C.A. 1930. 'Prince and Outcast at Dinner in London End Age-Old Barrier', Special Cable to *New York Times*, 30 November.

Sivaraj, N. 1943. *War and Peace in the Pacific New York*. New York: International Secretariat, Institute of Pacific Relations.

———. 1995. 'Memoirs of Dr. Ambedkar', in N. Rattu (ed.), *Reminiscences and Remembrances of Dr B.R. Ambedkar*. New Delhi: Falcon Books.

———. 2009. 'Address by the President Rao Bahadur N. Sivaraj', in *Report of the Proceedings of the Third Session of the All Indian Depressed Classes Conference, Nagpur, 18 and 19 July 1942*. New Delhi: Gautam Book Centre.

Slate, N. 2012. 'The Dalit Panthers: Race, Caste, and Black Power in India', in N. Slate (ed.), *Black Power, Beyond Borders*. New York: Palgrave Macmillan.

Teltumbde, Anand. 2017. 'Bridging the Unholy Rift', in B.R. Ambedkar, *India and Communism*. New Delhi: Left Word Books.

Thakur, V. 2016. 'When India Proposed a Casteist Solution to South Africa's Racist Problem'. *Wire*, 4 April. Available at https://thewire.in/27045/exploring-casteism-in-indias-foreign-policy, accessed 4 April 2016.

Uesugi, Saichiro. 1983. 'BLL's Appeal to the Second World Conference to Combat Racism and Racial Discrimination'. *Buraku Liberation News*, 16: 146–8. Available at http://www.blhrri.org/old/blhrri_e/news/news016.pdf, accessed 15 October 2018.

Vahed, Goolam. 2015. 'India and South Africa at the United Nations, 1946–1955'. *AlterNation*, Special Edition 15: 54–84.

Yengde, Suraj and Anand Teltumbde (eds). 2018. *The Radical in Ambedkar Critical Reflections*. New Delhi: Penguin Random House.

Zelliot, Eleanor. 1992. *From Untouchable to Dalit: Essays on the Ambedkar Movement*. New Delhi: Manohar.

11

Foregrounding Social Justice in Indian Historiography

Interrogating the Poona Pact

KARTHIK RAJA KARUPPUSAMY

Babasaheb Ambedkar was treated as an untouchable in the dominant historiographical tradition of Modern India, but his marginalization is not a singular anomaly by any measure. Historical events such as the Non-Brahmin Movement in Maharashtra and Tamil Nadu of the twentieth century, Magad Satyagraha of 1927, Poona Pact of 1932, and the mass conversion of Dalits to Buddhism in 1956 instantly come to one's mind as some of the worst victims of historiographical neglect.[1] Often, events associated with the caste-subaltern struggles were swiftly thrown to the margins by academic historians. Often these events were deemed irrelevant in the trajectory of India's march towards 'freedom' or 'modernity' or else these occurrences slip through methodological potholes of straightjacketed 'class' analysis. The embedded caste hierarchies and the anti-caste struggles mounted against them remain, by and large, conspicuous in the historiography of 'Modern India' by its absences.

This chapter, in a way, explores, elaborates, and follows the implication of such neglects and erasures by taking up the framing of the Poona Pact in dominant historiography. This historiographical

---

[1] One glaring exception, Mani (2005).

analysis proceeds by weighing written history not only by its presences but also searches in its absences. It further seeks to explore the dialectic nature of both presences and absences and to investigate its internal logic and function. I take framing as an inescapable act from which even an ardent advocate of positivist or 'objective' history cannot be credited with a taintless escape.[2] The chapter interrogates the dominant historiography for how it frames Ambedkar and his movements against the agency of upper-caste nationalist leader Gandhi, at the instance of RTC and Poona Pact negotiations of 1932. These events had a profound impact on the constitutional and electoral framework of not only British-ruled colonial India but also its post-independent iteration. An attempt to contextualize Gandhi, by placing him in his ideological and sociopolitical trappings to derive an enriched understanding of the Poona Pact, in particular, and the operation of caste power, in general, has been made. An effort to take stock of Gandhi's social vision for the lower castes and untouchables were made by juxtaposing his words and deeds. It will help us to overthrow the long shadow cast by the memorialization of Gandhi in academic discourses, including history writing.

The Flow of Paper

The conflict between Ambedkar and Gandhi in the RTC of 1931, followed by the Poona Pact of 1932, were moments where the everydayness of caste violence and contradiction that runs deep in the social fabric of the subcontinent came to the national canvas in a dramatic way. Decoding the conflict, its historiographical representation, and its relation to caste power were the chief foci of the investigation. This chapter proceeds by presenting a brief historical contextualization of the Poona Pact, followed by a series of political, cultural, and intellectual movements that substantiate its continuing historical significance in the anti-caste discourse of Dalit subalterns. Then, through survey of the Poona Pact as framed by the dominant historiography, I problematize how the 'general' histories privilege a Gandhian vantage point at the cost of Ambedkar's while representing the Poona Pact as written history.

---

[2] Bagade (2015).

The overwhelming presence of Gandhi makes an analysis of his social vision inevitable. Through this, I arrive at the argument that Gandhi's foundational belief in the fourfold varna-based social order and his political commitment to keep Hindus in one fold is crucial to understand his opposition to Dalit political representation through separate electorates. My analysis offers one plausible way of problematizing or, more precisely, casteing[3] the dominant historiographical understanding of the Poona Pact, especially in bringing out the relationship between history writing and configuration of caste power.

Contextualizing the Poona Pact

From the second decades of the twentieth century onwards, enfranchisement[4] and political representation[5] of Depressed Classes have become a pressing concern for their leaders in step with the top-down process of democratization introduced by the colonial government. In the 1920s, through his firebrand activism, critical journalism, and intellectual engagement with the caste problem, Ambedkar grew in stature as the spokesperson of the then depressed classes. When the Simon Commission came to India, numerous depressed classes organizations welcomed and willingly testified before it. An overwhelming majority of the associations representing the interests of the Depressed Classes demanded for separate electorates.[6] This attitude can be contrasted with that of the Indian National Congress, which did a black flag demonstration with the slogan 'Go back, Simon' for its non-inclusion of Indian (read *upper-caste*) representatives.

---

[3] Casteing can be taken as an act of rereading/rewriting the existing narrative with a mode of analysis that takes the differential power distribution along caste lines and relations as consequential (as opposed to taking for granted) in the way events unfold.

[4] Ambedkar had appeared before the Southborough Franchise Committee as early as 1919 to argue for measures to enable Depressed Classes to vote. See Zelliot (2015).

[5] Ambedkar and G.A. Gawai, a fellow Maharashtrian Mahar, demanded for separate electorate for the Depressed Classes in their testimony to Southborough Franchise Committee in 1919.

[6] Zelliot (2015: 101).

A series of RTCs were convened in London for discussing India's future constitution with various stakeholders from British India and also the princely states. For this purpose, along with Dewan Bahadur R. Srinivasan, Ambedkar was nominated to the RTC to represent the interests of the Depressed Classes. In Ambedkar's words, 'For the Untouchables it was a landmark in their history. The Untouchables were for the first time allowed to be represented separately by two delegates' and was deemed important enough 'to have the right to be consulted in the framing of a constitution of India'[7]

Ambedkar, in his Nagpur conference just before leaving for the First RTC, declared that 'he would be satisfied with joint electorates provided that there was adult franchise and reserved seats'.[8] Ambedkar, sensing that his demand for adult suffrage was not likely to be conceded, claimed separate electorates for the Depressed Classes. Gandhi, who was absent from the First RTC, was sent as the sole representative of the Indian National Congress after the conclusion of the Gandhi-Irwin pact.[9] Gandhi, while prepared to grant separate electorates for Muslims and Sikhs based on 'historical grounds', was staunchly against the demand of separate electorates for untouchables. Gandhi's opposition was so total that Ambedkar later commented, 'It would not be unfair if it was said that the main purpose for which Mr. Gandhi came to the RTC was to oppose the demands of the Untouchables.'[10] Gandhi claimed 'to represent the vast mass of the Untouchables' and dismissed Ambedkar's demand for separate electorates as a mistaken idea. Gandhi, in addition, threatened to stake his life if untouchables were offered a separate electorate.[11] Ambedkar stood his ground and asserted that he was fully qualified to represent the interest of the Depressed Classes and the claim of Congress to represent the Depressed Classes more

[7] Ambedkar (2016: 39).

[8] Zelliot (2015: 103).

[9] This was a truce reached between the colonial government and the Indian National Congress (Congress) by, amongst other things, agreeing to the suspension of civil disobedience by Congress and in return, participation of the Congress in the second RTC held in London. This enabled the representation of Congress in Second RTC.

[10] Ambedkar (2016: 69).

[11] Omvedt (2013: 171).

than he does was merely a 'false claim'.[12] This pushed the Second RTC to an impasse as far as the question of apportioning political representation to different communities was concerned. When the chairperson of the Minorities Committee, British PM Ramsay MacDonald, proposed to arbitrate, all the delegates accepted the proposal to give a signed requisition authorizing him to arbitrate, except for Ambedkar.[13] When Gandhi returned to Bombay, a black flag demonstration was held against him by 8,000 Depressed Class demonstrators, overwhelming the meagre depressed class cadres Congress had mobilized 'to show their faith in Gandhi'.[14] On 16 August 1932, the British Government announced 'the Communal award', which provided separate electorates to not only Muslims and Sikhs but also to Depressed Classes amongst others.

Following up his threat of resisting separate electorates with his life, Gandhi wrote to British PM Ramsay MacDonald that unless the British government 'of its own motion or under pressure of public opinion, revise their decision and withdraw their scheme of communal electorates for the Depressed Classes, whose representatives should be elected by the general electorate under the common franchise.'[15]

If not, then Gandhi threatened that he will fast unto death.[16] MacDonald, in return, emphasized to Gandhi that Depressed Classes were, in fact, given double votes 'in order that their membership of the Hindu Community should remain unimpaired'.[17] Ambedkar, in his statement, on a day before the proposed fast of Gandhi, accused Gandhi of desperately trying to deprive the little the untouchables have got.[18] Gandhi initiated his fast, heedless of anyone's reasoning, on 20 September 1932. The fast continued for six days. There were intense negotiations between caste Hindu leaders such as Madan Mohan Malaviya, Tej Bahadur Sapru, and C. Rajagopalachari and Ambedkar as the representative of

---

[12] Ambedkar (2016: 64).

[13] Ambedkar did not sign a requisition as he felt 'the demands of the Untouchables were so reasonable that no arbitration was necessary'; Ambedkar (2016: 73).

[14] Keer (2016: 191–2).

[15] Ambedkar (2016: 81).

[16] Ambedkar (2016: 81).

[17] Ambedkar (2016: 83).

[18] Ambedkar (2016: 298).

Foregrounding Social Justice in Indian Historiography   257

untouchables to arrive at a solution that is agreeable to both parties. On 24 September 1932, the Poona Pact[19] was sealed by the signatures of twenty-three people, all in total, representing either Hindus or Depressed Classes, the interesting fact being that Gandhi was not one of them. The Poona Pact, amongst other things, replaced separate electorates with an increased number of reserved seats with a two-tier election system where, first, Depressed Classes will elect a panel of four members from their own community, then, one of the four will be elected by the general constituency. This effectively made depressed class candidates dependent on the Caste Hindu votes as depressed class population is in minority without exception in all the constituencies. The demand of separate electorate by leaders of the Depressed Classes, the process of representation of the interests of the Depressed Classes in the RTCs of 1930–2, the grant of separate electorate in the form of Ramsay MacDonald award, and its reversal through Gandhi's fast represent a prime strand of political history of the Dalits. We have situated the Poona Pact in its historical setting to offer the backdrop for our analysis of its representation in the dominant historiography. While viewing the Poona Pact as a historical event of significance, one should not overlook its contemporary significance in the political, cultural, and intellectual expressions and assertion of the Dalit subaltern.

Poona Pact as a Historical Memory

The memory of the Poona Pact looms large in the political-cultural discourse of Dalit subalterns. In the *Chamcha Age*, Kanshi Ram memorializes the Poona Pact as the decisive moment that gave rise to 'the era of stooges' posing a challenge to the real Dalit representation. Kanshi Ram declares,

> Poona Pact made Dalits helpless. By rejecting separate electorate, Dalits were deprived of their genuine representation in legislatures. Several and various kind of *chamchas* were born in the last fifty years. As and when India's high-caste Hindu rulers felt the need of *chamchas* and when the authority of the upper castes got endangered by real and genuine dalit leaders, *chamchas* were brought to the fore in all other fields.[20]

[19] Ambedkar (2016: 87–9).
[20] Kanshi Ram, in Mani (2005: 362).

For this situation, he squarely places the blame on the Poona Pact that negates the right of separate electorates for Dalits that was hard won by Ambedkar from the colonial British Government.[21] Gopal Guru brings to our attention the Marathi songs sung by Dalit activists that poignantly recollect how Babasaheb gave up his demand for saving Gandhi's life.[22] The recent cultural resurgence and assertion in Tamil Nadu, precipitated by the effort of Film Director Pa. Ranjith, through the platform of 'The Casteless Collective', recollected the memory and the loss that goes with Gandhi's fast and the resultant Poona Pact through a powerful rap song that encapsulates Babasaheb's life narrative.[23] One of the most popular digital platforms for anti-caste discourse was even named after the RTCs,[24] signifying the historical importance of the negotiation for separate electorates. As late as 2018, a fascinating and in-depth book, *The Making of India's Electoral System*, with a point-blank focus on the Poona Pact and its implication for Dalit futures, made its appearance.[25] These instances demonstrate the recurring significance that the Poona Pact came to acquire, in the anti-caste discourse of the caste subalterns. Let us, now, turn our attention as to how the RTC and the Poona Pact is framed in dominant historiography.

Poona Pact in Mainstream Historiography

Though history is generally defined and thought of as writing about the *past*, it could often prove to be deceptive. Written histories cannot be seen as solely about things that were past. Consciousness about one's present, one's own sociopolitical location in that present, the ideology one identifies with, and the sources of funding of one's present and future projects, amongst other things, mediates the history one writes and its attendant teleology. The dominant

[21] Ram (1982).

[22] Guru (2017: 95–100).

[23] Casteless Collective. 2018. 'Jai Bhim Anthem' YouTube [video]. Available at https://www.youtube.com/watch?v=ZhYRz-v6fTc, accessed 14 April 2018.

[24] Round Table India. Available at http://roundtableindia.co.in/, accessed 11 April 2018.

[25] Vundru (2018).

historiography is circumscribed by its commitment, in ways that are implicit and explicit, to variants of nationalism, labelled as communal and secular. A rule of thumb that equates nationalism itself with the Congress and, in turn, Congress to Gandhi proves to be an implicit schema underwriting modern Indian history writing.

With this context, we are going to approach three texts, Sumit Sarkar's *Modern India* (1989), Bipan Chandra's *India's Struggle for Independence* (1989), and Sekhar Bandyopadhyay's *From Plassey to Partition* (2004).

Methodological Note

I take, as the representative of dominant historiography, three key histories of modern India: Sumit Sarkar's *Modern India*,[26] Bipan Chandra's *India's Struggle for Independence*,[27] and Sekhar Bandyopadhyay's *From Plassey to Partition*.[28] Specifically, these three works were chosen because of their exceptional acceptance in both academic as well as popular circles as authoritative general histories of modern India. In addition, they serve as textbooks in schools, colleges, and also for civil service examinations, which makes them incomparably highly circulated and consumed, thereby possessing a palpable role in shaping the popular historical common sense.

A text is a reflection of that period's social equilibrium as much as an individual's scholarship. Two of the books under consideration were written in the 1980s, the period that witnessed the rise of subaltern studies. Sumit Sarkar, a Marxist scholar, was intent on 'writing a history from below'. Sumit Sarkar starts his *Modern India*[29] with a promise that he is making an attempt to explore the possibilities of a '*history from below* as distinct from the usual tendency in the historiography of Indian nationalism to concentrate on the activities, ideals, or factional manoeuvres of leaders'.[30]

Nevertheless, the story of 'modern' India starts from 1885, which, not so co-incidentally, is the year Indian National Congress

[26] Sarkar (1989).
[27] Chandra et al. (1989).
[28] Bandyopadhyay (2006).
[29] Sarkar (1989).
[30] Sarkar (1989: Introduction).

was established. Sarkar considered this simply as a 'convenience'. Later, Sarkar clarified, in his preface to the second edition, that he did not imply the start of 'modern' from 1885. 'The date, as I hinted in the preface, was there only because there had been plans for a collective venture in which another historian was to have written a volume ending in 1885.'[31]

Sarkar's *Modern India*, in its short reference to the Poona Pact of 1932, records:

> Gandhi began a 'fast unto death' on the untouchable separate electorate issue on 20 September, and was able to secure an agreement between caste Hindu and untouchable leaders (Poona Pact) by which the Award was modified. The Hindu joint electorate was retained with reserved seats for untouchables who were given greater representation than by MacDonald.[32]

This can be read in line with the Marxist approach, which sees the caste question and the Dalit question in particular as a diversion.[33] Even a scholar like Sumit Sarkar, who later became more sensitive than most other historians to the presence of *non-upper caste* narratives in his later historiographical interventions,[34] treats the Poona Pact in an offhand manner. His reference to this moment in the making of 'modern India' itself seems merely incidental and largely non-consequential. The separate electorate and the reversal of it through Gandhi's coercive act of fasting, as established by the Poona Pact, was itself written in just to play an auxiliary role to Gandhi's Harijan upliftment, which according to Sarkar, then became 'Gandhi's principal concern'. In effect, the Poona Pact is seen as the springboard for Gandhi's campaign against untouchability, thereby denying the Poona pact any significance of its own.

---

[31] This detail from Sarkar, while presented to exonerate him from the charge of conflating the dawn of 'modern' with the coming of Indian National Congress, ends up revealing how structural that assumption was throughout academia and the publishing industry.

[32] Sarkar (1989: 328).

[33] 'However, this (poona pact) was a great blow to the freedom movement. For this led to the diversion of the people's attention from the objective of full independence to the mundane issue of upliftment of Harijans.' Namboodiripad (1986: 492).

[34] Sarkar (1997).

Foregrounding Social Justice in Indian Historiography   261

Sarkar, in his later career in the 1990s, coming out of the subaltern studies, critiques particularly Partha Chatterjee's *The Nation and its Fragments*,[35] and generally the thrust of the subaltern project in the following words that can also stand as a critique of his own work a decade ago: 'Even more surprisingly, the book tells the reader nothing about the powerful anti-caste movements associated with Phule, Periyar, or Ambedkar. No book can be expected to cover everything, but silences of this magnitude are dangerous in a work that appears on the surface comprehensive enough to serve as a standard introduction to colonial India for non-specialist and newcomers.'[36]

Later that same decade, Bipan Chandra, along with few other scholars, wrote a hagiographical account of the nationalist movement, placing Congress firmly at its centre, which did not have any space for politics that were at odds with it. He asserted that all the movements that happened in the colonial period were 'integral' to the Indian national movement except 'the only one which may be said to have formed part of an alternative stream of politics were communal and casteist movements which were not nationalist or anti-imperialist but in fact betrayed loyalist pro colonial tendencies'.[37]

Regardless of its partisan nature, Bipan Chandra's *India's Struggle for Independence*[38] is probably the most popular and celebrated history book on modern India. It is unmistakably the holy grail for millions of students who aspire to appear for the Civil Services. Published in 1989, it continues to be widely read as the political history of modern India. Unlike Sarkar, Bipan Chandra does deal with the Poona Pact in some detail.[39] However, as the saying goes, the devil is in the details.

Here, the question of agency should be foregrounded to see how the agency of upper-caste nationalists were exaggerated while Ambedkar's agency was undermined with impunity. The Poona Pact was seen as something that precipitated suddenly from the minds of the British. Chandra writes: 'The British Policy of "Divide and Rule" found another expression in the announcement of the

[35] Chatterjee (1993).
[36] Sarkar (2002: 412).
[37] Chandra et al. (1989: 28).
[38] Chandra et al. (1989).
[39] Bipan devotes around two pages in Chandra et al. (1989: 290–1), whereas Sarkar (1989: 328–30) has disposed it off in a mere few lines, in addition, subsuming it under the head (Gandhi's) 'Harijan Campaign'.

262 Karthik Raja Karuppusamy

Communal Award in August 1932.... The Award declared the
Depressed Classes (Scheduled Castes of today) also to be a minority community entitled to separate electorate and thus separated
them from the rest of the Hindus'.[40]

Bipan Chandra frames the award of separate electorates for the
Depressed Classes within the framework of the British policy of
'Divide and Rule'. This historiographical articulation tricks the
unsuspecting reader into experiencing merely the agency of the
British as well as Gandhi, thereby effectively erasing any Dalit initiative in this matter. The story of the Poona Pact starts with the
communal award as 'another expression' of the British divide-and-
rule policy, then it is stopped by the noble act of Gandhi's fast, and
then finally ends with Gandhi setting out 'to redeem his pledge'
to uplift the untouchables out of their miserable lives. Gandhi's
vision and Bipan's historiography converge in the matter of denying the Dalit agency, the former in the political and the latter in
historical change. If one is not convinced by the subtle point of
framing, the following extract can be of help in understanding how
Ambedkar was undermined as follows:

> While many political Indians saw the (Gandhi's) fast as a diversion
> from the ongoing political movement, all were deeply concerned and
> emotionally shaken. Mass meetings took place everywhere. The 20th
> of September was observed as a day of fasting and prayer. Temples,
> wells, etc., were thrown open to the Depressed Classes all over the
> country ... Political leader of different political persuasions includ-
> ing Madan Mohan Maliviya, M.C. Rajah and *B. R. Ambedkar, now
> become active.*[41]

Ambedkar, as a legal expert and activist of the first order for the
cause of Dalits, (then Depressed Classes), was foremost in engaging with the British on diverse issues that concerns the present
and future stakes of Dalits. Years before the award of separate
electorates, Ambedkar demanded it in his evidence to the Simon
Commission in 1928 as the only means to secure adequate representation for the Dalits in the absence of universal adult franchise.[42]
And further, as an active participant in the First RTC held in 1930,

---

[40] Chandra et al. (1989: 290).
[41] Chandra et al. (1989: 291). Emphasis added.
[42] Bandyopadhyay (2004).

Foregrounding Social Justice in Indian Historiography 263

he vocally advocated for separate electorate for untouchables, after his demand of universal adult franchise was not entertained. As an injustice to the facts of history, Chandra introduces Ambedkar as someone who became 'active' after Gandhi's fast.

Further, we are told, as the justification of Gandhi's opposition to the right of political self-representation of Dalits, as follows by Chandra in an endorsing way: 'What was needed was not the protection of the so-called interests of the Depressed Classes in terms of seats in the legislatures or jobs but the 'root and branch' eradication of untouchability.'[43]

Particularly, this kind of framing can be seen as a classic case of camouflaging the teleology of Gandhian enunciations by over-writing it with the politically correct of the contemporary. While Ambedkar asks for the appropriate provision to ensure Dalit representation as a means of Dalit empowerment, Gandhi who pleads for 'root and branch' eradication of untouchability has other things in mind. If one cares to dig a little deeper, then the context in which Gandhi uttered the phrase 'root and branch' can be seen as something wildly inconsistent with what Chandra wants us to believe.

> Because the Brahminism went down, it drew down with it all the other classes, and I have not a shadow of doubt in my mind that, if the Brahminism does not revive, the Hinduism must perish, and for me the infallible test of the revival of the Brahminism, that is, Hinduism, is the root and branch removal of untouchability.[44]

Sekhar Bandyopadhyay's *From Plassey to Partition*[45] was first published in 2004 and has slowly came to occupy dominance in circulation by partially replacing Bipan Chandra as the standard textbook for Civil Service exams. This story is about 'the establishment and functioning of colonial rule and also the emergence of a pluralist and polyphonic nationalism in India'. While this makes it apparent that this is yet another story of how nationalism came into existence in defiance of the colonial, there is one key word that sets it apart from the rest: polyphonic. The word 'polyphonic' comes to life in Bandyopadhyay's general 'history of modern India' by incorporating a section titled 'Many Voices of a Nation'. While

[43] Chandra et al. (1989: 291).
[44] Gandhi, M.K., as quoted in Tendulkar (1992: 196).
[45] Bandyopadhyay (2006).

talking about his calculated move away from the nationalist frames that generally history narrative tends to surrender to: 'This narrative seeks to take the discussion of nationalism beyond that constricted discursive space where nation-state is situated at the center and the existence of a homogeneous nation is uncritically accepted and it is supposed to have spoken in one voice.'[46]

According to Bandyopadhyay, the First RTC 'achieved very little' because of the non-participation of the Congress and the second one was not noteworthy as negotiations at the Minority Committee 'broke down'. What this 'broke down' refers to is that the demand for separate electorates by the Depressed Classes was not accepted by Gandhi, as the sole representative of the Congress in the second RTC. The dominant historiography of Modern India does not attribute much importance to the political significance of RTCs held between 1930 and 1932. The reason is the absence of the Congress in the first and the third editions, and more importantly, the exposition of the Congress' unwillingness to grant the legitimate share of political rights to the then Depressed Classes who were historically labouring under the tyranny of caste Hindus. The Congress, which prides itself as the champion of democracy, sent a sole representative, Mr Gandhi, which runs counter to any possible imagination of representation of the Congress. But what the Congress, through the words and actions of Gandhi, tried, though unsuccessfully, at the second RTC was to keep the *Varnashrama* puzzle in order. One observer recalls: 'To the utter dislike of Gandhi, the Minorities which included the dalits hammered out an agreement for their representation and right in the new Constitution. They met Prime Minister on 12 November 1931 and handed over the agreement to him. This was a victory for Ambedkar, after the unrelenting attempts of Gandhi to isolate the dalits.'[47]

Moral Victory?

On 26 September 1932, the *Hindu* in its editorial about the Poona Pact, without ever referring to Dr Ambedkar, celebrated 'Mahatmaji', for 'his inspiring and heroic lead' that gave rise to 'universal rejoicing in the country'. The claim of the Depressed

[46] Bandyopadhyay (2006: xi).
[47] Vundru (2018: 33).

Foregrounding Social Justice in Indian Historiography   265

Classes to their fair share of political power in the form of separate electorates and double vote (exclusive voting in addition to the provision to vote with general Hindu electorate) was equated with a 'calamity', which was countered by Gandhi like a 'miracle'.[48] Later, numerous studies emerged that equate the Poona Pact to a moral victory of Gandhi's universalist perspective over Ambedkar's separatist tendency. Accordingly, it was dubbed as Gandhi's 'finest hour'.[49] In a similar vein, Bandyopadhyay writes,

> The differences persisted when the Communal Award in September 1932 recognized the right to separate electorate for the untouchables—now called the Scheduled Castes—and Gandhi embarked on his *epic fast* unto death to get it revoked. Ambedkar now had little choice but to *succumb to the moral pressure* to save Mahatma's life and accepted a compromise, known as the Poona Pact, which provided for 151 reserved seats for the Scheduled Castes in joint electorate. For the time being, it seemed as if all conflicts had been resolved.[50]

It is historically naive, if not positively mischievous, to equate this settlement with the *moral force* of the actor. Ambedkar, in his statement on 19 September 1932, questioning the rationale of Gandhi's fast, writes: 'Whether, he knows it or not, the Mahatma's act will result in nothing but terrorism by his followers against the Depresses Classes all over the country.'[51]

In relation to the nature of Gandhi's fast, Omvedt writes: 'Though directed against Ambedkar, the pressure that came through the fast-to-death was one brought by Gandhi's Caste hindu followers—the fear of a wide village backlash against Dalits. As a result, this fast at least genuinely represented a kind of moral blackmail.'[52]

Ambedkar's words materialized as letters threatening his life for not accepting the Mahatma's demand.[53] While fasting itself is a form of coercion that bypasses other legitimate methods of persuasions, in this case, it was also underwritten by actual physical violence,

---

[48] *Hindu* (2017: 191–2).
[49] Kumar (1987).
[50] Bandyopadhyay (2006: 355). Emphasis added.
[51] Ambedkar (2016: 302).
[52] Omvedt (2008: 54).
[53] Vundru (2018: 56).

266 Karthik Raja Karuppusamy

not only to Ambedkar himself, who was the chief protagonist, but also to the Depressed Classes population, for whose interest Ambedkar was fighting tooth and nail.[54]

Gandhi for Reserved Seats?

Bandyopadhyay writes, very much in the steps of Chandra, that, 'Gandhi, though opposed to separate electorates, was not averse to the idea of reserved seats'.[55] While Bandyopadhyay can be said to leave out Gandhi's original opposition to reservation of seats for the Depressed Classes, Chandra positively states that Gandhi 'did not object to the demand for a larger number of the reserved seats of the Depressed Classes' as chronologically before his fast against separate electorates.[56] Ambedkar, as early as 1945 in his masterpiece *What Congress and Gandhi did to the Untouchables*, reveals that this pretension is a 'gross error'. According to Ambedkar, Gandhi's argument in the second RTC in London was as follows: 'Whatever his views are today, while in London he was totally opposed to any system of Special representation for the Depressed Classes whether by joint Electorates or by Separate Electorates.'[57]

This effectively means that there will be no reserved seats, let alone separate electorates, for the Depressed Classes according to the scheme of Gandhi. Dhananjay Keer substantiates the account of Gandhi proposing that the Depressed Classes give up reservation, with his characteristic tint of humour.

> Gandhi suggested a novel method to win the support of Ambedkar. He said that if the Untouchable candidates failed in the general election held on the basis of joint electorates without reservation of seats, the Depressed Classes should prove their bona fides in a

[54] Even M.C. Rajah, who reversed his support of separate electorates in favour of joint electorates to support Gandhi, recognized the violent consequences that were inherent in Gandhi's fast: 'If he (Gandhi) dies, for the next thousand of years, we shall be where we have been, if not worse. There will be such a strong feeling against us that we brought about his death that the mind of the whole Hindu community and whole civilised community will kick us downstairs further still.' See Vundru (2018: 56).

[55] Bandyopadhyay (2006: 324).

[56] Chandra et al. (1989: 289).

[57] Ambedkar (2016: 301).

Court of Law. Gandhi sometimes showed a knack of speaking absurd things with distinction, and Ambedkar therefore laughed heartily at the novel but meaningless idea.[58]

All the above accounts, to greater or lesser extent, are soaked in the Gandhian voice, rationale, and circuit of action, whereas Ambedkar's stances were seen as adjunct, if not altogether dispensable. Such framing was feasible by a specific economy of privileging a certain aspect of Gandhism while avoiding others. Gandhi's moral power was emphasized while his concrete positions in terms of caste subalterns were muted.

As these instances are numerous, delving into Gandhi's social vision will provide useful pointers on what was unwritten, opening up other possibilities of representing Gandhi in the above encountered historical narratives.

Gandhi's Faith on Varnavyavastha and his Fast against Separate Electorates

The literature on M.K. Gandhi is breathtaking. There has been a continuous stream of Gandhian literature, which was set forth in his own lifetime, then only to increase considerably after his death. There were numerous biographies, mostly hagiographical some critical. Apart from biographies, there were efforts to project Gandhi as philosopher, Gandhi as critical traditionalist, Gandhi as critic par excellence of modernity, Gandhi as environmentalist, Gandhi as feminist, and so on. But one aspect of the 'Mahatma' was left for the shadows of history. These studies on 'Mahatma' Gandhi, more often than not, gloss over or swiftly sidestep his foundational belief in the Varnashrama Dharma, that is, the defense of hereditary occupational division amongst castes. While it is natural that the hagiographers of Gandhi can be charged with such accusations, sadly, academic historians also do not fare better. While other political actors who were not a part of Gandhi's camp were systematically reduced to their immediate group interest, Gandhi was afloat because his actions were considered to be beyond such petty qualms of contextualization. However, his firm belief and even firmer advocacy, even under untenable situations, of Varnashrama

[58] Keer (2016: 191).

Dharma as the 'eternal law' that is based on hereditary 'aptitudes and karma', as the unqualified and ultimate solution for all the predicament of not only of Indian society but of the world, was not a convenient position for many scholars to manoeuvre. So, by an unspoken academic consensus, it was swept under the rug.[59] Numerous nationalist histories and even Gandhian biographies touch their finish lines without saying much about Gandhi's approach towards the caste question and its ramifications. It is not to say that they have not heaped praises on Gandhi for his selfless battle against the 'sin' of untouchability. In the interest of the full picture, we need to probe further into this aspect of Gandhi and his metaphysics to enrich our understanding of his decisions and deeds, especially in relation to the RTCs and the Poona Pact. For these reasons of absences, I need to set out first, in clear terms, what views Gandhi had regarding varna/caste-based social order; second, what place Depressed Classes have at that social order; and third, how it possibly relates to his opposition to the Dalit self-representation through the arrangement of separate electorates. I argue, through the following exposition, that Gandhi's foundational belief in the varna-based social order is critical to understand his opposition to Dalit political representation through separate electorates.

The Spell of the Gandhian Phenomenon

Gandhi considered as an extraordinary phenomenon without par is a commonplace occurrence in modern Indian historiography. One illustrative instance of such profession is Ramachandra Guha's titling his book as *India after Gandhi*.[60] As a leader of the Indian nationalist mass movement and as a political thinker and practitioner, Gandhi is one of the important figures that history has to contend with. While there is no objection to that proposition, I raise the question: *In what terms?* Kiran, in his insightful analysis about how Gandhi was treated in the academic discourse, has the following to say, '(Gandhi's) politico-religious practice is also construed as *sue generis*, incapable of being grasped and much less critiqued within the generally accepted frameworks.

[59] One recent exception which takes the bull by its horns, though not necessarily convincing, see Kolge (2018).

[60] Guha (2007).

He has been so elevated to a level that ordinary mortals can hardly touch him.'[61]

This approach of placing a few beyond the reach of objective historical analysis does immeasurable harm in the journey of arriving at a full picture of the past. While the dominant trend in historiography confers an all-encompassing historical agency and legitimacy to Gandhi, it is often done at the cost of subsuming and submerging numerous subaltern groups that were voicing in tandem and often in opposition to Gandhi. Ambedkar, as a subaltern par excellence, was continuously silenced, marginalized, or disciplined in order to maintain the decorum of 'Mahatmaship', to use Babasaheb's terminology.[62] So, Kiran demands that we 'embed' Gandhi in 'the prevalent existing power-structures to shed more light on the history of the period which will in turn take us closer to the holistic understanding of the Gandhian personality itself.[63]

For example, the chapter titled 'The Age of Gandhian Politics' in Bandyopadhyay leaves us with no doubt as to the importance bestowed on Gandhi in the writing of a general history of modern India. As a result, the privileged personality, who was elevated to be the motivating spirit of an era, should be unpacked for his foundational beliefs and ideological moorings. This Bandyopadhyay does with the help of Ashish Nandy, Partha Chatterjee, and Bhikhu Parekh, who declared Gandhi as 'counter-modernist critic of the west', 'critique of civil society', and a 'Critique of Modern Civilization' respectively.[64] Further taking Hind Swaraj, Bandyopadhyay elucidates Gandhi's attack against the 'evil' Western modernity. While this trend of treating Gandhi as an extraordinary phenomenon is the norm, seldom is the underbelly interrogated. The fact that much of Gandhi's critic against modernity/West is anchored securely in his faith on Varnashrama Dharma is of little importance to these neo-Gandhian scholars.[65] Even when such interrogation was undertaken, the field of Indian historiography is so much saturated with a configuration of power,

---

[61] Kiran (2016: 4).

[62] Ambedkar (1938).

[63] Kiran (2016: 4–5).

[64] Bandyopadhyay (2006: 289).

[65] For example, to see how some scholars tend to sidestep Gandhi's foundational belief in idealized forms of varna, see Rathore (2017: 168–91).

where the Dalit-Bahujan critics[66] fail to reach the discipline's ear but whereas a white scholar[67] measures up so easily to evoke impassioned responses.[68]

The dominant historical narrative accepts unquestioningly the Gandhian claim of the 'untouchable' question to be of 'religious' nature; they neither reject such division nor do they interrogate the implications of such a discursive move. Gandhi, in his letter to Sir Samuel Hoare, the Secretary of State for India, regarding the issue of separate electorates in 1932, declared, 'For me the question of these classes is predominantly moral and religious. The political aspect, important though it is, dwindles into insignificance compared to the moral and religious issue'.[69] Gandhi, while insisting that his 'epic fast' is of moral and religious nature, impersonating a metaphorical ostrich,[70] denies recognizing the material realities around him. The political crowd around him also swiftly follows. In a jiff, the political becomes trivial, irrelevant, and disposable and the personal morality and sacrifice of Gandhi was the only matter that got the centre stage. Neither the larger political implications nor even the morality of such an approach was deemed questionable. The 'political radicals' of the Congress, for the moment, conveniently joined the bandwagon, privileging the personal (of Gandhi) over the political (rights of Dalits). It is an irony that a clique that has dogmatically asserted the primacy of political over social,[71] now suddenly, quite opportunistically, chooses to subordinate the political claims of caste-oppressed Depressed Classes to the personal whims of its party supremo. If one closely looks at this contradiction and reads it purposively, then it is revealed that the trajectory of Gandhi and the Congress was consistent in contesting the caste subaltern's claim to power in the 'ruthless pursuit of monopoly power' from the colonial power.[72]

[66] Aloysius (1997); Mani (2005).

[67] Anderson (2012).

[68] Chatterjee, Kaviraj, and Menon (2015).

[69] Ambedkar (2016: 77).

[70] As I found out, as an instructive lesson in perspective, ostriches do not bury their heads in the sand in times of crisis; rather, it might deceptively appear to a spectator that way as the ostrich turn her eggs using her beak by peeking into the shallow nests dug in the ground, several times a day.

[71] Ambedkar (2016: 1–17).

[72] Aloysius (1997: 191).

One unmistakable hallmark of the dominant historiography is conferring on Gandhi's voice the power to represent the unalloyed and authoritative reality. Many historians prefer to let Gandhi eclipse the historical moments with agile ease. Gandhi's utterances and course of actions becomes taken as a direct description of reality itself, to which even an addition of a footnote was considered a sacrilege. This unmeasured historical agency bestowed on Gandhi was done at the cost of other subaltern voices of resistance that braved the hegemonic discourse of Gandhi and the Congress. While the historical agency of subaltern castes was quelled by the hegemonic discourse of Brahminism then, it again faces further assault at the hands of secular/Marxist (read upper-caste) historians whose social location places them in a world where they let these unruly struggles and unsuccessful confrontations slip in to the oblivion of the history.[73] The battle of Dalit-Bahujan historians was to liberate those submerged historical realities from this double bind.

Gandhian Social Vision

As early as 1916, just after Gandhi arrived from South Africa, he had taken an unambiguous position on the caste question. In his speech on the caste system to an audience in Ahmedabad, Gandhi spoke thus,

> I have devoted much thought to the subject of the caste system and come to the conclusion that Hindu society cannot dispense with it, that it lives on because of the discipline of caste.... Of course, these caste restrictions have something of value in them.... It is vain to effort to replace this structure by one single community.[74]

In the same year, in a view to elaborate his view regarding the caste question, Gandhi wrote an essay titled *The Hindu Caste System* that was published in a Marathi monthly *Bharat Sevak*. It praises the ingeniousness of caste for being a strong foundation for the existence of Hindu society.

[73] This happens primarily due to the fact that many academics, like those belonging to the Subaltern Studies project, until recently, did not consider 'caste-based oppression as worthy of historical analysis'. See Jungum (2015: 63–70).

[74] Gandhi (1972: Vol. 13, 277–8).

The Hindu social structure has endured, I believe, on the foundation of the caste system.... The caste system contains within it the seed of Swaraj.... The caste system is a perfectly natural institution.... I am opposed to the movements which are being carried on for the destruction of the system.[75]

For Gandhi, caste meant 'merely an agency for ensuring self control. The caste defines the limits within which one may enjoy life; that is to say, we are not free to seek any happiness outside our caste.' This 'limit' is applicable to eating and marriage. And this 'self control is conducive to happiness in all circumstances'.[76] In Gandhi's scheme of Varnavyavastha, following one's hereditary occupation is the most essential of all attributes. In categorically advising the 'educated *Antyajas*'[77] to stick to their ancestral occupation, Gandhi reasons:

Antyajas are generally engaged in weaving, agriculture and sanitary duties. The first two provide clothing and food to the people and the last preserves public health. No society can live without all these three occupations. To call any of them low or base is evidence of sheer ignorance. *It should not be our desire, when educated, to leave our occupation;* our effort should be to ennoble it.[78]

For Gandhi, the principle of Varnavyavastha is not merely a belief, but a discovery. He equates and elevates the dogma of birth-based division of society into a law that merely corresponds to the design of nature. In numerous instances, Gandhi unapologetically equates the law of gravity to that of the law of varna. Gandhi's metaphysical imagination regarding the nature of varna in the aftermath of the Poona Pact in 1933 is as follows:

The varnas have an intimate relationship to one's profession. The pursuit of one's calling is one's dharma. He, who forsakes his, falls from his varna. He himself is destroyed, his spirit decays. That man causes confusion of varnas and thereby society is harmed and its organization breaks down. When everybody discards his varna, the

[75] Gandhi (1972: Vol. 13, 301).

[76] Gandhi (1972: Vol. 13, 302).

[77] Antyajas literally means 'the last-born' referring to the untouchable castes within the framework of Varnavyavastha.

[78] Gandhi (1972: Vol. 17, 519). Emphasis added.

Foregrounding Social Justice in Indian Historiography   273

mal-organization of society grows, chaos reigns and society perishes. If the Brahmin class abjures its work of imparting education, it falls from its pedestal. If a Kshatriya gives up his work of protecting the people, he dishonours his varna. If a Vaishya discards the earning of money, he falls from his varna. If a Shudra abandons serving, he falls. All stay in their places by remaining engrossed in their own duty. He falls who gives up his proper duty. A Shudra who does his appropriate duty is better than a Brahmin who discards his duty.[79]

But at the same time, as at other instances of his glorification of the varna order, Gandhi, this time too, asserts that 'there is no room for feeling of high and low where it is a question of an obligation.'[80] How much trust can one invest in the discourse of Gandhi asserting that there is no superiority or inferiority in the ideal varna order that he envisages? While the existing society cleavage on the varna and caste lines with its attendant dynamics of hierarchies were systematically explored and exposed by Ambedkar and other scholars, those were of little use to Gandhi in reconsidering his position. The beauty of Gandhi's ideal varna-based social order lies in its immunity from the various aspersions against the existing varna/caste-based order. Ambedkar, while attacking the caste-based social order's manifestations, unlike Gandhi, attributed the perversity of this system to the very idea itself.

Gandhi is a firm believer in the karma theory, which states that according to the past life's merit, one is either upgraded or degraded in the scale of fourfold Varnashrama Dharma. The Varnavyavastha consists of Brahmin, Kshatriya, Vaisya, and Sudra. Beyond the pale of the fourfold varna system were the class of people who were variously referred to as Antyajas, *Panchnamas*, and so on. In Gandhi's metaphysical construction, Brahmin to the Antyajas represent a descending credit of their past karma. Despite the numerous instances, where Gandhi utters a guarded statement that in the original pristine version of varnashrama, there was no question of superiority and inferiority, Gandhi was never tired of not only comparing but equating the Brahmin's privilege of inhabiting the sacred (Sanskrit literature and learning) with the *Bangi's* compulsion of shouldering the profane (from doing

[79] Gandhi (1972: Vol. 54, 130).

[80] Gandhi (1972: 130); Regarding Gandhi's ambiguous usage of words and concepts, see Rathore (2017: 183–4).

menial jobs, scavenging, and cleaning the toilets). It was propagated by Gandhi in numerous instances, in writing and speeches, that there is no concept of superiority and inferiority in his scheme of Varnavyavastha. Nevertheless, Gandhi himself betrayed his metaphysics while delineating his views in 'Caste system' published in *Young India*, in 1920.

> I am inclined to think that the law of heredity is an eternal law and any attempt to alter that law must lead us, as it has before led, to utter confusion. I can see very great use in considering a Brahmin to be always a Brahmin throughout his life. If he does not behave himself like a Brahmin, he will naturally cease to command the respect that is due to the real Brahmin. It is easy to imagine the innumerable difficulties if one were to set up a court of punishments and rewards, degradation and promotion. *If Hindus believe, as they must know that nature will, without any possibility of mistake, adjust the balance by degrading a Brahmin, if he misbehaves himself, by reincarnating him in a lower division and translating one who lives the life of a Brahmin in his present incarnation to Brahminhood in the next*[81]

To further substantiate this view, Gandhi's metaphysics essentially accepted and privileged the existing unequal configuration of power and wealth as something preordained and apportioned according to the accumulative credit of one's deeds (*karma*) in one's previous births (*transmigration*). Gandhi, by his own admission, fashions his understanding from the Gita. The idea of Karma as without inequality is an oxymoron, as Karma connotes a metaphysical hierarchy of good deeds then distributed through descending embodiments of Brahmin, Kshatriya, Vaisya, and Sudra respectively. There is a massive and continuous exercise of shifting of categories, obfuscations, discursively for the most part, while not giving too much credence to the existing material realities in Gandhian thought and action regarding the caste question.

The Future of 'Harijan' in Gandhian Social Blue Print

In the Gandhian scheme of things, one wonders, what would be the place of 'Harijans'? If untouchability was abolished, then what would be their identity? Gandhi answers: 'The religious status

---

[81] Gandhi (1972: Vol. 19, 84–5). Emphasis added.

Foregrounding Social Justice in Indian Historiography 275

would be the same as that of the caste Hindus. They will therefore be classed as Shudras instead of Atishudras.'[82]

In the above historical accounts, we were told that Gandhi had a different 'approach' from that of Ambedkar. The conflicts between Ambedkar and Gandhi were presented as a result of this different approach. But what they fail to elaborate is what the Gandhian 'approach' means to untouchables and what kind of emancipatory future it entails. The Gandhian resolution of the untouchable question envisages for them a status of 'Caste Hindu' and more precisely, a 'Sudra' identity. Then to understand what it means, we have to seek what is in store for the Sudra in the Gandhian imagination. The identity of Sudra, the servile class in the Chaturvarna order, is championed as the emancipatory fate, for the millions of untouchables, while also under the condition that they should not leave their hereditary occupation, even if they were educated. How should a Sudra be? Romanticizing poverty and pauperism for the Sudra and Sudra alone, Gandhi praises that

> the Shudra, who performs body-labour in a spirit of service and duty, who has nothing to call his own and who has no desire for ownership, is worthy of the world's homage; he is the lord of all because he is the greatest servant. The dutiful Shudra will, of course, repudiate any such claim, but the gods will shower their choicest blessings on him.[83]

When questioned about the appropriateness of calling a Sudra a Brahmin, if he got 'all the qualities of a Brahmin', Gandhi answers, 'He may not be called a Brahmin in this birth. And it is a good thing for him not to arrogate a varna to which he is not born. It is a sign of true humility.'[84]

The existing dominant historiographical consensus wants us to believe Gandhi's motive to oppose the representation for Depressed Classes 'for fear of permanently splitting the Hindu society'.[85] The possible connection between Gandhi's staunch belief in his metaphysics of the varna-based social order and his opposition to representation of Depressed Classes through separate electorates were never brought up.

---

[82] Gandhi (1972: Vol. 26, 64).
[83] Gandhi (1972: Vol. 59 66–7).
[84] Gandhi (1972: Vol. 35, 518–25).
[85] Bandyopadhyay (2006:355).

Even if the above connection was considered allegedly tenuous, the direct Gandhian sources, at least, should be taken seriously. But even they were brushed aside. One day after the commencement of his fast, Gandhi revealed his reason to Sardar Patel, as recorded by his personal secretary Mahadev Desai:

> The possible consequences of separate electorates fill me with horror. Separate electorates for all other communities will still leave room for me to deal with them, but I have no other means to deal with untouchables.... It will create division among Hindus so much so that it will lead to blood-shed. Untouchable hooligans will make common cause with the Muslim hooligans and kill caste Hindus.[86]

Gandhi's social location as an upper caste, his glorification of Brahmanism, and his firm belief in the varna social order are historical facts that reflects his full being. By brushing it under the carpet, historians and academicians are not doing him any favour. So, accordingly, the above account sought to bring forth the context, historical and ideological, in which Gandhi took his decisions about the separate electorates for Depressed Classes. In this scenario, we need to cross-examine why there is a paucity of analyses that links Gandhi and his view on varna-based social order, which is so central to his sociopolitical practices.

What's at Stake?

In our analysis of textbooks by Sumit Sarkar, Bipan Chandra, and Sekhar Bandyopadhyay, we witness that their histories were all framed under the dominance of the nationalist paradigm, though opposed to their own promise, safely wrapped in the Gandhian spell in varying degrees. All of them being scholars of high repute, quite justifiably considering their length and breadth of their work, one wonders how come they have all missed attributing a crucial place to the Poona Pact, an event that was so consequential and controversial in the history of twentieth-century colonial India. How can we account for this collective failure? The answer may lie in the caste factor. As late as 2017, a history of modern India

---

[86] Gandhi as quoted in Mani (2005: 359).

contends: 'Generally, there is widespread ignorance and denial of caste-based oppression and violence in academic disciplines'.[87] All three of these works, though different in their ideological orientation, have one methodological feature in common. All three texts declare that primarily, they are an effort to collate all the new research findings that happened in the field. This reveals the fact that caste as a factor was not taken seriously enough, not only in these texts in hand, but also in the larger field of academic historical research. But, even if one considers these textbooks as mere collations of existing and new findings, does it offer an excuse for the authors to absolve themselves from this negligence? Is it ethically defensible for a historian to record the dominance as it is and leave it at that? The answer will be negative.

The Poona Pact is seen, by the Dalit-Ambedkarites, in present times, as a ploy of the hegemonic *upper-caste* nationalist complex, spearheaded by Gandhi, to co-opt the Dalits from getting access to political representation in their own terms. There is a renewed understanding of what happened then, in terms of the perversity of the power dynamic involved in the garb of religion and morals, exposing the operation of naked upper-caste power. But the surprising aspect is that this perspective is not entirely novel. Even during the Poona Pact and after it, in quite strong terms, Ambedkar exposed the bankruptcy of the Poona Pact from a pragmatic and normative perspective as a contentious critic and dutiful historian.[88] Ambedkar had left enough testimony and evidence to historians that it was not because of happy agreement or harmonious reconciliation, but due to arrogant upper-caste power, that he had to concede. Instead of interrogating the unfair configuration of *upper-caste* power, to recover and reconstruct the narrative from the vantage point of the caste-oppressed, the dominant histories failed, in the name of *objective* history or the excuse of *general* history, by simply reproducing the dominance and subalternity as historical realities. I conclude my chapter by pronouncing that the historical injustice need not and should not be re-enacted in the historiographical too by keeping the seductiveness of hegemonic discourse of the oppressive actors intact. If that was kept intact, then it will

[87] Jungum (2017: 4).
[88] Ambedkar (2016).

serve for a continuing ideological foundation for the oppression of the present.[89]

References

Aloysius, G. 1997. *Nationalism without a Nation in India*. New Delhi: Oxford University Press.

Ambedkar, B.R. 1938. 'Is Gandhi a Mahatma?' *Chittra* J, Dipavali Special Number (1938). Available at http://velivada.com/2017/04/15/is-gandhi-a-mahatma-what-dr-ambedkar-said/, accessed 2 May 2018.

———. 2016. *Dr. Babasaheb Ambedkar Writings and Speeches*. Vol. 9. Bombay: Government of Maharashtra.

Anderson, Perry. 2012. *Indian Ideology*. New Delhi: Three Essay Collective.

Bagade, Umesh. 2015. *Ambedkar's Historical Method*. New Delhi: Critical Quest.

Bandyopadhyay, Sekhar. 2004. *Caste, Culture and Hegemony: Social Dominance in Colonial Bengal. Book*. New Delhi: SAGE Publications.

———. 2006. *From Plassey to Partition, A History of Modern India*. Delhi: Orient Longman.

Chandra, Bipan, Mridula Mukherjee, Aditya Mukherjee, K.N. Panikkar, and Sucheta Mahajan. 1989. *India's Struggle for Independence 1857–1947*. New Delhi: Penguin Books.

Chatterjee, Partha. 1993. *The Nation and Its Fragments, Colonial and Postcolonial Histories*. New Jersey: Princeton University Press.

Chatterjee, Partha, Sudipta Kaviraj, and Nivedita Menon. 2015. *The Indian Ideology: Three Responses to Perry Anderson*. Ranikhet: Permanent Black.

Gandhi, M.K. 1972. *Collected Volumes of Mahatma Gandhi (CWMG)*. Ahmedabad: Navajivan Press.

Guha, Ramchandra. 2007. *India After Gandhi: The History of World's Largest Democracy*. New Delhi: Harper Collins.

Guru, Gopal. 2017. 'Ethics in Ambedkar's Critique of Gandhi.' *Economic and Political Weekly*, 52 (15): 95–100.

Hindu. 2017. *The First Hundred, Editorials for The Hindu, 1878–1978*. Chennai: Kasturi and Sons Lmt.

Jungum, Chinnaiah. 2015. 'Politics of Identity and the Project of Writing History in Postcolonial India, A Dalit Critique.' *Economic and Political Weekly*, 50 (40): 63–70.

---

[89] Recognizing that this 'seductiveness' itself is very much conditioned, if not generated, by one's social location and its attendant ramifications is a crucial first step in avoiding such a reproduction.

———. 2017. *Dalits and The Making of Modern India*. New York: Oxford University Press.

Keer, Dhananjay. 2016. *Dr. Babasaheb Ambedkar, Life and Mission*. Mumbai: Popular Prakashan.

Kiran, M. 2016. *Gandhi's Varnavyavastha*. New Delhi: Critical Quest.

Kolge, Nishikant. 2018. *Gandhi against Caste*. Oxford University Press.

Kumar, Ravinder. 1987. 'Gandhi, Ambedkar and the Poona Pact, 1932', in Jim Masselos (ed.), *Struggling and Ruling: The Indian National Congress 1885–1985*. New Delhi: Sterling Publications.

Mani, Braj Ranjan. 2005. *Debrahmanising History: Dominance and Resistance in Indian Society*. New Delhi: Manohar Publishers.

Moon, Vasant. 2002. *Dr. Babasaheb Ambedkar*. New Delhi: National Book Trust.

Namboodiripad, E.M.S. 1986. *A History of Indian Freedom Struggle*. Trivandrum: Social Scientist Press.

Omvedt, Gail. 2008. *Ambedkar, Toward an Enlightened India*. Gurgaon: Penguin Books.

———. 2013. *Dalits and the Democratic Revolution, Dr. Ambedkar and the Dalit Movement in Colonial India*. New Delhi: SAGE Publications.

Ram, Kanshi. 1982. *Chamcha Age, Era of the Stooges*. New Delhi: Kanshi Ram.

Rathore, Aakash Singh. 2017. *Indian Political Theory, Laying the Groundwork for Svaraj*. New York: Routledge.

Sarkar, Sumit. 1989. *Modern India: 1885–1947*. New York: Palgrave Macmillan.

———. 1997. *Writing Social History*. New Delhi: Oxford University Press.

———. 2002. 'The Decline of Subaltern in Subaltern Studies', in David Ludden (ed.), *Reading Subaltern Studies: Critical History, Contested Meaning, and the Globalisation of South Asia*. New Delhi: Orient Blackswan.

Tendulkar, D.G. 1992. *Mahatma, Life of Mohantdas Karamchand Gandhi, Volume Three*. New Delhi: Government of India.

Vundru, Raja Sekhar. 2018. *Ambedkar, Gandhi and Patel, The Making of India's Electoral System*. New Delhi: Bloomsbury.

Zelliot, Eleanor. 2015. *From Untouchables to Dalits, Essays on the Ambedkar Movement*. Delhi: Manohar Publishers.

12

Ambedkar and the Metaphysics of Social Justice

AJAY VERMA

If we wished to explore B.R. Ambedkar's views on the relationship between philosophy, religion, and politics, we would first want to be clear about what these terms might signify for him. We can get an idea from a passage of his on the philosophy of religion from his article, 'Philosophy of Hinduism':

> What is the philosophy of Hinduism? This is a question which arises in its logical sequence. But apart from its logical sequence its importance is such that it can never be omitted from consideration. Without it no one can understand the aims and ideals of Hinduism. It is obvious that such a study must be preceded by a certain amount of what may be called clearing of the ground and defining of the terms involved. At the outset it may be asked what does this proposed title comprehend? Is this title of the Philosophy of Hinduism of the same nature as that of the Philosophy of Religion? I wish I could commit myself one way or the other on this point. Indeed I cannot. I have read a good deal on the subject, but I confess I have not got a clear idea of what is meant by Philosophy of Religion. This is probably due to two facts. In the first place while religion is something definite, there is nothing definite as to what is to be included in the term philosophy. In the second place *Philosophy and Religion have been adversaries* if not actual antagonists as may be seen from the story of the philosopher and the theologian. According to the story, the two were engaged in disputation and the theologian accused the philosopher that he was 'like a blind man in a dark room, looking for a

Ambedkar and the Metaphysics of Social Justice   281

black cat which was not there'. In reply the philosopher charged the theologian saying that 'he was like a blind man in the dark room, looking for a black cat which was not there but he declared to have found there'.[1]

Based on the above ideas on religion and philosophy, I will claim that the caste system receives implicit philosophical, metaphysical support from Indian classical thought systems. These systems attempted to provide grounds for religious thought as it developed under the aegis of Hinduism. Religion cannot survive without making certain metaphysical assertions that support particular belief systems that a particular religion stands on. These metaphysical beliefs are supposed to be immune to any logical scrutiny because religion is considered a matter of faith, which immediately provides religion a shelter against philosophical questioning. But in the West, the philosophy of religion has been a thriving sub-discipline of philosophy where the metaphysical beliefs that a religion adheres to are put to logical scrutiny instead of bypassing them. Can we examine some of the possible arguments in favour of varna hierarchy in just the same way as some beliefs are scrutinized in Western philosophy? This is what the present chapter attempts to do. We devote most attention to Purusa Sukta, which is the heart and soul of the caste system as it came to make its appearance in Hindu society. In the last part of the chapter, an attempt is also made to demonstrate that an inevitable outcome of the varna system is the dehumanization of whole sections of society. This, clearly, bears serious implications for the idea of social justice.

Is the Vedic View of Self Substantialist?

Beliefs and assumptions regarding cosmogony or the beginning of the universe are some of the most common features of any religion. Based on such assumptions, belief systems regarding creation and sustenance, appearance and reality, and so on are forged further. Since these beliefs pertain to the very beginning of everything whatsoever, such beliefs conjure up a historical narrative that projects well into our present and future. Further proceeding from there, religious systems conjecture and project a moral order in

---

[1] Ambedkar (2019: 3).

the universe or alternatively provide us clues to formulate moral commands for oneself based on these very same creation myths. If we examine some of these religious moral systems closely, we find that there are certain religions that have definite metaphysical views regarding the ultimate substance of the world and the self. These views bear influence upon the moral role of the self in the world with an imagined moral order inherent in it. Thus, the moral commands advocated in these religions are justified on the basis of certain views regarding the nature of the world and concomitant view of the self. These metaphysical views are often founded upon certain metaphysical contemplations or conjectures as found in their respective holy books or both.

Idealism does not find much favour among orthodox schools of Indian philosophy. There are any numbers of conjectures regarding the ultimate substance of the universe in Indian philosophical and religious texts. But these surmises regarding the ultimate stuff of the universe also entail notions regarding the nature of other things that are arisen from the very same stuff or substance, including the self. Such resultant notions have serious implications for the social and political structures in a given society. Because once we have definite views about the substance that goes into making of a thing, we would tend to have strict definitions of what those things are. We could call such notions as substantialist notion of self and the world. But as opposed to this, Buddhism presents an example of the other category of religions that deny any definite notions that could be attached to the nature of the world or the nature of the self and probably the only one to do so in such unequivocal terms. As described earlier, moral notions are derivatives of their metaphysical postulates pertaining to the nature of the world and the self. For Buddhism though, there can be no way of deriving these ethical commands analytically on the basis of particular notions regarding the nature of world and self, both of which are impermanent and thus vacuous of any abiding substance. With no definite notion of nature of the world and the self, no definite moral commands could be metaphysically deduced therefore within Buddhism. Following such a philosophical position, the only possible way to make sense of the world and the self would be to understand them as a mere contingent coming together of various factors that go on to constitute different objects and selves in the world. That being the case, any moral assumptions can at best be contingent and provisional in nature depending upon the context.

Hinting obliquely towards the importance of metaphysical presupposition regarding substance and the self that together form the notion of permanent substantial selves, Dipankar Gupta writes, 'Though there is no way by which those in a caste society can actually distinguish unfailing natural markers of difference, yet they justify caste stratification on the ground that different castes are built of different natural substances'.[2] The caste system in this sense is one of many examples where, historically, social practices that created extreme inequality were attributed not to society but to the very nature of the world or divinity.

Buddhism, as both religion and a philosophy, focuses on human predicament in terms of one's experiential/existential reality and drives the motive of their enquiry based upon their empirical observation that there is suffering in the world. This is for them the first and foremost truth about the world. It might be said that if suffering is a part of the nature of the world then, that is the end of the matter. The substantialist view would interpret this to mean that suffering is a part of the nature of the world and the self. Following this, pain would become an inevitable part of our existence. Furthermore, if we have any metaphysical notions regarding the nature of the self or the world and if different selves were to have any substantial or essential nature (*svabhava*), then a way of putting them into a hierarchy could easily be devised on that basis. In that case, no remedy or alleviation of suffering would ever be possible. But since the theory of *nisvabhavata* (no self-nature) as propounded in the *shunyavadi* tradition of Buddhism states that there is no essential nature that could be ascribed to the self or the world, suffering in the world should be viewed as a contingent factor about the world and not a necessary part of it. If suffering is only a contingent feature of the world, there could always be a promise of getting rid of it through human effort and diligence. Needless to say that notions of human predicament, suffering, and alleviation of it and notions of affirmative action would differ widely depending upon whether we choose to hold the substantialist or non-substantialist view of the self.

One of the most robust examples of substantial view of the self and the world is found in Purusa Sukta of the Rig Veda. According

---

[2] Gupta (2000: 19).

to Purusha Sukta, the world of human selves has its origin in the metaphysical principle named Purusha, which is considered to be some primeval absolute self defined in the Rig Veda, defined as:

Om sahasra shirsha purushaha
sahasrakshas sahasrapat
sa bhumim vishvato vritva
atyatishthad dhashangulam

Translation: *The Purusha (the Supreme Being) has a thousand heads, a thousand eyes, and a thousand feet. He has enveloped this world from all sides and has (even) transcended it by ten angulas or inches.*[3]

Text Two

purusha evedagam sarvam
yadbhutam yaccha bhavyam
utamritatva syeshanaha
yadanne natirohati

Translation: *All this is verily the Purusha. All that which existed in the past or will come into being in the future (is also the Purusha). Also, he is the Lord of immortality. That which grows profusely by food (is also the Purusha).*[4]

Everything on this account is therefore supposed to have come into existence emanating substantially from the Purusha, including the plant and animal kingdom and also knowledge and gods. But then comes the most infamous part of the sukta:

Text Thirteen

brahmanosya mukhamasit
bahu rajanyah kritaha
uru tadasya yadvaishyaha
padhyagam shudro ajayata

---

[3] 'Purusha Sukta'. n.d. The Full Wiki. Available at http://maps. thefullwiki.org/Purusha_sukta, accessed 20 June 2019.
[4] 'Purusha Sukta'. n.d. The Full Wiki. Available at http://maps. thefullwiki.org/Purusha_sukta, accessed 20 June 2019.

Translation: From His face (or the mouth) came the brahmanas. From His two arms came the rajanya (the kshatriyas). From His two thighs came the vaishyas. From His two feet came the shudras.[5]

As seen from earlier, different varnas are supposed to be coeval and co-extensive with four different parts of the body of the Purusa. That means, in terms of their substance, there is continuity from origin of humanity into the present moment of our being in terms of what substance is most definitive of us. Surprisingly, the varna distinction is invoked to justify the morality of an action in several scriptures and even some philosophical texts of classical Indian thought systems. Most famous of these texts is the Bhagvad Gita, which has been commented upon by most of the *acharya*s of the *Vedanta* tradition, including Shankara and Ramanuja. But these philosophical traditions have elaborate accounts of theories of knowledge of their own. Shankara is so tenacious about logical rules of debate and what should count as evidence in an argument that he goes on to say that even if hundreds of holy scriptures declare that fire is cold, one should not believe it since it contradicts the direct evidence from experience. Add this also to the fact that Shankara being a part of the *Uttara Mimamsa* school of thought adheres to the verbal authority of the Vedas. Therefore, from the above two statements, it follows that conjectures offered in the Vedas on such important matters as cosmogony should adhere to the rule of logic and empirical evidence.

Julius Lipner, citing a pandit, states the following:

> It is on the basis of the cognitive authority of the Vedas (*vedaprama atvāt*) that other [Hindu] scriptures have such authority'. And another pandit declared: 'Having first accepted the things of scripture as true, one should then establish them by reasoning.... Reasoning conforms to scripture, not scripture to reasoning. Scripture is self-validating (*svata pramāṇaka*) whereas reasoning exists to understand scripture'. So the old approach had its champions while the new was gaining ground.[6]

Steven T. Katz states the following with respect to the authority of the Vedas in Indian philosophy:

[5] Stephen Knapp. n.d. 'The Purusha Sukta'. Available at https://www.stephen-knapp.com/purusha_sukta.htm, accessed 20 June 2019.

[6] Lipner (1994: 57).

Samkara emphasizes that the scope of scriptures is indeed restricted, its jurisdiction being valid only within the epistemological framework of the phenomenal world.... scripture as a means of knowledge must be compatible with the other means of knowledge. More specifically, it cannot produce statements that contradict statements derived from perception and inference. The result is that, speaking hypothetically, in any case in which scripture contradicts perception and inference, its statements must be regarded as invalid.[7]

Citing a passage from Shankara regarding the authority of the scriptures, he further writes:

The scripture seeks not to alter things, but to supply information about things unknown, as they are.... Things in the world are known to possess certain fixed characteristics such as grossness or fineness. By citing them as examples the scriptures seek to tell us about some other thing which does not contradict them. They would not cite an example from life if they wanted to convey an idea of something contradictory to it. Even if they did, it would be to no purpose, for the example would be different from the thing to be explained. You cannot prove that fire is cold, or that the sun does not give heat, even by citing a hundred examples, for the fact would already be known to be otherwise through another means of knowledge. And one means of knowledge does not contradict another, for it only tells us about those things that cannot be known by any other means.[8]

Taking this view regarding the conflict between direct experience and scriptural authority as the benchmark, one could attempt to examine possible arguments given in the Purusha Sukta for the origin of the four varnas.

Can Vedic Authority Be Immune to Reasoning?

Rig Veda being the oldest of world philosophical texts, it would not be wrong to say that such argument or rather conjecture on the nature of the self as emanating from the ultimate substantial self appears for the first time in a philosophical text but it is not the only time. We find similar pieces of reasoning making

[7] Katz (2000: 82–3).
[8] Katz (2000: 82–3).

their appearance in some of Plato's texts as well where he compares the four limbs of society with four different prototypes. But interestingly, the metaphysical idea of the primeval Purusha is not according to the Purusha Sukta an *eidos* or the idea of a perfect human being that all mortals on earth could aspire for. Rather, this metaphysical principle, namely, Purusha, is imagined to have real parts that could function as prototypes for the whole body of a particular human being who is completely determined in terms of his or her vocation depending upon which body part of Purusha s/he is supposed to have arisen from. As pointed out earlier, distinction and hierarchy is followed by all the orthodox systems of classical Indian philosophy. All these schools of philosophy mostly follow a rigorous system of reasoning, argumentation, and justification of our knowledge-claims. If we follow the different principles of justification of knowledge-claims in the *Pramana* system, followed by different schools of Indian philosophy, then *Upamana* or analogy would probably be the closest to any justification of system supposedly being offered in the Purusha Sukta. But a closer scrutiny of Upamana as a pramana would make it clear that the idea and description of Purusha is not being used in Purusha Sukta in accordance with Upamana pramana to justify the system. In other words, analogy as a system of justification could never be good enough to derive the hierarchy on the basis of Purusha Sukta.

The real object of comparison in Purusha is not the idea of Purusha in toto but the qualities, functions, or vocations associated with different body parts of Purusha. The head, which is associated with knowledge and learning, is supposed to be a prototype for the entire personhood of Brahmins. The chest and upper limbs, associated with the idea of valour, are supposed prototypes for Kshatriyas and so on. But strangely enough, it is not only the head of the Brahmin that is endowed with some special ability, but the entire body, including chest, abdomen, and lower limbs, are supposed embodiments of knowledge. Following this, the entire body stands on a metaphysical platform that is elevated high above all other. Furthermore, analogies work on the criteria of knowing the characteristics of a particular object named. Seeing these characteristics or qualities being empirically instantiated in some object that we come across, we come to know what an object is that we otherwise encounter for the first time. But in Purusha Sukta, the object of cognition is not somebody's Brahminhood in virtue of appearance of certain characteristics. Rather, a Brahmin, who is what s/he is by virtue of birth, is considered to be on a higher pedestal in virtue of a supposed affiliation to the prototype of Purusa's head. Thus, the point that emerges here is that justification of the varna system on the basis of Purusha Sukta is anything but philosophically justifiable on the basis of the pramana system recognized in the orthodox classical thought systems of India, especially if it is binding upon the Vedas not to be in violation of the empirical evidence.

This condition is not adhered to though by the early Mimamsa school *Prabhakara*s. According to them, the Vedas are the works that have an intrinsic validity not amenable to further reasoning with regard to scriptural authority of the Vedas. The *Bhatta*s leave the scope for interpretation and insinuation while interpreting the Vedic texts so far as any given interpretation is in consonance with the other statements in the same texts. But surprisingly, this hierarchy is held to be real and is taken seriously even by different orthodox schools of thought, including *Nyaya*, who are thoroughgoing realists, and Advaita Vedanta, who are generally considered more as idealists. The main focus of enquiry of the Nyāya school is, among others, to lay down the rules of logic and reasoning and also spelling out good reasoning from bad. For them, *brahminatva* is a *jati* or universal and is subject to perception, which means that one could see that somebody is a Brahmin since the universal belonging to Brahminhood is inherent in the person concerned, just like the chairness of the chair. This hierarchy of which has its own serious social implications, is held and taken seriously by most of the orthodox schools of Indian philosophy without much regard for existential human predicament that becomes inevitable for a person in virtue of such category or identity affiliations. Furthermore, if the distinctions based on such prototypes are to be taken seriously, like many important thinkers such as Gandhi and Radhakrishnan among others do, then no real emergence from one's social predicament is possible except in virtue of charity, which only the higher class has a liberty to show towards the supposed lower ones.

If we look at the hierarchy from the point of view of analytic and synthetic distinction, then these distinctions could be viewed as arising from the meaning ascribed to the terms 'Brahmin' and 'Sudras'. It is not that if one is deemed to be untouchable for some empirical reason (or say, for example, on account of some infectious disease and is quarantined temporarily), that one becomes a Sudra, in which case it would be an example of contingent or synthetic proposition. Rather, by Purusa Sukta's account, one is untouchable because one belongs to the prototype of. Untouchability on account of some contingent reasons, if there were any, could be removable, but untouchability on account of one's very being as an instantiation of some fantastic prototype could not be so. In other words, in the hierarchy of the vocation advocated in Purusa Sukta and accepted by orthodox systems of Indian philosophy, one is not held at a lower pedestal because of something culpable either avowed or done by the person. Rather, one is forced to choose a particular vocation, which may or may not interest one, by virtue of one's metaphysical affiliation to a certain identity that is not reflexively adhered to by the person. In a synthetic proposition, identity is ascribed on the basis of qualities; in analytic propositions, qualities are ascribed to persons by virtue of their identity (objectively forced upon them). Thus, any notions of identity that are formed on the basis of the meaning imbued or insinuated and further reified in a term are always inevitably constitutive of objective identities that are imposed upon a person from outside and often without subjective acceptance of the same.

Buddhist Critique of Essentialism

Buddhist systems of thought, whether in their *Mahayana* or *Hinayana* garb, are always critical of formulation of any philosophical claims that do not have their roots in human existential experience. Human perceptions are of a particular nature on this account, not because the world is essentially of a particular nature. Rather, human perceptions have an appearance of a particular kind because of the nature of human sensibility. If the human perceptions had their basis in the nature of the world and if the world had an essential nature and a pre-structured schema of relationships of its own (*nama, jati adi yojana*), then there would have been no way to unlock further vistas leading from our present human condition to a prospective better one. But if human experiences have a particular nature because of certain modes of human sensibility, then we can change our predicaments by modifying our sensibilities in accordance with desirability or undesirability of particular human experiences. In other words, if there is pain in the world not because of the nature of the world but because of the mode of human sensibility and understanding, then there is certainly a way out of it. Alternatively, the same applies to the nature of the self as well. If we ascribe a certain essential nature to the self or objectively define it in some way, then there would be no hope for redemption. To avoid such an impasse, Buddhists not only do not ascribe any definite nature to the self but deny acceptance of any metaphysical platform for any essentialist notions of the self to be formed at all through their no-soul theory.

Having pondered upon the illegibility of Purusa Sukta as the principle of derivation for the varna system, let us look at what view of selfhood or person it presents before us. As pointed out earlier, different parts of the body of Purusa are supposed to be the prototype of different varnas as generally understood. These parts are supposed to be personified in the entire person. But an implication of such quadrifurcation of different faculties and arranging them in a hierarchy of social positions could be even more appalling. As Ambedkar writes:

> In the scheme of Manu the Brahmin is placed at the first in rank. Below him is the Kshatriya. Below Kshatriya is the Vaishya. Below Vaishya is the Shudra and Below Shudra is the Ati-Shudra (the Untouchables). This system of rank and gradation is, simply another way of enunciating the principle of inequality so that it may be truly said that Hinduism does not recognize equality. This inequality in status is not merely the inequality that one sees in the warrant of precedence prescribed for a ceremonial gathering at a King's Court. It is a permanent social relationship among the classes to be observed— to be enforced—at all times in all places and for all purposes.[9]

If Brahmins represent the mind of the society, it would mean by default that the faculty of thinking and making judgements lies therefore *by nature* with that varna. It would further follow from it that the remaining three varnas should act in accordance with the judgement of Brahmins. This is an appalling proposal as it takes the liberty of ideas away from the other three varnas. Actually, this results in dehumanization of the other varnas, specially the last rung in the ladder, namely, the Sudras.

---

[9] Moon (1987:102–7).

Generally, the way we value the lives of different organisms depends upon our view of their level of intelligence. Our evaluation of intelligence of the other is probably an important marker of what treatment we may want to offer to a particular human being or species for that matter. We have no remorse about felling trees or harvesting of crops because we do not believe they have any intelligence level or sensibility quotient at all. From this observation, we could even probably conclude that our evaluation of the level of intelligence of a certain organism also consciously or subconsciously shapes our perception of their sensitivity index. We do not believe that plants are capable of having feelings like pain or pleasure. We believe animals are more sensitive to feelings; therefore, some of us are a little more hesitant in killing them for any purpose. Some of us are willing to grant them certain rights in virtue of their capability of feeling sensations, if not emotions. What emerges therefore from this observation is that our view of the other has an inevitable influence upon our recognition of worth and respect of the other. Once we understand this, it should not be difficult to understand subsequently for us that our lack of recognition of intelligence of the other would have inevitable bearing upon how we view the worth and respectability of that person. One could argue therefore that considering Brahminhood to be the prototype of the head of humanity or the site of social intelligence leads to dehumanization of the rest of society, most importantly among them, the Sudras. Needless to say, such mythological beliefs considered literally for our understanding of society would put one section of society in the position of moral and legal regulator and legislator of the life and actions of the entire society, thus violating some of the most fundamental principles of democracy.

This position is, in a certain sense, also reminiscent of Cartesian dualism where the mind is visualized as a pilot in a ship where the ship is representative of the material body. The pilot is in a position of control and command over the material ship and, therefore, in a superior position in comparison. Similarly, any substantial basis of social division would inevitably result in substance quadrilism (just like Cartesian dualism) of sorts. It may be pointed out here that the varnas other than the Sudras may not have the same kind of grievances against the varna system because Kshatriyas, the warrior class, still wield control over the political executive powers even if it is under the direction of the Brahmins. Similarly, the

292 Ajay Verma

Vaishyas or the merchant class would have the direct possession and control over the resources, and thus, their position is no less powerful. It is mainly the last in the rung that stands divested of any political power or control over resources, namely, Sudras. Their position is reduced to that of an accessory, almost an inanimate lifeless object that has some instrumental value but no intrinsic worth of their own.

Ambedkar's Critique of Metaphysics of Self

One could connect the earlier discussion at this point to some of the fundamental ideas Ambedkar propounded on religion. I will enumerate a few from them that are more useful for our present discussion:

1. Religion is necessary for a free society.
2. Humans and morality must be the centre of religion. If not, religion is a cruel superstition.
3. The function of religion is to reconstruct the world and to make it happy and not to explain its origin or its end.
4. Nothing is infallible. Nothing is binding forever.
5. Nothing is final.
6. Nothing is permanent or *sanatan*. Everything is subject to change.[10]

One could see clearly here that there were reasons why Ambedkar propounded and adhered to these ideas on religion though he never explicates them in any overt way in his various essays and books. We can also see that all these demands that Ambedkar maintains a religion should fulfil to have any socially engaging and politically redemptive role can only be fulfilled by Buddhism. Thus, Ambedkar proposes to look afresh at the philosophy of religion in terms of an enquiry into questions regarding religion and ethics. He proposes to view religion as a mode of engagement with one's intimate self, which, in his view, should be self-constituted. From such notion of self alone could emerge a socially engaged self that is dominantly Other-oriented and therefore constituted, motivated, and driven by social contingencies and a political self that asserts itself

[10] Ambedkar (2019: 442).

with its moral agency and engages in one's emancipatory goals. This requirement, namely, one's intimate self, which is freely self-constituted, can only be fulfilled if we grant that self does not have any essential nature except for its nothingness, which allows it to engage itself in a continual process of defining and redefining itself.

Ambedkar writes in his TBHD:

> It is on the impermanence of the nature of all things that the possibility of all other things depends. If things were not subject to continual change, but were permanent and unchangeable, the evolution of all of life from one kind to the other, and the development of living things, would come to a dead stop. If human beings [had not] died or changed, but had continued always in the same state, what would the result have been? The progress of the human race would have come to a dead halt.[11]

Comparing the revolution in earlier society and the modern one Ambedkar states, 'At one end of the Revolution was the antique society with its Religious ideal in which the end was Society. At the other end of the Revolution is the modern Society with its Religious ideal in which the end is the individual.'[12] But is there any scope within the conception of the self as a free individual so far as we have substantialist models of the self, specially the kind we find in Purusa Sukta? An individual in the true sense of the term would be the one who is independent to define his or her identity. Only a philosophy allowing any scope for identities with subjective approval would be conducive to the conception of the self that could be truly free in that sense. We find such models only to a certain extent available within Buddhism where self is viewed as conditionally arisen and therefore subject to change.

References

Ambedkar, B.R. 2019. *Dr. Babasaheb Ambedkar: Writings and Speeches*, Hari Narake (ed.). Vol. 3. New Delhi: Dr Ambedkar Foundation.

Gupta, Dipankar. 2000. *Interrogating Caste: Understanding Hierarchy and Difference in Indian Society*. New Delhi: Penguin Books India.

[11] Rathore and Verma (2011: 130).
[12] Ambedkar (2019: 22).

Katz, Steven T. 2000. *Mysticism and Sacred Scriptures*. New York: Oxford University Press.

Lipner, Julius. 1994. *Hindus: Their Religious Beliefs and Practices*. London: Routledge.

Moon, Vasant (ed.). 1987. *Dr. Babasaheb Ambedkar, Writings and Speeches*. Vol. 3. Bombay: Government of Maharashtra.

Rathore, Aakash Singh, and Ajay Verma (eds). 2011. *B.R. Ambedkar's The Buddha and His Dhamma: A Critical Edition*. New Delhi: Oxford University Press.

Index

Abdullah, Omar 240
acharyas 285
acquisitory method 173–4, 192–3
activism in foreign countries 246
activists 36; in Nepal Tharu and
    Magar 105
Ad Dharm xxxiv, 118–19, 121,
    125–9, 134, 138, 140–1; and
    Ambedkar 138; and Christianity
    128; Juergensmeyer on 129;
    movement of xxxiv, 119,
    121, 128
Adi Granth 125
Adityanath, Yogi 163
adivasis 42, 84–5
Advaita Vedanta 288
African-American community
    234–6, 245
Agnivesh, Swami 164
Ahmadiyya movement 123
Ain, Muluki 94
Akhlaq, Mohammad, killing of 212
All India Backward and Minorities
    Central Employees Federation
    (BAMCEF) 242

All India Scheduled Caste
    Federation (AISCF) 224–5,
    228, 230–2, 238, 243
Alliance of Hindu organizations 74
Aloysius, G. 204
alternative faith 138, *see also*
    Ad Dharm; Buddhism
Ambedkar Bhimrao Ramji xxiii,
    xxxi, 1–2, 6, 20, 31, 41, 49,
    76, 116, 197–200, 202, 210,
    212–13, 216, 218–19, 222, 252,
    258, 261–2, 269; battles in
    life of 153; Constitution and
    148; conversion to Buddhism
    199; and Dalit empowerment
    263; and foreign policy 224; as
    'fountainhead of social justice'
    54; and Gandhi, conflict
    between 253–4, 265–6, 275;
    Granger on 236; Haragopal on
    200; installation of statues of
    213; as internationalist 224–7;
    interview in New York Times
    231; as Law Minister 141, 203–
    4, 228; in London for DSc 227;

political imagination of 223;
resigns from Nehru's cabinet
230; Rodrigues on democracy
and 155; and Russia 240; and
scholarship from Maharaja of
Baroda 226; and UN 231–7, 242;
in US 226; vision of 197; as
visionary and realist 26
Ambedkar International
Associations 244
Ambedkar International Missions
244
American Revolutions 151
Annihilation of Caste (AC) 10, 17,
19, 41, 45, 88, 108, 117, 138, 236
anti-caste movements 216, 225,
253, 258, 261
anti-casteists 74
anti-nationals, branding as 165, 213
anti-racists 74
Anti-Untouchability League 77, 79
Antyajas 272–3
Appadurai, Arjun 80
appropriation 212–16
armed forces, selection process
in 171, 175,178
Arya Samaj 83, 123, 125–6
assertions 57, 64, 123, 128, 212–16,
219, 257–8
Ati-Sudras 235
atrocities: caste based 36, 50–3,
56–61, 63–7, 206–8, 233, 246;
colonial 233; and judgment
against victims 60; non-
registration of cases on 60–1,
206–7
Atrocities Act of 1989 36–7, 41
attacks: on Dalits in Andhra
Pradesh 207; in Laxmipet 207;
by Rod community 206–7
attitudes 3–10, 19, 39, 41, 62, 67,
117, 207, 254
authority 59–60, 108, 118, 120,
149–51, 155, 158–9, 161, 164,

166, 285; meaning of 150;
of scriptures 286

Backward and Minorities
Central Employees Federation
(BAMCEF) 242
Bahishkrit Hitkarini Sabha 153
Bahujan Samaj Party 242
Bahuns, in Nepal 100
Bandyopadhyay, Sekhar 228, 259,
262–6, 269, 276; on Gandhi 269;
'Many Voices of a Nation' of
263
beef festivals 83, *see also*
gaurakshas
belief structures 12
Bengaluru Declaration xxiii, xxiii–
xxxi, xxxv, xxxvii, 68, 166, 202,
217–19; Preamble of xxiii; social
security in xxx
Bhagats 118, 126
Bhagavata Purana 84
Bharatiya Janata Party (BJP) 157,
161, 163, 165; minorities and
165; Muslims in 157
Bishwakarma, Mom 96
Bishwakarma, Ruplal 106
Biswakarma, Tilak 96
B.K., Amar 96
black population 233, 235
black slavery 225, 235
Bourdieu, Pierre 5
Brahmin class 30, 103, 107, 122–3,
227, 236–7, 273–5, 287–8, 290–1;
in colonial rural Panjab 120
Brahminism 84, 119, 231, 263, 271,
274, 288, 291
British Government 256, 258
Buddha 11, 17–19, 110, 119
Buddha and His Dhamma,
The (TBHD) 11–13, 17, 20;
Ambedkar in 293
Buddhism 8, 11, 17–18, 20–1, 128,
210, 215–17, 243, 252, 282–3,

292–3; in Nepal 104; Nepal Dalits conversion to 105
Buddhist: alternative 7; identity 216
Buraku Liberation League (BLL) 242–3
bureaucracy 98, 174, 193

capitalism 30, 230–1
caste xxviii, xxxii–xxxvi, 27–30, 32–5, 37–8, 50–3, 56–7, 59–68, 71–5, 80–3, 116–25, 131–3, 175–8, 202–4, 213–17, 236–8, 240–2, 244–7, 252–4, 270–7; conflicts 64, 68; consciousness of 75–6, 80; culturalisation of 80; discrimination 56, 72–4, 76, 82, 105, 178, 210, 215, 241; Gandhi on 271; groups 30, 50, 60–1, 64, 83, 100, 236; as harmful institution 202; Hindu votes 229, 257; hierarchies xxxii, xxxiv, 27–31, 34–5, 45, 60, 75, 119, 125, 141; Hindu leaders 256; Hindus and 117; Hindus of upper xxxiii, 7, 62, 67, 71, 77–8, 217, 236, 260, 264, 275–6; Interrogating 153–4; as *jati* 30–1, 35, 41, 80, 82, 288; materiality of 30–1; mechanisms of 76; occupations 120; ridden Hindu society 149; stratification 283; system 53, 56, 61, 63, 200, 202, 236, 241, 271–2, 274, 281, 283
'caste laws' xxxiii, 66
caste-affected citizens and NGOs 244
caste-based: discrimination in Nepal 109; occupational vocations 203
Caste-Coalition 60–4
casteism xxxiii–xxxiv, 74, 76, 80–1, 83, 86, 119

Casteless Collective, The 258
caste-subaltern struggles 252
Castoriadis, Cornelius 7
Chaing KaiShek 238
Chamars 120–1, 123–5, 127–9, 132, 137, 141; Ad Dharm and 128; as siris 132
Chandra, Bipan 259, 261–3, 266, 276
charity 10, 15, 162, 288; 'mother cow' and 163
Chatterjee, Partha 261, 269
chaturvarna order 6, 275
Chauhan, Digree Prasad 84
China–Japan conflict 239
Christian missionaries 35, 123, 127
Christianity 105, 121, 123, 127, 138–9; in rural Panjab 128
Christians 82, 121, 123, 126–7, 140, 182; conversions by 163; in Nepal 105
Churhas 120–3, 125, 127, 129, 132, 137, 140; Ad Dharm and 128; as siris 132
citizens xxiv, xxix, 52, 54–5, 139, 151–2, 154, 157, 160, 193, 200–1, 241, 244
civil rights 53, 57, 77, 201; movements 225; violation of 57
Civil Rights (PCR) Act, 1976 53
civil services 55, 62, 261, 263; in Nepal 100
civil society organizations 36, 52
class system 50–1, 62, 252
coercion 18, 265
colonialism 93, 239
Common Faith, A 14
Communal Award 256, 262, 265
communal influence 164
Communism 230–1
communities xxiv, 20, 60–1, 63–4, 67, 72–4, 105, 122–30, 153–5, 165, 174, 191–3, 223–4, 256–7;

categories of 181; representation in services 182

compassion 1, 15, 18, 38–40, 44, 215

Congress 117, 227–9, 232, 234, 237, 254–6, 259, 261, 264, 266, 270–1

Constituent Assembly 54, 63, 107–8, 152, 201, 228–9, 232

Constitution xxv, xxvii, xxxi, xxxiv–xxxv, 52, 54–5, 147–51, 153–4, 159, 164–6, 169–70, 200–1, 229, 232, 255

constitutional: morality 157–8, 162, 165–6; values xxiv–xxv, 55–6, 170

constitutionalism 147, 166, 170, 198; task of 152, 166

conversion xxxiv, 2, 17, 19, 35, 105, 119, 122–9, 138, 140; Buddhist 216–17; of lower castes to Sikhism 121; politics of 119; Social Constraints of 19–20; Zelliot on 217

conviction rate 58–60

counter-rituals xxxiii, 72, 75, 81–4, 86–7

court trials, and loopholes 59, 64

cow protection 211

crimes 57–8, 60–1

criminal justice system 53, 56, 59, 65

cultural awakening, Mohan and 162

Cultural Inheritance 79–81

customary: mode of behaviour 78; morality 5

Dabholkar, Narendra 163, 206

Dadri incident 212, *see also* atrocities; violence

Dagis 121, 123, 127–8

Dalit activists 95, 104–5, 164, 258; in Nepal 95, 100, 104–5

Dalit assertions 207, 213–14, 219; Guru on 207

Dalit Commission 108–9

Dalit movement 103, 106, 108, 214, 224–5, 241, 243–4; counter publics' of 224; in Nepal 103–8;

Dalit Mukti Morcha 84

Dalit Panthers 246–7

Dalit Shoshit Samaj Sangharsh Samittee (DS-4) 242

Dalit-Ambedkarites 277

Dalit-Bahujan critics 270

Dalit–Muslim Unity 211–12

Dalits xxxii–xxxvi, 3–4, 27–39, 41–5, 51–3, 55–8, 60–1, 63–4, 66–8, 93–8, 100–1, 103–5, 107–10, 205–8, 210–14, 216, 218–19, 245–7, 257–8, 262–5; capabilities 43; constituency 228; conversion to Buddhism in Nepal 105; diaspora activism 246; empowerment 263; expelling and 206; and government policy 109; in Gujarat 211; human rights 240; Identity 214, 243–4; middle class xxxiv; migration and 103; in Nepal 91, 94, 104, 107–10; organizations 36; Politics 213–14, 228; reservations 95; self-reliance and capabilities 43; self-representation 268; social movement in Nepal 105; students 209–10, 213; subalterns 253, 257; as target for cow protection 211; and temple entry issue 206; in UP 163; userping land of 206; as victims 61, 207

Damodar Valley project 239

dehumanization xxxvii, 281, 290–1

democracy 16, 30, 54, 93, 152, 155, 157; Ambedkar on 148, 155–7, 160–1, 198–9; multi-party

Index

system in 156; principles of 156; and social order 223

democratic: government' 155, 199; Institutions xxv–xxvi; movements 51, 215; practices 16, 199; society 50, 56, 66, 148–9, 155, 165

democratization 209–10, 254

denial of justice 55, 60–6

depressed classes 77–9, 153, 198, 201, 231, 233, 254–7, 262, 264, 266, 268, 270, 275–6; Ambedkar on 77; and jobs in legislature 263; organizations 254; representation of 275

Dewey, John 3–5, 12, 14, 16, 76

dhamma 17–19, 21

dharma 158, 162–3, 268, 272

differentiation 171–4, 177, 192, 236

Directive Principles 159–60, 200

disability xxx, 52–3; abolition of 149

disadvantaged groups xxxii, 35, 39, *see also* depressed classes; untouchables

discrimination xxiv, 52–3, 55–6, 65–6, 72–4, 76, 81–2, 105, 109, 151–2, 200–2, 206–11, 213, 215, 241, 243–4

Divide and Rule policy 261–2

Dividing Labour and Labourers 129–38

division of labour 10, 117, 137, 202

dominant groups 80–1

Du Bois, W.E.B. 226, 233–6

Dumont 27, 80

Durga pooja 84

Dussehra 84

economic: democracy 152, 159–60, 200; empowerment 202; power 67, 148, 154

Economic and Social Council 240

'Educate-Agitate-Organise' 209

education xxix, 9, 12, 31–2, 34, 43, 172–3, 178, 180, 189, 203, 225, 227; access to 9, 12, 156, 207; institutions xxiv, xxvii, 32, 138, 209–10, 212

egalitarian: agenda 203, 215–16; society xxxi, 56, 198, 215, 218

elected representatives 155, 158, 173

Election Commission of India xxv, 155

elections 108, 148, 157, 161, 174, 228; in Nepal 100; State funding of xxv; two-tier system 257

electoral representation 172

emancipation 19, 238; Marks on 139–41

empowerment 50, 55, 59, 63–4

endogamy 81, 236

entitlements 134, 137, 148, 160, *see also* rights

equal accessibility xxvii, xxx, 67, 153

equality 15–17, 54, 62, 64, 68, 124–5, 148–51, 153, 155, 160, 162, 164–6, 169, 197–201, 215; values of 15

Equality Act (EA) 73–4

Equality and Human Rights Commission (EHRC), UK 72

Essentialism 289–92

ethics 2, 15, 17–18, 21, 200, 215, 292

evaluation, 'Merits' of 175–7; vs. acquisition 171–5; methods of 172, 175–7, 181, 192

exclusion 9, 11, 44, 49, 51, 66, 122, 126, 154, 160, 192; of Jews 139; in Nepal 95, 101

executives 159; selection process in 171–2, 175, *see also* judiciary

exploitation xxxiv, 11, 52, 106, 149, 164, 205; and Article 46 of Constitution 201

'extended compassion' 39–40, 43–5

festive rituals xxxiii, 84, *see also* counter-rituals

first information report (FIR) 58–60

forced labour 152, 200, *see also* black slavery; slavery

foreign affairs 224, 246

foreign policy xxxv–xxxvi, 222–5, 230, 236, 238, 240, 246; Ambedkar and 228; and international human rights movements 224

fraternity 15–18, 54, 148–9, 153, 164–6, 197, 199, 201, 205, 215

free social order, Ambedkar and 148

freedom xxiv–xxv, 16, 51, 66–7, 150, 158, 162, 198, 201, 209, 217

freedom of speech and expression 200

French Revolution 148, 151, 153

From Plassey to Partition 259, 263

fundamental rights xxiv–xxv, 67, 149–52, 164, 200–1; Ambedkar on 150–1

Gandhi, M.K. 38–9, 42, 45, 76, 78–9, 117, 126, 128, 147, 215, 223, 228, 237, 253–60, 262–7, 269–77; belief in *karma* theory 273; and caste 78, 270; criticism of 228; and reserved seats 266–7; right of political self-representation and 263; and *varna* social order 275–6; and *Varnavyavastha* 267–8; and Harijan upliftment 260

Gandhi-Irwin pact 255

Gandhism 231, 267

gauraksha campaign 211–12

gender: discrimination xxiv, 215; inequalities 214

'general category' (GC) 175–8, 180–1, 184

George, Goldy 84

Ghadar Party 124

global: Dalit appeal 246; policy dialogue xxxvi, 223; social justice movements 225, *see also* foreign policy

governance xxix–xxx

government: actions xxxii, 27, 41, 68; employment 32, 175

Government Equalities Office (GEO), UK 72

gram panchayat politics 32

Gramsci, Antonio 8

Granger, Lester B. 222, 236

Guha, Ramachandra 198, 268

Gujarati caste phenomena, Vertovec on 81

Gujars 123

Gupta, Dipankar 28

Guru, Gopal 80, 93, 207, 258

gurus 93, 106, 126, 162, 207

habitual conduct 71, 76, 83

Haragopal, G. 200–1

Harijans 116, 274–6

Harlem Renaissance 226

hegemony 214

hereditary occupation 78, 272, 275

hierarchies/hierarchization xxxi, xxxii, xxxiv, 10, 12, 27–8, 30–1, 34–5, 45, 75–6, 80, 85–6, 117–19, 136, 138–9, 141, 165, 193, 252, 281, 283, 287–90; Brahminical ideas of 7; Dumont on caste and 80; in Nepal 103; organization of 9, 92

'higher' castes xxxii, 28–9, 31–3, 34, 36–9, 41, 43–5; absence of empathy in 39; change and 45; in Nepal 95; perpetrators 61

higher education 101, 156, 189–90, 209, 213

Hind Swaraj 269

Index

Hindu Adoption and Maintenance Act, 1956 204
Hindu Caste System, The 271
Hindu Code Bill 203–4, 230
Hindu Janajagruti Samiti (HJS) 163
Hindu Marriage Act, 1955 204
Hindu Minority and Guardianship Act, 1956 204
Hindu Rashtra 163, 166
Hindu/Hindus 123, 125–7, 175, 178, 180, 198; in CG services 180; reformers 21; religion and scripture 116; social order 54, 56, 213; society xxxvi, 9, 20, 51, 68, 198, 203, 271, 275, 281
Hindu Succession Act, 1956 204
Hindu Temples 74, 140; and lower castes entering 79
Hinduism xxxiv, xxxvi, 13, 82, 119, 123, 125–7, 216–17, 263, 280–1, 290; Ambedkar and 217; philosophy of 280; Shastras in 117; untouchability of 129
Hindutva, Chauhan on cultural imperialism of 82, 84
Hoare, Samuel 270
Holi 84–6
Holika, ritual burning as counter-ritual 84–5
'Hindu' SCs, STs, and OBCs (HSSOs) 181, 191, 193; in CG services 184
Human Development xxix
human rights xxxiii, xxxvi, 49–51, 53–7, 65–6, 72, 149, 152, 164, 223, 243; violations xxxiii, 49–53, 55, 57, 66

'ideal society' 6, 16
Idealism 282
identity xxxiii, 20–1, 50, 60–1, 73–6, 81–2, 123–4, 127, 129, 131–2, 212–16, 226, 243–5, 274–5, 288–9; Ambedkarite

Buddhist 216; in Nepal 94–5; politics of 20, 213
ignorance 39, 92, 277
immigrant communities 226
inclusiveness 156
Independent Labour Party (ILP) 148, 228
India after Gandhi 268
Indian Constitution 2, 49, 53, 76, 105, 149–53, 165, 199, 201, 213, 240; Ambedkar and 148, 159; as cosmopolitan 166; objectives of 159; RSS on 52, 164, 197, 218
Indian National Congress 117, 254–5, 259
Indian nationalist mass movement 268
Indian philosophy 282, 285, 287–9
Indian society 9, 50–1, 65, 117, 152, 164, 201, 209, 229, 268
India's Struggle for Independence 259
indifferentism 10
individualism 18
industrialization 14, 238
inequalities 31–2, 34, 49, 51, 54, 153, 156, 158–61, 169, 177, 197, 200, 205, 216–17, 290; abolishing 151; graded 6, 10, 117; group 49, 51
injustices 11, 34, 39, 50, 164, 206, 215, 263
institutions xxiv, xxvii–xxviii, xxxi, 64, 66, 162, 191, 193, 198, 200, 208, 210, 212, 218; Gujaratis and 81; of hereditary hierarchy 117; higher learning 210; NDA and dismantling of 218; possibilities of modern 14
inter-caste marriages 117, 202; in Nepal 105
inter-caste relations 31–5, 40
inter-community relations 174, 192

302 *Index*

International Dalit Conference held in Kuala Lumpur 242
international Dalit solidarity 246
Irrigation and Navigation Commission. *See* River Control Board, Central Water Power Commission
Islam 125; conversion of lower castes to 121; conversion to 138
isolations 87, 155
Izsák-Ndiaye 241

jajmani system 32, 35, 131
Janajatis (tribals0, in Nepal xxxiii, 97, 99, 213
jatis. See caste
Jat-Pat Todak Mandal 116, 125
Jatts 122, 124, 135, 137; as Sikhs 126
Jews 139, 226, 235; Nazi attrocities against 233
judiciary xxvi, 59–62, 64–7, 155, 159, 176–8; selection process in 171–2, 175; and violation of rights 159
Juergensmeyer, Mark 124, 128–30
justice 15, 67; principle of 16, 54; State as machinery for 65

Kabir 118, 121, 125–7
Kalburgi, M.M. 206
Karamchedu massacre 207
karma theory 162, 273–4
karuna 11, 15
Kashmir issue 198, 224, 238
Katz, Steven T. 285
Kaviraj, Sudipta 44
Keer, Dhananjay 266
Kessinger, Tom 141
Khairlanji massacre in Maharashtra 207
Khalid, Umar 164
Khatris 123, 126
King Jr, Martin Luther 44, 235

Kolis or Kolis 121
Korean War 238–9
Kshatriyas 30, 95, 273–4, 285, 287, 290–1
Ku-Klux-Klan 233
Kumar, Madhav 108
Kurmi community 64
Kutanas 121

land reforms, Teltumbde on 208
landless labour movement 141
landlessness 34, 208
Laski, Harold, Ambedkar on 157
laws, implementation of 52–7, 60, 68, 172
legislature 155, 159, 171–2; Dalits in 257; depressed classes and jobs in 263; interventions by 50; selection process in 172–3
liberty 15–17, 51, 54, 148–52, 158, 161, 164–6, 197–201, 205, 288, 290
Lipner, Julius 285
Locke, John 158
love 40; Nussbaum on 40
love *jihad* 163, 212
lower-caste xxxiv, 12, 27–8, 32–3, 51, 119, 122, 126–8, 132, 138, 140; groups xxxiii, 50–1, 66, 68; Hindus in Panjab 127; religious identity 123; in rural Panjab 118–19, 121, 123
lower-caste minorities (Msso) 178, 181; in CG services 181
lynchings xxiv, 44; in Dadri 212

MacDonald, Ramsay 256–7, 260
Madhav, Ram 162
Magad Satyagraha 153, 252
Mahadalit 101
Mahars 20
Mahatma Gandhi National Rural Employment Guarantee Act. *See* MGNREGA

Index

Mahishasura 83–4

Mahishasuravadh 84

maitri 11, 15

Making of India's Electoral System, The 258

Malaviya, Madan Mohan 256, 262

Mangoo Ram 124–7, 130; Ad Dharm and 125; and Ambedkar 128

manual scavenging, in Gujarat 211

Manusmriti 7, 83, 216

Manuvadis 216

Maoist Revolution 92

Maoists 104–5, 107, 109; 'People's War 104, 107

marginalization 3, 252

marginalized xxxv–xxxvi, 50, 55–6, 63–5, 205, 210, 213–14, 217–18, 223–4, 228, 245–6, *see also* depressed classes; untouchables

marriage: law of 203; rituals xxxiii

Marriott, McKim 85

Marx, Karl 138–40; on human emancipation 140; on property and citizen 139

Masihs 121, 128

material realities 27, 30–1, 34, 270, 274

materiality 30–2, 35–6, 40

Matsumoto, Jiichiro, Buraku leader 243

Mayawati 106

Mazbis 121, 123, 126–8

Mbembe, Achille 86–7

menial labourers 122, 137, 140; in Rural Panjab 120

merit 9, 172, 175, 192, 209; 'evaluation' of 177; a failure 177–81

MGNREGA (Mahatma Gandhi National Rural Employment Guarantee Act) 33–4, 42–3; on local power dynamics 43

migration 82, 103; and Nepal 96, 101–3

Mill, John Stuart 15, 18

Millennial Dalit diaspora 245

minorities xxiv, xxvi–xxvii, xxix–xxx, 149, 151, 153, 156–9, 161, 163–5, 175, 177–8, 180–1, 191, 193, 241–2; in CG services 180; and Constituent Assembly 229; Muslim 218; in Parliament 165; State and 161; undergraduate enrolment of 189; in UP 163

Mochis 121, 123, 127–8

Modern India xxiii

Modi, Narendra 162

mono-race rule, of Nazis 228

Montevideo Convention 171

Moolnivasis, (indigenous people) 84

moral conscience of society 67–8

moral values 15, 19, 215

morality 5, 17–18, 157–8, 162, 165–6, 198, 200, 205, 215, 270, 285, 292, *see also* social ethics

Muni, S.D. 92

Muralidharan, E. 187

Muslims 42, 99, 123, 125–7, 157, 165, 211–12, 229, 255–6; BJP and 165; 'love jihad' 163; mob attack on 212; and nationality issue 218; in Nepal 99; undergraduate enrolment of 189

Mussalis or Kutanas 121, 123, 127–8

Nabha, Kahn Singh 126

Nagpur conference 255

Namdev 118, 125–7

Nanak, Guru 119

Nandy, Ashish 269

Naqvi, Mukhtar Abbas 180

Nation and its Fragments, The 261

nation building 162, 204–6

National Association for the Advancement of Colored People (NAACP) 235, 242
National Council of Hindu Temples 74
National Crime Record Bureau (NCRB) 52
National Dalit Commission xxxiv
National Democratic Alliance 212
National Human Rights Commission 65
nationalism 78, 192–3, 204–6, 259, 263–4
Natrajan, Balmurli 80
Negroes 233–4
'Nehru doctrine' 227
Nehru, Jawaharlal xxxi, 38–9, 44–5, 54, 204, 229, 233, 237–8, 240; and Ambedkar 229; and Communist Russia 240
Nepal 91–2; Ambedkar's influence on 109–10; caste and State law in 93; Caste-Based Discrimination and Untouchability (Offence and Punishment) Act, 2011 109; Chhetri (Kshatriya) in 100; for *chuwachut mukta* or 'untouchability-free' 109; civil war 108; Dalit activists and Ambedkar in 104–5; Dalits and Constitution of 109; Dalits and Government Policy 108–9; Dalits of xxxiv, 91, 94–101, 104–6, 108, 110; Dalits scholars 96; Gurungs 103, 105; Hill Dalits of 97–8, 100; identity politics in 100; Janajatis 97, 99, 213; Khas-Aryas xxxiii, 99–100; Madheshis xxxiii, 99, 106; Magars upgraded as Chhetri 94; Manandhars of Kathmandu 94; multiparty system 99; Muluki Ain 94; political movements in 106; political parties of

106; representation in politics 98; revolution 1990 107; Sanskritization in 94; social security 109; Tarai Dalits in 97–9, 101
Nepal Communist Party (United Front) 107
Nepal Dalit Commission 97
Nepal Dalit movement 106
Nepalis 92–3, 96, 99, 103, 106–7
neutralism 222, 236
Non-Brahmin Movement in Maharashtra and Tamil Nadu 252
non-government organizations (NGOs) 240–1, 243–4
Nordic race 228
Nussbaum, Martha C. 38–41, 43–5
Nyaya 288

Omvedt, Gail 228, 265
oppression 3, 49–50, 81, 149–50, 157, 164, 209, 229; denial on 277; in Nepal 95; systematic 72
Other Backward Classes (OBCs) xxiv–xxx, 42, 175–7, 184–5, 187, 189; in CG services 184–5, 187; and judiciary 177; quota and representation of 176, 187; undergraduate enrolment of 189

Pacific Relations Committee 225, 246
panchayati raj 33, 61
Panchnamas 273
pan-Indian polity 205
Pansare, Govind 206
Panjab 119–20; Ad Dharm identity for untouchables in 127; caste labour in rural 120–2; Dalits of xxxiv, 119, 138; society 118, 140
Panjab Alienation of Land Act in 1952 141
Parekh, Bhikhu 269

Index

Pariyar, Bishnu 96
Pariyar, Mitra 96
parliamentary democracy 15, 155, 158, 160–1, 230
Patel, Sardar 276
Pathans 122–3
patriarchy xxxi, 149, 203
Periyar 261
Phule, Jyotiba xxvi, 209, 225, 235, 261
place of birth, for discrimination 52, 151–2
plurality 87, 209
police, villagers on 61
political: capacity 33–4, 40, 43, 138; democracy 159–60, 169, 200–1; imagination 223; justice xxxi–xxxii; movements 106, 225, 262; opportunities 14–15; organizations 198, 200, 214; parties xxv, 68, 104, 106, 148, 155, 157, 173, 214, 217; pessimism 14; power xxxiv, 64, 117, 148, 193, 214, 216, 265, 292; realism 12; revolutions 8; structures 39, 148, 154, 217, 282
political rights xxxiv, 153, 198, 217, 264; movements 225
polygamy 204
Poona Pact xxxvi, 77, 252–62, 264–5, 268, 272, 276–7; Kanshi Ram and 257
poverty 11, 34, 39, 101, 108, 156, 158, 160, 204
Prabhakaras 288
Prachanda (Pushpa Kamal Dahal) 106–7
preamble xxiii–xxiv, 149, 164
prejudice 78, 80, 223; in Nepal 101
priestly class 51
privileged 155–6, 165, 201, 205, 216, 223, 231, 269, 274
Proletarian Workers' Association, Nepal 107

Property, equalization of 202
proselytizing 123, *see also* conversion
public goods, and community status 154
public opinion 155, 256
Purusa Sukta 281, 283–90, 293

Quest for Equity 218

Raavan 83–4; worship of 83
race xxiii, 52, 73, 151–2, 200, 236, 246–7, 293
Racial Discrimination 74, 236, 243
Radhakrishnan 288
Rajagopalachari, C. 256
Rajah, M.C. 262
Rajbhoj, P.N. 243
Rajputs 122–3
Ram, Kanshi 242–3, 257
Ramanuja 285
Ramdasia or Raidasia 121, 127
Rana regime 103
Rangretas 121
Ranjith, Pa. 258
rape 57, 206
Rashtriya Swayamsevak Sangh (RSS) and BJP 161–3
Ravidas, Bhagat 118, 121, 125–8, 138, 244
Ravidasia Sikh 121, 126
Rawls, John 44
rebellion 12
reforms xxiv–xxvi, 66, 203, 226
Rege, Sharmila 209
regulatory mechanism 51, 56
religion xxx–xxxii, xxxv–xxxvi, 2, 4, 6, 8, 17–21, 117–19, 127, 129, 149, 151–4, 198–200, 280–1, 292; and human predicament 283; as mode of engagement 292; necessity of 17–19; philosophy of 280–1, 292; as social force 4–5

religious: identities xxiv, 121, 216; practices 54; rituals xxxiii, 81, 83; sanctions 78

representation 148, 176, 181–2, 191–3, 257; Ambedkar on 155; in CG jobs by community 178, 180, 187; Dalits and 147, 262–4; Gandhi's opposition to 275; in higher education in Nepal 101; of minorities 165; untouchables and 148, 260

representativeness 174, 182, 182–5, 189–91, 193; Education and 189–90; kinds of 182; and Power 190

Republican Party of India 243

reservations xxv–xxvii, xxxiv–xxxv, 175–6, 178, 180, 182, 185, 187, 191, 255, 257, 260, 265–6; in educational institutions 32; in Nepal 100, 104; policy of 177–8, 181, 191, 201; and representativeness 182–7

resistance 8, 30, 209, 212, 215, 271

revolution 8, 107, 293

Rig Veda 283–4, 286

rights xxiv–xxv, xxix–xxx, xxxiii–xxxiv, 50–7, 64–8, 72–3, 148–53, 156, 158–61, 164, 197–8, 203, 217–18, 223–4, 226–7, 233–4, 242–3; revolutions and 151

rituals xxxiii, 39, 75, 80–83, 85, 87; and caste 81–2; of status reversals 86

River Control Board, Central Water Power Commission 239

Rodrigues, Valerian xxiii, 16, 155

Round Table Conference: Bandyopadhyay on 264; nomination of Ambedkar to 255

Round Table Conference (RTCs) 153, 253, 255–8, 262, 264, 266, 268

RTI Act 185; Muralidharan and 187

runaway marriages 83

Rural India xxix, xxxii, 27–8, 34, 37, 40, 44–5, 208; Theories of Change in 38–46

Safeguarding the People xxiv–xxv

Sagar, Tarun 158

Samkara 285–6

sanatan 13, 292

Sanatan Sanstha 163

Sankaran, S.R. 201

Sanskritization 3, 93–4

Sapru, Tej Bahadur 256

Sapru Committee 229

Sarkar, Sumit 259–61, 276

Sartre, Jean Paul 87

satyagrahas 38, 79

Savarkar, V.D. 162

Scheduled Castes (SCs) xxiv, xxvi–xxx, 52–3, 175–7, 181–2, 184, 189, 224, 230–3, 236, 241, 262, 265; Ambedkar on 210; in CG services 184; and judiciary 177

Scheduled Castes and Scheduled Tribes (Prevention of Atrocity [PoA]) Act, 1989 53, 211; cases under 57–8; Amendment Act, 2015 53, 58–9

scheduled tribes (STs) xxiv, xxvi–xxx, 42, 52–3, 59, 66, 175–7, 181, 184, 189; in CG services 184; GER of 189; and judiciary 177

scholars 80, 213–15, 236, 260–1, 268, 273, 276; anti-caste movements and 215; and anti-progressive groups 214; avoidance among 213; generation of 209; Marxist 214; moral value and 215; neo-Gandhian 269; Nepali Dalit 92, 96

Second World Conference to Combat Racism and Racial Discrimination in 1983 243 segregation 9, 154, 233–4, *see also* differentiation; exclusion

Self: Ambedkar and metaphysics of 292–3; criticality on 214

separate electorate 128, 130, 198, 254–8, 260, 262–8, 270, 275–6; and Dalit representation 257; demand for 255; Gandhi and 265; Patel on 276

sepidari system 131

73rd Amendment to the Constitution 33

sex 52, 151–2

Shah, Amit 157, 162

Shankara 285–6

Shastras 7, 118–19

shuddhi or 'purification' campaign 125

Shudras 236, 273, 275, 285, 290

Sikh Council UK 74

Sikhism 123, 125–8; caste in 119; conversion to 121, 138

Sikhs 121, 123, 125–7, 129, 255–6; institutions 125; restrictions in langar 126

Simon Commission 254, 262

Singh, Giani Ditt 126

Singh Sabha 123, 125–6

siri 131–3, 135–6, 140; cultivators and 133, 135, 137

Sivaraj, N 225, 232–3

slavery 84, 163, 198, 231, 235

social: action xxxv, 4–6, 12; activism 206, 214; actors 4–5, 12; belonging 75; change xxxiii, 12, 14, 17, 159, 216; class 59–61; contract 18; democracy 50, 54, 66, 155, 159–60, 165, 201; disabilities 66, 149, 152, 164; divisions 10, 236, 291; efficiency 9; endosmosis' 16; ethics 2, 18, 200; evils 52; exclusion 49–51; force 4–5, 7; group/community 182;

imaginaries 4–8; injustice 50, 52, 200, 237; life 3, 6, 13–14, 19, 45, 49–50, 157, 199, 207; opportunities 14; oppressions xxxiii, 50, 66, 68; order 4, 7, 51, 54, 56, 61, 64, 147–8, 213, 216, 268, 273, 275–6; problems 62, 66, 202, 214; recognition 1, 21; reforms 202; relationships xxxii, 12, 21, 56, 68, 79, 81, 87, 149, 216; revolutions 12; rights 149, 234; scientists 26, 28, 76, 93, 197; security xxx, 109; structure 5, 9, 56, 65, 148, 154, 272; suffering 11; transformation 3, 54, 199, 216; values xxxii, 2, 7

Social Conference, Madras 237

social discrimination xxxv, 28, 34, 51, 197, 206–11, 215; Ambedkar on 202; resistance against 215; Thorat on 208

social inequalities 50, 200, 213, 217, 236; abolishing 152; among Hindus 4

social justice xxvi–xxviii, 1, 52, 56, 64; access to xxxiii, 56, 66; conception of 149, 164; principles of 54, 62

socialism 201–2, 231

socialist movements 243

sociality 5, 12, 15, 18, 20–1

society: contemporary, 49–53, 55–6, 63, 65, 68; and kinship 20; Turner on 85

solidarity 10–11, 15, 17, 35, 75, 86–7, 235, 245–7

South East Asia Treaty Organization (SEATO) 240

Sovereign Right, Indian 227, 231

special representation 217, 266

Srinivasan, R. 255

Standing Committee on Social Justice and Empowerment 59

State 171; Ambedkar on 158–61;
functionaries 58–9; in Indian
Constitution 164
stigmatization 44, 72, 80, 154
Struggle for Independence 261
struggles 36, 164, 213, 219, 226,
252, 271; Aloysius on 204–5
sub-castes, abolition of 202
Sudarshan, K.S. 164
Sudras 30, 235, 273–5, 288–92
suffering 11, 39, 77, 82, 178, 232–3,
283
Sunam, Ramesh 96
Sunni Anjumans 123
sunyata 13–14
Supreme Court 150, 170, 176, 207
sustainable development goals
(SDGs) 50
sympathy 10, 15, 40, 155,
165, 235

Tagore, Rabindranath 39
Taylor, Charles 7
Taylor, Frederick Winslow 226
Teltumbde, Anand 191, 208, 228
Thakkar, A.V. 76
Third Worldism 227, 239
Thorat, S.K. 105, 208
transformation 19–20, 68; of norms
and belief 68; self 19
transgression xxxiii, 79, 81, 83–4,
206, 208
tribals or Janajatis 99, 213
Trutiya Ratna 209
Tsundur massacre 207
Turner, Victor 85
tyranny, of caste Hindus 125,
149–50, 159, 164, 233, 241

UML party 108
Una Dalit Atyachar Ladat Samiti
(UDALS) 212
Una incident xxxv, 210–12
unfair representation 223, 227

United Nations 224–5; and caste
issues 241; and civil society
241; permanent membership
to 238
United Nations Organization
(UNO) 224
universal access to education xxvii,
156
universal adult franchise 262–3
universalism 21; of Hindutva 82
universality 20
untouchability 52–3, 77–9, 129,
149, 152–4, 198, 200, 211,
213, 231, 235, 237, 246, 263,
289; abolition of 152–3, 200;
Ambedkar on 154; in Nepal 95,
104, 109
Untouchability (Offences) Act,
1955 53
untouchables 7, 62, 66–7, 121,
124–7, 129–30, 153–4, 198, 217,
227, 234–6, 255–6, 262–3, 265–6,
275–6; as complainant and
abuses 62; displacement for 125;
and Hinduism 138; as infection
of caste system 7; of Panjab and
Ad Dharm 138; representative
of 256–7; as stigma 199
upper-caste 3, 67–8, 83, 99,
176–7, 180, 205–7, 232, 257,
276; Brahminical nationalism'
205, 261; groups 67; Hindus
(UCH) 175, 178, 180–1, 184,
187, 190–3, 229; Hindus in CG
services 187; men and rape 206;
representation in services 177;
value adaptation of 3
Uttara Mimamsa 285

Vaisya 273–4
Valmikis 121, 125, 244
values 15; egalitarian 4
varna system/*varna*-based social
order xxxvi, 268, 275–6, 281,

288, 290–1; challenged by Ambedkar 76; Gandhi and 254

Varnashrama Dharma xxxvi, 30, 76, 254, 267–9, 272–3, 275–6, 281, 285–6, 288, 290–1

Varnavyavastha 267, 272–4

Vedic Authority 286–9

Vemula, Rohith, suicide of 209–10, 212

victims 7, 12, 50, 57–60, 62–3, 65–6, 68, 74, 241; and forced compromise 61, 66, *see also* denial of justice

village/villages 26–7, 29, 32, 34–7, 39–41, 43, 60, 62, 67, 123–4, 130–2, 136–7, 206–8, 211–12

violations 56–7, 65, 149, 164, 201, 288; of civil rights 57; community in 61; menials 119–20

violence 27–9, 36–7, 45, 50–3, 55–7, 63, 66–7, 147, 197, 205, 208; communal 205; costs of 37; in Muzaffarnagar 212

Vishva Hindu Parishad (VHP) 163

Vishwakarma 97, 104

weaker sections xxxiii–xxxiv, 52, 54–5, 66, 200, 205, 213–14

Weber, Max 5–6

What Congress and Gandhi Have done to the Untouchables 154, 237

White, Walter Francis 235

Wilkins, Roy 236

willful negligence 53, 59

Wilson, Woodrow 226

women xxiv–xxvii, xxx, 149, 156, 158, 164, 198, 203, 205, 213, 218; liberation of 203–4

World Conference against Racism in Durban 240

wrong dispositions 11

Yadav community 64

Zelliot, Eleanor 79, 199, 217, 225–6

Editor and Contributors

Editor

Aakash Singh Rathore is the author of *Ambedkar's Preamble: A Secret History of the Constitution of India* (2020) and a regular contributor to the *Indian Express* and *Outlook* magazine. Rathore has taught at Jawaharlal Nehru University (JNU), University of Delhi, and Jindal Global University, India; Rutgers University and University of Pennsylvania, USA; University of Toronto, Canada; Humboldt University of Berlin, Germany; and Libera Università Internazionale degli Studi Sociali (LUISS) Guido Carli, Italy.

His twenty previous books range in theme from political philosophy, law, and religion to literature, sports, and wine. These include *Hegel's India: A Reinterpretation, with Texts* (2017) and *B.R. Ambedkar's The Buddha and His Dhamma: A Critical Edition* (2011). He is also the author of the forthcoming book, *B.R. Ambedkar: A Biography*.

Contributors

Krishna P. Adhikari is a research fellow at the Institute of Social and Cultural Anthropology (ISCA), University of Oxford, UK. He is currently leading a HEFCE GCRF-funded field project on 'Tackling Dalit Structural Disadvantage through Nepal's Educational Curriculum'. Among his publications are a book, *Nepalis in the United Kingdom: An Overview* (2012) and a journal article (2016) (with David Gellner) 'New Identity Politics and the 2012 Collapse

Editor and Contributors   311

of Nepal's Constituent Assembly: When the Dominant becomes "Other"' in *Modern Asian Studies*.

Arjun Bahadur B.K. is a social science researcher, educational practitioner, and an emerging Dalit scholar. He has written a number of published and unpublished articles on the Dalit movement and Dalit consciousness. His areas of interest include the Dalit movement, social exclusion/inclusion, discourse, identity politics, and Dalit representation. He has been involved as education practitioner in teaching and managing a Kathmandu-based private education institution. He continues to carry out research as an independent researcher.

Jagannatham Begari teaches at the Central University of Gujarat, Gandhinagar, India. His interdisciplinary research interests include democracy, movements, and marginality. He has authored two books, *Interrogating democracy and Human Rights: Telangana People's Movement* (2014) and *Mapping Human Rights and Subalterns in Modern India* (2017) and both the books are an attempt to understand marginalization, subalterns, the Telangana movement, and India's democracy. These two books have received great attention. Begari has also published articles in edited books and reputed journals like *Economic and Political Weekly*.

Meena Dhanda is professor of philosophy and cultural politics at the University of Wolverhampton, UK. She is an advocate of socially engaged philosophy. Her research focuses on understanding injustices, prejudices, and misrepresentations suffered by powerless groups, which she pursues through transdisciplinary studies, specifically connecting caste, class, gender, and race. Her work includes *The Negotiation of Personal Identity* and *Reservations for Women*, besides papers in international journals, book chapters, and reference works. She holds a doctorate from Oxford University where she was a Commonwealth scholar and a Rhodes junior research fellow. As principal investigator, she has led three transdisciplinary research projects: (*a*) for the University of Wolverhampton (*Black and Minority Ethnic Students' Experience*); (*b*) for the Leverhulme Trust Research Fellowship (*Caste Aside: Dalit Punjabi Identity and Experience*); and (*c*) for the UK Equality and Human Rights Commission (EHRC) (*Caste in Britain*) leading a consortium of experts from UK universities. Her two EHRC reports were used by the UK Government Equalities Office in its public consultation on how caste discrimination must be legally addressed in Britain. She is currently working on the philosophical foundations of anti-casteism.

Martin Fuchs is an anthropologist and a sociologist. He holds the Professorship for Indian Religious History at the Max Weber Centre for Advanced Cultural and Social Studies, University of Erfurt, Germany. He is currently co-director of the M.S. Merian – R. Tagore International Centre of Advanced Studies in the Humanities and Social Sciences 'Metamorphoses of the Political: Comparative Perspectives on the Long Twentieth Century' (ICAS:MP) in Delhi, India. He has taught at universities in Germany, Switzerland, Hungary and New Zealand and was the Founding Director of the New Zealand South Asia Centre at the University of Canterbury, Christchurch. His research focuses on cultural and social theory, urban anthropology, social (esp. Dalit) movements, struggles for recognition, religious individualization and normative transformations; he undertook long-term fieldwork in Dharavi, Mumbai. His books include *Theorie und Verfremdung: Max Weber, Louis Dumont und die Analyse der indischen Gesellschaft; Kampf um Differenz: Repräsentation, Subjektivität und soziale Bewegungen -Das Beispiel Indien; and,* as (co-)editor, *Kultur, soziale Praxis, Text: Die Krise der ethnographischen Repräsentation; India and Modernity: Decentring Western Perspectives; Konfigurationen der Moderne: Diskurse zu Indien; Religious Interactions in Modern India; Religious Individualisation: Historical Dimensions and Comparative Perspectives.*

Karen Gabriel is associate professor and head of the English Department at St. Stephen's College, University of Delhi, India. She is also founder-director, Center for Gender, Culture and Social Processes at St. Stephen's College. Her publications include *Melodrama and the Nation: Sexual Economies of Bombay cinema 1970–2000* (2010) and the edited volume *Gendered Nation.* She is currently working on a book on the political economy of pornography, and one on dystopic fiction. She has earned international fellowships and awards such as the prestigious European Union's International Incoming Marie Curie Fellowship, Scholar in Residence at the College of William and Mary (USA) the Leverhulme Fellowship, and the like.

David N. Gellner is professor of social anthropology and a fellow of All Souls College in the University of Oxford, UK. He is the author of *Monk, Householder, and Tantric Priest: Newar Buddhism and its Hierarchy of Ritual, The Anthropology of Buddhism and Hinduism: Weberian Themes,* and (with Sarah LeVine) *Rebuilding Buddhism: The Theravada Movement in Twentieth-Century Nepal.* He has edited many books, most recently *Borderland Lives in Northern South Asia, Religion, Secularism, and Ethnicity in Contemporary Nepal,* and *Global Nepalis: Religion, Culture, and Community in a New and Old Diaspora.*

Navyug Gill is assistant professor in the Department of History at William Paterson University of New Jersey, United States of America. Currently, he is completing on a book manuscript titled 'Labors of Division: Caste, Class and the Emergence of the Peasant in Colonial Panjab,' which investigates landholding peasants, landless labourers, and a new rule of capital amid the transformation of Panjabi society in the late nineteenth and early twentieth century. He also has a forthcoming article on re-thinking the material and cultural logic of capitalist accumulation in the colonial world. His broader interests include agrarian studies, political economy of debt, colonialism and postcolonial theory, global capitalism, and the space between equality and equity.

Karthik Raja Karuppusamy, a first-generation college student from a Sudra family, submitted his MPhil thesis 'The Nation in Historical Imagination' in 2018, and is theorizing how secular and communal conceptions of 'nation' is constructed, operationalized, and disseminated through state-sponsored NCERT history textbooks post Independence. Currently, he is a doctoral candidate and senior research fellow at the Centre for Political Studies at JNU, India. His research focuses on the political, legal, and socio-economic interface between Dalits and OBCs in Kongunad region of Tamil Nadu. Besides, he is also co-editing a volume on the 'Shudra question' with Professor Kancha Ilaiah Shepherd, former director, Centre for Study of Social Exclusion and Inclusive Policy at Maulana Azad National Urdu University, Hyderabad, which is soon to be published.

314   *Editor and Contributors*

James Manor is the Emeka Anyaoku Professor Emeritus of Commonwealth Studies in the School of Advanced Study, University of London, UK. He has previously taught at Yale, Harvard, and Leicester Universities; the Institute of Development Studies, University of Sussex; the Institute for Social and Economic Change, Bengaluru; and Savitribai Phule Pune University. His books include *Politics and State-Society Relations in India* (with Rob Jenkins); *Politics and the Right to Work: India's Mahatma Gandhi National Rural Employment Guarantee Act*; and (with E. Raghavan) *Broadening and Deepening Democracy: Political Innovation in Karnataka*.

Shailaja Menon teaches Modern Indian History at the School of Liberal Studies, Ambedkar University, New Delhi, India. Her research interests include exploring caste and gender in contemporary society, cultural studies, and urbanization.

G.C. Pal is currently Director at Indian Institute of Dalit Studies, New Delhi. He has MPhil/PhD in Social Psychology, and was a Post-Doctoral Visiting Fellow, TIFR and Senior Fellow, ICSSR, India. He has a book and over forty research papers published in national and international academic journals and edited books. His academic interest is to understand development issues from socio-psychological perspectives, with a focus on marginalized groups, and to explore research methodology. He has been engaged in interdisciplinary research, which includes social psychology of unemployment; human cognition and education; identity-based exclusion and violence; intersectionality of identities and deprivation; and public policies.

Ajay Verma is associate professor at Centre for Philosophy in JNU, India. His research interests include classical Indian philosophy, Buddhist studies, Ambedkarian studies, continental philosophy, and comparative philosophy. He has co-edited B.R. Ambedkar's *Buddha and His Dhamma: Critical Edition*. Apart from publishing research articles in national and international journals of philosophy, he has lectured extensively on TV channels on *swayamprabha* platform on different philosophical themes.

Prem Kumar (P.K.) Vijayan teaches at the Department of English, Hindu College, Delhi University, India. His research was on the relations between Hindu nationalism and masculinity, and has recently been published as a book, Gender and Hindu Nationalism: Understanding Masculine Hegemony. He has been involved, as an activist and as an academic commentator, on various issues, including higher education in India, the Maoist movement in India, Hindu nationalism, corruption, terrorism, sexual violence in the workplace, and literary theory, among others.

Suraj Yengde is a Shorenstein Center postdoctoral fellow at the Harvard Kennedy School, USA. Suraj is India's first Dalit PhD holder from an African university. Suraj is an academic activist in the transnational movement of Dalit rights. He is actively involved in building solidarities of Dalit, Black, Roma, indigenous, Buraku, and refugee people's solidarities in the Fourth World project of marginalized peoples. Currently, he is involved in developing a critical theory of Dalit and Black Studies. He is the author of *Caste Matters* and co-editor of *The Radical in Ambedkar: Critical Reflections*.